HENR\
SAINT A
FIRST MODERN
MISSIONARY TO THE
MOHAMMEDANS
1781-1812

BY
GEORGE SMITH

PREFACE

In the year 1819, John Sargent, Rector of Lavington, published *A Memoir of the Rev. Henry Martyn.* The book at once became a spiritual classic. The saint, the scholar, and the missionary, alike found in it a new inspiration. It ran through ten editions during the writer's life, and he died when projecting an additional volume of the Journals and Letters. His son-in-law, S. Wilberforce, afterwards Bishop of Oxford and of Winchester, accordingly, in 1837 published, in two volumes, *Journals and Letters of the Rev. Henry Martyn, B.D.*, with an introduction on Sargent's life. Sargent had suppressed what Bishop Wilberforce describes as 'a great variety of interesting materials'. Especially in the lifetime of Lydia Grenfell it was thought necessary to omit the facts which give to Henry Martyn's personality its human interest and intensify our appreciation of his heroism. On the lady's death, in 1829, Martyn's letters to her became available, and Bishop Wilberforce incorporated these in what he described as 'further and often more continuous selections from the journals and letters of Mr. Martyn.' But, unhappily, his work does not fully supplement that of Sargent. The *Journal* is still mutilated; the *Letters* are still imperfect.

Some years ago, on completing the *Life of William Carey*, who had written that wherever his friend Henry Martyn might go as chaplain the Church need not send a[vi] missionary, I began to prepare a new work on the first modern apostle to the Mohammedans. I was encouraged by his grand-nephew, a distinguished mathematician, the late Henry Martyn Jeffery, F.R.S., who had in 1883 printed *Two Sets of Unpublished Letters of the Rev. Henry Martyn, B.D., of Truro.* For a time I stopped the work on learning that he had come into possession of Lydia Grenfell's papers, and was preparing the book which appeared in 1890, *Extracts from the Religious Diary of Miss L. Grenfell, of Marazion, Cornwall.* Except her letters to Henry Martyn, which are not in existence now, all the desirable materials seemed to be ready. Meanwhile, the missionary bishop who most resembled Martyn in character and service, Thomas Valpy French, of Lahore and Muscat, had written to Canon Edmonds of S. Wilberforce's book as 'a work for whose reprint I have often pleaded in vain, and for which all that there is of mission life in our Church would plead, had it not been so long out of print and out of sight.'

My aim is to set the two autobiographies, unconsciously written in the Journals and Letters of Henry Martyn and in the Diary of Lydia Grenfell, in the light of recent knowledge of South Africa and India, Persia and Turkey, and of Bible work and missionary history in the lands of which, by his life and by his death, Henry Martyn took possession for the Master. Bengal chaplain of the East India Company, he was, above all, a missionary to the two divisions of Islam, in India and Persia, and in Arabia and Turkey. May this book, written after years of experience in Bengal, lead many to enter on the inheritance he has left to the Catholic Church!

Then came another of priestly garb and mien,
A young man still wanting the years of Christ,
But long since with the saints....
A poet with the contemplative gaze
And listening ear, but quick of force and eye,
Who fought the wrong without, the wrong within,
And, being a pure saint, like those of old,
Abased himself and all the precious gifts
God gave him, flinging all before the feet
Of Him whose name he bore—a fragile form
Upon whose hectic cheek there burned a flush
That was not health; who lived as Xavier lived,
And died like him upon the burning sands,
Untended, yet whose creed was far from his
As pole from pole; whom grateful England still
Loves.

The awakened gaze
Turned wholly from the earth, on things of heaven

He dwelt both day and night. The thought of God
Filled him with infinite joy; his craving soul
Dwelt on Him as a feast; as did the soul
Of rapt Francesco in his holy cell
In blest Assisi; and he knew the pain,
The deep despondence of the saint, the doubt,
The consciousness of dark offence, the joy
Of full assurance last, when heaven itself
Stands open to the ecstasy of faith.

The relentless lie
Of Islam ... he chose to bear, who knew
How swift the night should fall on him, and burned
[xii]To save one soul alive while yet 'twas day.
This filled his thoughts, this only, and for this
On the pure altar of his soul he heaped
A costlier sacrifice, this youth in years,
For whom Love called, and loving hands, and hope
Of childish lives around him, offering these,
Like all the rest, to God.

Yet when his hour
Was come to leave his England, was it strange
His weakling life pined for the parting kiss
Of love and kindred, whom his prescient soul
Knew he should see no more?

... The woman of his love
Feared to leave all and give her life to his,
And both to God; his sisters passed away
To heaven, nor saw him more. There seemed on earth
Nothing for which to live, except the Faith,
Only the Faith, the Faith! until his soul
Wore thin her prison bars, and he was fain
To rest awhile, or work no more the work
For which alone he lived.
      A Vision of Saints. By LEWIS MORRIS.

[1]
CHAPTER I
CORNWALL AND CAMBRIDGE, 1781-1803

Writing half a century ago, as one who gratefully accepted the guidance of the Church of England, from the evangelical and philanthropic side of which he sprang, Sir James Stephen declared the name of Henry Martyn to be 'in fact the one heroic name which adorns her annals from the days of Elizabeth to our own'. The past fifty years have seen her annals, in common with those of other Churches, adorned by many heroic names. These are as many and as illustrious on the side which has enshrined Henry Martyn in the new Cathedral of Truro, as amongst the Evangelicals, to whom in life he belonged. But the influence which streams forth from his short life and his obscure death is the perpetual heritage of all English-speaking Christendom, and of the native churches of India, Arabia, Persia, and Anatolia in all time to come. His *Journal*, even in the mutilated form published first by his friend Sargent, is one of the great spiritual autobiographies of Catholic literature. It is placed beside the *Confessions*[2] of Augustine and the *Grace Abounding* of Bunyan. The *Letters* are read along with those of Samuel Rutherford and William Cowper by the most saintly workers, persuasive preachers, and learned scholars, who, even in these days of searching criticism, attribute to the young chaplain-missionary their early inspiration and renewed consecration, even as he traced his to Brainerd, Carey, and Charles Simeon.

2

Born in Truro on February 18, 1781, Henry Martyn came from a land the oldest and most isolated in Great Britain; a Celtic people but recently transformed from the rudest to the most courteous and upright; a family created and partly enriched by the great mining industry; and a church which had been the first, in these far-western islands, to receive the teaching of the Apostles of Jesus Christ.

The tin found in the lodes and streams of the Devonian Slates of West Cornwall was the only large source of supply to the world down to Henry Martyn's time. The granite porphyries which form the Land's End had come to be worked only a century before that for the 'bunches' of copper which fill the lines of fault and fissure. It was chiefly from the deeper lodes of Gwennap, near Truro, that his family had drawn a competence. The statement of Richard Carew, in his *Survey of Cornwall*, was true of the dim centuries before Herodotus wrote, that the 'tynne of the little angle (Cornwall) overfloweth England, watereth Christendom, and is derived to a great part of the world besides'.[1] Tyrian and Jew, Greek and Roman, as navigators, travellers, and capitalists, had in the[3] darkness of prehistoric days dealings with the land described in an Elizabethan treatise on Geography as a foreign country on that side of England next to Spain. London itself is modern compared with the Cornish trade, which in its latest stage assumed the Latin name *Stannum*, and the almost perfect economic laws administered by the Lord Warden of the Stannaries since King John leased the mines to the Jews, and Edward I., as Earl of Cornwall, established the now vexed 'royalties' by charter. Even in the century since Henry Martyn's early days, fourteen of the Cornish mines have yielded a gross return of more than thirteen millions sterling, of which above one-fifth was clear profit.

Whether the Romans used the Britons in the mines as slaves or not, the just and democratic system of working them—which was probably due to the Norman kings, and extorted the admiration of M. Jars, a French traveller of the generation to which Henry Martyn's father belonged—did not humanise the population. So rude were their manners that their heath-covered rocks bore the name of 'West Barbary.' Writing two centuries before Martyn, Norden described the city of his birth as remarkable for its neatness, which it still is, but he added, there is not a town 'more discommendable for the pride of the people.' The Cornish miner's life is still as short as it is hard and daring, in spite of his splendid physique and the remarkable health of the women and children. But the perils of a rock-bound coast, the pursuits of wrecking and smuggling, added to the dangers of the mines, and all isolated from the growing civilisation of England, had combined, century after century, to make Cornwall a byword till John Wesley and George Whitfield visited it. Then the miner became so changed, not less really because rapidly, that the feature of the[4]whole people which first and most continuously strikes a stranger is their grave and yet hearty politeness. Thomas Carlyle has, in his *Life of Sterling*, pictured the moral heroism which Methodism, with its 'faith of assurance,' developes in the ignorant Cornish miner, a faith which, as illustrated by William Carey and taught by the Church of England, did much to make Henry Martyn what he became. John Wesley's own description in the year of Henry Martyn's birth is this: 'It pleased God the seed there sown has produced an abundant harvest. Indeed, I hardly know any part of the three kingdoms where there has been a more general change.' The Cornishman still beguiles the weary hours of his descent of the ladder to his toil by crooning the hymns of Charles Wesley. The local preacher whose eloquent earnestness and knowledge of his Bible have delighted the stranger on Sunday, is found next day two hundred fathoms below the sea, doing his eight hours' work all wet and grimy and red from the iron-sand, picking out the tin of Bottallack or the copper of Gwennap. Long before Henry Martyn knew Simeon he had become unconsciously in some sense the fruit of the teaching of the Wesleys.

During fifty-five years again and again John Wesley visited Cornwall, preaching in the open air all over the mining county and in the fishing hamlets, till two generations were permanently changed. His favourite centre was Gwennap, which had long been the home of the Martyn family, a few miles from Truro. There he found his open-air pulpit and church in the great hollow, ever since known as 'Wesley's Pit,' where, to this day, thousands crowd every Whit-Monday to commemorative services. Wesley's published journal, which closes with October 1790,[5] when Henry Martyn was nearly ten years of age, has more frequent and always more appreciative references to Gwennap than to any other town. On July 6, 1745, we find him writing:

At Gwennap also we found the people in the utmost consternation. Word was brought that a great company of tinners, made drunk on purpose, were coming to do terrible things—so that abundance of people went away. I preached to the rest on 'Love your enemies.'

By 1774 we read 'the glorious congregation was assembled at five in the amphitheatre at Gwennap.' Next year we find this:

'At five in the evening in the amphitheatre at Gwennap. I think this is the most magnificent spectacle which is to be seen on this side heaven. And no music is to be heard upon earth comparable to the sound of many thousand voices when they are all harmoniously joined together singing "praises to God and the Lamb." Four-and-twenty thousand were present, frequently, at that spot. And yet all, I was informed, could hear distinctly in the fair, calm evening.' Again: 'I think this is my *ne plus ultra.* I shall scarce see a larger congregation till we meet in the air.'

We are thus introduced to the very spot where Henry Martyn was born: 'About noon I preached in the piazza adjoining to the Coinage Hall in Truro. I was enabled to speak exceeding plain on "Ye are saved through faith."' In the evening of the same day Wesley preached in the fishing village of Megavissey, 'where I saw a very rare thing—men swiftly increasing in substance, and yet not decreasing in holiness.'

From such a land and such influences sprang the first missionary hero of the Church of England in modern[6] times. The Martyn family had for more than a century been known locally as one of skilled miners, described by their ablest representative in recent times[2] as 'mine agents or mine captains who filled positions of trust.' Martin Luther had a similar origin. There is no evidence that any of them went underground, although that, if true, would justify the romance for which Martyn's first biographer is responsible. His great-grandfather was Thomas Martyn, his grandfather was John Martyn of Gwennap Churchtown, and his grand-uncle was the surveyor, Thomas Martyn (1695-1751), who published the map of Cornwall described as a marvel of minute and accurate topography, due to a survey on foot for fifteen years. Mr. Jeffery quotes from some manuscript notes written by his father:

John, an elder brother of Thomas Martyn, was the father of John Martyn, who was born at Gwennap Churchtown, and, when young, was put as an accountant at Wheal Virgin Mine. He was soon made cashier to Ralph Allen Daniell, Esq., of Trelissick. Mr. Martyn held one-twenty-fourth of Wheal Unity Mine, where upwards of 300,000*l* was divided. He then resided in a house opposite the Coinage Hall (now the Cornish Bank), Truro, a little below the present Market House. Here Henry Martyn was born February 18, 1781, and was sent thence to Dr. Cardew's School in 1788.

The new Town Hall stands on the site of the house.

The boy bore a family name which is common in Southwest England, and which was doubtless derived, in the first instance, from the great missionary monk of Celtic France, the founder of the Gallic Church, St. Martin, Bishop of Tours. Born in what is now Lower Hungary, the son of[7] a pagan soldier of Rome, St. Martin, during his long life which nearly covered the fourth century, made an impression, especially on Western or Celtic Christendom, even greater than that of the Devonshire Winfrith or Boniface on Germany long after him. It was in the generation after his death, when St. Martin's glory was at its height, that the Saxon invasion of Britain led to the migration of British Christians from West and South England to Armorica, which was thence called Brittany. The intercourse between Cornwall and Britannia Minor became as close as is now the case between the Celtic districts of the United Kingdom and North America. Missionaries continually passed and repassed between them. St. Corentin, consecrated Bishop of Quimper in Brittany or French Cornwall, by the hands of St. Martin himself, was sent to Cornwall long before Pope Gregory despatched St. Augustin to Canterbury, and became a popular Cornish saint after whom St. Cury's parish is still named. On the other side, the Early British Church of Cornwall, where we still find Roman Christian inscriptions, kept up a close fellowship with the Church in Ireland. The earliest martyrs and hermits of the Church of Cornu-Gallia were companions of St. Patrick.

Certainly there is no missionary saint in all the history of the Church of Christ whom, in his character, Henry Martyn so closely resembled as his namesake, the apostle of the Gallic peoples. In the pages of the bishop's biographer, Sulpicius Severus, we see the same self-consecration which has made the *Journal* of Henry Martyn a stimulus to the noblest spirits of modern Christendom; the same fiery zeal, often so excessive as to defeat the Divine mission; the same soldier-like obedience and[8] humility; the same prayerfulness without ceasing, and faith in the power of prayer; the same fearlessness in preaching truth however disagreeable to the luxurious and vicious of the time; and, above all on the practical side, the same winning loveableness and self-sacrifice for others which have made the story of St. Martin dividing his cloak with the beggar second only, in Mediæval art, to the Gospel records of the Lord's own acts of tender grace and Divine self-emptying. As we trace, step by step, the unceasing service of Henry Martyn to men for love of his Master, we shall find a succession of modern parallels to the act of St. Martin, who, when a lad of eighteen with his regiment at Amiens, himself moneyless, answered the appeal of a beggar, shivering at the city gates in a cruel winter, by drawing his dagger, dividing his military cloak, and giving half of it to the naked man. If the legend continues to run, that the boy saw in a dream Christ Himself in the half-cloak saying to the attendant angels, 'Martin, still a catechumen, has clothed Me with this garment,' and forthwith sought baptism—that is only a form of the same spirit which, from the days of Paul to our own, finds inspiration in the thought that we are compassed about by a great cloud of witnesses.

Henry Martyn was baptised in the old church of St. Mary, now part of the unfinished cathedral. He was the third of four children. The eldest, a half-brother, John, was born fifteen years before him. The second and fourth were his own sisters, Laura and Sally; the former married Mr. Curgenven, nephew of the Vicar of Lamorran of that name; the latter married a Mr. Pearson. Short-lived as Henry himself proved to be, all three died before him. To both the sisters—and especially to the younger,[9] who proved to be to him at once sister, mother, and spiritual guide to Christ—there are frequent allusions in his *Journals and Letters*. His mother, named Fleming, and from Ilfracombe, died in the year after his birth, having transmitted her delicate constitution to her children. It was through his father, as well as younger sister, that the higher influences were rained on Henry Martyn. In the wayward and often wilful years before the boy yielded to the power of Christ's resurrection, the father's gentleness kept him in the right way, from which any violent opposition would have driven one of proud spirit. A skilled accountant and practical self-trained mathematician, the father encouraged in the boy the study of science, and early introduced him to the great work of Newton. Valuing the higher education as few in England did at that time, John Martyn ever kept before the lad the prospect of a University course. Looking back on these days, and especially on his last visit home before his father's unexpected death, Henry Martyn wrote when he was eighteen years of age:

The consummate selfishness and exquisite irritability of my mind were displayed in rage, malice, and envy, in pride and vain-glory and contempt of all; in the harshest language to my sister, and even to my father, if he happened to differ from my mind and will. Oh, what an example of patience and mildness was he! I love to think of his excellent qualities, and it is frequently the anguish of my heart that I ever could be so base and wicked as to pain him by the slightest neglect.

Truro was fortunate in its grammar school—'the Eton of Cornwall'—and in the headmaster of that time, the Rev. Cornelius Cardew, D.D., whose portrait now adorns the cit[10]y's council chamber. The visitor who seeks out the old school in Boscawen Street now finds it converted into the ware-room of an ironmonger. All around may still be seen the oak panels on which successive generations of schoolboys cut their names. A pane of glass on which Henry Martyn scratched his name, with a Greek quotation and a Hebrew word, probably on his last visit to the spot before he left England for ever, is reverently preserved in the muniment room of the corporation buildings. There also are the musty folios of the dull history and duller divinity which formed the school library of that uncritical century, but there is no means of tracing the reading of the boys. Into this once lightsome room, adorned

5

only by a wood-carving of the galleon which formed the city arms, was the child Henry Martyn introduced at the age of seven. Dr. Clement Carlyon, who was one of his fellow-pupils, writes of him as 'a good-humoured plain little fellow, with red eyelids devoid of eyelashes'. But we know from Mrs. Sherwood, when she first met him in India—where his hair, a light brown, was raised from his forehead, which was a remarkably fine one—that although his features were not regular, 'the expression was so luminous, so intellectual, so affectionate, so beaming with Divine charity, as to absorb the attention of every observer'. His sensitive nature and violent passionateness when roused, at once marked him out as the victim of the older boys. In a happy moment Dr. Cardew put 'little Henry Martyn' under the care of one of them, who became his protector, tutor, and friend, not only at school but at college, and had an influence on his spiritual as well as intellectual life next only to that of his father, sister, and Charles Simeon. That 'upper boy'—named Kempthorne, son of Admiral Kempthorne, of Helston—delighted to recall|11| to his first biographer, Sargent, 'the position in which he used to sit, the thankful expression of his affectionate countenance, when he happened to be helped out of some difficulty, and a thousand other little incidents of his boyish days.' This boy-friend 'had often the happiness of rescuing him from the grasp of oppressors, and has never seen more feeling of gratitude evinced than was shown by him on those occasions.'

Even at seven Henry's natural cleverness was so apparent that high expectations of his future were formed. Dr. Cardew wrote of his proficiency in the classics as exceeding that of most of his school-fellows, but he was too lively and too careless to apply himself as some did who distanced him. 'He was of a lively, cheerful temper, and, as I have been told by those who sat near him, appeared to be the idlest among them, being frequently known to go up to his lesson with little or no preparation, as if he had learnt it by intuition.' The delicacy of his constitution naturally kept him from joining in the rougher games of his fellows. Such was the impression made by his progress at school that, when he was fifteen years of age, not only Dr. Cardew and his father, but many of his father's friends, urged him to compete for a vacant scholarship of Corpus Christi College, Oxford. With only a letter to the sub-rector of Exeter College, the usual Cornish College, the boy found himself in the great University city. The examiners were divided in opinion as to the result, but a majority gave it in favour of one with whom Henry Martyn was almost equal. Had he become a member of that University at fifteen, with character unformed and knowledge immature or superficial, it is not likely that Oxford would have gained what, at a riper stage, Cambridge fell|12| heir to. His own comment, written afterwards like Augustine's in the *Confessions*, was this: 'The profligate acquaintances I had in Oxford would have introduced me to scenes of debauchery, in which I must, in all probability, from my extreme youth, have sunk for ever.' He returned to school for two years, to extend his knowledge of the classics. He spent his leisure in shooting, and in reading travels and Lord Chesterfield's *Letters*. His early private Journal reflects severely on that time as spent in 'attributing to a want of taste for mathematics what ought to have been ascribed to idleness; and having his mind in a roving, dissatisfied, restless condition, seeking his chief pleasure in reading and human praise.'

ST. JOHN'S COLLEGE, CAMBRIDGE, IN 1797

In this spirit he began residence in St. John's College, Cambridge, in the month of October 1797, as a pensioner or unassisted student. To that University he was attracted by Kempthorne, who had been his protector at school, and had just distinguished himself at St. John's, coming out Senior Wrangler. Alike from the idleness to which he was tempted by other fellow-students who were new to him, and from the variety of study with no other motive than to win glory of men, his friend gradually weaned his fickle and impulsive genius. But for two years he halted between two opinions. He was ever restless because ever dissatisfied with himself, and his want of inward peace only increased the natural irritability of his temper. He indulged in bursts of passion on slight provocation, and sometimes on none at all, save that of an uneasy conscience. Like Clive about the same age, Henry Martyn on one occasion hurled a knife at his friend, Cotterill, who just escaped, leaving it quivering in the panel of the dining-hall. The father and younger sister at |15|home prayerfully watched over him, and by letter sought to guide him. On his periodical visits to Truro he was able at least to report success in his examinations, and at the close of 1799 he came out first, to his father's delight. The providence of God had made all things ready for the completion of His eighteen years' work in the convictions and character of Henry Martyn, on his return to college. To him, at the opening of the new century, all things became new.

Cambridge, first of all, had received—unconsciously to its leading men for a time—that new spirit which has ever since identified its University with the aggressive missionary philanthropy of the nineteenth century. For nearly the whole period of Martyn's life, up to that time, Charles Simeon, the Eton boy, Fellow of King's College, and Christian gentleman, who had sought the position only that he might preach Christ after the manner of St. Paul, had, from the pulpit of Trinity Church, been silently transforming academic life. He had become the trusted agent of Charles Grant and George Udny, the Bengal civilians who were ready to establish an eight-fold mission in Bengal as soon as he could send out the men. Failing to find these, he had brought about the foundation of the Church Missionary Society on April 12, 1799. Some years before that, Charles Grant exchanged his seat in the Bengal council for one of the 'chairs' of the Court of Directors. He became their chairman, and it was to Simeon that he turned for East India chaplains. Cambridge, even more than London itself, had become the centre of the spiritual life of the Church of England.

First among the fellow-students of Henry Martyn, though soon to leave for India when he entered it, was his|16| future friend, Claudius Buchanan, B.A. of 1796 and Fellow of Queen's College, of which Isaac Milner was president. Magdalene College—which had sent David Brown to Calcutta in 1786, to prepare the way for the other four, who are for ever memorable as 'the Five Chaplains'—had among its students of the same standing as Martyn, Charles Grant's two distinguished sons, of whom one became Lord Glenelg and a cabinet minister, and the younger, Robert, was afterwards Governor of Bombay, the still valued hymnologist, and the warm friend of Dr. John Wilson. Thomason—seven years older than Martyn, and induced afterwards, by his example, to become a Bengal chaplain—was Simeon's curate and substitute in the closing years of the last century, when to Mr. Thornton of Clapham, who had warned him against preaching five sermons a week, as casting the net too often to allow time to mend it, he drew this picture of college life: 'There are reasons for fearing the mathematical religion which so prevails here. Here, also, is everything that can contribute to the ease and comfort of life. Whatever pampers the appetite and administers fuel to sloth and indolence is to be found in abundance. Nothing is left to want or desire. Here is the danger; this is the horrible precipice.' Corrie and Dealtry, also of the Five Chaplains, and afterwards first and second Bishops of Madras, were of Martyn's Cambridge time, the latter graduating before, and the former just after him.

Hardly had Henry Martyn returned to college in January 1800 when he received from his half-brother news of the death of their father, whom he had just before left 'in great health and spirits.' The first result was 'consternation,' and then, as he told his sister,|17|

I was extremely low-spirited, and, like most people, began to consider seriously, without any particular determination, that invisible world to which he had gone and to which I must one day go. As I had no taste at this time for my usual studies, I took up my Bible. Nevertheless I often took up other books to engage my attention, and should have continued to do so had not Kempthorne advised me to make this time an occasion of serious reflection. I began with the Acts, as being the most amusing, and when I was entertained with the narrative I found myself insensibly led to inquire more attentively into the doctrines of the Apostles.... On the first night after, I began to pray from a precomposed form, in which I thanked God in general for having sent Christ into the world. But though I prayed for pardon I had little sense of my own sinfulness; nevertheless, I began to consider myself a religious man.

The college chapel service at once had a new meaning for the student whom death had shaken and the Book of the Acts of the Apostles had awakened. 'The first time after this that I went to chapel I saw, with some degree of surprise at my former inattention, that in the Magnificat there was a great degree of joy expressed at the coming of Christ, which I thought but reasonable.' His friend then lent him Doddridge's *Rise and Progress of Religion in the Soul*, but, because the first part of that book 'appeared to make religion consist too much in humiliation, and my proud and wicked heart would not bear to be brought down into the dust,' he could not bear to read it. 'Soon, however,' as he afterwards told his sister, who had prayed for this very thing all her life, as Monica had agonised for Augustine,[18] 'I began to attend more diligently to the words of our Saviour in the New Testament, and to devour them with delight. When the offers of mercy and forgiveness were made so freely, I supplicated to be made partaker of the covenant of grace with eagerness and hope, and thanks be to the ever-blessed Trinity for not leaving me without comfort.' The doctrines of the Apostles, based on the narrative of the Acts, and confirming the teaching of the family in early youth, were seen to be in accord with the words of the Master, and thus Henry Martyn started on the Christian life an evangelical of the Evangelicals. In the preaching and the personal friendship of the minister of Trinity Church he found sympathetic guidance, and so 'gradually acquired more knowledge in divine things.' All the hitherto irregular impulses of his fervent Celtic nature received the baptism of the Holy Spirit, and became centred in the living, reigning, personal Christ. All the restless longings of his soul and his senses found their satisfaction for ever in the service of Him who had said 'He that loveth his life shall lose it. If any man serve Me, let him follow Me, and where I am there shall also My servant be.' All the pride of his genius, his intellectual ambition, and his love of praise became purged by the determination thenceforth to know nothing save the Crucified One.

His first temptation and test of honest fitness for such service was found in the examination for degrees, and especially for the greatest honour of all, that of Senior Wrangler. If we place his conversion to Christ at the close of his nineteenth year, we find that the whole of his twentieth was spent in the necessary preparation for the competition, and in the accompanying spiritual struggles. It is not surprising that, when looking back on that year from higher experiences, he should be severe in his self-examination. But the path of duty clearly lay in hard[19] and constant study, and not alone in religious meditation. It was not surprising that the experienced convert should afterwards pronounce the former worldly, and lament that 'the intenseness with which I pursued my studies' prevented his growth in contrition, and in a knowledge of the excellency of Christ. But so severe a judge as his friend and fellow-student John Sargent, who knew all the facts, and became not less saintly than himself, declares that there was no reason, save his own humility, for his suspecting a want of vitality at least in his spiritual life in this critical year. His new-found life in Christ, and delight in the Bible, reacted on his whole nature, elevating it to that degree of spontaneous energy free from all self-consciousness which is the surest condition, divine and human, of success. He himself used to tell how, when he entered the Senate House, the text of a sermon he had recently heard quieted his spirit: 'Seekest thou great things for thyself? Seek them not, saith the Lord.'

Henry Martyn was not fully twenty years of age when, in January 1801, he came out Senior Wrangler and first Smith's (mathematical) Prizeman. His year was one of the most brilliant in the recent history of the University. Woodall of Pembroke was second. Robert Grant was third, and Charles Grant (Lord Glenelg) fourth Wrangler. They distanced him in classics, once his strongest point. But the boy who entered college believing that geometry was to be learned by committing Euclid[3] to memory had[20] given the whole strength of his powers during three years to the college examinations, so as to please his father and win the applause of his fellows. Until recently it was possible for a student to enter the University ignorant of mathematics, and to come out Senior Wrangler, as the late Professor Kelland used to tell his Edinburgh class. Such was the reverence for Newton that the Leibnizian methods were not recognised in the University studies till the reform of the Cambridge course was introduced by Dean Peacock and his contemporaries. In those earlier days, Dr. Carlyon,[4] who had been one of his school-fellows, tells us high Wranglers won their places by correct book-work rapidly produced in oral examination from four set treatises by Wood and Vince, on optics, mechanics, hydrostatics, and astronomy; problem papers were answered by the best men. Martyn's grand-nephew, himself a distinguished mathematician, remarks that he sprang from a family of calculators, and so had the patience and taste necessary for mathematical attainments. There is no evidence that he pursued science even at Cambridge except as a tutor; he does not appear to have been a mathematical examiner even in his own college.

[21]

The truth is seen in his own comment on a success which at once won for him admiration and deference in circles that could not appreciate the lofty Christian aims of his life: 'I obtained my highest wishes, but was surprised to find that I had grasped a shadow.' He was called to other service, and for that he brought his University triumph with him to the feet of Christ. He was too cultured, however, to despise learning or academic reputation, for they might be made weapons for the Master's use, and we shall find him wielding both alike in home and foreign missions. His genius and learning found expression in the study, the translation, and the unceasing application to the consciences of men, of the Word of God. His early love of the classics of Greece and Rome prevailed over his later mathematical studies to make him an ardent philologist, with the promise, had he lived, of becoming an Orientalist of the type of Sir William Jones. If he was known in his college as 'the man who had not lost an hour' when University honours alone were his object, how much would not his unresting perseverance have accomplished, when directed by the highest of all motives, had he been spared to the age of William Carey or John Wilson?

The time had come for the brilliant student to decide on his profession. The same ambition which had stimulated him to his college successes, had led him to resolve on studying the law, as the most lucrative. 'I could not consent to be poor for Christ's sake,' was his own language at a later period. But Christ himself had changed all that, as effectually as when the young lawyer Saul was stricken down after the martyr testimony of Stephen. The year 1801 was to him one of comparative solitude, both in[22] Cornwall and at the University, where he cultivated the fruitful grace of meditation, learning to know and to master himself, as he came to know more and more intimately, and to submit himself to, Christ Jesus. He was admitted to the inner circle of Simeon's friends, and to unreserved intercourse with men of his own age who had come to Christ before him. Especially was he drawn to John Sargent, one year his senior, who was about to leave the university for the Temple, that he might by the study of law prepare himself to administer worthily the family estate to which he was to succeed. His son-in-law, the late Bishop S. Wilberforce, has left us a charming picture[5] of this saintly man, of whom Martyn wrote, even at college, 'Sargent seems to be outstripping us all.' While Simeon ever, by his counsels and his example, impressed on the choice youth whom he gathered around him the attractiveness of the Christian ministry,[6]Sargent bewailed that only a painful sense of duty to others kept him from it, and in a few years he succeeded in entering its consecrated ranks. Among such friends, and with his own heart growing in the experience of the power of the Holy Spirit, Henry Martyn was constrained, notwithstanding his new humbleness of mind, to hear and obey the divine call. He who had received such mercy must tell it abroad; he who had known such love must bring others to share the sweetness. Hence he writes to his sister:

When we consider the misery and darkness of the unregenerate world, oh! with how much reason shall we burst out into thanksgiving to God, who has called us in His mercy through Christ Jesus! What are we, that we[23] should thus be made objects of distinguishing grace! Who, then, that reflects upon the rock from which he was hewn, but must rejoice to give himself entirely and without reserve to God, to be sanctified by His Spirit. The soul that has truly experienced the love of God, will not stay meanly inquiring how much he shall do, and thus limit his service, but will be earnestly seeking more and more to know the will of our Heavenly Father, and that he may be enabled to do it. Oh, may we both be thus minded! may we experience Christ to be our all in all, not only as our Redeemer, but also as the fountain of grace. Those passages of the Word of God which you have quoted on this head, are indeed awakening; may they teach us to breathe after holiness, to be more and more dead to the world, and alive unto God, through Jesus Christ. We are as lights in the world; how needful then that our tempers and lives should manifest our high and heavenly calling! Let us, as we do, provoke one another to good works, not doubting that God will bless our feeble endeavours to His glory.

The next year, 1802, saw Martyn Fellow of his College and the winner of the first University prize for a Latin essay, open to those who had just taken the Bachelor of Arts degree. It ended in his determination to offer himself to the Church Missionary Society. He had no sooner resolved to be a minister of Christ than he began such home mission work as lay to his hands among his fellow members of the University, and in the city where, at a recent period, one who closely resembled him in some points, Ion Keith-Falconer, laboured. When ministering to a dying man he found that the daughters had removed to another house, where they were cheerful, and one of the students was reading a play to them.[24] 'A play! when their father was lying in the agonies of death! What a species of consolation! I rebuked him so sharply, and, I am afraid, so intemperately, that a quarrel will perhaps ensue.' This is the first of those cases in which the impulsively faithful Christian, testifying for his Master, often roused hatred to himself. But the student afterwards thanked him for his words, became a new man, and went out to India, where he laboured for a time by his side. After a summer tour—during which he walked to Liverpool, and then through Wales, ascending Snowdon—Henry Martyn found himself in the old home in Truro, then occupied by his brother. From the noise of a large family he moved to Woodbury: 'With my brother-in-law[?] I passed some of the sweetest moments in my life. The deep solitude of the place favoured meditation; and the romantic scenery around supplied great external sources of pleasure.'

Along the beautiful coast of Cornwall and Devon there is no spot more beautiful than Woodbury. It is henceforth sacred as Moulton in Carey's life, and St. Andrews in Alexander Duff's, for there Henry Martyn wrestled out his deliberate dedication to the service of Christ in India and Persia. The Fal river is there just beginning to open out into the lovely estuary which, down almost to Falmouth town and Carrick Road, between Pendennis and St. Mawes, is clothed on either side with umbrageous woods. On the left shore, after leaving the point from which is the best view of Truro and its cathedral, now known as the Queen's View, there is Malpas, and further on are the sylvan glories of Tregothnan. On the right shore, sloping down to the ever-moving tide, are the oaks, ilexes, and firs which inclose Woodbury, recently rebuilt. There the Cambridge scholar of twenty-one roamed and read his Bible (especially Isaiah);[25] 'and from this I derived great spirituality of mind compared with what I had known before.' He returned to Cambridge and its tutorial duties, ready to become Simeon's curate, and ultimately to go abroad when the definite call should come. In the first conversation which he had with him, Simeon, who had been reading the last number of the *Periodical Accounts* from Serampore, drew attention to the results of William Carey's work, in the first nine years of his pioneering, as showing what a single missionary could accomplish. From this time, in his letters and journals, we find all his thoughts and reading, when alone, revolving around the call to the East.

1803, January 12 to 19.—Reading Lowth on Isaiah—Acts—and abridged Bishop Hopkins' first sermon on Regeneration. On the 19th called on Simeon, from whom I found that I was to go to the East Indies, not as a missionary, but in some superior capacity; to be stationed at Calcutta, or possibly at Ceylon. This prospect of this world's happiness gave me rather pain than pleasure, which convinced me that I had before been running away from the world, rather than overcoming it. During the whole course of the day, I was more worldly than for some time past, unsettled and dissatisfied. In conversation, therefore, I found great levity, pride, and bitterness. What a sink of corruption is this heart, and yet I can go on from day to day in self-seeking and self-pleasing! Lord, shew me myself, nothing but 'wounds and bruises, and putrefying sores,' and teach me to live by faith on Christ my all.

St. John's, January 17, 1803.

My dear Sargent,—G. and H. seem to disapprove of my project much; and on this account I have been rather discouraged of late, though not in any degree convinced. It would be more satisfactory to go out with the[26] full approbation of my friends, but it is in vain to attempt to please man. In doubtful cases, we are to use the opinions of others no further than as means of directing our own judgment. My sister has also objected to it, on the score of my deficiency in that deep and solid experience necessary in a missionary.

February 4.—Read Lowth in the afternoon, till I was quite tired. Endeavoured to think of Job xiv. 14, and to have solemn thoughts of death, but could not find them before my pupil came, to whom I explained justification by faith, as he had ridiculed Methodism. But talk upon what I will, or with whom I will, conversation leaves me ruffled and discomposed. From what does this arise? From a want of the sense of God's presence when I am with others.

February 6.—Read the Scriptures, between breakfast and church, in a very wandering and unsettled manner, and in my walk was very weak in desires after God. As I found myself about the middle of the day full of pride and formality, I found some relief in prayer. Sat with H. and D. after dinner, till three, but though silent, was destitute of humility. Read some of S. Pearce's[8] life, and was much interested by his account of the workings of his mind on the subject of his mission. Saw reason to be thankful that I had no such tender ties to confine me at home, as he seemed to have; and to be amazed at myself, in not making it a more frequent object of reflection, and yet to praise God for calling me to minister in the glorious work of the conversion of the Gentiles.

March 27.—The lectures in chemistry and anatomy I was much engaged with, without receiving much instruction. A violent cold and cough led me to prepare myself for an inquiry into my views of death. I was enabled to rest composed on the Rock of Ages. Oh, what mercy shewn to the chief of sinners.[27]

April 22.—Was ashamed to confess to ——that I was to be Mr. Simeon's curate, a despicable fear of man from which I vainly thought myself free. He, however, asked me if I was not to be, and so I was obliged to tell him. Jer. i. 17.

May 8.—Expressed myself contemptuously of ——, who preached at St. Mary's. Such manifestations of arrogance which embody, as it were, my inward pride, wound my spirit inexpressibly, not to contrition, but to a sullen sense of guilt. Read Second Epistle to Timothy. I prayed with some earnestness.

June 13 to 24.—Passed in tolerable comfort upon the whole; though I could on no day say my walk had been close with God. Read Sir G. Staunton's *Embassy to China*, and was convinced of the propriety of being sent thither. But I have still the spirit of worldly men when I read worldly books. I felt more curiosity about the manners of this people than love and pity towards their souls.

St. John's, June 30, 1803.

Dear Sargent,—May you, as long as you shall give me your acquaintance, direct me to the casting down of all high imaginations. Possibly it may be a cross to you to tell me or any one of his faults. But should I be at last a castaway, or at least dishonour Christ through some sin, which for want of faithful admonition remained unmortified, how bitter would be your reflections! I conjure you, therefore, my dear friend, as you value the good of the souls to whom I am to preach, and my own eternal interests, that you tell me what you think to be, in my life, spirit, or temper, not according to the will of God my Saviour. D. has heard about a religious young man of seventeen, who wants to come to College, but has only 20*l*.a year. He is very clever, and from the perusal of some poems which he has published, I am much interested about him. His name is H.K. White.[28]

July 17.—Rose at half-past five, and walked a little before chapel in happy frame of mind; but the sunshine was presently overcast by my carelessly neglecting to speak for the good of two men, when I had an opportunity. The pain was, moreover, increased by the prospect of the incessant watchfulness for opportunities I should use; nevertheless, resolved that I would do so through grace. The dreadful act of disobeying God, and the baseness of being unwilling to incur the contempt of men, for the sake of the Lord Jesus, who had done so much for me, and the cruelty of not longing to save souls, were the considerations that pressed on my mind.

July 18 to 30.—Gained no ground in all this time; stayed a few days at Shelford, but was much distracted and unsettled for want of solitude. Felt the passion of envy rankle in my bosom on a certain occasion. Seldom enjoyed peace, but was much under the power of corruption. Read Butler's *Analogy*; Jon. Edwards *On the Affections*, in great hopes that this book will be of essential use to me.

September 10.—Was most deeply affected with reading the account of the apostasy of Lewis and Broomhall, in the transactions of the Missionary Society. When I first came to the account of the awful death of the former, I cannot describe the sense I had of the reality of religion,—that there is a God who testifies His hatred of sin; 'my flesh trembled for fear of His judgments.' Afterwards, coming to the account of Broomhall's sudden turn to Deism, I could not help even bursting into tears of anxiety and terror at my own extreme danger;

because I have often thought, that if I ever should make shipwreck, it would be on the rocks of sensuality or infidelity. The hollowness of Broomhall's arguments was so apparent, that I could only attribute his fall to the neglect of inquiring after the rational foundation of his faith.

September 12.—Read some of the minor prophets, and Greek Testament, and the number of the [29]*Missionary Transactions.* H. drank tea with me in the evening. I read some of the missionary accounts. The account of their sufferings and diligence could not but tend to lower my notions of myself. I was almost ashamed at my having such comforts about me, and at my own unprofitableness.

September 13.—Received a letter from my sister, in which she expressed her opinion of my unfitness for the work of a missionary. My want of Christian experience filled me with many disquieting doubts, and this thought troubled me among many others, as it has often done: 'I am not only not so holy as I ought, but I do not strive to have my soul wrought up to the highest pitch of devotion every moment.'

September 17.—Read Dr. Vanderkemp's mission to Kafraria. What a man! In heaven I shall think myself well off, if I obtain but the lowest seat among such, though now I am fond of giving myself a high one.

St. John's, September 29, 1803.

How long it seems since I heard from you, my dear Sargent. My studies during the last three months have been Hebrew, Greek Testament, Jon. Edwards *On Original Sin*, and *On the Affections*, and Bishop Hopkins,—your favourite and mine. Never did I read such energetic language, such powerful appeals to the conscience. Somehow or other he is able to excite most constant interest, say what he will. I have been lately reading the first volume of the *Reports* of the Missionary Society, who sent out so many to Otaheite and the southern parts of Africa. You would find the account of Dr. Vanderkemp's mission into Kafraria infinitely entertaining. It appeared so much so to me, that I could read nothing else while it lasted. Respecting my own concerns in this way, no material change has taken place, either externally or internally, except that my sister thinks me unqualified, through want of religious experience, and that I find greater pleasure at the prospect[30] of it. I am conscious, however, of viewing things too much on the bright side, and think more readily of the happiness of seeing the desert rejoice and blossom as the rose, than of pain, and fatigue, and crosses, and disappointments. However it shall be determined for me, it is my duty to crush the risings of self-will, so as to be cheerfully prepared to go or stay.

October 1.—In the afternoon read in Law's *Serious Call*, the chapter on 'Resignation,' and prayed for it, according to his direction. I rather think a regular distribution of the day for prayer, to obtain the three great graces of humility, love, and resignation, would be far the best way to grow in them. The music at chapel led my thoughts to heaven, and I went cheerfully to Mrs. S.H. drank tea with me afterwards. As there was in the *Christian Observer* something of my own, the first which ever appeared in print, I felt myself going off to vanity and levity.

SECOND COURT, ST. JOHN'S COLLEGE, 1803

October 9.—Rose at six, which is earlier than of late, and passed the whole morning in great tranquillity. I prayed to be sent out to China, and rejoiced in the prospect of the glorious day when Christ shall be glorified on earth. At chapel the music of the chant and anthem seemed to be in my ears as the sounds of heaven, particularly the anthem, 1 Chron. xxix. 10. But these joys, alas! partake much of the flesh in their transitory nature. At chapel I wished to return to my rooms to read the song of Moses the servant of God, &c. in the Revelation, but when I came to it I found little pleasure. The sound of the music had ceased, and with it my joy, and nothing remained but evil temper, darkness, and unbelief. All this time I had forgotten what it is to be a poor humble soul. I had floated off the Rock of Ages into the deep, where I was beginning to sink, had not the Saviour stretched out His hand, and said to me, 'It is I!' Let me never be cheated out of my dependence on Him, nor ever forget my need of Him.

October 12.—Reading Paley's *Evidences.* Had my pride[33] deeply wounded to-day, and perceived that I was far from humility. Great bitterness and dislike arose in my mind against

12

the man who had been the unconscious cause of it. Oh, may I learn daily my hidden evils, and loathe myself for my secret abominations! Prayed for the man, and found my affections return.

October 19.—I wished to have made my approaching ordination to the ministry a more leading object of my prayers. For two or three days I have been reading some of St. Augustine's *Meditations*, and was delighted with the hope of enjoying such communion with God as this holy man. Blessed be God! nothing prevents, no earthly business, no earthly love can rightfully intrude to claim my thoughts, for I have professedly resigned them all. My mind still continues in a joyous and happy state, though at intervals, through want of humility, my confidence seems vain.

October 20.—This morning was almost all lost, by friends coming in. At noon I read the fortieth chapter of Isaiah. Amidst the bustle of common life, how frequently has my heart been refreshed by the descriptions of the future glory of the Church, and the happiness of man hereafter!

November 13.—I longed to draw very near to God, to pray Him that He would give me the Spirit of wisdom and revelation. I thought of David Brainerd, and ardently desired his devotedness to God and holy breathings of soul.

When a Fellow of St. John's, Henry Martyn occupied the three rooms in the highest storey of E block, entered from the right-hand corner of the Second Court before passing through the gateway into the Third Court. The Court is that pronounced by Ruskin the finest in the University, because of the beautiful plum-red hue of the old brick, going back to 1595, and the perfect architecture. From the same stair the fine College Library is entered.[34] The low roof was formed of reed, instead of lath, and plaster, down to a very recent date. On one occasion, while the outer roof was being repaired, the foot of a workman suddenly pushed through the frail inner ceiling above the study table, an incident which has enabled their present occupant[2] to identify the rooms. Here Martyn studied, and taught, and prayed, while hour after hour and quarter after quarter, from the spire of St. Clement's on the one side, and the tower of Trinity College on the other, the flight of time was chimed forth. When, a generation after, Alexander Duff visited Charles Simeon and his successor, Carus, and expressed surprise that so few Cambridge men had, by 1836, given themselves to foreign missions, Carus pointed to the exquisite beauty of the Cam, as it winds between Trinity and St. John's, as one explanation of the fact. Both forgot Henry Martyn, whose Cornish temperament was most susceptible to the seductive influence, and whose academic triumphs might have made the ideal life of a Fellow of St. John's an overpowering temptation. As we stand in these hallowed rooms, or wander through the four courts, and in the perfect gardens, or recall the low chapel—which has given place to Sir Gilbert Scott's, with a frescoed figure of Henry Martyn on its roof—we can realise the power of the motive that sent him forth to Dinapore and Cawnpore, Shiraz and Tokat.

Samuel Pearce—the 'seraphic' preacher of Birmingham, whom a weak body, like Martyn's, alone prevented from joining his beloved Carey at Serampore; Vanderkemp, the Dutch physician, who had given up all for the good of the Kafirs, and whom he was soon to see in the midst of his converts; David Brainerd, also like himself in the shortness[35] and saintliness of his career; the transactions of the London Missionary Society; the latest works on the East; and the experimental divinity of Augustine, Jonathan Edwards, and Law, with the writings of Bishops Butler and Hopkins, and Dr. Paley—these were the men and the books he used to train his spirit for the work of the ministry abroad, when he had fed it with the words of Jesus Christ, Isaiah, and Paul. He thus describes his examination for Deacon's orders, and his ordination by the Bishop of Ely on the title of his Fellowship, after which he became Mr. Simeon's curate, and took charge of the neighbouring small parish of Lolworth.

1803, October 22.—Went in a gig to Ely with B. Having had no time for morning prayer, my conversation was poor. At chapel, I felt great shame at having come so confidently to offer myself for the ministry of the Lord Jesus Christ, with so much ignorance and unholiness, and I thought it would be but just if I were sent off with ignominy. Dr. M., the examining chaplain, set me to construe the eleventh chapter of Matthew: Grotius: To turn the first article into Latin: To prove the being of a God, His infinite power and goodness: To give the evidence of Christianity to Jews and heathens: To shew the importance of the miracle of the resurrection of Christ. He asked an account, also, of the Pharisees, Sadducees, and Scribes, the places of the worship amongst the Jews, &c. After leaving the palace I was in very low spirits. I had now nothing to think of but the weight and difficulty of the work which lay before me, which never appeared so great at a distance. At dinner the conversation was frivolous. After tea I was left alone with one of the deacons, to whom I talked seriously, and desired him to read the Ordination Service, at which he was much affected. Retired to my room early, and besought God to give me a right and affecting sense of things. I seemed to[36] pray a long time in vain, so dark and distracted was my mind. At length I began to feel the shameful and cruel neglect and unconcern for the honour of God, and the souls of my brethren, in having trifled with men whom I feared were about to 'lie to the Holy Ghost.' So I went to them again, resolving to lay hold on any opportunity, but found none to do anything effectually. Went to bed with a painful sense of my hardness of heart and unsuitable preparation for the ministry.

October 23.—Rose early, and prayed, not without distraction. I then walked, but could not acquire a right and happy sense of God's mercy in calling me to the ministry; but was melancholy at the labours that awaited me. On returning, I met one of the deacons, to whom I spoke on the solemn occasion, but he seemed incapable of entertaining a serious thought. At half-past ten we went to the cathedral. During the ordination and sacramental services I sought in vain for a humble heavenly mind. The outward show which tended to inspire solemnity, affected me more than the faith of Christ's presence, giving me the commission to preach the gospel. May I have grace to fulfil those promises I made before God and the people! After dinner, walked with great rapidity to Cambridge. I went straight to Trinity Church, where my old vanities assailed my soul. How monstrous and horrible did they appear in me, now that I was a minister of holy things! I could scarcely believe that so sacred an office should be held by one who had such a heart within. B. sat with me in the evening, but I was not humbled; for I had not been near to God to obtain the grace of contrition. On going to prayer at night, I was seized with a most violent sickness. In the pain and disorder of my body, I could but commend myself faintly to God's mercy in Jesus Christ.

TRINITY CHURCH IN 1803.

October 24 to 29.—Busily employed in writing a sermon, and from the slow advances I made in it, was in general[39] very melancholy. I read on the Thursday night for the first time in Trinity Church.

October 30.—Rose with a heavy heart, and my head empty, from having read so little of the Scriptures this last week. After church, sat with ——— two hours conversing about the missionary plan. He considered my ideas on the subject to be enthusiastic, and told me that I had neither strength of body nor mind for the work. This latter defect I did not at all like; it was galling to the pride of my heart, and I went to bed hurt; yet thankful to God for sending me one who would tell me the truth.

December 3.—Employed all day in writing sermon. The incessant employment of my thoughts about the necessary business of my life, parishes, pupils, sermons, sick, &c., leave far too little time for my private meditations; so that I know little of God and my soul. Resolved I would gain some hours from my usual sleep, if there were no other way; but failed this morning in consequence of sitting up so late.

December 4.—Called at two or three of the parishioners' houses, and found them universally in the most profound state of ignorance and stupidity. On my road home could not perceive that men who have any little knowledge should have anything to do but instruct their wretched fellow-creatures. The pursuits of science, and all the vain and glittering employments of men, seemed a cruel withholding from their perishing brethren of that time and exertion which might save their souls.

December 22.—Married ———. How satisfactory is it to administer the ordinance of matrimony, where the couple are pious! I felt thankful that I was delivered from all desires of the comforts of the married life. With the most desirable partner, and every prospect of happiness, I would prefer a single life, in which there are so much greater opportunities for heavenly-mindedness.

[40]

14

When appointed classical examiner of his college at this time, he jealously examined himself:

Did I delight in reading of the retreat of the ten thousand Greeks; and shall not my soul glory in the knowledge of God, who created the Greeks, and the vast countries over which they passed! I examined in Butler's *Analogy* and in Xenophon: how much pride and ostentatious display of learning was visible in my conduct—how that detestable spirit follows me, whatever I do!

He opened the year 1804, after preaching in Trinity Church, and visiting two men whom he exhorted to think on their ways, with a review of his new-found life.

Nevertheless, I judge that I have grown in grace in the course of the last year; for the bent of my desires is towards God more than when I thought I was going out as a missionary, though vastly less than I expected it would have been by this time.

This year he received into his fellowship the young poet, Henry Kirke White, whom Wilberforce had, at Simeon's request, sent to St. John's. Southey declares that Chatterton is the only youthful poet whom Kirke White does not leave far behind him. 'The Star of Bethlehem' is certainly a hymn that will live. The sickly youth followed close in Martyn's steps, becoming the first man of his year, but the effort carried him off almost before his friend reached India.

Had Martyn been of canonical age for ordination at the close of 1803, there can be little doubt that he would at once have been sent out by the Church Missionary Society, which could find only German Lutherans as its agents abroad, until 1813, when another Fellow of St. John's, and a Wrangler, the Rev. William Jowett, offered his services,[41] and was stationed at Malta. But when ordained he lost the little that he had inherited from his father, and saw his younger sister also without resources. There was a tradition in the family of his half-brother John, that Henry and his sisters litigated with him, and farther lessened the patrimony. However that may have been, while in India Henry set apart the proceeds of his Fellowship at St. John's for the maintenance of his brother's family, and bequeathed all he had to his children. Mr. H. Thornton, of Clapham, was executor, and duly carried out his instructions, starting the nephews in life. Another incident at this time foreshadows the self-denial of his Indian career. By opening the door of his room suddenly he had disfigured the face of his Cambridge landlady, whose husband was a clergyman. He left to her the interest of 1,000*l.* as an amend, and she enjoyed this annuity through a very long life.

The Senior Wrangler was not allowed to preach in the church where he had been baptised, nor in any church of his native county, save in his brother-in-law's. On August 8, 1804, he thus wrote to his friend 'R. Boys, Esq., Bene't Coll., Cambridge,' after preaching at Plymouth for his cousin:

The following Sunday it was not permitted me to occupy the pulpit of my native town, but in a neighbouring church I was allowed to testify the Gospel of the grace of God. But that one sermon was enough. The clergy seem to have united to exclude me from their churches, so that I must now be contented with my brother-in-law's two little churches about five miles from Truro. The objection is that 'Mr. Martyn is a Calvinist preacher in the dissenting way, &c.' My old schoolmaster, who has always hitherto been proud of his pupil, has offered his services for any time to a curate near this place, rather than, as he said, he should apply to me for assistance.

[42]

It is interesting to remember, remarks Mr. Moule, who has published this letter for the first time, that 'always now, as the anniversary of Martyn's death recurs, a sermon is preached in the cathedral of Truro, in which the great work of Missions is set forth, and his illustrious share in it commemorated.'

As confidential adviser of Charles Grant in the Court of Directors, in the appointment of chaplains, Simeon always sought to attract the best of his curates to that career, and it would appear from the *Journal* that so early as the beginning of 1803 he had hinted at this to Martyn. Now the way was plain. Martyn could no longer support himself as one of those volunteer missionaries whose services the two great missionary societies of the Church of England have always been happy to enjoy, nor could he relieve his sister out of the subsistence allowance of a missionary. Mr. Grant's offer of a Bengal chaplaincy seemed to come to him as the solution. But a new element had entered into his life, second only to his spiritual loyalty. He had learned to love Lydia Grenfell.

FOOTNOTES:

[1]See the *Statistical Society's Journal*, September, 1888, for invaluable notes on the 'System of Work and Wages in the Cornish Mines,' by L.L. Price, M.A., of Oriel College, Oxford.

[2]The late Henry Martyn Jeffery, M.A., F.R.S., in 1883.

[3]Rev. Henry Bailey, D.D., Canon of Canterbury, supplies us with this story from the lips of the late Rev. T.H. Shepherd, who was the last surviving Canon of the Collegiate Church in Southwell:—

'Henry Martyn had just entered the College as a Freshman under the Rev. Mr. Catton. I was the year above him, *i.e.* second year man; and Mr. Catton sent for me to his rooms, telling me of Martyn, as a quiet youth, with some knowledge of classics, but utterly unable as it seemed to make anything of even the First Proposition of Euclid, and desiring me to have him into my rooms, and see what I could do for him in this matter. Accordingly, we spent some time together, but all my efforts appeared to be in vain; and Martyn, in sheer despair, was about to make his way to the coach office, and take his place the following day back to Truro, his native town. I urged him not to be so precipitate, but to come to me the next day, and have another trial with Euclid. After some time light seemed suddenly to flash upon his mind, with clear comprehension of the hitherto dark problem, and he threw up his cap for joy at his *Eureka*. The Second Proposition was soon taken, and with perfect success; but in truth his progress was such and so rapid, that he distanced every one in his year, and, as everyone knows, became Senior Wrangler.'

[4]*Early Years and Late Reflections*, vol. iii. p. 5.

[5]Introduction to *Journals and Letters of Henry Martyn*, 1837.

[6]See the delightful *Charles Simeon*, by H.C.G. Moule, M.A. (1892), published since this was written.

[7]Rev. Mr. Curgenven, curate of Kenwyn and Kea.

[8]William Carey's most intimate friend. See p. 46 of *Life of William Carey*, D.D., 2nd ed. (John Murray).

[9]Rev. A. Caldecott, M.A., Fellow and Dean of St. John's College.

[43]

CHAPTER II

LYDIA GRENFELL

Twenty-six miles south-west of Truro, and now the last railway station before Penzance is reached for the Land's End, is Marazion, the oldest, the warmest, and long the dullest, of English towns. This was the home of Lydia Grenfell; this was the scene of Henry Martyn's wooing. Running out from the town is a natural causeway, uncovered at low tide, and leading to the most romantic spot on a romantic coast—the granite rock known to the Greek geographers as Ictis, and to English legend and history as St. Michael's Mount. Here it was that Jack slew the giant, Cormoran; here that the Phœnician, and possibly Israelite, traffickers found the harbour, and in the town the market, where they bought their copper and their tin; here that St. Michael appeared, as on the larger rock off Normandy, to the earliest Christian hermits, followed by the Benedictines; and here that King John made a fortress which both sides in the Great Rebellion held and took alternately. Since that time, possessed by the St. Aubyn family, and open to all the world, St. Michael's Mount has been a unique retreat in which castle and chapel, cemetery and garden, unite peacefully, to link the restlessness of the nineteenth century with the hermit saintliness and angel-ophanies of the fifth. It was the last spot of English, of[44] Cornish, ground seen by Henry Martyn, and he knew that the windows of his beloved looked upon its grassy castellated height.

In the one ascending street of Marazion on the shore, there still stands the plain substantial Grenfell House, now boarded up and falling to ruin for want of the freehold tenure. Opposite it is the parish church, now on the site of the old chapel of ease of the neighbouring St. Hilary, which Lydia Grenfell deserted for the then warmer evangelical service of the little Wesleyan chapel. That is hidden in a lane, and is still the same as when she worshipped there, or only a little enlarged. The Grenvilles, Grenviles, or Grenfells, were

16

long a leading family connected with Cornwall as copper-buyers and smelters. One, Pascoe Grenfell, was a Governor of the Bank of England. Mr. Pascoe Grenfell, of Marazion (1729-1810), Commissary to the States of Holland, was father (1) of Emma, who became wife of Martyn's cousin, Rev. T. Martyn Hitchins; (2) of Lydia Grenfell; and (3) of Pascoe Grenfell, D.C.L., M.P. for Marlow and Penryn. This Pascoe's four daughters—Lydia Grenfell's nieces—each became the wife of a remarkable man. The eldest, in 1825, married Mr. Carr Glyn, M.P. for Kendal, and the first Lord Wolverton; the second, Lord Sidney Godolphin Osborne; the third, Mr. James Anthony Froude; and the fourth, Charles Kingsley.

ST. MICHAEL'S MOUNT AT FULL TIDE.

Lydia Grenfell, born in 1775, died in her sister's house, the old Vicarage of Breage, in 1829. She was thus six years older than Henry Martyn. As the sister of his cousin by marriage he must have known her early. He evidently did not know, till it was too late, that she had been engaged to a Mr. Samuel John, solicitor, of Penzance, who was unworthy of her and married someone else.[47] This engagement and its issue seem to have weighed on her very sensitive conscience; it became to her very much what Henry Martyn's hopeless love for her proved to be to himself. In the years from October 19, 1801, to 1826, she kept a diary not less devout, but far more morbid than his own. The two journals form, where they meet, a pathetic, even tragic, tale of affection, human and divine. Her bulky memoranda[10] contain few incidents of interest, rather severe introspections, incessant communings and heart-searchings, abstracts of sermons, records of visits to the sick and poor, but also a valuable residuum by which her relations with Martyn can be established beyond controversy. They show that she was as saintly as himself. She weighed every thought, every action, as in the immediate presence of God.

When Henry Martyn, at nineteen, entered on the higher life, he must have known Lydia Grenfell as the sister of Mrs. T.M. Hitchins, the cousin with whom his correspondence shows him to have been on most intimate, and even affectionate, terms. At that time the difference of age would seem slight; her it would affect little, if at all, while common experience suggests that it would be even attractive to him. With the ardour of a young disciple—which in his case grew, year by year, till he passed away—he sought spiritual counsel and communion. On his visits to Cornwall he found both in his younger sister, but it is evident that, from the first, the riper spiritual life of Lydia Grenfell attracted him to her. His triumph, at twenty, as Senior Wrangler put him quite in a position to dream of winning her. His unexpected poverty was relieved by his[48] Fellowship of St. John's. In those days, however, that would have ceased with marriage. When it became more than probable that he would receive an appointment to Bengal, through Mr. Charles Grant—either as minister of the Mission Church founded by Kiernander, or as a chaplain of the East India Company— he was face to face with the question of marrying.

In these days the course followed by missionary societies as the result of experience is certainly the best. A missionary and a chaplain in India should, in ordinary circumstances, be married, but it is not desirable that the marriage take place for a year or longer, until the young minister has proved the climate, and has learned the native language, when the lady can be sent out to be united to him. At the beginning of the modern missionary enterprise, a century ago, it was difficult to find spiritual men willing to go to India on any terms, and they did well in every case to go out married. All the conditions of time, distance, society, and Christian influence were then different. If the missionary's or chaplain's wife is worthy of his calling, she doubles his usefulness, notwithstanding the cares and the expense of children in many cases, alike by keeping her husband in a state of efficiency on every side, by her own works of charity and self-sacrifice—especially among the women, who can be reached in no other way—and by helping to present to the idolatrous or Mussulman community the powerful example of a Christian home. Henry Martyn's principles and instincts were right in this matter. As a chaplain, at any rate, he was in a position to marry at once. As India or Bengal then was, Lydia, had she gone out with him, or soon after him, would have proved to be a much needed force in Anglo-Indian society,[49] an influence on the native communities whom he sought to bring to Christ. Above all, as a man born with a weak body, with habits of incessant and intense application to study and to duty, Henry Martyn required one with the influence of a wife to keep him in life and to prolong his Indian service. It was the greatest calamity of his whole career that Lydia did not accompany him. But, since he learned to love her with all the rich devotion of his passionate nature, we cannot consider it 'a bitter misfortune,' as some do, that he ever knew her. His love for Lydia, in the fluctuations of its hope, in the ebb and flow of its tenderness, and in the transmutation of its despair into faith and resignation to the will of God, worked out a higher elevation for himself, and gives to his *Journals and Letters* a pure human interest which places them above the *Confessions of St. Augustine.*

The first allusion to the possibility of marriage we find in his *Journal* of January 23, 1803, and again in June 12 of the same year:

I was grieved to find that all the exertions of prayer were necessary against worldly-mindedness, so soon had the prospect of the means of competent support in India filled my heart with concern about earthly happiness, marriage, &c.; but I strove earnestly against them, and prayed for grace that, if it should please God to try my faith by calling me to a post of opulence, I might not dare to use for myself what is truly His; as also, that I might be enabled to keep myself single, for serving Him more effectually. Nevertheless, this change in my circumstances so troubled me, that I could have been infinitely better pleased to have gone out as a missionary, poor as the Lord and His Apostles.

[50]

His friend Sargent's 'approaching marriage with a lady of uncommon excellence rather excited in me a desire after a similar state; but I strove against it,' he wrote on July 10. Next day, on the top of the coach from London to Bath, in the cold of a high wind, he was 'most dreadfully assailed by evil thoughts, but at the very height prayer prevailed, and I was delivered, and during the rest of the journey enjoyed great peace and a strong desire to live for Christ alone, forsaking the pleasures of the world, marriage, &c.' At Plymouth he spent two days 'with my dear cousin T.H.,' Lydia's sister. After Truro, Kenwyn, and Lamorran, near Truro, of which his sister Sarah's husband was vicar, he rode to St. Hilary.

1804, July 29. (Sunday.)—Read and prayed in the morning before service with seriousness, striving against those thoughts which oppressed me all the rest of the day. At St. Hilary Church in the morning my thoughts wandered from the service, and I suffered the keenest disappointment. Miss L.G. did not come. Yet, in great pain, I blessed God for having kept her away, as she might have been a snare to me. These things would be almost incredible to another, and almost to myself, were I not taught by daily experience that, whatever the world may say, or I may think of myself, I am a poor, wretched, sinful, contemptible worm.

Called after tea on Miss L.G., and walked with her and ——, conversing on spiritual subjects. All the rest of the evening, and at night, I could not keep her out of my mind. I felt too plainly that I loved her passionately. The direct opposition of this to my devotedness to God in the missionary way, excited no small tumult in my mind. In conversation, having no divine sweetness in peace, my cheerfulness was affected, and, consequently, very hurtful [51] to my conscience. At night I continued an hour and a half in prayer, striving against this attachment. I endeavoured to analyse it, that I might see how base, and mean, and worthless such a love to a speck of earth was, compared with divine love. Then I read the most solemn parts of Scripture, to realise to myself death and eternity; and these attempts were sometimes blest. One while I was about to triumph, but in a moment my heart had wandered to the beloved idol. I went to bed in great pain, yet still rather superior to the evening; but in dreams her image returned, and I awoke in the night with my mind full of her. No one can say how deeply this unhappy affection has fixed itself; since it has nothing selfish in it, that I can perceive, but is founded on the highest admiration of her piety and manners.

July 30.—Rose in great peace. God, by secret influence, seemed to have caused the tempest of self-will to subside. Rode away from St. Hilary to Gwennap in peace of mind, and meditated most of the way on Romans viii. I again devoted myself to the Lord, and with more of my will than last night. I was much disposed to think of subjects entirely placed beyond the world, and had strong desires, though with heavy opposition from my corrupt nature, after that entire deadness to the world which David Brainerd manifested. At night I found myself to have backslidden a long way from the life of godliness, to have declined

18

very much since my coming into Cornwall, but especially since I went to St. Hilary. Sat up late, and read the last chapter and other parts of Revelation, and was deeply affected. Prayed with more success than lately.

July 31.—Read and prayed this morning with increasing victory over my self-will. Romans vii. was particularly suitable; it was agreeable to me to speak to God of my own corruption and helplessness. Walked in the afternoon to Redruth, after having prayed over the Epistle to the[52] Ephesians with much seriousness. On the road I was enabled to triumph at last, and found my heart as pleased with the prospect of a single life in missionary labours as ever. 'What is the exceeding greatness of His power to usward who believe!'

After preaching to crowds in his brother-in-law's church at Kenwyn and Lamorran, on the two subsequent Sundays, he walked to St. Hilary:

1804, August 26.—Rose early, and walked out, invited by the beauty of the morning. Many different pleasing thoughts crowded on my mind, as I viewed the sea and rocks, Mount and bay, and thought of the person who lived near it; but, for want of checking my natural spirits, and fixing on one subject of thought, I was not much benefited by my meditations. Walked in the evening with Mrs. G. and Lydia up the hill, with the most beautiful prospect of the sea, &c.; but I was unhappy, from feeling the attachment to Lydia, for I was unwilling to leave her.

August 27.—Walked to Marazion, with my heart more delivered from its idolatry, and enabled to look steadily and peacefully to God. Reading in the afternoon to Lydia alone, from Dr. Watts, there happened to be, among other things, a prayer on entire preference of God to the creature. Now, thought I, here am I in the presence of God, and my idol. So I used the prayer for myself, and addressed it to God, who answered it, I think, for my love was kindled to God and divine things, and I felt cheerfully resigned to the will of God, to forego the earthly joy which I had just been desiring with my whole heart. I continued conversing with her, generally with my heart in heaven, but every now and then resting on her. Parted with Lydia, perhaps for ever in this life, with a sort of uncertain pain, which I knew would increase to greater violence afterwards, on reflection. Walked to St. Hilary, determining, in great tumult and[53] inward pain, to be the servant of God. All the rest of the evening, in company or alone, I could think of nothing but her excellences. My efforts were, however, through mercy, not in vain, to feel the vanity of this attachment to the creature. Read in Thomas à Kempis many chapters directly to the purpose; the shortness of time, the awfulness of death and its consequences, rather settled my mind to prayer. I devoted myself unreservedly to the service of the Lord, to Him, as to one who knew the great conflict within, and my firm resolve, through His grace, of being His, though it should be with much tribulation.

August 28.—Rose with a heavy heart, and took leave of St. Hilary, where all the happier hours of my early life were passed. —— and ——accompanied me in the chaise a few miles; but the moment they left me I walked on, dwelling at large on the excellence of Lydia. I had a few faint struggles to forget her, and delight in God, but they were ineffectual. Among the many motives to the subjection of self-will, I found the thought of the entire unworthiness of a soul escaped from hell to choose its own will before God's, most bring my soul to a right frame. So that, while I saw the necessity of resigning, for the service of God, all those joys, for the loss of which I could not perceive how anything in heaven or earth could be a compensation, I said, Amen!

August 29.—I walked to Truro, with my mind almost all the way taken up with Lydia. But once reasoning in this way—If God made me, and wills my happiness, as I do not doubt, then He is providing for my good by separating me from her; this reasoning convinced my mind. I felt very solemnly and sweetly the excellence of serving God faithfully, of following Christ and His Apostles, and meditated with great joy on the approach of the end of this world. Yet still I enjoyed, every now and then, the thought of walking hereafter with her, in the realms of glory, conversing on the things of God. My mind the[54] rest of the evening was much depressed. I had no desire to live in this world; scarcely could I say where I would be, or what I would do, now that my self-will was so strongly counteracted. Thus God waits patiently my return from my backsliding, which I would do immediately. If He were to offer me the utmost of my wishes, I would say, 'Not so, Lord! Not my will, but Thine be done.'

August 30.—Passed the morning rather idly, in reading lives of pious women. I felt an indescribable mixture of opposing emotions. At one time, about to ascend with delight to God, who had permitted me to aspire after the same glory, but oftener called down to earth by my earthly good. Major Sandys calling, continued till dinner conversing about India. I consented to stay a day with him at Helston, but the thought of being so near Marazion renewed my pain, especially taken in connection with my going thither on the subject of my departure. After dinner, walked in the garden for two hours, reasoning with my perverse heart, and, through God's mercy, not without success. You preach up deadness to the world, and yet not an example of it! Now is the time, my soul, if you cannot feel that it is best to bear the cross, to trust God for it. This will be true faith. If I were put in possession of my idol, I should immediately say and feel that God alone was, notwithstanding, the only good, and to Him I should seek immediately. Again I weighed the probable temporal consequence of having my own will gratified; the dreadful pain of separation by death, after being united, together with the distress I might bring upon her whom I loved. All these things were of small influence till I read the Epistle to the Hebrews, by which my mind, made to consider divine things attentively, was much more freed from earthly things. 'Let us come boldly to the throne of grace, that we may obtain mercy, and find grace to help in time of need,' was very precious and comforting to me. I have found grace to help in this time of need; I still[55] want a humble spirit to wait upon the Lord. I almost called God to witness that I duly resigned my pleasure to His, as if I wished it to be remembered. In the evening had a serious and solemn time in prayer, chiefly for the influences of the Spirit, and rose with my thoughts fixed on eternity; I longed for death, and called on the glorious day to hasten; but it was in order to be free from the troubles of this world.

August 31.—Passed the morning partly in reading and writing, but chiefly in business. Rode to Rosemundy, with my mind at first very unhappy, at the necessity of mortifying my self-will, in the same particulars as for some days. In conversing on the subject of India with Major Sandys, I could not help communicating the pain I felt at parting with the person to whom I was attached; but by thus dwelling on the subject my heart was far more distressed than ever. Found my mind more easy and submissive to God at night in prayer.

St. Hilary Church, in which Henry Martyn preached, is one of the oldest in England, containing, in the tower of Edward III.'s reign, two stones with inscriptions of the time of the Emperor Flavius Constantinus, who was killed by Honorius in 411. What Lydia Grenfell thought of Martyn's sermon on that day, August 26, thenceforth memorable to both, we find in her *Diary* of that date:

1804, August 26.—Heard H.M. on 'Now then we are ambassadors for Christ, as though God did beseech you by us: we pray you, in Christ's stead, be ye reconciled to God. For He hath made Him to be sin (*i.e.* sin-offering) for us, Who knew no sin; that we might be made the righteousness of God in Him.' Exordium on the honourable employment of a minister of the Gospel. In the text two things were implied. First, we were at enmity with God. Second, we were unable to restore ourselves to His[56] favour. There were two things expressed in the text—the means of reconciliation, and God's invitation to be reconciled; a threefold address to saints, backsliders, and sinners; and a farewell address. A precious sermon. Lord, bless the preacher, and those that heard him!

At that time, in 1804, the lady was still preoccupied, in conscience or heart, or both, by her imaginary ties to Mr. S. John. But six months before that she had heard of his approaching marriage, though, in fact, that did not take place till 1810. All that time, if she did not feel, to one to whom her heart had been more closely united than to any 'earthly object,' as she had written in her *Diary*, what Mr. H.M. Jeffery describes as the attachment of a widow with the responsibility of a wife, her scrupulous introspective habit was an obstacle to a healthy attachment. The preacher, younger than herself, was in 1804 evidently to her only an interesting and gracious second cousin, or perhaps a little more.

On his way back to London Henry Martyn again visited Plymouth, where he learned from his cousin 'that my attachment to her sister was not altogether unreturned, and the discovery gave me both pleasure and pain.' He left them, his thoughts 'almost wholly occupied with Lydia.' London, Cambridge, his reading and his walking, his work and even his sleep, bring him no rest from the absorbing passion. His *Journal* is full of it, almost every day. Fortescue's poems recall the happy mornings at St. Hilary, but his pensive meditation subsided into a more profitable one on the vanity of the world: 'they marry and are given in marriage,' and at the end of a few years what are they more than myself?—looking forward to the same dissolution, and expecting their real happiness in another[57] life. 'The fashion of this world passeth away,' Amen. 'Let me do the will of God while I am in it.'

The first day of the year 1805 led him to review the past five years, and to renew his self-dedication to God the Father, Son, and Holy Ghost, to be His servant for ever. The time for his departure to India was at hand, and his last act, on leaving London for Cambridge, to complete his arrangements for sailing, was deliberately to engage himself to Lydia Grenfell in the following letter to her sister.[11] It is thus referred to in his *Journal*:

I was in some doubt whether I should send the letter to Emma, as it was taking a very important step, and I could scarcely foresee all the consequences. However, I did send it, and may now be said to have engaged myself to Lydia.

18 Brunswick Square (London), January 11, 1805.

My dear Mrs. Hitchins,—How unaccountable must my long silence appear to you after the conversation that passed between us in the carriage! You may well wonder that I could forbear, for three whole months, to inquire about the 'beloved Persis.' Indeed, I am surprised at my own patience, but, in truth, I found it impossible to discover what it is which I wish or ought to say on the subject, and therefore determined to defer writing till I could inform you with certainty of my future destination. But I have it not yet in my power to do this, for no actual appointment has been made for me yet. I came to town the beginning of this week to inquire into the present state of the business, and learned from Mr. Grant that the situation he intended to procure, and to which he had[58] no doubt of getting me nominated, was not in the Army, but at Fort William, near Calcutta. Thus it pleases God to suspend the declaration of His mind, and I can believe that He acts wisely. These apparent delays serve to check my youthful impetuosity, and teach me to look up to God, and wait for Him. If the chaplaincy at Fort William should be given me, it would seem to be His design not to call me to the peculiar work of a missionary, but to fix my station among the English. At present my own inclination remains almost unbiassed, as to the particular employment or place God shall assign me, whether to pass my days among the natives, or the more polished inhabitants of Calcutta, or even to remain at home.

But you will easily conceive that the increasing probability of my being settled in a town rather tends to revive the thoughts of marriage, for I feel very little doubt in my own mind, that in such a situation it would be expedient for me on the whole to marry, if other circumstances permitted it. It is also as clear that I ought not to make an engagement with any one in England, till I have ascertained by actual observation in India, what state of life and mode of proceeding would be most conducive to the ends of my mission. But why do I mention these difficulties? If they were removed, others would remain still more insurmountable. The affections of the beloved object in question must still be engaged in my favour, or even then she would not agree to leave the kingdom, nor would any of you agree to it, nor would such a change of climate, it may be thought, suit the delicacy of her constitution.

Must I, then, yield to the force of these arguments, and resolve to think of her no more? It shall certainly be my endeavour, by the help of my God, to do it, if need be; but I confess I am very unwilling to go away and hear of her only accidentally through the medium of others. It is this painful reflection that has prompted a wish, which I do not mention without some hesitation, and that is my[59] wish of corresponding with her. It is possible you may instantly perceive some impropriety in it which escapes my notice, and indeed there are some objections which I foresee might be made, but instead of anticipating them, I will leave you to form your own opinion. In religion we have a subject to write upon of equal interest to us both, and though I cannot expect she would derive any advantage from my letters, it is certain I should receive no small benefit from hers. But I leave it with yourself; if you disapprove of the measure, let the request be forgotten. It will be best for her never to know I had made it, or if she does, she will, I hope, pardon a liberty to which I have been drawn only by the love of her excellence.

N.B.—I remember *Leighton*; take care not to forget it nor the desired MS.

On June 1 he wrote in his *Journal*:

My departure from my friends, and my deprivation of the sweetest delight in society, for ever in this life, have rather dejected me to-day. Ah! Nature, thou hast still tears to shed for thyself.... I seem to be hankering after something or other in this world, though I am sure I could not say there is anything which I believed could give me happiness. No! it is in God above. Yet to-night I have been thinking much of Lydia. Memory has been at work to unnerve my soul, but reason, and honour, and love to Christ and to souls, shall prevail. Amen. God help me!

Two days after, at the Eclectic Society, after a discussion on the symptoms of 'the state of the nation,' the subject of marriage, somehow or other, came to be mentioned.

Mr. Cecil spoke very freely and strongly on the subject. He said I should be acting like a madman if I went out unmarried. A wife would supply by her comfort and counsel the entire want of society, and also be a preservative[60] both to character and passions amidst such scenes. I felt as cold as an anchorite on the subject as to my own feelings, but I was much perplexed all the rest of the evening about it. I clearly perceived that my own inclination upon the whole was not to marriage. The fear of being involved in worldly cares and numberless troubles, which I do not now foresee, makes me tremble and dislike the thoughts of such connection. When I think of Brainerd, how he lived among the Indians, travelling freely from place to place, can I conceive he would have been so useful had he been married? I remember also that Owens, who had been so many years in the West Indies as a missionary, gave his advice against marriage. Schwartz was never married, nor St. Paul. On the other hand, when I suppose another in my circumstances, fixed at a settlement without company, without society, in a scene and climate of such temptation, I say without hesitation, he ought to be married. I have recollected this evening very much my feelings when I walked through Wales; how I longed there to have some friend to speak to; and the three weeks seemed an age without one. And I have often thought how valuable would be the counsel and comfort of a Christian brother in India. These advantages would be obtained by marrying. I feel anxious also that as many Christians as possible should go to India, and anyone willing to go would be a valuable addition. But yet voluntary celibacy seems so much more noble and glorious, and so much more beneficial in the way of example, that I am loth to relinquish the idea of it. In short, I am utterly at a loss to know what is best for the interests of the Gospel. But, happily, my own peace is not much concerned in it. If this opinion of so many pious clergymen had come across me when I was in Cornwall, and so strongly attached to my beloved Lydia, it would have been a conflict indeed in my heart to oppose so many arguments. But now I feel, through grace, an astonishing difference. I hope I am not seeking an[61]excuse for marriage, nor persuading myself I am indifferent about it, in order that what is really my inclination may appear to be the will of God. But I feel my affections kindling to their wonted fondness while I dwell on the circumstances of a union with Lydia. May the Lord teach His weak creature to live peacefully and soberly in His love, drawing all my joys from Him, the fountain of living waters.

June 4.—The subject of marriage made me thoughtful and serious. Mr. Atkinson, whose opinion I revere, was against my marrying. Found near access to my God in prayer. Oh, what a comfort it is to have God to go to. I breathed freely to Him my sorrows and cares, and set about my work with diligence. The Lord assisted me very much, and I wrote more freely than ever I did. Slept very little in the night.

June 5.—Corrie breakfasted with me, and went to prayer; I rejoiced to find he was not unwilling to go to India. He will probably be my fellow-labourer. Most of this morning was employed in writing all my sentiments on the subject of marriage to Mr. Simeon. May the Lord suggest something to him which may be of use to guide me, and keep my eye single. In my walk out, and afterwards, the subject was constantly on my mind. But, alas! I did not guard against that distraction from heavenly things which I was aware it would occasion. On reflection at home, I found I had been talking in a very inconsistent manner, but was again restored to peace by an application to Christ's blood through the Spirit. My mind has all this day been very strongly inclined to marriage, and has been consequently uncomfortable, for in proportion to its want of simplicity it is unhappy. But Mr. Cecil said to-day, he thought Lydia's decision would fully declare the will of God. With this I am again comforted, for now hath the Lord taken the matter into His own hands. Whatever He decides upon, I shall rejoice; and though I confess I[62] think she will not consent to go, I shall then have the question finally settled.

Discussion in the evening was about my marriage again; they were all strenuous advocates for it. Wrote at night with great freedom, but my body is very weak from the fatigue I have already undergone. My mind seems very active this week; manifestly, indeed, strengthened by God to be enabled to write on religious subjects with such unusual ease, while it is also full of this important business of the marriage. My inclination continues, I think, far more unbiassed than when I wrote to Mr. Simeon.

June 7.—Oh, the subtlety of the devil, and the deceitfulness of this corrupted heart! How has an idol been imperceptibly raised up in it. Something fell from Dr. F. this evening against my marriage which struck me so forcibly, though there was nothing particular in it, that I began to see I should finally give up all thoughts about it. But how great the conflict! I could not have believed it had such hold on my affections. Before this I had been writing in tolerable tranquillity, and walked out in the enjoyment of a resigned mind, even rejoicing for the most part in God, and dined at Mr. Cecil's, where the arguments I heard were all in favour of the flesh, and so I was pleased; but Dr. F.'s words gave a new turn to my thoughts, and the tumult showed me the true state of my heart. How miserable did life appear without the hope of Lydia! Oh, how has the discussion of the subject opened all my wounds afresh! I have not felt such heartrending pain since I parted with her in Cornwall. But the Lord brought me to consider the folly and wickedness of all this. Shall I hesitate to keep my days in constant solitude, who am but a brand plucked from the burning? I could not help saying, 'Go, Hindus, go on in your misery; let Satan still rule over you; for he that was appointed to labour among you is consulting his ease.' No, thought I; hell and[63] earth shall never keep me back from my work. I am cast down, but not destroyed; I began to consider, why am I so uneasy? 'Cast thy care upon Him, for He careth for you.' 'In everything, by prayer,' &c. These promises were graciously fulfilled before long to me.

June 8.—My mind continued in much the same state this morning, waiting with no small anxiety for a letter from Mr. Simeon, hoping, of course, that the will of God would coincide with my will, yet thinking the determination of the question would be indifferent to me. When the letter arrived I was immediately convinced, beyond all doubt, of the expediency of celibacy. But my wish did not follow my judgment quite so readily. Mr. Pratt coming in, argued strongly on the other side, but there was nothing of any weight. The subject so occupied my thoughts that I could attend to nothing else. I saw myself called to be less than ever a man of this world, and walked out with a heavy heart. Met Dr. F., who alone of all men could best sympathise, and his few words were encouraging. Yet I cannot cordially acquiesce in all the Lord's dealings, though my reason and judgment approve them, and my inclination would desire to do it. Dined at Mr. Cecil's, where it providentially happened that Mr. Foster came in. To them I read Mr. Simeon's letter, and they were both convinced by it. So I went away home, with nothing to do but to get my heart easy again under this sacrifice. I devoted myself once more to the entire and everlasting service of God, and found myself more weaned from this world, and desiring the next, though not from a right principle. Continued all the evening writing sermon, and reading *Pilgrim's Progress*, with successions of vivid emotions of pain and pleasure. My heart was sometimes ready to break with agony at being torn from its dearest idol, and at other times I was visited by a few moments of sublime and enraptured joy. Such is the conflict; why have my friends mentioned this subject? It has torn open[64] old wounds, and I am again bleeding. With all my honours and knowledge, the smiles and approbation of men, the health and prosperity that have fallen to my lot, together with that freedom from doubts and fears with which I was formerly visited, how much have I gone through in the last two or three years to bring my mind to be willing to do the will of God when it should be revealed! My heart is pained within me, and my bodily frame suffers from it.

June 9. (Sunday.)—My heart is still pained. It is still as a bullock unaccustomed to the yoke; the Lord help me to maintain the conflict. Preached this morning at Long Acre Chapel on Matt. xxviii., the three last verses. There was the utmost attention. In the interval between morning and afternoon, passed most of the time in reading and prayer. Read Matthew iii., and considered the character of John the Baptist. Holy emulation seemed to spring up in my mind. Then read John xvii. and last chapter, and Rev. i., all of which were blessed to my soul. I went into the church persuaded in my feelings—which is different from being persuaded in the understanding—that it was nobler and wiser to be as John the Baptist, Peter, John, and all the Apostles, than to have my own will gratified. Preached on Eph. ii. 18. Walked a little with Mr. Grant this evening. He told me I should have great trials and temptations in India; but I know where to apply for grace to help.

Cecil's final opinion, that Lydia Grenfell's decision would fully declare the will of God, was not borne out by the result, as we shall see. Meanwhile, let us trace the steps which led to the final appointment to India, and the farewell.

On his first visit to London at the beginning of the year 1804, by the Telegraph coach, the Cambridge recluse was[65] distracted by the bustle of the great city, as he walked about the streets and called at the booksellers'. Dr. Wollaston, the British Museum, and the Gresham Lecture on Music, of which he was passionately fond, occupied his first two days. At the old India House, since swept away from Leadenhall Street, he met Mr. Charles Grant, who, as he took him to Clapham, the evangelical centre which Sir James Stephen has made so famous,[11] gave him much information on the state of India, such as this:

It would be absolutely necessary to keep three servants, for three can do no more than the work of one English; that no European constitution can endure being exposed to mid-day heat; that Mr. Schwartz, who was settled at Tanjore, did do it for a time, walking among the natives. Mr. Grant had never seen Mr. Schwartz, but corresponded with him. He was the son of a Saxon gentleman (the Saxon gentlemen never enter the ministry of the Church), and had early devoted himself to the work of a missionary amongst the Indians. Besides the knowledge of the Malabar tongue, in which he was profoundly skilled and eloquent, he was a good classic, and learnt the English, Portuguese, and Dutch. He was a man of dignified and polished manners, and cheerful.

This was the first opportunity that 'the Clapham sect' had to satisfy themselves that the Senior Wrangler was worthy of the commendation of Charles Simeon. Accordingly they dined with William Wilberforce at Broomfield.

We conversed about my business. They wished me to fill the church in Calcutta very much; but advised me to wait some time, and to cherish the same views. To Mr. Wilberforce I went into a detail of my views, and the reasons that had operated on my mind. The conversation[66] of Mr. Wilberforce and Mr. Grant during the whole of the day, before the rest of the company, which consisted of Mr. Johnston, of New South Wales, a French Abbé, Mrs. Unwin, Mr. H., and other ladies, was edifying; agreeable to what I should think right for two godly senators, planning some means of bringing before Parliament propositions for bettering the moral state of the colony of Botany Bay. At evening worship Mr. W. expounded Sacred Scripture with serious plainness, and prayed in the midst of his large household.

In *The Life of William Wilberforce*, by his sons, we find this passage introduced by the remark, 'It is delightful to contrast with his own language the observation of one who, with as holy and as humble a soul, was just entering on his brief but glorious course:' Martyn 'drank tea at Mr. Newton's'; the old man was very civil to me, and striking in his remarks in general.' Next day:

Read Isaiah. At one, we went to hear the charge delivered to the missionaries at the New London Tavern, in Cheapside. There was nothing remarkable in it, but the conclusion was affecting. I shook hands with the two missionaries, Melchior Rayner and Peter Hartwig, and almost wished to go with them, but certainly to go to India. Returned, and read Isaiah.

From the ever recurring distractions of his soul, caused now by 'a despicable indulgence in lying in bed,' and again by the interruptions of visitors, he sought refuge frequently in fasting and ascetic self-denial, and occasionally in writing verse:

Composed some poetry during my walk, which often has a tendency to divert my thoughts from the base distractions of this life, and to purify and elevate it to higher|67|subjects.... On my way to Mr. Simeon's, heard part of the service in King's Chapel. The sanctity of the place, and the music, brought heaven and eternal things, and the presence of God, very near to me.

He seems to have competed for the Seatonian Prize. He was an ardent lover of Nature.

Walked out before breakfast, and the beauties of the opening spring constrained me to adoration and praise. But no earthly object or operation can produce true spirituality of heart. My present failing is in this, that I do not feel the power of motives.

Of another walk he writes:

I was led to think a good while on my deficiency in human learning, and on my having neglected those branches which would have been pleasing and honourable in the acquisition. Yet I said, though with somewhat of melancholy, 'What things were gain to me, those I counted loss for Christ.' Though I become less esteemed by man, I cannot but think (though it is not easy to do so) that it must be more acceptable to God to labour for souls, though the mind remains uninformed; and, consequently, that it must be more truly great and noble, than to be great and notable among men for learning. In the garden afterwards I rejoiced exceedingly at the prospect of a death fast approaching, when my powers of understanding would be enlarged inconceivably. They all talked to me in praise of my sermon on Sunday night; but praise is exceedingly unpleasant to me, because I am slow to render back to God that glory which belongs to Him alone. Sometimes it may be useful in encouraging me, when I want encouragement; but that at present is not the case; and in truth, praise generally produces pride, and pride presently sets me far from God.|68|

Oh, what a snare are public ministrations to me! Not that I wish for the praise of men, but there is some fear and anxiety about not getting through. How happy could I be in meeting the people of my God more frequently were it not for this fear of being unprofitable! But since God has given me natural gifts, let this teach me that all I want is a spiritual frame to improve and employ them in the things of God!

Mr. K. White, of Nottingham, breakfasted with me. In my walk was greatly cast down, except for a short time on my return, when, as I was singing, or rather chanting, some petitions in a low, plaintive voice, I insensibly found myself sweetly engaged in prayer.

Such outpourings of his heart must be read in the light of a time when even the Churches had not awoke to their duty, and the most theologically orthodox were too often the most indifferent, or opposed, to the Lord's command.

1804, January 13.—Walked out in the evening in great tranquillity, and on my return met with Mr. C., with whom I was obliged to walk an hour longer. He thought it a most improper step for me to leave the University to preach to the ignorant heathen, which any person could do, and that I ought rather to improve the opportunity of acquiring human learning. All our conversation on the subject of learning, religion, &c., ended in nothing; he was convinced he was right, and all the texts of Scripture I produced were applicable, according to him, only to the times of the Apostles. How is my soul constrained to adore the sovereign mercy of God, who began His work in my proud heart, and carried it on through snares which have ruined thousands—namely, human learning and honours: and now my soul, dost thou not esteem all things but dung and dross, compared with the excellency of the knowledge of Christ Jesus my Lord? Yea, did not gratitude constrain me,|69| did not duty and fear of destruction, yet surely the excellency of the service of Christ would constrain me to lay down ten-thousand lives in the prosecution of it. My heart was a little discomposed this evening at the account of the late magnificent prizes proposed by Mr. Buchanan and others in the University, for which Mr. C. has been calling me to write; but I was soon at rest again. But how easily do I forget that God is no respecter of persons; that in the midst of the notice I attract as an enthusiast He judges of me according to my inward state. Oh, my soul, take no pleasure in outward religion, nor in exciting wonder, but in the true circumcision of the heart.

January 16.— ——told me of many contemptuous insulting things that had been said of me, reflecting, some on my understanding, some on my condition, sincerity, inconsistent conduct. It was a great trial of my patience, and I was frequently tempted, in the course of the evening, to let my natural spirit rage forth in indignation and revenge; but I remembered Him of whom it was said, 'Who, when He was reviled, reviled not again; but committed Himself to Him that judgeth righteously.' As I was conscious I did not deserve the censures which were passed upon me, I committed myself to God; and in Him may I abide until the indignation be overpast!

In July 1804 he again visited London on his way to Cornwall, and to see Mr. Charles Grant.

Dined with Mr. Wilberforce at Palace Yard. It was very agreeable, as there was no one else. Speaking of the slave trade, I mentioned the words, 'Shall I not visit for these things?' and found my heart so affected that I could with difficulty refrain from tears. Went with Mr. W. to the House of Commons, where I was surprised and charmed with Mr. Pitt's eloquence. Ah, thought I, if these powers of oratory were now employed in recommending the Gospel!

[70]

On his way back to Cambridge, through London, he

Went to St. Paul's, to see Sir W. Jones's monument; the sight of the interior of the dome filled my soul with inexpressible ideas of the grandeur of God, and the glory of heaven, much the same as I had at the sight of a painted vaulted roof in the British Museum. I could scarcely believe that I might be in the immediate enjoyments of such glory in another hour. In the evening the sound of sacred music, with the sight of a rural landscape, imparted some indescribable emotions after the glory of God, by diligence in His work. To preach the Gospel for the salvation of my poor fellow-creatures, that they might obtain the salvation which is in Christ Jesus, with eternal glory, seemed a very sweet and precious employment. Lydia then, again, seemed a small hindrance.

His duties as examiner, tutor, and in charge of Lolworth, and home mission work in Wall's Lane, the hospital and almshouse, left him little leisure, and that he gave to the Bengali grammars of Halhed and Carey, to Carey's Bengali New Testament, to Arabic grammars, and to the missionary accounts in the *Christian Observer*, for which, also, he wrote. Referring, evidently, to Carey's convert, he wrote:

The account of a Brahmin preaching the Gospel delighted me most exceedingly. I could not help blessing God for thus glorifying Himself.... I was much pained and humbled at reflecting that it has never yet, to my knowledge, pleased God to awaken one soul by my means, either in public or private,—shame be to myself.

Simeon gave me a letter from Mr. Brown of Calcutta, which gave me great delight on many accounts. Speaking of me, he says, 'Let him marry, and come out at once.' I thought of Lydia with great tenderness, but without pain at my determination to go out single. I found great[71] affection in prayer for my dear brethren at Calcutta, for the establishing of Christ's Kingdom among the poor Gentiles, and for my being sent among them, if it were His will.

Thinking my mind was in need of recreation, I took up Lord Teignmouth's *Life of Sir William Jones*, and read till tea.

Low spirits at church, through being about to preach old sermons, which I feel so ashamed of offering to God, that I believe I shall rather leave everything undone, than not write one new one at least every week.

Mr. Thomason preached on Heb. xii. to my edification.

Dr. Milner and Lord C. called. I was introduced as having been Senior Wrangler; but how contemptible did these paltry honours appear to me! Ah, thought I, you know not how little I am flattered by these intended compliments.

In the hall was much affected by the sight of Lord B., whose look of meekness and humility riveted my attention, and almost melted me to tears. If there is one disposition in the world I wish for more than another, it is this; but the bias of my corrupted nature hurries me violently against it.

Mr. Grant's summons to him 'to sail for St. Helena in eight or ten days,' reached him a month before his twenty-fourth birthday, before which he could not legally receive full ordination, in the Chapel Royal at St. James's.

Felt more persuaded of my call than ever; indeed, there was scarcely a shadow of a doubt left. Rejoice, O my soul, thou shalt be the servant of thy God in this life, and then in the next for all the boundless ages of eternity.

Not till August 31 was it possible for the fleet which convoyed the East Indiamen, in that year of war with France and Napoleon's Continental allies, to see the last of[72] Ireland. The seven months were spent by Henry Martyn in elaborate preparations for what proved to be nearly a year's voyage, and in repeated farewells the anguish of which is reflected in his *Journal* and correspondence. Having previously taken his M.A. degree, he received that of Bachelor of Divinity by mandate, which required the assent of all the heads of colleges, and then a grace to pass the senate, and the presenting of a petition to the King. Dr. Gilchrist, the Orientalist who had just returned from his long career in Calcutta, where he had been a colleague of Carey in the College of Fort William, gave him lessons in Hindustani pronunciation.

On my mentioning my desire of translating some of the Scriptures with him, he advised me by all means to desist till I knew much more of the language, by having resided some years in the country. He said it was the rock on which missions had split, that they had attempted to write and preach before they knew the language. The Lord's Prayer, he said, was now a common subject of ridicule with the people, on account of the manner in which it had been translated. All these are useful hints to me.

The mode of appointing to Indian chaplaincies has varied so much since the time of Charles Grant and Simeon, that it is interesting to see what was done in Henry Martyn's case.

1805, April 1.—Went to Lord Hawkesbury's office, but, being too early, I went into St. James's Park, and sat down on a bench to read my Bible. After a little time a person came and sat down on the same bench; on entering into conversation with him I found he had known better days. He was about seventy years of age, and of a very passionate and disappointed spirit. He spoke sensibly on several[73] subjects, and was acquainted with the Gospel; but was offended at my reminding him of several things concerning it. On my offering him some money, which I saw he needed, he confessed his poverty; he was thankful for my little donation, and I repeated my advice of seeking divine consolation.

April 2.—Breakfasted with ——. Our conversation was on the most delightful subject to me, the spread of the Gospel in future ages. I went away animated and happy. Went with Mr. Grant towards the India House. He said that he was that day about to take the necessary steps for bringing forward the business of the chaplains, and that by to-morrow night I should know whether I could go or not. In prayer at night my soul panted after God, and longed to be entirely conformed to His image.

April 3.—After dinner, passed some time in prayer, and rejoiced to think that God would finally glorify Himself, whatever hindrance may arise for a time. Going to Mr. Grant's, I found that the chaplaincies had been agreed to, after two hours' debate, and some obloquy thrown upon Mr. Grant by the chairman, for his connection with Mr. Wilberforce and *those people*. Mr. G. said that though my nomination had not taken place, the case was now beyond danger, and that I should appear before the court in a couple of days in my canonicals. I felt very indignant at this, not so much, I think, from personal pride, as on account of the degradation of my office. Mr. G. pleasantly said, I must attend to my appearance, as I should be much remarked, on account of the person who had nominated me. I feel this will be a trial to me, which I would never submit to for gain; but I rejoice that it will be for my dear and blessed Lord.

April 4.—Went down to Cambridge.

April 6.—Passed most of the morning in the Fellows' garden. It was the last time I visited this favourite retreat, where I have often enjoyed the presence of God.[74]

April 7. (Sunday.)—Preached at Lolworth on Prov. xxii. 17; very few seemed affected at my leaving them, and those chiefly women. An old farmer of a neighbouring parish, as he was taking leave of me, turned aside to shed tears; this affected me more than anything. Rode away with my heart heavy, partly at my own corruption, partly at the thoughts of leaving this place in such general hardness of heart. Yet so it hath pleased God, I hope, to reserve them for a more faithful minister. Prayed over the whole of my sermon for the evening, and when I came to preach it, God assisted me beyond my hopes. Most of the younger people seemed to be in tears. The text was 2 Sam. vii. 28, 29. Took leave of Dr. Milner; he was much affected, and said himself his heart was full. Mr. Simeon commended me to God in prayer, in which he pleaded, amongst other things, for a richer blessing on my soul. He perceives that I want it, and so do I. Professor Parish walked home with me to the college gate, and there I parted from him, with no small sorrow.

April 8.—My young friends in the University, who have scarcely left me a moment to myself, were with me this morning as soon as I was moving, leaving me no time for prayer. My mind was very solemn, and I wished much to be left alone. A great many accompanied me to the coach, which took me up at the end of the town. It was a thick, misty morning, so the University, with its towers and spires, was out of sight in an instant.

April 24.—Keenly disappointed at finding no letter from Lydia; thus it pleased God, in the riches of His grace, to quash at once all my beginnings of entanglement. Oh, may it be to make me more entirely His own. 'The Lord shall be the portion of mine inheritance, and of my cup.' Oh, may I live indeed a more spiritual life of faith! Prayed that I might obtain a more deep acquaintance with the mysteries of the Gospel, and the offices of Christ; my soul was solemnised. Went to Russell Square, and found from[75] Mr. Grant that I was that day appointed a chaplain to the East India Company, but that my particular destination would depend on the government in India. Rather may I say that it depends on the will of my God, who in His own time thus brings things to pass. Oh, now let my heart be spiritualised; that the glorious and arduous work before me may fill all my soul, and stir me up to prayer.

April 25.—Breakfasted with the venerable Mr. Newton, who made several striking remarks in reference to my work. He said he had heard of a clever gardener, who would sow the seeds when the meat was put down to roast, and engage to produce a salad by the time it was ready; but the Lord did not sow oaks in this way. On my saying that perhaps I should never live to see much fruit, he answered, I should have a bird's eye view of it, which would be better. When I spoke of the opposition that I should be likely to meet with, he said, he supposed Satan would not love me for what I was about to do. The old man prayed afterwards, with sweet simplicity. Drank tea at C. Our hearts seemed full of the joy which comes from the communion of saints.

April 26.—Met D. at Mr. Grant's, and was much affected at some marks of love expressed by the people at Cambridge, at the time of my leaving them. He said that as I was going down the aisle they all rose up to take their last view.

May 4.—Waiting this morning on the Archbishop of Canterbury at Lambeth Palace. He had learnt from somebody my circumstances, the degree I had taken, and my object in going to India. He spoke much on the importance of the work, the small ecclesiastical establishment for so great a body of people, and the state of those English there, who, he said, 'called themselves very civil, and wished me all the success I desired. I then proceeded to the India House, and received directions to attend on Wednesday to be[76] sworn in. Afterwards walked to Mr. Wilberforce's at Broomfield.

May 8.—Reading Mr. Grant's book.[13] The state of the natives, and the prospects of doing good there, the character of Schwartz, &c., set forth in it, much impressed my mind, and I found great satisfaction in pleading for the fulfilment of God's promises to the heathen. It seemed painful to think of myself at all, except in reference to the Church of Christ. Being somewhat in danger of distraction this evening, from many concurrent circumstances, I found a very short prayer answered by my being kept steady. Heard from Mr. Parry this evening, that in consequence of an embargo laid on all the ships by government, who had taken the best seamen from the Company's ships, on account of the sailing of the French and Spanish fleets, I should not be able to go before the middle of June, if so soon.

May 15.—Read prayers at Mr. Newton's, and preached on Eph. ii. 19-21. The clerk threw out very disrespectful and even uncivil things respecting my going to India; though I thought the asperity and contemptuousness he manifested unsuitable to his profession, I felt happy in the comfortable assurance of being upright in my intentions. The sermon was much praised by some people coming in, but happily this gives me little satisfaction. Went home and read a sermon of Flavel's, on knowing nothing but Christ.

May 17.—Walked out, and continued in earnest striving with my corruption. I made a covenant with my eyes, which I kept strictly; though I was astonished to find the difficulty I had in doing even this.

May 22.—Endeavoured to guard my thoughts this morning in a more particular manner, as expecting to pass it, with Sargent, in prayer for assistance in the ministry. Called at Mr. Wilberforce's, when I met Mr. Babington. The extreme kindness and cordiality of these two was very[77] pleasing to me, though rather elating. By a letter from B. to-day, learnt that two young men of Chesterton had come forward, who professed to have been awakened by a sermon of mine on Psalm ix. 17. I was not so affected with gratitude and joy as I expected to be; could not easily ascribe the glory to God; yet I will bless Him through all my ignorance that He has thus owned the ministry of one so weak. Oh, may I have faith to go onward, expecting to see miracles wrought by the foolishness of preaching. H., to whom I had made application for the loan which Major Sandys found it inconvenient to advance, dined with me, and surprised me by the difficulty he started. After dinner went to the India House to take leave. Mr. ——, the other chaplain, sat with me before we were called in, and I found that I knew a little of him, having been at his house. As he knew my character, I spoke very freely to him on the subject of religion. Was called in to take the oaths. All the directors were present, I think. Mr. Grant, in the chair, addressed a charge to us, extempore. One thing struck my attention, which was, that he warned us of the enervating effects of the climate.

I felt more acutely than ever I did in my life the shame attending poverty. Nothing but the remembrance that I was not to blame supported me. Whatever comes to me in the way of Providence is, and must be, for my good.

May 30.—Went to the India House. Kept the covenant with my eyes pretty well. Oh, what bitter experience have I had to teach me carefulness against temptation! I have found this method, which I have sometimes had recourse to, useful to-day—namely, that of praying in ejaculations for any particular person whose appearance might prove an occasion of sinful thoughts. After asking of God that she might be as pure and beautiful in her mind and heart as in body, and be a temple of the Holy Ghost, consecrated to the service of God, for whose glory[78] she was made, I dare not harbour a thought of an opposite tendency.

June 6.—How many temptations are there in the streets of London!

June 14.—Sent off all my luggage, as preparatory to its going on board. Dined at Mr. Cecil's; he endeavoured to correct my reading, but in vain. 'Brother M.,' says he, 'you are a humble man, and would gain regard in private life; but to gain public attention you must force yourself into a more marked and expressive manner.' Generally, to-night, have I been above the world; Lydia, and other comforts, I would resign.

June 16.—I thought it probable, from illness, that death might be at hand, and this was before me all the day; sometimes I was exceedingly refreshed and comforted at the thought, at other times I felt unwilling and afraid to die. Shed tears at night, at the thought of my departure, and the roaring sea, that would soon be rolling between me and all that is dear to me upon earth.

Mrs. T.M. Hitchins, his cousin's wife, having asked him for some of his sermons, he replied:

London: June 24, 1805.

The arguments you offer to induce me seem not to possess that force which I look for in your reasoning. Sermons cannot be good memorials, because once read they are done with—especially a young man's sermons, unless they possess a peculiar simplicity and spirituality; which I need not say are qualities not belonging to mine. I hope, however, that I am improving and I trust that—now I am removed from the contagion of academic air—I am in the way of acquiring a greater knowledge of men and of my own heart—I shall exchange my jejune scholastic style for a simple spiritual exhibition of profitable truth. Mr. Cecil has been taking a great deal of pains with me.[79] My insipid, inanimate manner in the pulpit, he says, is intolerable. Sir, said he, it is cupola-painting, not miniature, that must be the character of a man that harangues a multitude. Lieut. Wynter called on me last Saturday, and last night drank tea with me. I cannot but admire his great seriousness. I feel greatly attached to him. He is just the sort of person, of a sober thoughtful cast, that I love to associate with. He mentioned Lydia, I do not know why, but he could not tell me half enough about her, while she was at Plymouth, to satisfy my curiosity. Whitsun-week was a time of the utmost distress to me on her account. On the Monday at the Eclectic, Mr. Cecil, speaking of celibacy, said, I was acting like a madman in going out without a wife. So thought all the other ten or eleven ministers present, and Mr. Foster among the rest, who is unmarried. This opinion, coming deliberately from so many experienced ministers, threw me into great perplexity, which increased, as my affections began to be set more afloat, for then I was less able than before to discern the path of duty. At last I wrote to Simeon, stating to him the strongest arguments I heard in favour of marriage in my case. His answer decided my mind. He put it in this way. Is it necessary? To this I could answer, No. Then is it expedient? He here produced so many weighty reasons against its expediency, that I was soon satisfied in my mind. My turbulent will was, however, not so easily pacified. I was again obliged to undergo the severest pain in making that sacrifice which had cost me so dear before. Better had it been if those wounds had never been torn open. But now again, through the mercy of God, I am once more at peace. What cannot His power effect? The present wish of my heart is that there may be *never* a necessity of marriage, so that I may henceforth have no one thing upon earth for which I would wish to stay another hour, except it be to serve the Lord my Saviour in the work of the ministry. Once more, therefore,[80] I say to Lydia, and with her to all earthly schemes of happiness, Farewell. Let her live happy and useful in her present situation, since that is the will of God. How long these thoughts may continue, I cannot say. At times of indolence, or distress, or prevalent corruption, the former wishes, I suppose, will occur and renew my pain: but pray, my dear sister, that the Lord may keep in the imaginations of the thoughts of my heart all that may be for the glory of His great name. The only objection which presented itself to my advisers to marriage was the difficulty of finding a proper person to be the wife of a missionary. I told them that perhaps I should not have occasion to search a long time for one. Simeon knows all about Lydia. I think it very likely that he will endeavour to see her when she comes to town next winter.

(*Addendum at the commencement, before the Address.*)

I never returned my acknowledgment for the little hymn book, which is a memento of both. It is just the sort of thing. Instead of sending the books I intended, I shall inclose in the tea-caddy a little *Pilgrim's Progress* for you, and another for Lydia.

July 2 was spent with Corrie in prayer, and converse 'about the great work among the heathen.' Martyn gave a final sitting for his miniature for his sister, to 'the painter lady, who still repeated her infidel cavils; having nothing more to say in the way of argument, I thought it right to declare the threatenings of God to those who reject the Gospel.' On the 8th he sat for his picture, for his friend Bates, to Russel. After his farewell to Sargent, and riding back,

Though I was in good health a moment before, yet as I was undressing I fainted and fell into a convulsive fit; I lost my senses for some time, and on recovering a little[81] found myself in intense pain. Death appeared near at hand, and seemed somewhat different and more terrible than I could have conceived before, not in its conclusion, but in itself. I felt assured of my safety in Christ. Slept very little that night, from extreme debility. Tenth, I went to Portsmouth, where we arrived to breakfast, and find friends from Cambridge. Went with my things on board the Union at the Motherbank. Mr. Simeon read and prayed in the afternoon, thinking I was to go on board for the last time. Mr. Simeon first prayed, and then myself. On our way to the ship we sung hymns. The time was exceedingly solemn, and our hearts seemed filled with solemn joy.

As tidings from Lord Nelson were waited for, the fleet—consisting of fifteen sail under convoy of the Belliqueuse, Captain Byng—went no farther than Plymouth, and then anchored off Falmouth.

The coast of Devonshire and Cornwall was passing before me. The memory of beloved friends, then, was very strong and affecting.... I was rather flurried at the singularity of this providence of God, in thus leading me once more to the bosom of all my friends.... I have thought with exceeding tenderness of Lydia to-day; how I long to see her; but if it be the Lord's will, He will open a way. I shall not take any steps to produce a meeting.

So he wrote on July 20. On the same day, the Rev. T.M. Hitchins wrote to him, thus: 'Lydia, from whom we heard about ten days ago, is quite well. She is much interested in your welfare.' Mrs. Hitchins wrote: 'Lydia, whom I heard lately from, is well, and never omits mentioning you in her letters—and, I may venture to say, what you will value still more, in her prayers also.' Martyn wrote to Mr. Hitchins on the 23rd:|82| 'A great work lies before me, and I must submit to many privations if I would see it accomplished. I should say, however, that poverty is not one of the evils I shall have to encounter; the salary of a chaplain, even at the lowest, is 600 rupees a month. Give my kind love to mama—as also to Miss L. Grenfell.' A postscript to the letter stated that the writer had taken his place in the coach for Marazion: 'Trust to pass some part of the morning at Miss Grenfell's.' He thus records in his *Journal* the interviews which resulted in what amounted to a brief engagement:

I arrived at Marazion in time for breakfast, and met my beloved Lydia. In the course of the morning I walked with her, though not uninterruptedly; with much confusion I declared my affection for her, with the intention of learning whether, if ever I saw it right in India to be married, she would come out; but she would not declare her sentiments, she said that the shortness of arrangement was an obstacle, even if all others were removed. In great tumult I walked up to St. Hilary, whence, after dining, I returned to Mr. Grenfell's, but, on account of the number of persons there, I had not an opportunity of being alone with Lydia. Went back to Falmouth with G. I was more disposed to talk of Lydia all the way, but roused myself to a sense of my duty, and addressed him on the subject of religion. The next day I was exceedingly melancholy at what had taken place between Lydia and myself, and at the thought of being separated from her. I could not bring myself to believe that God had settled the whole matter, because I was not willing to believe it.

To Miss Lydia Grenfell, Marazion

Union, Falmouth Harbour: July 27, 1805.

... As I was coming on board this morning, and reading Mr. Serle's hymn you wrote out for me, a sudden|83| gust of wind blew it into the sea. I made the boatmen immediately heave to, and recovered it, happily without any injury except what it had received from the sea. I should have told you that the Morning Hymn, which I always kept carefully in my pocket-book, was one day stolen with it, and other valuable letters, from my rooms in college. It would be extremely gratifying to me to possess another copy of it, as it always reminded me most forcibly of the happy day on which we visited the aged saint. The fleet, it is said, will not sail for three weeks, but if you are willing to employ any of your time in providing me with this or any other manuscript hymns, the sooner you write them, the more certain I shall be of receiving them. Pardon me for thus intruding on your time; you will in no wise lose your reward. The encouragement conveyed in little compositions of this sort is more refreshing than a cup of cold water. The Lord of the harvest, who is sending forth me, who am most truly less than the least of all saints, will reward you for being willing to help forward even the meanest of His servants. The love which you bear to the cause of Christ, as well as motives of private friendship, will, I trust, induce you to commend me to God, and to the word of His grace, at those sacred moments when you approach the throne of our covenant God. To His gracious care I commend you. May you long live happy and holy, daily growing more meet for the inheritance of the saints in light. I remain, with affectionate regard, yours most truly,

H. MARTYN.

July 28.—(Sunday.)—Preached in the morning, on board, on John iii. 3. In the afternoon, at Falmouth Church, on 1 Cor. i. 20 to 26.

July 29.—My gloom returned. Walked to Lamorran; alternately repining at my dispensation, and giving it up to the Lord. Sometimes—after thinking of Lydia for a|84| long time together, so as to feel almost outrageous at being deprived of her—my soul would feel its guilt, and flee again to God. I was much relieved at intervals by learning the hymn, 'The God of Abraham praise.'

The lady's *Diary* has these passages, which show that her sister, Mrs. Hitchins, had rightly represented the state of her heart as not altogether refusing to return Martyn's affection:

1805, July 25.—I was surprised this morning by a visit from H.M., and have passed the day chiefly with him. The distance he is going, and the errand he is going on, rendered his society particularly interesting. I felt as if bidding a final adieu to him in this world, and all he said was as the words of one on the borders of eternity. May I improve the opportunity I have enjoyed of Christian converse, and may the Lord moderate the sorrow I feel at parting with so valuable and excellent friend—some pains have attended it, known only to God and myself. Thou God, that knowest them, canst alone give comfort.... Oh, may we each pursue our different paths, and meet at last around our Father's throne; may we often meet now in spirit, praying and obtaining blessings for each other. Now, my soul, return to God, the author of them.

July 26.—Oh, how this day has passed away! Nothing done to any good purpose. Lord, help me! I feel Thy loved presence withdrawn; I feel departing from Thee. Oh, let Thy mercy pardon, let Thy love succour, me. Deliver me from this temptation, set my soul at liberty, and I will praise Thee. I know the cause of all this darkness, this depression; dare I desire what Thou dost plainly, by the voice of Thy providence, condemn? O Lord, help me to conquer my natural feelings, help me to be watchful as Thy child. Oh, leave me not; or I fall a prey to this corroding care. Let me cast every care on Thee.[85]

Gurlyn, July 30.—Blessed Lord, I thank Thee for affording me the retirement I so much delight in; here I enjoy freedom from all the noise and interruption of a town. Oh, may the Lord sanctify this pleasure. Oh, may it prove the means of benefiting my soul. Oh, may I watch against the intrusions of vain thoughts; else, instead of an advantage, I shall find solitude ruinous to my soul.

August 4.—This evening my soul has been pained with many fears concerning an absent friend, yet the Lord sweetly supports me, and is truly a refuge to me. It is a stormy and tempestuous night; the stillness and retirement of this place add to the solemnity of the hour. I hear the voice of God in every blast—it seems to say, 'Sin has brought storm and tempest on a guilty world.' O my Father and my God, Thou art righteous in all Thy judgments, merciful in all Thy ways. I would humbly trust in Thee, and confide all who are dear to me into Thy hands. The anxieties of nature, the apprehensions of affection, do Thou regulate, and make me acquiesce in whatever is Thy will.

August 5.—My mind is relieved to-day by hearing the fleet, in which I thought my friend had sailed, has not left the port. Oh, how frequently do unnecessary pains destroy our peace. Lord, look on me to-night, pardon my sins and make me more watchful and fight against my inward corruption. Oh, it is a state of conflict indeed!

He thus wrote to Mrs. Hitchins:

Falmouth: July 30, 1805.

'My dearest Cousin,—I am exceedingly rejoiced at being permitted to send you one more letter, as the former, if it had been the last, would have left, I fear, a painful impression on your mind. It pleased God to restore peace to my mind soon after I came on board—as I thought—finally. I was left more alone with God, and found blessed seasons of intercourse with Him. But when your letter came,[86] I found it so sympathising, so affectionate, that my heart was filled with joy and thankfulness to God for such a dear friend, and I could not refrain from bowing my knees immediately to pray that God might bless all your words to the good of my soul, and bless you for having written them. My views of the respective importance of things continue, I hope, to rectify. The shortness of time, the precious value of immortal souls, and the plain command of Christ, all conspire to teach me that Lydia must be resigned—and for ever—for though you suggest the possibility of my hereafter returning and being united to her, I rather wish to beware of looking forward to anything in this life as the end or reward of my labours. It would-be a temptation to me to return before being necessitated. The rest which remaineth for the people of God is in another world, where they neither marry nor are given in marriage. But while I thus reason, still a sigh will ever and anon escape me at the thought of a final separation from her. In the morning when I rise, before prayer puts grace into exercise, there is generally a very heavy gloom on my spirits—and a distaste for everything in earth or heaven. You do not seem to suppose that any objection would remain in her mind, if I should return and other obstacles were removed—which opinion of yours is, no doubt, very pleasing to me—but if

32

there*were* anything more than friendship, do you think it at all likely she could have spoken and written to me as she has? However, do not suppose from this that I wish to hear from you anything more on this subject—in the hope of being gratified with an assurance to the contrary. I cannot tell what induced me to take my leave of the people in the west when I was last there, as it was so probable we should be detained; were it not for having bid them adieu, I believe I should pay them another visit—only that I could not do it without being with Lydia again, which might not perhaps answer any good purpose, and more probably would renew the pain.[87]

If, in India, I should be persuaded of the expediency of marriage, you perceive that I can do nothing less than make her the offer, or rather propose the sacrifice. It would be almost cruel and presumptuous in me to make such an application to her, especially as she would be induced by a sense of duty rather than personal attachment. But what else can be done? Should she not, then, be warned of my intention—before I go? If you advance no objection, I shall write a letter to her, notwithstanding her prohibition. When this is done no further step remains to be taken, that I know of. The shortness of our acquaintance, which she made a ground of objection, cannot now be remedied.

The matter, as it stands, must be left with God—and I do leave it with Him very cheerfully. I pray that hereafter I may not be tempted to follow my will, and mistake it for God's—to fancy I am called to marriage, when I ought to remain single—and you will likewise pray, my dear cousin, that my mind may be always under a right direction.

His *Journal* thus continues:

July 31.—Went on board this morning in extreme anguish. I could not help saying, 'Lord, it is not a sinful attachment in itself, and therefore I may commune more freely with Thee about it.' I sought for hymns suitable to my case, but none did sufficiently; most complained of spiritual distress, but mine was not from any doubt of God's favour, for I felt no doubt of that.

August 1.—Rose in great anguish of mind, but prayer relieved me a little. The wind continuing foul, I went ashore after breakfast; but before this, sat down to write to Lydia, hoping to relieve the burden of my mind. I wrote in great turbulence, but in a little time my tumult unaccountably subsided, and I enjoyed a peace to which I have been for some time a stranger. I felt exceedingly willing to leave her, and to go on my way rejoicing. I[88] could not account for this, except by ascribing it to the gracious influence of God. The first few Psalms were exceedingly comfortable to me. Received a letter this evening from Emma, and received it as from God; I was animated before, but this added tenfold encouragement. She warned me, from experience, of the carefulness it would bring upon me; but spoke with such sympathy and tenderness, that my heart was quite refreshed. I bowed my knees to bless and adore God for it, and devoted myself anew to His beloved service. Went on board at night; the sea ran high, but I felt a sweet tranquillity in Him who stilleth the raging of the sea. I was delighted to find that the Lascars understood me perfectly when I spoke to them a sentence or two in Hindustani.

August 5.—Went ashore. Walked to Pendennis garrison; enjoyed some happy reflections as I sat on one of the ramparts, looking at the ships and sea.

August 7.—Preached at Falmouth Church, on Psalm iii. 1, with much comfort; after church, set off to walk to St. Hilary. Reached Helston in three hours in extraordinary spirits. The joy of my soul was very great. Every object around me called forth praise and gratitude to God. Perhaps it might have been joy at the prospect of seeing Lydia, but I asked myself at the time, whether out of love to God I was willing to turn back and see her no more. I persuaded myself that I could. But perhaps had I been put to the trial, it would have been otherwise. I arrived safe at St. Hilary, and passed the evening agreeably with R. 8th. Enjoyed much of the presence of God in morning prayer. The morning passed profitably in writing on Heb. ii. 3. My soul seemed to breathe seriously after God. Walked down with R. to Gurlyn to call on Lydia. She was not at home when we called, so I walked out to meet her. When I met her coming up the hill, I was almost induced to believe her more interested about me than I had conceived. Went away in the expectation[89] of visiting her frequently. Called on my way (from Falmouth) at Gurlyn. My mind not in peace; at night in prayer, my soul was much overwhelmed with fear, which caused me to approach God in fervent petition, that He would make me perfectly upright, and my walk consistent with the high character I am called to assume.

August 10.—Rose very early, with uneasiness increased by seeing the wind northerly; walked away at seven to Gurlyn, feeling little or no pleasure at the thought of seeing Lydia; apprehension about the sailing of the fleet made me dreadfully uneasy; was with Lydia a short time before breakfast; afterwards I read the 10th Psalm, with Horne's Commentary, to her and her mother; she was then just putting into my hand the 10th of Genesis to read when a servant came in, and said a horse was come for me from St. Hilary, where a carriage was waiting to convey me to Falmouth. All my painful presentiments were thus realised, and it came upon me like a thunderbolt. Lydia was evidently painfully affected by it; she came out, that we might be alone at taking leave, and I then told her, that if it should appear to be God's will that I should be married, she must not be offended at receiving a letter from me. In the great hurry she discovered more of her mind than she intended; she made no objection whatever to coming out. Thinking, perhaps, I wished to make an engagement with her, she said we had better go quite free; with this I left her, not knowing yet for what purpose I have been permitted, by an unexpected providence, to enjoy these interviews. I galloped back to St. Hilary, and instantly got into a chaise with Mr. R., who had been awaked by the signal gun at five in the morning, and had come for me. At Hildon I got a horse, with which I rode to Falmouth, meeting on the road another express sent after me by R. I arrived about twelve, and instantly went on board; almost all the other ships were under weigh, but the Union had got entangled in the chains. The commodore[90]expressed his anger as he passed, at this delay, but I blessed the Lord, who had thus saved His poor creature from shame and trouble. How delusive are schemes of pleasure; at nine in the morning I was sitting at ease, with the person dearest to me on earth, intending to go out with her afterwards to see the different views, to visit some persons with her, and to preach on the morrow; four hours only elapsed, and I was under sail from England! The anxiety to get on board, and the joy I felt at not being left behind, absorbed other sorrowful considerations for a time; wrote several letters as soon as I was on board. When I was left a little at leisure, my spirits began to sink; yet how backward was I to draw near to my God. I found relief occasionally, yet still was slow to fly to this refuge of my weary soul. Was meditating on a subject for to-morrow. As more of the land gradually appeared behind the Lizard, I watched with my spy-glass for the Mount (St. Michael's), but in consequence of lying to for the purser, and thus dropping astern of the fleet, night came on before we weathered the point. Oh, let not my soul be deceived and distracted by these foolish vanities, but now that I am actually embarked in Christ's cause, let a peculiar unction rest upon my soul, to wean me from the world, and to inspire me with ardent zeal for the good of souls.

TO MISS LYDIA GRENFELL.

Union, Falmouth: August 10, 1805.

My dear Miss Lydia,—It will perhaps be some satisfaction to yourself and your mother, to know that I was in time. Our ship was entangled in the chain, and was by that means the only one not under weigh when I arrived. It seems that most of the people on board had given me up, and did not mean to wait for me. I cannot but feel sensibly this instance of Divine mercy in thus preserving me from the great trouble that would have attended the loss of my[91] passage. Mount's Bay will soon be in sight, and recall you all once more to my affectionate remembrance.... I bid you a long Farewell. God ever bless you, and help you sometimes to intercede for me.

H. MARTYN.

The lady alludes thus, in her *Diary*, to these events, in language which confesses her love, as she did not again confess it till after his death:[114]

August 8.—I was surprised again to-day by a visit from my friend, Mr. Martyn, who, contrary to every expectation, is detained, perhaps weeks longer. I feel myself called on to act decisively—oh how difficult and painful a part—Lord, assist me. I desire to be directed by Thy wisdom, and to follow implicitly what appears Thy will. May we each consider Thy honour as entrusted to us, and resolve, whatever it may cost us, to seek Thy glory and do Thy will. O Lord, I feel myself so weak that I would fain fly from the trial. My hope is in Thee—do Thou strengthen me, help me to seek, to know, and resolutely to do, Thy will, and that we may be each divinely influenced, and may principle be victorious over feeling. Thou, blessed Spirit, aid, support, and guide us. Now may we be in the armour of God, now may we flee from temptation. O blessed Jesus, leave me not, forsake me not.

August 9.—What a day of conflict has this been! I was much blessed, as if to prepare me for it, in the morning, and expected to see my friend, and hoped to have acted[92] with Christian resolution. At Tregembo I learnt he had been called on by express last night. The effect this intelligence had on me shows how much my affections are engaged. O Lord, I lament it, I wonder at myself, I tremble at what may be before me—but do not, O Lord, forsake me. The idea of his going, when at parting I behaved with greater coolness and reserve than I ever did before, was a distress I could hardly bear, and I prayed the Lord to afford me an opportunity of doing away the impression from his mind. I saw no possibility of this—imagining the fleet must have sailed—when, to my astonishment, I learnt from our servant that he had called again this evening, and left a message that he would be here to-morrow. Oh, I feel less able than ever to conceal my real sentiments, and the necessity of doing it does not so much weigh with me. O my soul, pause, reflect—thy future happiness, and his too, the glory of God, the peace of my dear mother—all are concerned in what may pass to-morrow; I can only look and pray to be directed aright.

August 10.—Much have I to testify of supporting grace this day, and of what I must consider Divine interference in my favour, and that of my dear friend, who is now gone to return no more. My affections are engaged past recalling, and the anguish I endured yesterday, from an apprehension that I had treated him with coolness, exceeds my power to express; but God saw it, and kindly ordered it that he should come and do away the idea from my mind. It contributed likewise to my peace, and I hope to his, that it is clearly now understood between us that he is free to marry where he is going, and I have felt quite resigned to the will of God in this, and shall often pray the Lord to find him a suitable partner.

Went to meeting in a comfortable frame, but the intelligence brought me there—that the fleet had probably sailed without my friend—so distressed and distracted my[93] mind, that I would gladly have exchanged my feelings of yesterday for those I was now exercised with; yet in prayer I found relief, and in appealing to God. How unsought by me was his coming here. I still felt anxiety beyond all expression to hear if he arrived in time or not. Oh, not for all the world could offer me would I he should lose his passage!—yet stay, my soul, recollect thyself, are not all events at the Lord's disposal? Are not the steps of a good man ordered by the Lord? Cast then this burden on Him who carest for thee, my soul. Oh, let not Thy name, great God, be blasphemed through us—surely we desire to glorify it above all things, and would sacrifice everything to do so; enter then my mind this night, and let me in every dark providence trust in the Lord.

August 11.—A day of singular mercies. O my soul, how should the increasing goodness of God engage thee to serve Him with more zeal and ardour. I had a comfortable season in prayer before breakfast, enjoying sweet liberty of spirit before God my Saviour, God, the sinner's friend and helper. Went to church, but could get no comfort from the sermon; the service I found in some parts quickening. On my return I found a letter from my excellent friend, dated on board the Union. Oh, what a relief to my mind! By a singular providence this ship was prevented sailing by getting entangled in the chain; every other belonging to the fleet was under weigh when he reached Falmouth, and his friends there had given over the hope of his arriving in time. Doth not God care for His people, and order everything, even the most trifling, that concerns them? The fleet must not sail till the man of God joined it;—praised be the name of the Lord for this instance of His watchful care. And now, my soul, turn to God, thy rest. Oh, may the remembrance of my dear friend, whilst it is cherished as it ought, be no hindrance to my progress in grace and holiness. May God alone fill my thoughts, and may my regard for my friend be sanctified, and be a[94] means of stimulating me to press forward, and animate me in devoting myself entirely to God. Lord, I would unfeignedly adore Thee for all the instances of Thy loving kindness to me this week. I have had many remarkable answers to prayer, many proofs that the Lord watches over me, unworthy as I am. O Divine Saviour, how shall I praise Thee? Walked this evening to a little meeting at Thirton Wood. I was greatly refreshed and comforted. Oh, what a support in time of trouble is the Lord God of Israel! I am about retiring to rest—oh, may my thoughts upon my bed be solemn and spiritual. The remembrance of my dear friend is at times attended with feelings most painful, and yet, when I consider why he is gone, and Whom he is serving, every burden is removed, and I rejoice on his account, and rejoice that the Lord has such a faithful servant employed in the work. Oh, may I find grace triumphant over every feeling of my heart. Come, Lord Jesus, and dwell with me.

August 12.—Passed a sweet, peaceful day, enjoying much of His presence whose favour giveth life, and joy, and peace. Visited several of the poor near me, and found ability to speak freely and feelingly to them of the state of their souls. My dear absent friend is constantly remembered by me, but I find not his remembrance a hindrance to my soul in following after God—no, rather does it stimulate me in my course. Thus hath the Lord answered my prayers, as it respects myself, that our regard might be a sanctified one. Oh, bless the Lord, my soul, for ever! praise Him in cheerful lays from day to day, and hope eternally to do so.

August 13.—Awoke early and had a happy season. Visited a poor old man in great poverty, whose mind seemed disposed to receive instruction, and in some measure enlightened to know his sinful state and need of Christ; I found it a good time whilst with him. This evening my spirits are depressed; my absent friend is present to my remembrance, possessing more than common sensibility and[95] affection. What must his sufferings be? but God is sufficient for him. He that careth for the falling sparrow will not forget him—this is my never-failing source of consolation.

August 15.—My soul has been cold in duties to-day. Oh, for the spirit of devotion! Great are the things God has wrought for me; oh, let these great things suitably impress my soul. I have had many painful reflections to-day respecting my absent friend, fearing whether I may not be the occasion of much sorrow to him and possibly of hindering him in the work. I could not do such violence to my feelings as to treat him with reserve and distance, yet, in his circumstances, I think I ought to. O Lord, if in this I have offended, forgive me, and oh, do away from his mind every improper remembrance of me. Help me to cast my cares on Thee to-night, and help me with peace.

Marazion, September 2.—My mind has been exercised with many painful anxieties about my dear friend, but I have poured out my soul to God, and am relieved; I have left my sorrows with Him. Isaiah (41st chapter) has comforted me. Oh, what pleasure did that permission give me when my heart was overburdened to-day. 'Produce your cause'—what a privilege to come to God as a friend. I disclose those feelings to Him I have no power to any earthly friend. Those I could say most to seem to avoid the subject that occupies my mind; I have been wounded by their silence, yet I do not imagine them indifferent or unconcerned. It is well for me they have seemed to be so, for it has made me more frequent at a throne of grace, and brought me more acquainted with God as a friend who will hear all my complaints. Oh, how sweet to approach Him, through Christ, as my God. 'Fear not,' He says, 'for I am with you: be not dismayed, I am thy God, I will strengthen thee, yea (O blessed assurance!) I will help thee, yea, I will uphold thee with the right hand of My righteousness;' and so I find it—glory be to God! Lord,[96] hear the frequent prayers I offer for Thy dear servant, sanctify our mutual regard; may it continue through eternity, flowing from our love to Thee.

September 3.—Still no letters from Stoke, and no intelligence whether the fleet has sailed—this is no small exercise of my patience, but at times I feel a sweet complacency in saying, 'Thou art my portion, O Lord.' I have often felt happy in saying this, but it is in a season such as this, when creature comforts fail, that we may know whether we are sincere in saying so. Ah! how do we imperceptibly cleave to earth, and how soon withdraw our affections from God. I am sensible mine would never fix on Him but by His own power effecting it. I rest on Thy power, O God most high, retired from human observation.

When the commodore opened his sealed despatches off the Lizard, it was found that the fleet was to linger still longer at Cork, whence Henry Martyn wrote again to Lydia's sister, Mrs. Hitchins. On Sunday, when becalmed in Mount's Bay, and he would have given anything to have been ashore preaching at Marazion or St. Hilary, he had taken for his text Hebrews xi. 16: 'But now they desire a better country, that is, an heavenly.'

36

Cork Harbour: August 19, 1805.

The beloved objects were still in sight, and Lydia I knew was about that time at St. Hilary, but every wave bore me farther and farther from them. I introduced what I had to say by observing that we had now bid adieu to England, and its shores were dying away from the view. The female part of my audience were much affected, but I do not know that any were induced to seek the better country. The Mount continued in sight till five o'clock, when it disappeared behind the western boundary of the[97] bay. Amidst the extreme gloom of my mind this day I found great comfort in interceding earnestly for my beloved friends all over England. If you have heard from Marazion since Sunday, I should be curious to know whether the fleet was observed passing....

We are now in the midst of a vast number of transports filled with troops. It is now certain from our coming here that we are to join in some expedition, probably the Cape of Good Hope, or the Brazils; anywhere for me so long as the Lord goes with me. If it should please God to send me another letter from you, which I scarcely dare hope, do not forget to tell me as much as you can about Lydia. I cannot write to her, or I should find the greatest relief and pleasure even in transmitting upon paper the assurances of my tenderest love.

Cove of Cork: August 28, 1805.

My dearest Cousin,—I have but a few minutes to say that we are again going to sea—under convoy of five men of war. Very anxiously have I been expecting to receive an answer to the letter I sent you on my arrival at this port, bearing date August 16; from the manner in which I had it conveyed to the post-office, I begin to fear it has never reached you. I have this instant received the letter you wrote me the day on which we sailed from Falmouth. Everything from you gives me the greatest pleasure, but this letter has rather tended to excite sentiments of pain as well as pleasure. I fear my proceedings have met with your disapprobation, and have therefore been wrong—since it is more probable you should judge impartially than myself.

I am now fully of opinion that, were I convinced of the expediency of marriage, I ought not in conscience to propose it, while the obstacle of S.J. remains. Whatever others have said, I think that Lydia acts no more than consistently by persevering in her present determination.[98] I confess, therefore, that till this obstacle is removed my path is perfectly clear, and, blessed be God! I feel very, very happy in all that my God shall order concerning me. Let me suffer privation, and sorrow and death, if I may by these tribulations enter into the kingdom of God. Since we have been lying here I have been enjoying a peace almost uninterrupted. The Spirit of adoption has been drawing me near to God, and giving me the full assurance of His love. My prayer is continually that I may be more deeply and habitually convinced of His unchanging, everlasting love, and that my whole soul may be altogether in Christ. The Lord teaches me to desire Christ for my all in all—to long to be encircled in His everlasting arms, to be swallowed up in the fulness of His love. Surely the soul is happy that thus bathes in a medium of love. I wish no created good, but to be one with Him and to be living for my Saviour and Lord. Oh, may it be my constant care to live free from the spirit of bondage, and at all times have access to the Father. This I now feel, my beloved cousin, should be our state—perfect reconciliation with God, perfect appropriation of Him in all His endearing attributes, according to all that He has promised. This shall bear us safely through the storm. Oh, how happy are we in being introduced to such high privileges! You and my dear brother, and Lydia, I rejoice to think, are often praying for me and interested about me. I have, of course, much more time and leisure to intercede for you than you for me—and you may be assured I do not fail to employ my superior opportunities in your behalf. Especially is it my prayer that the mind of my dear cousin, formed as it is by nature and by grace for higher occupations, may not be rendered uneasy by the employments and cares of this.

Hearing nothing accurately of the India fleet after its departure from Mount's Bay, Lydia Grenfell thus[99] betrayed to herself and laid before God her loving anxiety:

1805, September 24.—Have I not reason ever, and in all things, to trust and bless God? O my soul, why dost thou yield to despondency? why art thou disquieted? O my soul, put thy trust in God, assured that thou shalt yet praise Him, who is the help of thy countenance and thy God in Christ Jesus. My mind is under considerable anxiety, arising from the uncertainty of my dear friend's situation, and an apprehension of his being ill. Oh, how soon is my soul filled with confusion! yet I find repose for it in the love of Jesus—oh, let me then raise my eyes to Him, and may His love be shed abroad in my heart; make me in all things resigned to Thy will, to trust and hope and rejoice in Thee.

November 1.—My dear absent friend has too much occupied my thoughts and affections, and broken my peace—but Jesus reigns in providence and grace, and He does all things well. Yes, in my best moments I can rejoice in believing this, but too often I yield to unbelieving fears and discouragements. The thought that we shall meet no more sinks at times my spirits, yet I would say and feel submissive—Thy will be done. Choose for my motto, on entering my thirty-first year, this Scripture: 'Our days on the earth are as a shadow, and there is none abiding.'

November 4.—I think of my friend, but blessed be God for not suffering my regard to lead me from Himself.

November 16.—I have been employed to-day in a painful manner, writing[15](perhaps for the last time) to too dear a friend. I have to bless God for keeping me composed whilst doing so, and for peace of mind since, arising from a conviction that I have done right; and oh, that I may now be enabled to turn my thought from all below to [100] that better world where my soul hopes eternally to dwell. Blessed Lord Jesus, be my strength and shield. Oh, let not the enemy harass me, nor draw my affections from Thee.

November 17.—Felt great depression of spirits to-day, from the improbability of ever seeing H.M. return. I feel it necessary to fly to God, praying for submission to His will, and to rest assured of the wisdom and love of this painful event. O my soul, rise from these cares, look beyond the boundary of time. Oh, cheering prospect, in that blest world where my Redeemer lives I shall regain every friend I love—with Christian love again. Be resigned then, my soul, Jesus is thine, and He does all things well.

FOOTNOTES:

[10]Deposited by Henry Martyn Jeffery, Esq., in the Truro Museum of the Royal Institution, where the MS. may be consulted.

[11]Hitherto unpublished. We owe the copy of this significant letter to the courtesy of H.M. Jeffery, Esq., F.R.S., for whom Canon Moor, of St. Clement's, near Truro, procured it from the friend to whom Mrs. T.M. Hitchins had given it.

[12]*Essays in Ecclesiastical Biography.*

[13]The *Observations on the State of Society among the Asiatic Subjects of Great Britain,* written in 1792.

[14]The parallel between Henry Martyn and David Brainerd, so close as to spiritual experience and missionary service, hereditary consumption and early death, is even more remarkable in their hopeless but purifying love. Brainerd was engaged to Jerusha, younger daughter of the great Jonathan Edwards. 'Dear Jerusha, are you willing to part with me?' said the dying missionary on October 4, 1747.... 'If I thought I should not see you and be happy with you in another world, I could not bear to part with you. But we shall spend a happy eternity together!' See J.M. Sherwood's edition (1885) of the *Memoirs of Rev. David Brainerd,* prefaced by Jonathan Edwards, D.D., p. 340.

[15]This letter never reached its destination, but was captured in the Bell Packet.
[101]

CHAPTER III

THE NINE MONTHS' VOYAGE—SOUTH AMERICA—SOUTH AFRICA, 1805 1806

The East India fleet had been detained off Ireland 'for fear of immediate invasion, in which case the ships might be of use.' The young chaplain was kept busy enough in his own and the other vessels. In one of these, the Ann, there was a mutiny. Another, the Pitt, was a Botany Bay ship, carrying out 120 female convicts. Thanks to Charles Simeon, he was able to supply all with Bibles and religious books. But even on board his own transport, the Union, the captain would allow only one service on the Sabbath, and denied permission to preach to the convicts. The chaplain's ministrations between decks were continued daily, amid the indifference and even opposition of all save a few.

At last, on August 31, 1805, the Indiamen of the season and fifty transports sailed out of the Cove of Cork under convoy of the Diadem, 64 guns, the Belliqueuse, 64 guns, the Leda and Narcissus frigates, on a voyage which, after two months since lifting the anchor at Portsmouth, lasted eight and a half months to Calcutta. The Union had H.M. 59th Regiment on board. Of its officers and men, and of the East India Company's cadets and the officers commanding them, he succeeded in inducing only five to[102] join him in daily worship. His own presence and this little gathering caused the vessel to be known in the fleet as 'the praying ship.' The captain died during the voyage to the Cape. One of the ships was wrecked, the Union narrowly escaping the same fate. Martyn's *Journal* reveals an amount of hostility to himself and of open scoffing at his message which would be impossible now. He fed his spirit with the Word of God, which he loved to expound to others. Leighton, especially the too little known *Rules for Holy Living*, was ever in his hands. Augustine and Ambrose delighted him, also Hooker, Baxter, Jonathan Edwards, and Flavel, which he read to any who would listen, while he spoke much to the Mohammedan Lascars. He worked hard at Hindustani, Bengali, and Portuguese. Not more faithfully reflected in his *Journal* than the tedium of the voyage and the often blasphemous opposition of his fellows are, all unconsciously, his own splendid courage, his untiring faithfulness even when down with dysentery and cough, his watchful prayerfulness, his longing for the spread of Christ's kingdom. As the solitary young saint paced the deck his thoughts, too, were with the past—with Lydia, in a way which, even he felt, did not leave him indisposed for communion with God. From Funchal, Madeira, he wrote to Lydia's sister: 'God knows how dearly I love you, and Lydia and Sally (his younger sister), and all His saints in England, yet I bid you all an everlasting farewell almost without a sigh.' His motto throughout the voyage was the sentence in which Milner characterises the first Christians:

'To Believe, to Suffer, and to Love.'

Meanwhile Lydia Grenfell was thus committing to her *Diary* these melancholy longings:[103]

November 22.—Yesterday brought me most pleasing intelligence from my dear friend, for which I have and do thank Thee, O Lord my God. He assures us of his being well, and exceedingly happy—oh, may he continue so. I have discovered that insensibly I have indulged the hope of his return, which this letter has seemed to lessen. I see it is my duty to familiarise my mind to the idea of our separation being for ever, with what feelings the thought is admitted, the Lord—whose will I desire therein to be done—only knows, and I find it a blessed relief to look to Him for comfort. I can bear testimony to this, that the Lord does afford me the needful support. I have been favoured much within this day or two, and seem, if I may trust to present feelings, to be inspired to ask the Lord's sovereign will and pleasure concerning me and him. I look forward to our meeting only in another state of existence, and oh, how pure, how exalted will be our affection then! here it is mixed with much evil, many pains, and great anxieties. Hasten, O Lord, Thy coming, and fit me for it and for the society of Thy saints in light. I desire more holiness, more of Christ in my soul, more of His likeness. Oh, to be filled with all Thy fulness, to be swallowed up in Thee!

November 23.—Too much has my mind been occupied to-day with a subject which must for ever interest me. O Lord, have mercy on me! help can only come from Thee. Let Thy blessed Word afford me relief; let the aids of Thy Spirit be vouchsafed. Restore to me the joys of Thy salvation.

November 24.—Passed a night of little sleep, my mind restless, confused, and unhappy. In vain did I endeavour to fix my thoughts on spiritual things, and to drive away those distressing fears of what may befall my dear friend. Blessed for ever be the Lord that on approaching His mercy-seat, through the blood of Jesus, I found peace, rest, and an ability to rely on God for all things. I have through the day enjoyed a sense of the Divine presence, and a [104]blessed nearness to the Lord. To-night I am favoured with a sweet calmness; I seem to have no desire to exert myself. O Lord, animate, refresh my fainting soul. I see how dangerous it is to admit any worldly object into the heart, and how prone mine is to idolatry, for whatever has the preference, that to God is an idol. Alas! my thoughts, my first and last thoughts, are now such as prove that God cannot be said to have the supreme place in my affections; yet, blessed be His name, I can resign myself and all my concerns to His disposal, and this is my heart's desire. Thy will be done.

December 11.—I seem reconciled to all before me, and consider the Lord must have some great and wise purposes to answer by suffering my affections to be engaged in the degree they are. If it is only to exercise my submission to His will, and to make me more acquainted with His power to support and comfort me, it will be a great end answered, and oh, may I welcome all He appoints for this purpose. The mysteries of Providence are unfathomable. The event must disclose them, and in this I desire to make up my mind from henceforth no more to encourage the least expectation of meeting my dear friend in this world. O Lord, when the desire is so strong, how impossible is it for me to do this; but Thou art able to strengthen me for it. Oh, vouchsafe the needful help.

December 16.—I have had many distressing feelings to-day, and struggled with my heart, which is at times rent, I may say, by the reflection that I have bidden adieu for ever in this life to so dear a friend; but the blessed employment the Lord has assisted me in, and the thought that he is serving my blessed Lord Jesus, is most consolatory. Oh, may I never more seek to draw him back from the work. Lord, Thou knowest all things, Thou knowest that I would not do this.

December 26.—Went early to St. Hilary, where I had an opportunity of reading the excellent prayers of our|105| Church. I have been blest with sweet peace to-day—a solemn expectation of entering eternity. I feel a sadness of spirit at times (attended with a calm resignation of mind, not unpleasing) at the remembrance of my friend, whom I expect no more to see till we meet in heaven. Oh, blessed hope that there we shall meet! Lord, keep us each in the narrow way that leads to Thee.

December 31.—The last in 1805—oh, may it prove the most holy to my soul. I am shut out from the communion of Thy saints in a measure; oh, let me enjoy more communion with my God. Thou knowest my secret sorrows, yea, Thou dost calm them by causing me to have regard to a future life of bliss with Thee, when I shall see and adore the wisdom of Thy dealings with me. Oh, my idolatrous heart!

These passages occur in Henry Martyn's *Journal*:

December 4.—Dearest Lydia! never wilt thou cease to be dear to me; still, the glory of God, and the salvation of immortal souls, is an object for which I can part with thee. Let us live then for God, separate from one another, since such is His holy will. Hereafter we shall meet in a happier region, and if we shall have lived and died, denying ourselves for God, triumphant and glorious will our meeting be....

December 5.—My mind has been running on Lydia, and the happy scenes in England, very much; particularly on that day when I walked with her on the sea-shore, and with a wistful eye looked over the blue waves that were to bear me from her. While walking the deck I longed to be left alone, that my thoughts might run at random. Tender feelings on distant scenes do not leave me indisposed for communion with God; that which is present to the outward senses is the greatest plague to me. Went among the soldiers in the afternoon, distributing oranges to those who are scorbutic. My heart was for some hours expanding with joy and love; but I have reason to|106| think that the state of the body has great influence on the frames and feelings of the mind. Let the rock of my consolations be not a variable feeling, but Jesus Christ and His righteousness.

The fleet next touched at San Salvador, or Bahia, from which Henry Martyn wrote to Mrs. Hitchins, his cousin, asking her to send him by Corrie, who was coming out as chaplain, 'your profile and Cousin Tom's and Lydia's. If she should consent to it, I should much wish for her miniature.' The request, when it reached her, must have led to such passages in her *Diary* as these:

1806, February 8.—I have passed some days of pain and weakness, but now am blessed again with health. During the whole of this sickness I was afflicted with much deadness of soul, and have had very few thoughts of God. I felt, as strength returned, the necessity of more earnest supplications for grace and spiritual life. I have ascertained this sad truth, that my soul has declined in spiritual fervour and liveliness since I have admitted an earthly object so much into my heart. Ah! I know I have not power to recall my affections, but God can, and I believe He will, enable me to regulate them better. This thought has been of great injury to me, as I felt no murmuring at the will of God, nor disposed to act therein contrary to His will. I thought I might indulge secretly my affection, but it has been of vast disadvantage to me. I am now convinced, and I do humbly (relying on strength from on high) resolve no more to yield to it. Oh, may my conversation be in heaven, and the glories of Immanuel be all my theme.

February 15.—I have been much exercised yesterday and to-day—walking in darkness, without light—and I feel the truth of this Scripture: 'Your sins have separated between you and your God.' I have betrayed a most unbecoming impatience and warmth of temper. My dear[107] absent friend, too, has been much in my mind. How many times have I endured the pain of bidding him farewell! I would not dare repine. I doubt not for a moment the necessity of its being as it is, but the feelings of my mind at particular seasons overwhelm me. My refuge is to consider it is the will of God. Thy will, my God, be done.

Henry Martyn did not lose a day in discharging his mission to the residents and slaves of that part of the coast of Brazil, in the great commercial city and seat of the metropolitan. His was the first voice to proclaim the pure Gospel in South America since, three hundred years before, Coligny's and Calvin's missionaries had been there silenced by Villegagnon, and put to death. Martyn was frequently ashore, almost fascinated by the tropical glories of the coast and the interior, and keenly interested in the Portuese dons, the Franciscan friars, and the negro slaves. After his first walk through the town to the suburbs, he was looking for a wood in which he might rest, when he found himself at a magnificent porch leading to a noble avenue and house. There he was received with exuberant hospitality by the Corrè family, especially by the young Señor Antonio, who had received a University training in Portugal, and soon learned to enjoy the society of the Cambridge clergyman. In his visits of days to this family, his exploration of the immediate interior and the plantations of tapioca and pepper, introduced from Batavia, and his discussions with its members and the priests on Roman Catholicism, all conducted in French and Latin, a fortnight passed rapidly. He was ever about his Master's business, able in speaking His message to men and in prayer and meditation.[108] 'In a cool and shady part of the garden, near some water, I sat and sang,

O'er the gloomy hills of darkness.

I could read and pray aloud, as there was no fear of anyone understanding me. Reading the eighty-fourth Psalm,

O how amiable are Thy tabernacles,

this morning in the shade, the day when I read it last under the trees with Lydia was brought forcibly to my remembrance, and produced some degree of melancholy.' Refreshed by the hospitality of San Salvador, he resumed the voyage with new zeal for his Lord and for his study of such authorities as Orme's *Indostan* and Scott's *Dekkan*, and thus taking himself to task: 'I wish I had a deeper conviction of the sinfulness of sloth.'

Thus had he taken possession of Brazil, of South America, for Christ. As he walked through the streets, where for a long time he 'saw no one but negro slaves male and female'; as he passed churches in which 'they were performing Mass,' and priests of all colours innumerable, and ascended the battery which commanded a view of the whole bay of All Saints, he exclaimed, 'What happy missionary shall be sent to bear the name of Christ to these western regions? When shall this beautiful country be delivered from idolatry and spurious Christianity? Crosses there are in abundance, but when shall the doctrine of the Cross be held up?' In the nearly ninety years that have gone since that time, Brazil has ceased to belong to the house of Braganza, slavery has been abolished, the agents of the Evangelical churches and societies of the United States of America and the Bible societies have been sent in answer to his prayer; while down in the far south Captain Allen Gardiner, R.N., by his death for the savage people, has brought about results that extorted the admiration of Dr. Darwin. As Martyn went back to the ship for the last[109] time, after a final discussion on Mariolatry with the Franciscans, rowed by Lascars who kept the feast of the Hijra with hymns to Mohammed, and in converse with a fellow-voyager who declared mankind needed to be told nothing but to be sober and honest, he cried to God with a deep sigh 'to interfere in behalf of His Gospel; for in the course of one hour I had seen three shocking examples of the reign and power of the devil in the form of Popish and Mohammedan delusion and that of the natural man. I felt, however, in no way discouraged, but only saw the necessity of dependence on God.'

Why did Henry Martyn's preaching and daily pastoral influence excite so much opposition? Undoubtedly, as we shall see, both in Calcutta and Dinapore, his Cornish-Celtic temperament, possibly the irritability due to the disease under which he was even then suffering, disabled him from disarming opposition, as his friend Corrie, for instance, afterwards always did. But we must remember to whom he preached and what he preached, and the time at which he preached, in the history not only of the Church of England, but of Evangelical religion. He had himself been brought out of spiritual darkness under the influence of Kempthorne and Charles Simeon, by the teaching of Paul in his letters to the Roman and the Galatian converts. To him sin was exceeding sinful. The Pauline doctrine of sin and its one remedy was the basis not only of his theology, but of his personal experience and daily life. After a brief ministry to the villagers of Lolworth and occasional sermons to his fellow students in Cambridge, this Senior Wrangler and Classic, yet young convert, was put in spiritual charge of a British regiment and Indiaman's crew, and was the only chaplain in a force of eight thousand soldiers, some with[110] families, and many female convicts. At a time when the dead churches were only beginning to wake up, after the missions of the Wesleys and Whitfield, of William Carey and Simeon, this youthful prophet was called to reason of temperance, righteousness, and judgment to come, with men who were practically as pagan or as sceptical as Felix.

His second address at sea, on September 15, was from Paul's sermon in the synagogue of Antioch in Pisidia (Acts xiii. 38-39): *Through this man is preached unto you the forgiveness of sins, &c.*[110] It was a full and free declaration of God's love in Jesus Christ to sinful man, which he thus describes in his *Journal:* 'In the latter part I was led to speak without preparation on the all-sufficiency of Christ to save sinners who came to Him with all their sins without delay. I was carried away with a Divine aid to speak with freedom and energy. My soul was refreshed, and I retired seeing reason to be thankful!' But the next week's experience resulted in this: 'I was more tried by the fear of man than I have ever been since God called me to the ministry. The threats and opposition of those men made me unwilling to set before them the truths which they hated; yet I had no species of hesitation about doing it. They had let me know that if I would preach a sermon like one of Blair's they should be glad to hear it; but they would not attend if so much of hell was preached.' Strengthened by our Lord's promise of the Comforter (John xiv. 16), he next Sunday took for his text Psalm ix. 17: *The wicked shall be turned into hell, and all the nations that forget God.* He thus concluded:[111]

Pause awhile, and reflect! Some of you, perhaps, by this time, instead of making a wise resolve, have begun to wonder that so heavy a judgment should be denounced merely against forgetfulness. But look at the affairs of common life, and be taught by them. Do not neglect, and want of attention, and not looking about us to see what we have to do—do not any of these bring upon us consequences as ruinous to our worldly business as any ACTIVE misbehaviour? It is an event of every day, that a man, by mere laziness and inattention to his business, does as certainly bring himself and family to poverty, and end his days in a gaol, as if he were, in wanton mischief, to set fire to his own house. So it is also with the affairs of the soul: neglect of that—forgetfulness of God, who only can save it— will work his ruin, as surely as a long and daring course of profligate wickedness.

When any one has been recollecting the proper proofs of a future state of rewards and punishments, nothing, methinks, can give him so sensible an apprehension of punishment or such a representation of it to the mind, as observing that, after the many disregarded checks, admonitions, and warnings which people meet with in the ways of vice, folly, and extravagance warnings from their very nature, from the examples of others, from the lesser inconveniences which they bring upon themselves, from the instructions of wise and good men—after these have been long despised, scorned, ridiculed—after the chief bad consequences (temporal consequences) of their follies have been delayed for a great while, at length they break in irresistibly like an armed force: repentance is too late to relieve, and can serve only to aggravate their distress: the case is become desperate; and poverty and sickness, remorse and anguish, infamy and death, the effects of their own doings, overwhelm them beyond possibility of remedy or escape. This is an account of what is, in fact, the general constitution of Nature.[112]

But is the forgetfulness of God so light a matter? Think what ingratitude, rebellion, and atheism there is at the bottom of it! Sirs, you have 'a carnal mind, which is enmity against God.' (Rom. viii. 7.) Do not suppose that you have but to make a slight effort, and you will cease to forget Him: it is your nature to forget Him: it is your nature to hate Him: so that nothing less than an entire change of heart and nature will ever deliver you from this state of enmity. Our nature 'is not subject to the law of God, neither indeed can be. They that are in the flesh cannot please God.' (Rom. viii. 7, 8.) From this state let the fearful menace in the text persuade you to arise! Need we remind you again of the dreadfulness of hell—of the certainty that it shall overtake the impenitent sinner? Enough has been said; and can any of you be still so hardened, and such enemies to your souls, as still to cleave to sin? Will you still venture to continue any more in the hazard of falling into the hands of God? Alas! 'Who among us shall dwell with the devouring fire? Who among us shall dwell with everlasting burnings?' (Isa. xxxiii. 14.) 'Can thine heart endure, or can thine hands be strong, in the days that I shall deal with thee? I the Lord have spoken it, and will do it!' (Ezek. xxii. 14.) Observe, that men have dealt with sinners—ministers have dealt with them—apostles, prophets, and angels have dealt with them: at last, God will take them in hand, and deal with them! Though not so daring as to defy God, yet, brethren, in all probability you put on repentance. Will you securely walk a little longer along the brink of the burning furnace of the Almighty's fury? 'As the Lord liveth, and as thy soul liveth, there is but a step between thee and death!' (1 Sam. xx. 3.) When you lie down you know not but you may be in it before the morning; and when you rise you know not but God may say, 'Thou fool, this night thy soul shall be required of thee!' When once the word is given to cut you down,[113] the business is over. You are cut off from your lying refuges and beloved sins—from the world—from your friends—from the light—from happiness—from hope, for ever! Be wise, then, my friends, and reasonable: give neither sleep to your eyes, nor slumber to your eyelids, till you have resolved, on your knees before God, to forget Him no more. Go home and pray. Do not dare to fly, as it were, in the face of your Maker, by seeking your pleasure on His holy day; but if you are alarmed at this subject, as well you may be, go and pray to God that you may forget Him no more. It is high time to awake out of sleep. It is high time to have done with hesitation: time does not wait for you; nor will God wait till you are pleased to turn. He hath bent His bow, and made it ready: halt no more between two opinions: hasten—tarry not in all the plain, but flee from the wrath to come. Pray for grace, without which you can do nothing. Pray for the knowledge of Christ, and of your own danger and helplessness, without which you cannot know what it is to find refuge in Him. It is not our design to terrify, without pointing out the means of safety. Let us then observe, that if it should have pleased God to awaken any of you to a sense of your danger, you should beware of betaking yourselves to a refuge of lies.

But, through the mercy of God, many among us have found repentance unto life—have fled for refuge to the hope set before them—have seen their danger, and fled to Christ. Think with yourselves what it is now to have escaped destruction; what it will be to hear at the last day our acquittal, when it shall be said to others, 'Depart from Me, ye cursed, into everlasting fire.' Let the sense of the mercy of God gild all the path of life. On the other hand, since it is they who forget God that are to bear the weight of His wrath, let us beware, brethren, how we forget Him, through concern about this world, or through unbelief, or through sloth. Let us be punctual in all our engagements[114] with Him. With earnest attention and holy awe ought we to hear His voice, cherish the sense of His presence, and perform the duties of His worship. No covenant relation or Gospel grace can render Him less holy, less jealous, or less majestic. 'Wherefore let us have grace, whereby we may serve God acceptably, with reverence and godly fear; for our God is a consuming fire.'

The officers had seated themselves behind the preacher, that they might retire in case of dislike, and one of them employed himself in feeding the geese; so it had happened in the case of the missionary Paul, and Martyn wrote: 'God, I trust, blessed the sermon to the good of many. Some of the cadets and soldiers were in tears.' The complement[117] of this truth he soon after displayed to them in his sermon on the message through Ezekiel xxxiii. 11. *As I live, saith the Lord, I have no pleasure in the death of the wicked.*

Men have been found in all ages who have vented their murmurs against God for the severity of His final punishment, as well as for the painful continuance of His judgments upon them in this life, saying, 'If our state be so full of guilt and misery as is represented, and God is determined to avenge Himself upon us, be it so; then we must take the consequences.' If God were to reply to this impious complaint only by silence; if He were to suffer the gloom of their hearts to thicken into tenfold darkness, and give them up to their own malignity, till they died victims to their own impiety and despair, the Lord would still be righteous, they would then only eat of the fruit of their doings. But, behold, the Lord gives a very unexpected message, with which He bids us to follow men,[115] to interrupt their sad soliloquies, to stop their murmurs. 'Say unto them,' saith He, 'As I live, saith the Lord God, I have no pleasure in the death of the wicked, but that the wicked turn from his way and live. Turn ye, turn ye, from your evil ways; for why will ye die?'

Behold the inseparable connexion—we must turn, or die. Here there is a question put by God to sinners. Let sinners then answer the question which God puts to them,—'Why will ye die?' Is a motive not strong enough to induce you to forego a momentary pleasure? Is it a light thing to fall into the hands of the living God? Is a life of godliness so very intolerable as not to be repaid by heavenly glory? Turn ye at His reproof—'Why will ye die?' Is it because there is no hope? God has this very hour testified with an oath that it is His desire to save you. Yea, He at this moment expostulates with you and beseeches you to seek Him. 'Why will ye die?' You know not why. If, then, you are constrained—now accustomed as you are to self-vindication—to acknowledge your unreasonableness, how much more will you be speechless in the last day when madness will admit of no palliation, and folly will appear without disguise!

Are any returned to God? Do any believe they are really returned?—then here they have consolation. It is a long time before we lose our slavish dread of God, for our natural prejudices and mistakes become inveterate by habit, and Satan opposes the removal of them. But come now, and let us reason together. Will ye also dishonour your God by accounting Him more willing to destroy than to save you? *Will* ye think hardly of God? Oh, that I had been able to describe as it deserves, His willingness to save! Oh, that I could have borrowed the pen of a seraph, and dipped it in a fount of light! Could plainer words be needed to describe the wonders of His love? Hearken, my beloved brethren! Hath He no pleasure in the death of the wicked, and will He take pleasure in yours? Hath He[116] promised His love, His tenderness to those who turn from their wicked ways, and yet, when they are turned, straightway forgot His promise? Harbour no more fearful, unbelieving thoughts. But the reply is often that the fear is not of God, but of myself, lest I have not turned away from my evil ways. But this point may surely be ascertained, brethren; and if it may, any further refinements on this subject are derogatory to God's honour. Let these words convince you that, if you are willing to be saved in His way, He is willing to save you. It may be you will still be kept in darkness, but darkness is not always the frown of God; it is only Himself—thy shade on thy right hand. Then tremble not at the hand that wipes away thy tears; judge Him not by feeble sense, but follow Him, though He lead thee by a way that thou knewest not.

There are some of you who have reason to hope that you have turned from the error of your ways. Ye have tasted that the Lord is gracious. It is but a taste, a foretaste, an antepast of the feast of heaven. It was His pleasure that you should turn from your ways; it is also His good pleasure to give you the kingdom. Then what shall we recommend to you, but gratitude, admiration, and praise? 'Praise the Lord, O Jerusalem; praise thy God, O Zion.' Let each of us abundantly utter the memory of His great goodness, and sing aloud of His righteousness. Let each say, 'Awake, lute and harp; I myself will awake right early.' Let us join the chorus of angels, and all the redeemed, in praising the riches of His love in His kindness towards us through Christ Jesus.

As the fleet sailed from San Salvador, the captains were summoned to the commodore, to learn that Cape Town and the Dutch settlement formed the object of the expedition, and that stout resistance was expected. This gave new zeal to the chaplain, were that possible, in his dealings[117]with the officers and men of his Majesty's 59th, and with the cadets, to whom he taught mathematics in his unrewarded friendliness. Many were down with dysentery, then and long a peculiarly fatal disease till the use of ipecacuanha. His constant service made him also for some time a sufferer.

1805, December 29. (Sunday.)—My beloved spake and said unto me, Rise up, &c. (Cant. ii. 10, 11). Ah! why cannot I rise and go forth and meet my Lord? Every hindrance is removed: the wrath of God, the guilt of sin, and severity of affliction; there is nothing now in the world that has any strong hold of my affections. Separated from my friends and country for ever in this life, I have nothing to distract me from hearing the voice of my beloved, and coming away from this world and walking with Him in love, amidst the flowers that perfume the air of Paradise, and the harmony of the happy spirits who are singing His praise. But alas! my heart is cold and slothful. Preached on 2 Peter iii. 11, taking notice at the end of these remarkable circumstances, that made the text particularly applicable to us. It was the last Sabbath of a year, which had been memorable to us from our having left our country, and passed through many dangers. Secondly, within a few days they were to meet an enemy on the field of battle. Thirdly, the death of the captain. I was enabled to be self-collected, and in some degree tender. There was a great impression; many were in tears. Visited and conversed with Mr. M. twice to-day, and marked some passages for him to read. His heart seems tender. There was a considerable number on the orlop in the afternoon. Expounded Matt. xix. and prayed. In the evening Major Davidson and M'Kenzie came to my cabin, and stayed nearly three hours. I read Romans vi. and vii., and explained those difficult chapters[118] as well as I could, so that the Major, I hope, received a greater insight into them; afterwards I prayed with them. But my own soul after these ministrations seemed to have received harm rather than good. It was an awful reflection that Judas was a preacher, perhaps a successful one. Oh, let my soul tremble, lest, after preaching to others, I myself should be a castaway.

1806. January 4.—Continued to approach the land; about sunset the fleet came to an anchor between Robben Island and the land on that side, farthest from Cape Town, and a signal was immediately given for the 59th Regiment to prepare to land. Our men were soon ready, and received thirty-six rounds of ball cartridge; before the three boats were lowered down and fitted, it was two in the morning. I stayed up to see them off; it was a melancholy scene; the privates were keeping up their spirits by affecting to joke about the approach of danger, and the ladies sitting in the cold night upon the grating of the after-hatchway overwhelmed with grief; the cadets, with M'Kenzie, who is one of their officers, all went on board the Duchess of Gordon, the general rendezvous of the company's troops. I could get to speak to none of my people, but Corporals B. and B. I said to Sergeant G., 'It is now high time to be decided in religion,' he replied with a sigh; to Captain S. and the cadets I endeavoured to speak in a general way. I this day signed my name as a witness to Captain O.'s and Major Davidson's wills; Captain O. left his with me; I passed my time at intervals in writing for to-morrow. The interest I felt in the outward scene distracted me very much from the things which are not seen, and all I could do in prayer was to strive against this spirit. But with what horror should I reflect on the motions of sins within me, which tempted me to wish for bloodshed, as something gratifying by its sublimity. My spirit would be overwhelmed by such a consciousness of depravity, but that I can pray still[119] deliberately against sin; and often the Lord manifested His power by making the same sinful soul to feel a longing desire that the blessed gospel of peace might soothe the spirits of men, and make them all live together in harmony and love. Yet the principle within me may well fill me with shame and sorrow.

Since, on April 9, 1652, Johan Anthonie van Riebeck by proclamation took formal possession of the Cape for the Netherlands East India Company, 'providing that the natives should be kindly treated,'[118] the Dutch had governed South Africa for nearly a century and a half. The natives had been outraged by the Boers, the Moravian missionaries had departed, the colony had been starved, and yet denied the rudiments of autonomy. The French Revolution changed all that, and very much else. The Stadtholder of the United Provinces having allied himself with Great Britain, Dumouriez entered Holland, and Pichegru marched the armies of France over its frozen waters in the terrible winter of 1794-5. To protect the trade with India from the French, Admiral Elphinstone thereupon took possession of the Cape, which was administered successively by General J.H. Craig, the Earl of Macartney, Sir George Young, and Sir Francis Dundas, for seven prosperous years, until the Treaty of Amiens restored it to the Batavian Republic in February 1803. It was then a territory of 120,000 square miles, reaching from the Cape to a curved line which extended from the mouth of the Buffalo River in Little Namaqualand to the present village of Colesberg. The Great Fish River was the eastern boundary. Now the Christian colonies and settlements of South Africa,[120] enjoying British sovereignty and largely under self-governing institutions, stretch north from the sea, and east and west from ocean to ocean, to the great river Zambesi—the base from which Christian civilisation, by missions and chartered companies, is slowly penetrating the explored wilds of Central Africa up the lake region to the Soudan and Ethiopia.

This less than a century's progress has been made possible by the expedition of 1806, in which Henry Martyn, almost alone, represented Christianity. After the three years' respite given by the virtual armistice of Amiens, Napoleon Bonaparte again plunged Europe and the world into war. William Pitt's last government sent out this naval armament under Sir Home Popham. The 5,000 troops were commanded by Sir David Baird, who had fought and suffered in India when the senior of the future Duke of Wellington. Henry Martyn has told us how the squadron of the sixty-three sail had anchored between Robben Island and the coast. The Dutch Governor, General Jan Willen Janssens, was more worthy of his trust than his predecessor ten years before. He had been compelled to send on a large portion of his force for the defence of Java, soon to fall to Lord Minto, the Governor-General, and had only 2,000 troops left. He had received only a fortnight's notice of the approach of the British fleet, which was reported by an American vessel. He drilled the colonists, he called French marines to his aid, he organised Malay artillery, he embodied even Hottentot sepoys, and made a reserve and refuge of Hottentot's Holland, from which he hoped to starve Cape Town, should Baird capture it. Both armies were equal in numbers at least.[121]

All was in vain. On January 8 was fought the battle of Blaauwberg (on the side of Table Bay opposite Cape Town), from the plateau of which the Dutch, having stood the musketry and field pieces, fled at the charge of the bayonet with a loss of 700 men. The British, having dropped 212, marched on Cape Town, halted at Papendorp, and there, on January 10, 1806, were signed the articles of capitulation which have ever since given the Roman-Dutch law to the colony. Sir David Baird and Sir Home Popham soon after received the surrender of Janssens, whose troops were granted all the honours of war in consideration of their gallant conduct. At the Congress of Vienna in 1815 Lord Castlereagh sacrificed Java to the Dutch, but kept South Africa for Great Britain. The surrender of the former, in the midst of the splendid successes of Sir Stamford Raffles, is ascribed to that minister's ignorance of geography. He knew equally little of the Cape, which he kept, beyond its importance to India, but God has overruled all that for the good of Equatorial, as well as South, Africa, as, thanks to David Livingstone, vacillating statesmen have begun to see.

Henry Martyn's *Journal* thus describes the battle and the battlefield.

1806, January.—Ten o'clock. When I got up, the army had left the shore, except the Company's troops, who remained to guard the landing-place; but soon after seven a most tremendous fire of artillery began behind a mountain abreast of the ship; it seemed as if the mountain itself were torn by intestine convulsions. The smoke rose from a lesser eminence on the right of the hill, and on the top of it troops were seen rushing down the farther declivity; then came such a long drawn fire of musketry, that I[122] could not have conceived anything like it. We all shuddered at considering what a multitude of souls must be passing into eternity. The poor ladies were in a dreadful condition, every peal seemed to go through their hearts; I have just been endeavouring to do what I can to keep up their spirits. The sound is now retiring, and the enemy are seen retreating along the low ground on the right towards the town. Soon after writing this I went ashore and saw M'K., &c., and Cecil, with whom I had an agreeable conversation on Divine things. The cadets of our ship had erected a little shed made of bushes and straw, and here, at their desire, I partook of their cheer. Three Highlanders came to the lines just as I arrived, all wounded in the hand. In consequence of their report of the number of the wounded, a party of East India troops, with slings and barrows, attended by a body of cadets with arms, under Major Lumsden, were ordered to march to the field of battle.

I attached myself to these, and marched six miles through the soft burning sand with them. The first we came to was a Highlander, who had been shot through the thigh, and had walked some way from the field and lay spent under some bushes. He was taken care of and we went on, and passed the whole of the larger hill without seeing anything. The ground then opened into a most extensive plain, which extended from the sea to the blue mountains at a great distance on the east. On the right was the little hill, to which we were attracted by seeing some English soldiers; we found that they were some wounded men of the 24th. They had all been taken care of by the surgeons of the Staff. Three were mortally wounded. One, who was shot through the lungs, was spitting blood, and yet very sensible. The surgeon desired me to spread a great-coat over him as they left him; as I did this, I talked to him a little of the blessed Gospel, and begged him to cry for mercy through Jesus Christ. The poor man feebly turned[123] his head in some surprise, but took no further notice. I was sorry to be obliged to leave him and go on after the troops, from whom I was not allowed to be absent, out of a regard to my safety. On the top of the little hill lay Captain F., of the grenadiers of the same regiment, dead, shot by a ball entering his neck and passing into his head. I shuddered with horror at the sight; his face and bosom were covered with thick blood, and his limbs rigid and contracted as if he had died in great agony. Near him were several others dead, picked off by the riflemen of the enemy. We then descended into the plain where the two armies had been drawn up.

A marine of the Belliqueuse gave me a full account of the position of the armies and particulars of the battle. We soon met with some of the 59th, one a corporal, who often joins us in singing, and who gave the pleasing intelligence that the regiment had escaped unhurt, except Captain McPherson. In the rear of the enemy's army there were some farm-houses, which we had converted into a receptacle for the sick, and in which there were already two hundred, chiefly English, with a few of the enemy. Here I entered, and found that six officers were wounded; but as the surgeon said they should not be disturbed, I did not go in, especially as they were not dangerously wounded. In one room I found a Dutch captain wounded, with whom I had a good deal of conversation in French. After a few questions about the army and the Cape, I could not help inquiring about Dr. Vanderkemp; he said he had seen him, but believed he was not at the Cape, nor knew how I might hear of him. The spectacle at these houses was horrid. The wounded soldiers lay ranged within and without covered with blood and gore. While the India troops remained here, I walked out into the field of battle with the surgeon. On the right wing, where they had been attacked by the Highland regiment, the dead and wounded seemed to have been strewed in great numbers, from the[124] knapsacks, &c. Some of them were still remaining; with a Frenchman whom I found amongst them I had some conversation. All whom we approached cried out instantly for water. One poor Hottentot I asked about Dr. Vanderkemp, I saw by his manner that he knew him; he lay with extraordinary patience under his wound on the burning sand; I did what I could to make his position comfortable, and laid near him some bread, which I found on the ground. Another Hottentot lay struggling with his mouth in the dust, and the blood flowing out of it, cursing the Dutch in English, in the most horrid language; I told him he should rather forgive them, and asked him about God, and after telling him of the Gospel, begged he would pray to Jesus Christ; but he did not attend. While the surgeon went back to get his instrument in hopes of saving the man's life, a Highland soldier came up, and asked me in a rough tone, 'Who are you?' I told him, 'An Englishman;' he said, 'No, no, you are French,' and was going to present his musket. As I saw he was rather intoxicated, and might in mere wantonness fire, I went up to him and told him that if he liked he might take me prisoner to the English army, but that I was certainly an English clergyman. The man was pacified at last. The surgeon on his return found the thigh bone of the poor Hottentot broken, and therefore left him to die. After this I found an opportunity of retiring, and lay down among the bushes, and lifted up my soul to God. I cast my eyes over the plain which a few hours before had been the scene of bloodshed and death, and mourned over the dreadful effects of sin. How reviving to my thoughts were the blue mountains on the east, where I conceived the missionaries labouring to spread the Gospel of peace and love.

At sunrise on the 10th, a gun from the commodore's ship was instantly answered by all the men-of-war, as the British flag was seen flying on the Dutch fort. The future[125] historian of the Christianisation of Africa will not fail to put in the forefront, at the same time, the scene of Henry Martyn, on his knees, taking possession of the land, and of all lands, for Christ.

I could find it more agreeable to my own feelings to go and weep with the relatives of the men whom the English have killed, than to rejoice at the laurels they have won. I had a happy season in prayer. No outward scene seemed to have power to distract my thoughts. I prayed that the capture of the Cape might be ordered to the advancement of Christ's kingdom; and that England, while she sent the thunder of her arms to the distant regions of the globe, might not remain proud and ungodly at home; but might show herself great indeed, by sending forth the ministers of her Church to diffuse the gospel of peace.

Thus on Africa, as on South America, North India, Persia and Turkey, is written the name of Henry Martyn.

The previous government of the Cape by the British, under Sir Francis Dundas, had been marked by the arrival, in 1799, of the London Missionary Society's agents, Dr. Vanderkemp and Kicherer. With the great chief Ngqika, afterwards at Graaff Reinet and then near Algoa Bay, the quondam Dutch officer, Edinburgh medical student, and aged landed proprietor, giving his all to Christ, had gathered in many converts. Martyn, who had learned to admire Vanderkemp from his books, was even more delighted with the venerable man. Driven by the Boers into Cape Town, the old missionary, and Mr. Reid, his colleague, were found in the midst of their daily services with the Hottentots and Kafirs. In such society, worshipping through the Dutch language, the India chaplain[126] spent the greater part of the five weeks' detention of the Union. 'Dear Dr. Vanderkemp gave me a Syriac Testament as a remembrance of him.' When Martyn and Reid parted, the latter for Algoa Bay, 'we spoke again of the excellency of the missionary work. The last time I had stood on the shore with a friend speaking on the same subject, was with Lydia, at Marazion.' In Isaiah, and Leighton, especially his *Rules for a Holy Life*, the missionary chaplain found comfort and stimulus.

February 5, 1806.—I am born for God only. Christ is nearer to me than father, or mother, or sister,—a nearer relation, a more affectionate friend; and I rejoice to follow Him, and to love Him. Blessed Jesus! Thou art all I want—a forerunner to me in all I ever shall go through, as a Christian, a minister, or a missionary.

February 13.—After breakfast had a solemn season in prayer, with the same impressions as yesterday, from Leighton, and tried to give up myself wholly to God, not only to be resigned solely to His will, but to seek my only pleasure from it, to depart altogether from the world, and be exactly the same in happiness, whether painful or pleasing dispensations were appointed me: I endeavoured to realise again the truth, that suffering was my appointed portion, and that it became me to expect it as my daily lot. Yet after all, I was ready to cry out, what an unfortunate creature I am, the child of sorrow and care; from my infancy I have met with nothing but contradiction, but I always solaced myself that one day it would be better, and I should find myself comfortably settled in the enjoyment of domestic pleasures, whereas, after all the wearying labours of school and college, I am at last cut off from all my friends, and comforts, and dearest hopes, without being permitted even to hope for them any more. As I walked the deck, I found that the conversation of others, and my[127] own gloomy surmises of my future trials, affected me far less with vexation, than they formerly did, merely from this, that I took it as my portion from God, all whose dispensations I am bound to consider and receive as the fruits of infinite wisdom and love towards me. I felt, therefore, very quiet, and was manifestly strengthened from above with might in my inner man; therefore, without any joy, without any pleasant considerations to balance my present sickness and gloom, I was contented from the reflection, that it was God who did it. I pray that this may be my state—neither to be anxious to escape from this stormy sea that was round the Cape, nor to change the tedious scene of the ship for Madras, nor to leave this world merely to get rid of the troubles of it, but to glorify God where I am, and where He puts me, and to take each day as an important trust for Him, in which I have much to do both in suffering and acting. Employed in collecting from the New Testament all the passages that refer to our walking in Christ.

February 18.—Completed my twenty-fifth year. Let me recollect it to my own shame, and be warned by it, to spend my future years to a better purpose; unless this be the case, it is of very little consequence to notice when such a person came into the world. Passed much of the morning in prayer, but could not succeed at all in getting an humble and contrite spirit; my pride and self-esteem seemed unconquerable. Wrote sermon with my mind impressed with the necessity of diligence: had the usual service, and talked much to a sick man. Read Hindustani.

February 27.—Rose once more after a sleepless night, and had in consequence a peevish temper to contend with. Had a comfortable and fervent season of prayer, in the morning, while interceding for the heathen from some of the chapters in Isaiah. How striking did those words Isaiah xlii. 8 appear to me,|128| 'I am the Lord, that is My name; and My glory will I not give to another, neither My praise to graven images.' Lord, is not Thy praise given to graven images in India? Here, then, is Thine own express word that it shall not continue to be so. And how easy is it for the mighty God that created the heavens and stretched them out, that spread forth the earth, and that which cometh out of it; that giveth breath unto the people upon it, and spirit to them that walk therein; to effect His purposes in a moment. What is caste? What are inveterate prejudices, and civil power, and priestly bigotry, when once the Lord shall set to His hand? Who knows whether even the present generation may not see Satan's throne shaken to its base in India? Learning Hindustani words in the morning; in the afternoon below, and much hurt at the cold reception the men gave me.

March 7.—Endeavoured this morning to consider Christ as the High Priest of my profession. Never do I set myself to understand the nature of my walk in Christ without getting good to my soul. Employed as usual through the day. Heard from M'Kenzie that they are not yet tired with inveighing against my doctrines. They took occasion also to say, from my salary, that 'Martyn, as well as the rest, can share the plunder of the natives in India; whether it is just or not he does not care.' This brought back the doubts I formerly had about the lawfulness of receiving anything from the Company. My mind is not yet comfortable about it. I see it, however, my duty to wait in faith and patience, till the Lord shall satisfy my doubts one way or other. I would wish for no species of connection with the East India Company, and notwithstanding the large sums I have borrowed on the credit of my salary, which I shall never be able to repay from any other means, I would wish to become a missionary, dependent on a society; but I know not how to decide. The Lord in mercy keep my soul in peace. Other thoughts have occurred to me since. A man who has unjustly|129| got possession of an estate hires me as a minister to preach to his servants, and pays me a salary: the money wherewith he pays me comes unjustly to him, but justly to me. The Company are the acknowledged proprietors of the country, the ruling power. If I were to refuse to go there, I might, on the same account, refuse to go to France, and preach to the French people or bodyguard of the emperor, because the present monarch who pays me is not the lawful one. If there were a company of Mohammedan merchants or Mohammedan princes in possession of the country, should I hesitate to accept an offer of officiating as chaplain among them, and receiving a salary?

March 14.—*Suavissima vita est indies sentire se fieri meliorem.* So I can say from former experience more than from present. But oh, it is the ardent desire of my soul to regard all earthly things with indifference, as one who dwells above with God. May I grow in grace; may the grace of God, which bringeth salvation, teach me to become daily more spiritual, more humble, more steadfast in Christ, more meek, more wise, and in all things to live soberly, righteously, and godly in this present world. How shall I attain to greater heavenly-mindedness? Rose refreshed after a good night's sleep, and wrote on a subject; had much conversation with Mr. B. upon deck; he seemed much surprised when I corrected his notions on religion, but received what I said with great candour. He said there was a minister at Madras, a Dane, with whom Sir D. Baird was well acquainted, who used to speak in the same manner of religion, whose name was Schwartz. My attention was instantly roused at the venerable name, and I eagerly inquired of him all the particulars with which he was acquainted. He had often heard him preach, and Mr. Jænicke had often breakfasted with him; Schwartz, he said, had a very commanding manner, and used to preach extempore in English at Madras; he died very poor. In|130| the afternoon had a service below, much of the evening M'Kenzie passed with me, and prayed.

March 26.—Passed much time before breakfast in sitting on the poop, through utter disinclination to all exertion. Such is the enervating effect of the climate; but after staying some hours learning Hindustani words, 2 Timothy ii. roused me to a bodily exertion. I felt strong in spirit, resolving, if I died under it, to make the body submit to robust exercise; so I walked the deck with great rapidity for an hour and a half. My animal spirits were altered instantly; I felt a happy and joyful desire to brave the enervating effects of India in the service of the blessed Lord Jesus. B. still delirious and dying fast: the first thing he said to me when I visited him this afternoon, was, 'Mr. Martyn, what will you choose for a kingdom?' I made no answer to this, but thought of it a good deal afterwards. What would I choose? Why, I do not know that anything would be a heaven to me, but the service of Christ, and the enjoyment of His presence.

In this spirit, coasting Ceylon, and getting his first sight of India at the Danish mission station of Tranquebar, on April 22, 1806, Henry Martyn landed at Madras. To Mr. Hitchins he afterwards wrote:

There was nothing remarkable in this first part of India which I visited; it was by no means so romantic as America. Vast numbers of black people were walking about with no dress but a little about their middle, but no European was to be seen except here and there one in a palanquin. Once I preached at Fort St. George, though the chaplains hardly knew what to make of such sort of preaching; they were, however, not offended. Finding that the people would bear to be addressed plainly, and not really think the worse of a minister for dealing closely with|131| their consciences, they determined, they said, to preach the Gospel as I did; but I fear that one, if not both, has yet to learn what the Gospel is. I breakfasted one day with Sir E. Pellew, the Port Admiral at Madras, and met S. Cole, his captain. I was perfectly delighted to find one with whom I could speak about St. Hilary and Marazion; we spoke of every person, place, and thing we could think of in your neighbourhood.

FOOTNOTES:

|16|*Twenty Sermons*, by the late Rev. Henry Martyn, B.D. Fourth edition (from first edition printed at Calcutta), London, 1822.

|17|*Five Sermons* (never before published), by the late Rev. Henry Martyn, B.D., with a prefatory letter on missionary enterprise, by the Rev. G.T. Fox, M.A., London, 1862.

|18|George M. Theal's *South African History*, Lovedale Institution Press, 1873.
|132|

CHAPTER IV

INDIA AND THE EAST IN THE YEAR 1806

Henry Martyn reached India, and entered on his official duties as chaplain and the work of his heart as missionary to North India, at a time when the Anglo-Indian community had begun to follow society in England, in a reformation of life and manners, and in a corresponding desire to do good to the natives. The evangelical reaction set in motion by the Pietists, Moravians, and Marrow-men, John Wesley and Whitfield, Andrew Fuller and Simeon, John Erskine and the Haldanes, had first affected South India and Madras, where Protestant Christian Missions were just a century old. The Danish-Halle men, led by Ziegenbalg and Schwartz, had found support in the Society for Promoting Christian Knowledge from the year 1709. So early as 1716 an East India Company's chaplain, the Rev. William Stevenson, wrote a remarkable letter to that society,|19| 'concerning the most effectual way of propagating the Gospel in this (South India) part of the world.' He urged a union of the several agencies in England, Denmark, and Germany into one common Society for Promoting the Protestant Missions, the formation of colleges in Europe to train missionaries, the raising of an annual income of|133| 3,000*l*, and the maintenance therewith of a staff of at least eight well-qualified missionaries. By a century and a half he anticipated the proposal of that union which gives strength and charity; the erection of colleges, at Tranquebar and Madras, to train native ministers, catechists, and schoolmasters, and the opening of free schools in every considerable place superintended by the European missionaries on the circle system. Another Madras chaplain, the Rev. George Lewis, was no less friendly and helpful to Ziegenbalg; he was Mr. Stevenson's predecessor, and wrote in 1712.

In North India—where the casteless races of the hills, corresponding to the Shanars around Cape Comorin, were not discovered till far on in the present century—almost everything was different. By the time that the Evangelical Church directed its attention to Calcutta, the East India Company had become a political, and consequently an intolerant, power. It feared Christian proselytism, and it encouraged Hindu and Mohammedan beliefs and institutions. Whereas, in Madras, it gladly used Schwartz, subsidised the mission with 500 pagodas or 225*l.* a year, and had always conveyed the missionaries' freight in its ships free of charge, in Bengal it kept out missionaries, or so treated them with all the rigour of the law against 'interlopers,' that William Carey had to begin his career as an indigo planter, and seek protection in Danish Serampore, where he became openly and only a preacher and teacher of Christ. North India, too, with Calcutta and Benares as its two Hindu centres, and Lucknow and Delhi as its two Mohammedan centres, Shiah and Soonni, was, and is, the very citadel of all the non-Christian world. The same Gospel which had proved the power of God to[134] the simple demonolators of the Dravidian south, must be shown to be the wisdom of God to the Koolin of Bengal, the Brahman of Kasi, the fanatical Muslim from Dacca, and ultimately to Peshawur and Cabul, Persia and Arabia. The Himalayan and Gangetic land—from which Buddhism overran Eastern and Southern Asia—must again send forth a missionary message to call Cathay to Christ.

The Christianising of North India began in 1758, the year after the battle of Plassey, when, as Governor, the conqueror, Clive, welcomed his old acquaintance, of the Cuddalore Mission, the Swede Kiernander, to Calcutta, and gave him a rent-free house for eight years. Even Burke was friendly with Clive, writing of him: 'Lord Clive once thought himself obliged to me for having done what I thought an act of justice towards him;'[29] and it is pleasant thus to be able in any way to link that name with the purely spiritual force which used the Plassey and the Mutiny wars, as it will direct all events, for making India Christ's. The first church, built in 1715 by the merchants and captains, had been destroyed by a hurricane; the second had been demolished by Suraj-ood-Dowlah, in the siege of Calcutta, two years before, and one of the two chaplains had perished in the Black Hole, while the other was driven away. For the next thirty years the few who went to the chaplains' church worshipped in a small bungalow in the old fort, where Kiernander opened his first school. By 1771-4 he had formed such a congregation of poor Christians—Portuguese, Roman Catholics, and Bengali converts—that he built and extended the famous Mission Church and School-house, at a cost of[135] 12,000*l.*, received from both his marriages. When, by becoming surety for another, the old man lost his all, and blindness added to his sorrows, he left an English congregation of 147 members, and a Native congregation of 119, half Portuguese or Eurasians, and half Bengali.

Kiernander's Mission Church was the centre of the religious life of Calcutta and Bengal. Six years after its foundation there came to Calcutta, from Madras, Mr. William Chambers—who had been converted by Schwartz—and John Christian Obeck, who had been one of the catechists of the Apostle of South India. Chambers had not been a year in the capital when he found out Charles Grant, at that time overwhelmed by a domestic sorrow, and brought him to Christ. Grant soon after went to Maldah as Commercial Resident, where he had as his subordinates, George Udny, Ellerton, W. Brown, W. Grant, J. Henry, and Creighton. These men, with their families, Sir Robert Chambers, of the Supreme Court, Mrs. Anne Chambers who was with her sons, Mrs. Chapman, and others less known, formed the nucleus of a Christian community which first supported Thomas as a medical missionary, then welcomed Carey, and, with the assistance of two Governor-Generals, Sir John Shore and Lord Wellesley, changed the tone of Anglo-Indian society. Sir William Jones, too, in his brief career of six years, set an example of all the virtues. Henry Martyn had two predecessors as Evangelical chaplains and missionary philanthropists, the Yorkshire David Brown, and the Scottish Claudius Buchanan.

51

David Brown, an early friend of Simeon and Fellow of Magdalen College, was recovering from a long illness in 1785, when a letter reached him from London, proposing[136] that he should seek ordination, and in ten days he accompanied Captain Kirkpatrick to Calcutta to superintend the Military Orphan School. The officers of the Bengal Army had unanimously resolved to tax themselves for the removal and prevention of the scandal caused by the number of boys and girls left destitute—no fewer than 500 at that time. This noble school, the blessings of which were soon extended to the white and coloured offspring of non-commissioned officers and soldiers also, was organised at Howrah by Brown, who then was made chaplain to a brigade, and afterwards one of the Fort William or Presidency chaplains. He found the Mission practically non-existent, owing to Kiernander's losses and old age. To save the buildings from sale by the sheriff, Charles Grant bought them for 10,000 rupees and vested them in himself, Mr. A. Chambers, and Mr. Brown, by a deed providing that they remain appropriated to the sole purposes of religion. Until the Society for Promoting Christian Knowledge could send out a minister, David Brown greatly extended the work of Kiernander. At one time it was likely that Henry Martyn would be sent out by Mr. Grant. Under the Church Missionary Society the Mission Church of Calcutta has ever since been identified with all that is best in pure religion and missionary enterprise in the city of Calcutta.

When sending out the Rev. A.T. Clarke, B.A. of Trinity College, Cambridge, who soon after became a chaplain, the Christian Knowledge Society, referring to Schwartz and Germany, fertile in missionaries, declared,[137] 'It has been the surprise of many, and the lamentation of more, that fortitude thus exemplified should not have inspired some of our own clergy with an emulation to follow and to imitate these champions of the Cross, thus seeking and thus contending to save them who are lost.' That was in 1789, when the Society and Dr. Watson, Bishop of Llandaff, along with Simeon, Wilberforce, and the other Clapham men, had before it, officially, the request of Charles Grant, Chambers and Brown to send out eight English missionaries on 350*l.* a year each, to study at Benares and attack Hinduism in its very centre. Not till 1817 was the first Church of England missionary, as such, the Rev. William Greenwood, to settle in Ceylon and then in Bengal. Even he became rather an additional chaplain to the invalid soldiers at Chunar.

After a career not unlike that of John Newton, who first directed his attention to India, Claudius Buchanan, whom his father had intended to educate for the ministry of the Church of Scotland, wandered to London, was sent to Queen's College, Cambridge, by Mr. Thornton of Clapham; there came under Simeon's influence, and was appointed to Bengal as a chaplain by Mr. Grant. That was in 1796. For the next ten years in Barrackpore and Calcutta as the trusted chaplain of Lord Wellesley, by his researches in South India, by his promotion of Bible translation, and by the interest in the Christianising of India which his generous prizes excited in the Universities and Churches of England and Scotland, Dr. Claudius Buchanan was the foremost ecclesiastic in the East. He at once gave an impulse to the silent revolution which David Brown began and the Serampore missionaries carried on. His Christian statesmanship commended him to all the authorities, and soon the new Cathedral of St. John, which Warren Hastings had erected to supersede the old Bungalow Church, became filled with an attentive and devout congregation, as well as the mission church. These two men[138] and William Carey formed the pillars of the College of Fort William, by which Lord Wellesley not only educated the young civilians and military officers in the Oriental languages, and in their duties to the natives, but developed a high ideal of public life and personal morality. Such was the growth of Christian feeling alike in the army and the civil service, and such the sense of duty to the rapidly increasing Eurasian community, as well as to the natives, that by 1803 Claudius Buchanan submitted to the Governor-General, the Archbishop of Canterbury, and Bishop Porteus, his *Thoughts on the Expediency of an Ecclesiastical Establishment for British India.* It took ten years, covering the whole period of Henry Martyn's activities and life, from this time for the proposal to be legislatively carried out in the East India Company's Charter of 1813.

Practically—except in Maldah residency during the influence of Grant, Udny, and Carey at the end of last century—the reformation was confined to Calcutta, as we shall see. It was a young lieutenant of the Company's army who was the first to draw the attention of the Governor-General, Sir John Shore, in 1794, to the total neglect of religion in Bengal. Lieutenant White wrote that he had been eleven years in the country without having had it in his power to hear the public prayers of the Church above five times. He urged the regular worship of God, the public performance of Divine service, and preaching at all the stations. He proposed[139] 'additional chaplains to the Company's complement for considerable places which now have none to officiate. Unless places were erected at the different stations for assembling to Divine service, it must be impossible for chaplains even to be able to do their duty, and to assemble the people together.' The letter delighted the Governor-General, who said of it to David Brown, 'I shall certainly recommend places to be made at the stations, and shall desire the General who is going up the country to take this matter in charge, and to fix on spots where chapels shall be erected.' Nothing was done in consequence of this, however. It was left to Martyn, and the other chaplains who were in earnest, to find or create covered places for worship at the great military stations. Claudius Buchanan himself could not hold regular services at Barrackpore, close to Calcutta, for want of a church, and that was supplied long after by adapting and consecrating the station theatre!

The figures in Buchanan's published Memoir on the Expediency of an Ecclesiastical Establishment, enable us to estimate exactly the spiritual destitution of the Protestant subjects of the British Government in Asia. Twelve years after Lieutenant White, Sir John Shore, David Brown, and Claudius Buchanan first raised the question, and when Henry Martyn began his ministrations to all classes, there were 676,557 Protestant subjects in India, Ceylon, Java, Sumatra, and Canton, Roman Catholics and Syrian Christians not included. In the three Presidencies of India alone there were 156,057, of whom 7,257 were civil and military officers and inhabitants, 6,000 were the Company's European troops, 19,800 were the King's troops, 110,000 were Eurasians, and 13,000 were 'native Protestant Christians at Tanjore.' In Bengal alone—that is, North India—there were fifty stations, thirty-one civil and nineteen military, many of which had been[140] 'without the offices of religion for twenty years past, though at each there reside generally a judge, a collector, a commercial resident, with families, together with their assistants and families, and a surgeon;' also indigo planters, tradesmen, and other European inhabitants and the alarmingly large number of Eurasians. In Bengal alone there were 13,299 European Protestants, of whom 2,467 were civil servants and military officers; of the whole 13,299, 'a tenth part do not return to England,' and desire Christian education and confirmation for their children. Yet 'at present there are but three churches in India, the chief of which was aided in construction by Hindu contribution.' The India *Journals and Letters* of Martyn must be read in the light of all this.

It was thus that the successive generations of soldiers and civilians who won for Christian England its Indian Empire in the century from Clive to Wellesley, Hastings, and Dalhousie, were de-Christianised. Not till the close of the Mutiny war in 1858 did John Lawrence, first as Lieutenant-Governor of the Punjab and then as Viceroy, and Sir Robert Montgomery as Lieutenant-Governor, lead the Queen's Government to do its duty, by erecting, or helping Christians to erect, a chapel in every station up to Peshawur and Burma—that, to use Buchanan's language in 1806, 'the English soldiers and our countrymen of all descriptions, after long absence from a Christian country, may recognise a church.' Including Ceylon, Buchanan's scheme proposed an annual expenditure of 144,000*l.* for four dioceses, with 50 English chaplains and 100 native curates, 200 schoolmasters and 4 colleges to train both Europeans and natives for the ministry; of this, Parliament to give 100,000*l.* The ecclesiastical establishment of India—without Ceylon, but including Church of Scotland chaplains, and grants to Wesleyans and Roman Catholics—now costs India itself 160,000*l.* a[141] year, while the annual value of the lands devoted to the non-Christian cults is many millions sterling. With all this, and the aid of the Additional Clergy and Anglo-Indian Evangelisation Societies, and of the missionaries to the natives, Great Britain does not meet the spiritual wants of the now enormous number and scattered communities of Christian soldiers and residents in its Indian Empire.

Henry Martyn went out to India at a time when the government of India had been temporarily entrusted to one of the only three or four incompetent and unworthy men who have held the high office of Governor-General. Sir George Barlow was a Bengal civilian of the old type, whom Lord Wellesley had found so zealous and useful in matters of routine that he had recommended him as provisional Governor General. But the moment that that proconsul had seated the East India Company on the throne of the Great Mogul, as has been said, and Lord Cornwallis, who had been hurried out a second time to undo his magnificent and just policy, had died at Ghazipore, Sir George Barlow showed the most disastrous zeal in opposition to all his former convictions. By withholding from Sindia the lamentable despatch of September 19, 1805, which Lord Cornwallis had signed when the unconsciousness of death had already weakened his efficiency, Lord Lake gave the civil authorities a final opportunity to consider their ways. But Barlow's stupidity—now clothed with the almost dictator's power of the highest office under the British Crown, as it was in those days—deliberately declared it to be his desire, not only to fix the limit of our empire at the Jumna, a river fordable by an enemy at all times, but to promote general anarchy beyond that frontier as the best security for British peace within it. The peace|142| of Southern Asia and the good of its peoples were postponed for years, till, with difficulty, the Marquis of Hastings restored the empire to the position in which Lord Wellesley had left it. Sir George Barlow is responsible for the twelve years' anarchy of British India, from 1805 to 1817. His administration, which became such a failure that he was removed to Madras, and was from even that province recalled, must rank as a blot on the otherwise unbroken splendour and benevolence to the subject races of the government of South Asia in the century and a half from Clive to Lord Lansdowne.

The man who, from dull stolidity more than from Macchiavellian craft, thus again plunged half India into a series of wars by chief upon chief and creed upon creed, was no less guilty of intolerance to Christianity within the Company's territories. On the one hand, in opposition to the views of Lord Wellesley, and even of the Court of Directors led by Charles Grant, he made the Company's government the direct manager of the Poori temple of Jaganath and its dancing girls; on the other, he would have banished the Serampore and all Christian missionaries from the country, but for the courageous opposition of the little Governor of that Danish settlement. All too late he was relieved by Lord Minto, whom the Brahmanised officials of 1807 to 1810 used for a final and futile effort to crush Christianity out of India, to the indignation of Henry Martyn, whose language in his *Journal* is not more unmeasured than the intolerance deserves. But in his purely foreign policy Lord Minto proved that he had not held the office of President of the Board of Control in vain. He once more asserted the only reason for the existence of a foreign power in India,|143| 'the suppression of intestine disorder,' clearing Bundelkhund of robber chiefs and military strongholds. Surrounded and assisted by the brilliant civilians and military officers whom Wellesley and Carey had trained—men like Mountstuart Elphinstone, Metcalfe and Malcolm—Lord Minto proved equal to the strain which the designs of Napoleon Bonaparte in the Treaty of Tilsit put upon our infant empire in the East. He sent Metcalfe to Lahore, and confined the dangerous power of Ranjeet Singh to the north of the Sutlej. He despatched Elphinstone to Cabul, introducing the wise policy which has converted Afghanistan into a friendly subsidised State; and through Malcolm he opened Persia to English influence, paving the way for the embassy of Wellesley's friend, Sir Gore Ouseley, and—unconsciously—for the kindly reception of Henry Martyn.

It was on April 22, 1806, at sunrise, that the young chaplain landed from the surf-boat on the sands of Madras. His experience at San Salvador had prepared him for the scene, and even for the crowds of dark natives, though not for 'the elegance of their manners.' 'I felt a solemn sort of melancholy at the sight of such multitudes of idolators. While the turbaned Asiatics waited upon us at dinner, about a dozen of them, I could not help feeling as if we had got into their places.' He visited the native suburb in which his Hindustani-speaking servants dwelt, and was depressed by its 'appearance of wretchedness.' His soul was filled with the zeal of the Old Testament prophets against idolatry, the first sight of which—of men, women, and children, mad upon their idols—produces an impression which he does not exaggerate: 'I fancy the frown of God to be visible.' He lost not a day in commending his Master to the people.|144| 'Had a good deal of conversation with a Rajpoot about religion, and told him of the Gospel.' The young natives pressed upon the new-comer as usual. 'Rose early, but could not enjoy morning meditations in my walk, as the young men would attach themselves to me.'

He was much in the society of the Rev. Dr. Kerr[20] and the other Madras chaplains; one of these was about to proceed to Seringapatam, where Martyn urged him to 'devote himself to the work of preaching to the natives.' This was ever foremost in his thoughts. He spent days in obtaining from Dr. Kerr 'a vast deal of information about all the chaplains and missionaries in the country, which he promised to put in writing for me.' Schwartz was not then dead ten years, and Dr. Kerr, who had known him and Guericke well, gave his eager listener many details of the great missionary.

Felt excessively delighted with accounts of a very late date from Bengal, describing the labours of the missionaries, and was rather agitated at the confusion of interesting thoughts that crowded upon me; but I reasoned, Why thus? God may never honour you with a missionary commission; you must expect to leave the field, and bid adieu to the world and all its concerns.

On his first Sunday in India, April 27, 1806, Henry Martyn assisted in the service in the church at Fort St. George, and preached from Luke x. 41, 42,|145| 'One thing is needful.'

There was much attention, and Lord William sent to Dr. Kerr afterwards to request a copy of the sermon; but I believe it was generally thought too severe. After dinner, went to Black Town to Mr. Loveless's chapel. I sat in the air at the door enjoying the blessed sound of the Gospel on an Indian shore, and joining with much comfort in the song of divine praise. With young Torriano I had some conversation respecting his entering the ministry, as he spoke the Malabar tongue fluently. Walked home at night enjoying the presence of God.

April 28.—This morning, at breakfast, Sir E. Pellew came in and said: 'Upon my word, Mr. Martyn, you gave us a good trimming yesterday.' As this was before a large company, and I was taken by surprise, I knew not what to say. Passed most of the day in transcribing the sermon. There was nothing very awakening in it. About five in the evening I walked to Dr. Kerr's, and found my way across the fields, which much resembled those near Cambridge; I stopped some time to take a view of the men drawing 'toddy' from the tree, and their manner of ploughing.

April 30.—Breakfasted at Sir E. Pellew's with Captain S. Cole of the Culloden. I had a good deal of conversation about our friends at St. Hilary and Marazion. Continued at home the rest of the day transcribing sermon, and reading Zechariah. In the evening drove with Dr. Kerr to Mr. Faulkner's, the Persian translator, five or six miles in the country. We had some useful conversation about the languages. On my return walked by moonlight in the grounds reflecting on the mission. My soul was at first sore tried by desponding thoughts: but God wonderfully assisted me to trust Him for the wisdom of His dispensations. Truly, therefore, will I say again, 'Who art thou, O great mountain? before Zerubbabel thou shalt become a plain.' How easy for God to do it! and it shall be done in good time: and even if I never should see a native|146| converted, God may design by my patience and continuance in the work to encourage future missionaries. But what surprises me is the change of views I have here from what I had in England.—There, my heart expanded with hope and joy at the prospect of the speedy conversion of the heathen! but here, the sight of the apparent impossibility requires a strong faith to support the spirits.

The 'Lord William' of the *Journal* is the Governor of Madras, Lord William Bentinck, whom, at the beginning of his Indian career, it is interesting to find thus pleasantly brought into contact with Henry Martyn—just as he became the fast friend of Alexander Duff, at the close of his long and beneficent services to his country and to humanity. In two months thereafter the Vellore Mutiny was to break out, through no fault of his, and he was to be recalled by an act of injustice for which George Canning and the Court of Directors atoned twenty years after by appointing him Governor-General.

After a fortnight off Madras, the Union once more set sail under the convoy of the Victor sloop-of-war. Every moment the young scholar had sought to add to his knowledge of Hindustani and Persian. He changed his first native servant for one who could speak Hindustani. He drove with Dr. Kerr to Mr. Faulkner's, the Persian translator to Government. 'We had some useful conversation about the languages.' On the voyage to Calcutta, he was 'employed in learning Bengali. Passed the afternoon on the poop reading

Sale's *Al Coran.*' Only missionary thoughts and aspirations ruled his mind, now despairing of his own fitness; now refreshed as he turned from the Church Missionary Society's reports to the evangelical prophecies of Malachi; again praying for the[147] young missionaries of the London Society as he passed Vizagapatam, and for 'poor India' as he came in sight of the Jaganath pagoda, 'much resembling in appearance Roche Rock in Cornwall ... the scene presented another specimen of that tremendous gloom with which the devil has overspread the land.' After taking a pilot on board in Balasore Roads, where Carey had first landed, the ship was driven out to sea by a north-wester, and Henry Martyn suffered from his first sunstroke. In three days she anchored in the Hoogli, above Culpee, and on May 13 bumped on that dreaded shoal, the James and Mary. 'The captain considered the vessel as lost. Retired as soon as possible for prayer, and found my soul in peace at the prospect of death.' She floated off, exchanging most of the treasure into a tender which lay becalmed off the Garden Reach suburb, then 'very beautiful.'

Henry Martyn landed at Calcutta in the height of the hot season, on May 16, 1806. Claudius Buchanan had passed him at the mouth of the Hoogli, setting out on the tour of the coasts of India, which resulted in the *Christian Researches.* David Brown was in his country retreat at Aldeen, near Serampore.

The man whom, next to his own colleagues, he first sought out was the quondam shoemaker of Hackleton, and poor Baptist preacher of Moulton, the Bengali missionary to whose success Charles Simeon had pointed him when fresh from the triumph of Senior Wrangler; the apostle then forty-five years of age, who was busy with the duties of Professor of Sanskrit, Bengali, and Marathi, in the College of Fort William, that he might have the Bible translated into all the languages of Asia, and preached in all the villages of North India.[148]

1806, May 16.—Went ashore at daylight this morning, and with some difficulty found Carey: Messrs. Brown and Buchanan being both absent from Calcutta. With him I breakfasted, joined with him in worship, which was in Bengali for the advantage of a few servants, who sat, however, perfectly unmoved. I could not help contrasting them with the slaves and Hottentots at Cape Town, whose hearts seemed to burn within them. After breakfast Carey began to translate, with a Pandit, from a Sanskrit manuscript. Presently after, Dr. Taylor came in. I had engaged a boat to go to Serampore, when a letter from Mr. Brown found me out, and directed me to his house in the town, where I spent the rest of the day in solitude, and more comfortably and profitably than any time past. I enjoyed several solemn seasons in prayer, and more lively impressions from God's Word. I felt elevated above those distressing fears and distractions which pride and worldliness engender in the mind. Employed at times in writing to Mr. Simeon, Mr. Brown's moonshi; a Brahmin of the name of B. Roy came in and disputed with me two hours about the Gospel. I was really surprised at him; he spoke English very well and possessed more acuteness, good sense, moderation, and acquaintance with the Scriptures than I could conceive to be found in an Indian. He spoke with uncommon energy and eloquence, intending to show that Christianity and Hinduism did not materially differ. He asked me to explain my system, and adduce the proofs of it from the Bible, which he said he believed was the Word of God. When I asked him about his idolatry, he asked in turn what I had to say to our worshipping Christ. This led to inquiries about the Trinity, which, after hearing what I had to say, he observed was actually the Hindu notion. I explained several things about the Jews and the Old Testament, about which he wanted information, with all which he was amazingly pleased. I feel much encouraged by this to go to instruct them. I see that they are a[149] religious people, as St. Paul called the Athenians, and my heart almost springs at the thought that the time is ripening for the fulness of the Gentiles to come in.

May 17.—A day more unprofitable than the foregoing; the depravity of my heart, as it is in its natural frame, appeared to me to-day almost unconquerable. I could not, however long in prayer, keep the presence of God, or the power of the world to come, in my mind at all. It sunk down to its most lukewarm state, and continued in general so, in spite of my endeavours. Oh, how I need a deep heartrending work of the Spirit upon myself, before I shall save myself, or them that hear me! What I hear about my future destination has proved a trial to me to-day. My dear brethren, Brown and Buchanan, wish to keep me here, as I expected, and the Governor accedes to their wishes. I have a great many reasons for not liking this; I almost think that to be prevented going among the heathen as a missionary would break my heart. Whether it be self-will or aught else, I cannot yet rightly ascertain. At all events I must learn submission to everything. In the multitude of my thoughts Thy comforts delight my soul. I have been running the hurried round of thought without God. I have forgotten that He ordereth everything. I have been bearing the burden of my cares myself, instead of casting them all upon Him. Mr. Brown came in to-day from Serampore, and gave me directions how to proceed; continued at home writing to E. In the afternoon went on board, but without being able to get my things away. Much of the rest of the day passed in conversation with Mr. Brown. I feel pressed in spirit to do something for God. Everybody is diligent, but I am idle; all employed in their proper work, but I tossed in uncertainty; I want nothing but grace; I want to be perfectly holy, and to save myself and those that hear me. I have hitherto lived to little purpose, more like a clod than a servant of God; now let me burn out for God.

FOOTNOTES:

|19|*An Abstract of the Annual Reports and Correspondence of the Society for Promoting Christian Knowledge from 1709 to 1814.* London, 1814, pp. 4-24.

|20|See a remarkable letter from Mr. Burke to Yuseph Emin, an Armenian of Calcutta, in Simeon's *Memorial Sketches of David Brown*, p. 334.

|21|Simeon thus introduced him to Dr. Kerr, in a private letter quoted by a later Madras chaplain, Rev. James Hough, in his valuable five volumes on *The History of Christianity in India*: 'Our excellent friend, Mr. Martyn, lived five months with me, and a more heavenly-minded young man I never saw.' In the same year, the Rev. Marmaduke Thompson, an evangelical chaplain, arrived in Madras *viâ* Calcutta.

|150|

CHAPTER V

CALCUTTA AND SERAMPORE, 1806

'Now let me burn out for God!' Such were the words with which Henry Martyn began his ministry to natives and Europeans in North India, as in the secrecy of prayer he reviewed his first two days in Calcutta. Chaplain though he was, officially, at the most intolerant time of the East India Company's administration, he was above all things a missionary. Charles Simeon had chosen him, and Charles Grant had sent him out, for this as well as his purely professional duty, and it never occurred to him that he could be anything else. He burned to bring all men to the same peace with God and service to Him which he himself had for seven years enjoyed. We find him recording his great delight, now at an extract sent to him from the East India Company's Charter, doubtless the old one from William III., 'authorising and even requiring me to teach the natives,' and again on receiving a letter from Corrie, 'exulting with thankfulness and joy that Dr. Kerr was preaching the Gospel. Eight such chaplains in India! this is precious news indeed.' Even up to the present time no Christian in India has ever recognised so fully, or carried out in a brief time so unrestingly, his duty to natives and Europeans alike as sinners to be saved by Jesus Christ alone.

Henry Martyn's first Sunday in Calcutta was spent in |151| worship in St. Johns, the 'new church,' when Mr. Jefferies read one part and Mr. Limerick another of the service, and Mr. Brown preached. Midday was spent with 'a pious family where we had some agreeable and religious conversation, but their wish to keep me from the work of the mission and retain me at Calcutta was carried farther than mere civility, and showed an extraordinary unconcern for the souls of the poor heathens.' In the evening, though unwell with a cold and sore throat, he ventured to read the service in the mission or old church of Kiernander. He was there 'agreeably surprised at the number, attention, and apparent liveliness of the audience. Most of the young ministers that I know would rejoice to come from England if they knew how attractive every circumstance is respecting the church.' Next day he was presented at the levée of Sir George Barlow, acting Governor-General, 'who, after one or two trifling questions, passed on.' He then spent some time in the College of Fort William, where he was shown Tipoo's library, and one of the Mohammedan professors—a colleague of Carey—chanted the Koran. Thence he was rowed with the tide, in an hour and a half, sixteen miles up the Hoogli to Aldeen, the house of Rev. David Brown in the suburb of Serampore, which became his home in Lower Bengal. On the next two Sundays he preached in the old church of Calcutta, and in the new church 'officiated at the Sacrament with Mr. Limerick.' It was on June 8 that he preached in the new church, for the first time, his famous sermon from 1 Cor. i. 23, 24, on|152| '*Christ crucified, unto the Jews a stumblingblock, and unto the Greeks foolishness; but unto them which are called, both Jews and Greeks, Christ the power of God, and the wisdom of God.*'

This is his own account of the immediate result:

1806, June 8.—The sermon excited no small ferment; however, after some looks of surprise and whispering, the congregation became attentive and serious. I knew what I was to be on my guard against, and therefore, that I might not have my mind full of idle thoughts about the opinions of men, I prayed both before and after, that the Word might be for the conversion of souls, and that I might feel indifferent, except on this score.

We cannot describe the sermon, as it was published after his death, and again in 1862, more correctly than by comparing it to one of Mr. Spurgeon's, save that, in style, it is a little more academic and a little less Saxon or homely. But never before had the high officials and prosperous residents of Calcutta, who attended the church which had become 'fashionable' since the Marquess Wellesley set the example of regular attendance, heard the evangel preached. The chaplains had been and were of the Arian and Pelagian type common in the Church till a later period. They at once commenced an assault on their young colleague and on the doctrines by which Luther and Calvin had reformed the Churches of Christendom. This was the conclusion of the hated sermon:

There is, in every congregation, a large proportion of Jews and Greeks. There are persons who resemble the Jews in self-righteousness; who, after hearing the doctrines of grace insisted on for years, yet see no occasion at all for changing the ground of their hopes. They seek righteousness 'not by faith, but as it were by the works of the law: for they stumble at that stumbling-stone' (Rom. ix. 32); or, perhaps, after going a little way in the profession of the Gospel, they take offence at the rigour of the practice|153| which we require, as if the Gospel did not enjoin it. 'This is a hard saying,' they complain; 'who can hear it?' (John vi. 60), and thus resemble those who first made the complaint, who 'went back and walked no more with Him.'

Others come to carp and to criticise. While heretics who deny the Lord that bought them, open infidels, professed atheists, grossly wicked men, are considered as entitled to candour, liberality, and respect, they are pleased to make serious professors of the Gospel exclusively objects of contempt, and set down their discourses on the mysteries of faith as idle and senseless jargon. Alas! how miserably dark and perverse must they be who think thus of that Gospel which unites all the power and wisdom of God in it. After God has arranged all the parts of His plan, so as to make it the best which in His wisdom could be devised for the restoration of man, how pitiable their stupidity and ignorance to whom it is foolishness! And, let us add, how miserable will be their end! because they not only are condemned already, and the wrath of God abideth on them, but they incur tenfold danger: they not only remain without a remedy to their maladies, but have the guilt of rejecting it when offered to them. This is their danger, that there is always a stumbling-block in the way: the further they go, the nearer are they to their fall. They are always exposed to sudden, unexpected destruction. They cannot foresee one moment whether they shall stand or fall the next; and when they do fall they fall at once without warning. Their feet shall slide in due time. Just shame is it to the sons of men, that He whose delight it was to do them good, and who so loved them as to shed His blood for them, should have so many in the world to despise and reject His offers; but thus is the ancient Scripture fulfilled—'The natural man receiveth not the things of the Spirit of God' (1 Cor. ii. 14).

Tremble at your state, all ye that from self-righteousness, or pride, or unwillingness to follow Him in the|154| regeneration, disregard Christ! Nothing keeps you one moment from perdition but the mere sovereign pleasure of God. Yet suppose not that we take pleasure in contradicting your natural sentiments on religion, or in giving pain by forcing offensive truths upon your attention—no! as the ministers of joy and peace we rise up at the command of God, to preach Christ crucified to you all. He died for His bitterest enemies:

therefore, though ye have been Jews or Greeks, self-righteous, ignorant, or profane—though ye have presumed to call His truths in question, treated the Bible with contempt, or even chosen to prefer an idol to the Saviour—yet return, at length, before you die, and God is willing to forgive you.

How happy is the condition of those who obey the call of the Gospel. Their hope being placed on that way of salvation which is the *power* and *wisdom* of God, on what a broad, firm basis doth it rest! Heaven and earth may pass away, though much of the power and wisdom of God was employed in erecting that fabric; but the power and wisdom themselves of God must be cut off from His immutable essence, and pass away, before one tittle of your hope can fail. Then rejoice, ye children of Wisdom, by whom she is justified. Happy are your eyes, for they see; and your ears, for they hear; and the things which God hath hidden from the wise and prudent, He hath revealed unto you. Ye were righteous in your own esteem; but ye 'count all things but loss for the excellency of the knowledge of Christ Jesus our Lord.' Then be not ashamed of the Gospel of Christ, 'which is the power of God unto salvation unto every one that believeth'; but continue to display its efficacy by the holiness of your lives, and live rejoicing in hope of the glory of God.

The opposition of the officers and many of the troops on board the transport had made the preacher familiar with attack and misrepresentation, but not less faithful in ex[155]pounding the Gospel of the grace of God as he himself had received it to his joy, and for his service to the death. But the ministrations of David Brown for some years might have been expected to have made the civilians and merchants of Calcutta more tolerant, if not more intelligent. They were, however, incited or led by the two other chaplains thus:

1806, June 16.—Heard that Dr. Ward had made an intemperate attack upon me yesterday at the new church, and upon all the doctrines of the Gospel. I felt like the rest, disposed to be entertained at it; but I knew it to be wrong, and therefore found it far sweeter to retire and pray, with my mind fixed upon the more awful things of another world.

June 22.—Attended at the new church, and heard Mr. Jefferies on the evidences of Christianity. I had laboured much in prayer in the morning that God would be pleased to keep my heart during the service from thinking about men, and I could say as I was going, 'I will go up to Thy house in the multitude of Thy mercies, and in Thy fear will I worship toward Thy holy temple.' In public worship I was rather more heavenly-minded than on former occasions, yet still vain and wandering. At night preached on John x. 11: 'I am the good shepherd;' there was great attention. Yet felt a little dejected afterwards, as if I always preached without doing good.

July 6.—Laboured to have my mind impressed with holy things, particularly because I expected to have a personal attack from the pulpit. Mr. Limerick preached from 2 Pet. i. 13, and spoke with sufficient plainness against me and my doctrines. Called them inconsistent, extravagant, and absurd. He drew a vast variety of false inferences from the doctrines, and thence argued against the doctrines themselves. To say that repentance is the gift of God[156] was to induce men to sit still and wait for God. To teach that Nature was wholly corrupt was to lead men to despair; that men thinking the righteousness of Christ sufficient to justify, will account it unnecessary to have any of their own: this last assertion moved me considerably, and I started at hearing such downright heresy. He spoke of me as one of those who understand neither what they say nor whereof they affirm, and as speaking only to gratify self-sufficiency, pride, and uncharitableness. I rejoiced at having the sacrament of the Lord's Supper afterwards, as the solemnities of that blessed ordinance sweetly tended to soothe the asperities and dissipate the contempt which was rising; and I think I administered the cup to —— and ——with sincere good-will. At night I preached on John iv. 10, at the mission church, and, blessed be God! with an enlarged heart. I saw —— in tears, and that encouraged me to hope that perhaps some were savingly affected, but I feel no desire except that my God should be glorified. If any are awakened at hearing me, let me not hear of it if I should glory.

August 24.—At the new church, Mr. Jefferies preached. I preached in the evening on Matt. xi. 28, without much heart, yet the people as attentive as possible.

August 25.—Called on Mr. Limerick and Mr. Birch; with the latter I had a good deal of conversation on the practicability of establishing schools, and uniting in a society. An officer who was there took upon him to call in question the lawfulness of interfering with the religion of the natives, and said that at Delhi the Christians were some of the worst people there. I was glad at the prospect of meeting with these Christians. The Lord enabled me to speak boldly to the man, and to silence him. From thence I went to the Governor-General's levée, and received great attention from him, as, indeed, from most others here. Perhaps it is a snare of Satan to stop my mouth, and make me unwilling to preach faithfully to|157| them. The Lord have mercy, and quicken me to diligence.

August 26.—At night Marshman came, and our conversation was very refreshing and profitable. Truly the love of God is the happiness of the soul! My soul felt much sweetness at this thought, and breathed after God. At midnight Marshman came to the pagoda, and awakened me with the information that Sir G. Barlow had sent word to Carey not to disperse any more tracts nor send out more native brethren, or in any way interfere with the prejudices of the natives. We did not know what to make of this; the subject so excited me that I was again deprived of necessary sleep.

August 28.—Enjoyed much comfort in my soul this morning, and ardour for my work, but afterwards consciousness of indolence and unprofitableness made me uneasy. In the evening Mr. Marshman, Ward, Moore, and Rowe came up and talked with us on the Governor's prohibition of preaching the Gospel, &c. Mr. Brown's advice was full of wisdom, and weighed with them all. I was exceedingly excited, and spoke with vehemence against the measures of government, which afterwards filled me justly with shame.

The earnestness of the young chaplain was such that 'the people of Calcutta,' or all the Evangelicals, joined even by the Baptist missionaries at Serampore, gave him no rest that he might consent to become minister of the mission or old church, with a chaplain's salary and house. Dr. Marshman urged that thus he might create a missionary spirit and organise missionary undertakings of more value to the natives than the preaching of any one man. But he remained deaf to the temptation, while he passed on the call to Cousin T. Hitchins and Emma, at Plymouth. His call was not to preach even in the metropolis of British|158| India, the centre of Southern Asia; but, through their own languages, to set in motion a force which must win North India, Arabia, and Persia to Christ, while by his death he should stir up the great Church of England to do its duty.

PAGODA, ALDEEN HOUSE

Serampore was the scene of his praying, his communing, and his studying, while every Sunday was given to his duties in Calcutta, as he waited five months for his first appointment to a military station. David Brown had not long before acquired Aldeen House, with its tropical garden and English-like lawn sloping down to the river, nearly opposite the Governor-General's summer-house and park of Barrackpore. Connected with the garden was the old and architecturally picturesque temple of the idol Radha-bullub, which had been removed farther inland because the safety of the shrine was imperilled by the river. But the temple still stands, in spite of the rapid Hoogli at its base, and the more destructive peepul tree which has spread over its massive dome. In 1854, when the present writer first visited the now historic spot, even the platform above the river was secure, but that has since disappeared, with much of the fine brick moulding and tracery work. Here was the young saint's home; ever since it has been known as Henry Martyn's Pagoda, and has been an object of interest to hundreds of visitors from Europe and America.

A BRICK FROM HENRY MARTYN'S PAGODA

Henry Martyn became one of David Brown's family, with whom he kept up the most loving correspondence almost to his death. But he spent even more time with the already experienced missionaries who formed the famous brotherhood a little farther up the right bank of the Hoogli. Carey thus wrote of him, knowing nothing of the fact that it was his own earlier reports which, in Simeon's hands, had first led Martyn to desire the |161|missionary career: 'A young clergyman, Mr. Martyn, is lately arrived, who is possessed of a truly missionary spirit. He lives at present with Mr. Brown, and as the image or shadow of bigotry is not known among us here, we take sweet counsel together and go to the house of God as friends.' Later on, the founder of the Modern Missionary enterprise, who desired to send a missionary to every great centre in North India, declared of the Anglican chaplain that, wherever he went no other missionary would be needed. The late

Mr. John Clark Marshman, C.S.I., who[162] as a lad saw them daily, wrote: 'A strong feeling of sympathy drew him into a close intimacy with Dr. Marshman, and they might be often seen walking arm in arm, for hours together, on the banks of the river between Aldeen House and the Mission House.' To the last he addressed Dr. Marshman, in frequent letters, as his 'dear brother,' anticipating the catholic tenderness of Bishop Heber.[22] Martyn attended those family lectures of Ward on the Hindus which resulted in his great book on the subject. In the Pagoda, 'Carey, Marshman, and Ward joined in the same chorus of praise with Brown, Martyn, and Corrie.' Martyn himself gives us these exquisite unconscious pictures of Christian life in Serampore, in which all true missionaries face to face with the common enemy have followed the giants of those days.

1806, May 19.—In the cool of the evening we walked to the mission-house, a few hundred yards off, and I at last saw the place about which I have so long read with pleasure. I was introduced to all the missionaries. We sat down about one hundred and fifty to tea, at several long tables in an immense room. After this there was evening service in another room adjoining, by Mr. Ward. Mr. Marshman then delivered his lecture on grammar. As his observations were chiefly confined to the Greek, and seemed intended for the young missionaries, I was rather disappointed, having expected to hear something about the Oriental languages. With Mr. M. alone I had much conversation, and received the first encouragement to be a missionary that I have met with since I came to this country. I blessed God in my heart for this seasonable supply of refreshment. Finding my sore throat and cough much[163] increased, I thought there might be some danger, and felt rather low at the prospect of death. I could scarcely tell why. The constant uneasiness I am in from the bites of the mosquitoes made me rather fretful also. My habitation assigned me by Mr. Brown is a pagoda in his grounds, on the edge of the river. Thither I retired at night, and really felt something like superstitious dread at being in a place once inhabited, as it were, by devils, but yet felt disposed to be triumphantly joyful that the temple where they were worshipped was become Christ's oratory. I prayed out aloud to my God, and the echoes returned from the vaulted roof. Oh, may I so pray that the dome of heaven may resound! I like my dwelling much, it is so retired and free from noise; it has so many recesses and cells that I can hardly find my way in and out.

May 20.—Employed in preparing a sermon for to-morrow, and while walking about for this purpose, my body and mind active, my melancholy was a little relieved by the hope that I should not be entirely useless as a missionary. In the evening I walked with Mr. Brown, to see the evening worship at a pagoda whither they say the god who inhabited my pagoda retired some years ago. As we walked through the dark wood which everywhere covers the country, the cymbals and drums struck up, and never did sounds go through my heart with such horror in my life. The pagoda was in a court, surrounded by a wall, and the way up to it was by a flight of steps on each side. The people to the number of about fifty were standing on the outside, and playing the instruments. In the centre of the building was the idol, a little ugly black image, about two feet high, with a few lights burning round him. At intervals they prostrated themselves with their foreheads to the earth. I shivered at being in the neighbourhood of hell; my heart was ready to burst at the dreadful state to which the Devil had brought my poor fellow-creatures. I would have given the world to have known the language,[164] to have preached to them. At this moment Mr. Marshman arrived, and my soul exulted that the truth would now be made known. He addressed the Brahmins with a few questions about the god; they seemed to be all agreed with Mr. Marshman, and quite ashamed at being interrogated, when they knew they could give no answer. They were at least mute, and would not reply; and when he continued speaking they struck up again with their detestable music, and so silenced him. We walked away in sorrow, but the scene we had witnessed gave rise to a very profitable conversation, which lasted some hours. Marshman in conversation with me alone sketched out what he thought would be the most useful plan for me to pursue in India; which would be to stay in Calcutta a year to learn the language, and when I went up the country to take one or two native brethren with me, to send them forth, and preach occasionally only to confirm their word, to establish schools, and visit them. He said I should do far more good in the way of influence than merely by actual preaching.

After all, whatever God may appoint, prayer is the great thing. Oh, that I may be a man of prayer; my spirit still struggles for deliverance from all my corruptions.

May 22.—In our walk at sunset, met Mr. Marshman, with whom I continued talking about the languages. Telling Mr. Brown about my Cambridge honours, I found my pride stirred, and bitterly repented having said anything about it. Surely the increase of humility need not be neglected when silence may do it.

May 23.—Was in general in a spiritual, happy frame the whole day, which I cannot but ascribe to my being more diligent and frequent in prayer over the Scriptures, so that it is the neglect of this duty that keeps my soul so low. Began the Bengali grammar, and got on considerably. Continued my letters to Mr. Simeon and Emma. At night we attended a conference of the missionaries on|165| this subject: 'Whether God could save sinners without the death of Christ.' Messrs. Carey, Marshman, and Ward spoke, Mr. Brown and myself. I offered what might be said on the opposite side of the question to that which the rest took, to show that He might have saved them without Christ. About fourteen of the Bengali brethren were present and spoke on the subject. Ram Roteen prayed.

Monday, May 26.—Went up to Serampore with Mr. Brown, with whom I had much enlivening conversation. Why cannot I be like Fletcher and Brainerd, and those men of modern times? Is anything too hard for the Lord? Cannot my stupid stony heart be made to flame with love and zeal? What is it that bewitches me, that I live such a dying life? My soul groans under its bondage. In the evening Marshman called; I walked back with him, and was not a little offended at his speaking against the use of a liturgy. I returned full of grief at the offences which arise amongst men, and determined to be more alone with the blessed God.

May 29.—Had some conversation with Marshman alone on the prospects of the Gospel in this country, and the state of religion in our hearts, for which I felt more anxious. Notwithstanding, I endeavoured to guard against prating only to display my experience; I found myself somewhat ruffled by the conversation, and derived no benefit from it, but felt desirous only to get away from the world, and to cease from men; my pride was a little hurt by Marshman's questioning me as the merest novice. He probably sees farther into me than I see into myself.

June 12.—Still exceedingly feeble; endeavoured to think on a subject, and was much irritated at being unable to write a word. Mrs. Brown, and afterwards Mr. Brown, paid me a visit. I came into the house to dinner, but while there I felt as if fainting or dying, and indeed really thought I was departing this life. I was brought back again to the pagoda, and then on my bed I began to pray as on the|166| verge of eternity. The Lord was pleased to break my hard heart, and deliver me from that satanic spirit of light and arrogant unconcern about which I groaned out my complaint to God. From this time I lay in tears, interceding for the unfortunate natives of this country; thinking with myself, that the most despised Soodra of India was of as much value, in the sight of God, as the King of Great Britain: through the rest of the day my soul remained in a spirit of contrition.

June 14.—A pundit came to me this morning, but after having my patience tried with him, I was obliged to send him away, as he knew nothing about Hindustani. I was exceedingly puzzled to know how I should ever be able to acquire any assistance in learning these languages. Alas! what trials are awaiting me. Sickness and the climate have increased the irritability of my temper, and occasions of trying it occur constantly. In the afternoon, while pleading for a contrite tender spirit, but in vain, I was obliged to cease praying for that tenderness of spirit, and to go on to other petitions, and by this means was brought to a more submissive state. Officiated at evening worship.

June 15.—Found my mouth salivated this morning from calomel. Attended the morning service at the mission-house; Mr. Marsdon preached. After service Marshman and Carey talked with me in the usual cheering way about missionary things, but my mind was dark. In the afternoon was rather more comfortable in prayer, and at evening worship was assisted to go through the duties of it with cheerfulness. Read some of Whitfield's *Sermons*.

June 19.—Rose in gloom, but that was soon dissipated by consideration and prayer. Began after breakfast for the first time with a moonshi, a Cashmerian Brahmin, with whom I was much pleased. In the boat, back to Serampore, learning roots. Officiated at evening worship. Walked at night with Marshman and Mr. Brown to the bazaar held at this time of the year, for the use of the[167] people assembling at Juggernaut. The booth or carriage was fifty feet high, in appearance a wooden temple, with rows of wheels through the centre of it. By the side of this a native brother who attended Marshman gave away papers, and this gave occasion to disputes, which continued a considerable time between Marshman and the Brahmins. Felt somewhat hurt at night at ——'s insinuating that my low spirits, as he called it, was owing to want of diligence. God help me to be free from this charge, and yet not desirous to make a show before men. May I walk in sweet and inward communion with Him, labouring with never-ceasing diligence and care, and assured that I shall not live or labour in vain.

June 24.—At daylight left Calcutta, and had my temper greatly exercised by the neglects and improper behaviour of the servants and boatmen. Arrived at Serampore at eight, and retired to my pagoda, intending to spend the day in fasting and prayer; but after a prayer in which the Lord helped me to review with sorrow the wickedness of my past life, I was so overcome with fatigue that I fell asleep, and thus lost the whole morning; so I gave up my original intention. Passed the afternoon in translating the second chapter of St. Matthew into Hindustani. Had a long conversation at night with Marshman, whose desire now is that I should stay at Serampore, give myself to the study of Hindustani for the sake of the Scriptures, and be ready to supply the place of Carey and Marshman in the work, should they be taken off; and for another reason—that I might awaken the attention of the people of God in Calcutta more to missionary subjects. I was struck with the importance of having proper persons here to supply the place of these two men; but could not see that it was the path God designed for me. I felt, however, a most impatient desire that some of my friends should come out and give themselves to the work; for which they are so much more fit in point of learning than any of the[168]Dissenters are, and could not bear that a work of such stupendous magnitude should be endangered by their neglect and love of the world. Marshman recommended that the serious people in Calcutta should unite in a society for the support of missions, and each subscribe fifty rupees a month for their maintenance. Ten members with this subscription could support sixty or seventy native brethren. He wished me also to see the duty of their all remaining in the country, learning the language, and instructing their servants. My mind was so filled and excited by the first part of our conversation, that I could not sleep for many hours after going to bed. He told me that the people were surfeited with the Gospel, and that they needed to be exhorted to duty.

June 26.—Employed in translating St. Matthew into Hindustani, and reading Mirza's translation; afterwards had moonshi a little. In the afternoon walked with Mr. Brown to see Juggernaut's car drawn back to its pagoda. Many thousands of people were present, rending the air with acclamations. The car with the tower was decorated with a vast number of flags, and the Brahmins were passing to and fro through the different compartments of it, catching the offerings of fruit, cowries, &c., that were thrown up to the god, for which they threw down in return small wreaths of flowers, which the people wore round their necks and in their hair. When the car stopped at the pagoda, the god and two attending deities were let down by ropes, muffled up in red cloths, a band of singers with drums and cymbals going round the car while this was performed. Before the stumps of images, for they were not better, some of the people prostrated themselves, striking the ground twice with their foreheads; this excited more horror in me than I can well express, and I was about to stammer out in Hindustani, 'Why do ye these things?' and to preach the Gospel. The words were on my lips—though if I had spoken thousands would have[169] crowded round me, and I should not have been understood. However, I felt my spirit more inflamed with zeal than I ever conceived it would be; and I thought that if I had words I would preach to the multitudes all the day, if I lost my life for it. It was curious how the women clasped their hands, and lifted them up as if in the ecstasy of devotion, while Juggernaut was tumbled about in the most clumsy manner before their eyes. I thought with some sorrow that Satan may exert the same influence in exciting apparently religious affections in professors of the Gospel, in order to deceive souls to their eternal ruin. Dr. Taylor and Mr. Moore joined us, and distributed tracts. Mr. Ward, we heard, was at a distance preaching. On our return we met Marshman going upon the same errand. In evening worship my heart was rather drawn out for the heathen, and my soul in general through the day enjoyed a cheering sense of

63

God's love. Marshman joined us again, and our conversation was about supporting some native missions.

June 30.—Went up to Serampore in the boat, learning roots. Spent the afternoon chiefly in prayer, of which my soul stood greatly in need through the snares into which my heart had been falling. Called at the mission-house, and saw Mr. Marsdon previous to the commencement of his missionary career. Now the plans of God are, I trust, taking another step forward.

July 2.—Mr. Brown proposed a prayer meeting between ourselves and the missionaries previous to the departure of Dr. Taylor for Surat. It was a season of grace to my soul, for some sense of the vast importance of the occasion dwelt upon my mind in prayer, and I desired earnestly to live zealously, labouring for souls in every possible way, with more honesty and openness. In the evening went to Marshman, and proposed it. There were at his house many agreeable sights; one pundit was translating Scripture into Sanskrit, another into Guzerati,[170] and a table was covered with materials for a Chinese dictionary. Employed with moonshi in Hindu Story-teller, and in learning to write the Persian characters.

July 3.—Rose with some happiness in my soul, and delight in the thought of an increase of labour in the Church of God. Employed morning as usual, and in thinking of subject for sermon. Was detained in the house at a time when I wanted prayer. In the evening walked with the family through Serampore, the native's part. At night we had a delightful spiritual conversation. Thus my time passes most agreeably in this dear family. Lord, let me be willing to leave it and the world with joy.

July 8.—Reading with moonshi all the morning. Spent the afternoon in reading and prayer, as preparatory to a meeting of the missionaries at night. At eight, ten of us met in my pagoda. It was, throughout, a soul-refreshing ordinance to me. I felt as I wished, as if having done with the world, and standing on the very verge of heaven, rejoicing at the glorious work which God will accomplish on the earth. The Lord will, I hope, hear our prayers for our dear brother, on whose account we met, previous to his departure for Surat. An idea thrown out by Carey pleased me very much, not on account of its practicability, but its grandeur, *i.e.* that there should be an annual meeting, at the Cape of Good Hope, of all the missionaries in the world.

July 9.—Dull and languid from the exertions and late hours of yesterday. Reading the Sermon on the Mount, in the Hindustani Testament, with moonshi. In the evening went to the mission-house, drank tea, and attended their worship. These affectionate souls never fail to mention me particularly in their prayers, but I am grieved that they so mistake my occasional warmth for zeal. It is one of the things in which I am most low and backward, as the Lord, who seeth in secret, knows too well. Oh, then, may any who think it worth while to take up my[171] name into their lips, pray for the beginning rather than the continuance of zeal! Marshman, in my walk with him, kindly assured me of his great regard and union of heart with me. I would that I had more gratitude to God, for so putting it into the hearts of His people to show regard to one so undeserving of it. At night had much nearness to God in prayer. I found it sweet to my spirit to reflect on my being a pilgrim on earth, with Christ for my near and dear friend, and found myself unwilling to leave off my prayer.

July 10.—Employed during the morning with moonshi. At morning and evening worship enjoyed freedom of access to God in prayer. Mr. Brown's return in the evening, with another Christian friend, added greatly to my pleasure. Marshman joined us at night, but these enjoyments, from being too eagerly entered into, often leave my soul carnally delighted only, instead of bringing me nearer to God. Wrote sermon at night.

July 12.—Most of this morning employed about sermon. In the afternoon went down to Calcutta with Mr. Brown and all his family; we passed the time very agreeably in singing hymns. Found Europe letters on our arrival, but were disappointed in not finding Corrie or Parson in the list of passengers. My letters were from Lydia, T.H. and Emma, Mr. Simeon, and Sargent. All their first letters had been taken in the Bell Packet. I longed to see Lydia's, but the Lord saw it good, no doubt, not to suffer it to arrive. The one I did receive from her was very animating, and showed the extraordinary zeal and activity of her mind. Mr. Simeon's letter contained her praises, and even he seemed to regret that I had gone without her. My thoughts were so occupied with these letters that I could get little or no sleep.

July 13. (Sunday.)—Talked to Mr. Brown about Lydia, and read her letter to him. He strongly recommended the measure of endeavouring to bring her here,[172] and was clear that my future situation in the country would be such as to make it necessary to be married. A letter from Colonel Sandys, which he opened afterwards, spoke in the highest terms of her. The subject of marriage was revived in my mind, but I feel rather a reluctance to it. I enjoy in general such sweet peace of mind, from considering myself a stranger upon earth, unconnected with any persons, unknown, forgotten, that were I never thrown into any more trying circumstances than I am in at present, no change could add to my happiness. At the new church this morning, had the happiness of hearing Mr. Jefferies preach. I trust God will graciously keep him, and instruct him, and make him another witness of Jesus in this place. My heart was greatly refreshed, and rejoiced at it all the day. At night preached at the missionary church, on Eph. ii. 1-3, to a small congregation. Sat up late with Mr. Brown, considering the same subject as we had been conversing on before, and it dwelt so much on my mind that I got hardly any sleep the whole night.

July 14.—The same subject engrosses my whole thoughts. Mr. Brown's arguments appear so strong that my mind is almost made up to send for Lydia. I could scarcely have any reasonable doubts remaining, that her presence would most abundantly promote the ends of the mission.

July 15.—Most of the day with moonshi; at intervals, thinking on subject for sermon. My affections seemed to be growing more strong towards Lydia than I could wish, as I fear my judgment will no longer remain unbiassed. The subject is constantly on my mind, and imagination heightens the advantages to be obtained from her presence. And yet, on the other hand, there is such a sweet happiness in living unconnected with any creature, and hastening through this life with not one single attraction to detain my desires here, that I am often very unwilling to exchange a life of celibacy for one of which I know nothing, except that it is in general a life of care.[173]

July 16.—Morning with moonshi; afterwards preparing myself for church. Preached at night, at missionary church, on Isa. lxiii. 1. Both in prayers and sermon I felt my heart much more affected than I expected, and there seemed to be some impression on a few of the people. I feel to be thankful to God, and grateful to the people, that they continue to hear me with such attention. My thoughts this day have been rather averse to marriage. Anxiety about the education and conversion of children rather terrifies me.

July 20. (Sunday.)—Preached at the new church on 2 Cor. v. 17. Mr. Marshman dined with us, and at four I went to the bazaar, to hear him preach to the natives. I arrived at the shed before him, and found the native brethren singing, after which one of them got up, and addressed the people with such firmness and mild energy, notwithstanding their occasional contradictions and ridicule, that I was quite delighted and refreshed. To see a native Indian an earnest advocate for Jesus, how precious! Marshman afterwards came, and prayed, sung, and preached. If I were to be very severe with him, I should say that there is a want of seriousness, tenderness, and dignity in his address, and I felt pained that he should so frequently speak with contempt of the Brahmins, many of whom were listening with great respect and attention. The group presented all that variety of countenance which the Word is represented as producing in a heathen audience—some inattentive, others scornful, and others seemingly melting under it. Another native brother, I believe, then addressed them. An Indian sermon about Jesus Christ was like music on my ear, and I felt inflamed to begin my work: these poor people possess more intelligence and feeling than I thought. At the end of the service there was a sort of uproar when the papers were given away, and the attention of the populace and of some Europeans was excited. Read prayers at night at the missionary church; Mr. Brown preached on the unspeakable gift.[174]

July 21.—Returned to Serampore rather in a low state of mind, arising from deprivation of a society of which I had been too fond.

July 22.—Read Hindustani without moonshi. Not being able to get to the pagoda from the incessant rain, I passed the latter part of the day in the house, reading the life of Francis Xavier. I was exceedingly roused at the astonishing example of that great saint, and began to consider whether it was not my duty to live, as he did, in voluntary poverty and celibacy. I was not easy till I had determined to follow the same course, when I should perceive that the kingdom of God would be more advanced by it. At night I saw the awful necessity of being no longer slothful, nor wasting my thoughts about such trifles as whether I should be married or not, and felt a great degree of fear, lest the blood of the five thousand Mohammedans, who, Mr. Brown said, were to be found in Calcutta capable of understanding a Hindustani sermon, should be required at my hand.

July 25.—The thought of the Mohammedans and heathens lies very heavy upon my mind. The former, who are in Calcutta, I seem to think are consigned to me by God, because nobody preaches in Hindustani. Employed the morning in sermon and Hindustani. In the afternoon went down to Calcutta. In the boat read Wrangham's Essay and some of Mr. Lloyd's letters, when young. What knowledge have some believers of the deep things of God! I felt myself peculiarly deficient in that experimental knowledge of Christ with which Mr. Lloyd was particularly favoured. Walked from the landing-place, a mile and a half, through the native part of Calcutta, amidst crowds of Orientals of all nations. How would the spirit of St. Paul have been moved! The thought of summoning the attention of such multitudes appeared very formidable, and during the course of the evening was the occasion of many solemn thoughts and prayer, that God would deliver me[175]from all softness of mind, fear, and self-indulgence, and make me ready to suffer shame and death for the name of the Lord Jesus.

July 26.—My soul in general impressed with the awfulness of my missionary work, and often shrinking from its difficulties.

July 28.—In the boat to Serampore we read Mitchell's Essay on *Evangelizing India*, and were much pleased and profited. Whatever plans and speculations may be agitated, I felt it my duty to think only of putting my hand to the work without delay. Felt very unhappy at having other work put upon me, which will keep me from making progress in the language. Nothing but waiting upon God constantly for direction, and an assurance that His never-ceasing love will direct my way, would keep me from constant vexation. I scarcely do anything in the language, from having my time so constantly taken up with writing sermons.

July 29.—Much of this morning taken up in writing to Lydia. As far as my own views extend, I feel no doubt at all about the propriety of the measure—of at least proposing it. May the Lord, in continuance of His loving-kindness to her and me, direct her mind, that if she comes I may consider it as a special gift from God, and not merely permitted by Him. Marshman sat with us in the evening, and as usual was teeming with plans for the propagation of the Gospel. Stayed up till midnight in finishing the letter to Lydia.

TO LYDIA GRENFELL.

Serampore: July 30, 1806.

My dearest Lydia,—On a subject so intimately connected with my happiness and future ministry, as that on which I am now about to address you, I wish to assure you that I am not acting with precipitancy, or without much[176] consideration and prayer, while I at last sit down to request you to come out to me in India.

May the Lord graciously direct His blind and erring creature, and not suffer the natural bias of his mind to lead him astray. You are acquainted with much of the conflict I have undergone on your account. It has been greater than you or Emma have imagined, and yet not so painful as I deserve to have found it for having suffered my affections to fasten so inordinately on an earthly object.

Soon, however, after my final departure from Europe, God in great mercy gave me deliverance, and favoured me throughout the voyage with peace of mind, indifference about all worldly connections, and devotedness to no object upon earth but the work of Christ. I gave you up entirely—not the smallest expectation remained in my mind of ever seeing you again till we should meet in heaven: and the thought of this separation was the less painful from the consolatory persuasion that our own Father had so ordered it for our mutual good. I continued from that time to remember you in my prayers only as a Christian sister, though one very dear to me. On my arrival in this country I saw no reason at first for supposing that marriage was advisable for a missionary—or rather the subject did not offer itself to my mind. The Baptist missionaries indeed recommended it, and Mr. Brown; but not knowing any proper person in this country, they were not very pressing upon the subject, and I accordingly gave no attention to it. After a very short experience and inquiry afterwards, my own opinions began to change, and when a few weeks ago we received your welcome letter, and others from Mr. Simeon and Colonel Sandys, both of whom spoke of you in reference to me, I considered it even as a call from God to satisfy myself fully concerning His will. From the account which Mr. Simeon received of you from Mr. Thomason, he seemed in his letter to me to|177|regret that he had so strongly dissuaded me from thinking about you at the time of my leaving England. Colonel Sandys spoke in such terms of you, and of the advantages to result from your presence in this country, that Mr. Brown became very earnest for me to endeavour to prevail upon you. Your letter to me perfectly delighted him, and induced him to say that you would be the greatest aid to the mission I could possibly meet with. I knew my own heart too well not to be distrustful of it, especially as my affections were again awakened, and accordingly all my labour and prayer have been to check their influence, that I might see clearly the path of duty.

Though I dare not say that I am under no bias, yet from every view of the subject I have been able to take, after balancing the advantages and disadvantages that may ensue to the cause in which I am engaged, always in prayer for God's direction, my reason is fully convinced of the expediency, I had almost said the necessity, of having you with me. It is possible that my reason may still be obscured by passion; let it suffice, however, to say that now with a safe conscience and the enjoyment of the Divine presence, I calmly and deliberately make the proposal to you—and blessed be God if it be not His will to permit it; still this step is not advancing beyond the limits of duty, because there is a variety of ways by which God can prevent it, without suffering any dishonour to His cause. If He shall forbid it, I think that, by His grace, I shall even then be contented and rejoice in the pleasure of corresponding with you. Your letter, dated December 1805, was the first I received (your former having been taken in the Bell Packet), and I found it so animating that I could not but reflect on the blessedness of having so dear a counsellor always near me. I can truly say, and God is my witness, that my principal desire in this affair is that you may promote the kingdom of God in my own heart, and be the means of extending it to the heathen.|178| My own earthly comfort and happiness are not worth a moment's notice. I would not, my dearest Lydia, influence you by any artifices or false representations. I can only say that if you have a desire of being instrumental in establishing the blessed Redeemer's kingdom among these poor people, and will condescend to do it by supporting the spirits and animating the zeal of a weak messenger of the Lord, who is apt to grow very dispirited and languid, 'Come, and the Lord be with you!' It can be nothing but a sacrifice on your part, to leave your valuable friends to come to one who is utterly unworthy of you or any other of God's precious gifts: but you will have your reward, and I ask it not of you or of God for the sake of my own happiness, but only on account of the Gospel. If it be not calculated to promote it, may God in His mercy withhold it. For the satisfaction of your friends, I should say that you will meet with no hardships. The voyage is very agreeable, and with the people and country of India I think you will be much pleased. The climate is very fine—the so much dreaded heat is really nothing to those who will employ their minds in useful pursuits. Idleness will make people complain of everything. The natives are the most harmless and timid creatures I ever met with. The whole country is the land of plenty and peace. Were I a missionary among the Esquimaux or Boschemen, I should never dream of introducing a female into such a scene of danger or hardship, especially one whose happiness is dearer to me than my own: but here there is universal tranquillity, though the multitudes are so great that a missionary needs not go three miles from his house without having a congregation of many thousands. You would not be left in solitude if I were to make any distant excursion, because no chaplain is stationed where there is not a large English Society. My salary is abundantly sufficient for the support of a married man, the house and number of people kept by each Company's servant being|179| such as to need no increase for a family establishment. As I must make the supposition of your coming, though it may be perhaps a premature liberty, I should give you some directions. This letter will reach you about the latter end of the year; it would be very desirable if you could be ready for the February fleet, because the voyage will be performed in far less time than at any other season. George will find out the best ship—one in which there is a lady of high rank in the service would be preferable. You are to be considered as coming as a visitor to Mr. Brown, who will write to you or to Colonel Sandys, who is best qualified to give you directions about the voyage. Should I be up the country on your arrival in Bengal, Mr. Brown will be at hand to receive you, and you will find yourself immediately at home. As it will highly expedite some of the plans which we have in agitation that you should know the language as soon as possible, take Gilchrist's *Indian Stranger's Guide*, and occasionally on the voyage learn some of the words.

If I had room I might enlarge on much that would be interesting to you. In my conversations with Marshman, the Baptist missionary, our hearts sometimes expand with delight and joy at the prospect of seeing all these nations of the East receive the doctrine of the Cross. He is a happy labourer; and I only wait, I trust, to know the language to open my mouth boldly and make known the mystery of the Gospel. My romantic notions are for the first time almost realised; for in addition to the beauties of sylvan scenery may be seen the more delightful object of multitudes of simple people sitting in the shade listening to the words of eternal life. Much as yet is not done; but I have seen many discover by their looks while Marshman was preaching that their hearts were tenderly affected. My post is not yet determined; we expect, however, it will be Patna, a civil station, where I shall not be under military command. As you are so kindly anxious[180] about my health, I am happy to say, that through mercy my health is far better than it ever was in England.

The people of Calcutta are very desirous of keeping me at the mission-church, and offer to any Evangelical clergyman a chaplain's salary and a house besides. I am of course deaf to such a proposal; but it is strange that no one in England is *tempted*by such an inviting situation. I am actually going to mention it to Cousin T.H. and Emma—not, as you may suppose, with much hope of success; but I think that possibly the chapel at Dock may be too much for him, and he will have here a sphere of still greater importance. As this will be sent by the overland despatch, there is some danger of its not reaching you. You will therefore receive a duplicate, and perhaps a triplicate by the ships that will arrive in England a month or two after. I cannot write now to any of my friends. I will therefore trouble you, if you have opportunity, to say that I have received no letters since I left England, but one from each of these—Cousin Tom and Emma, Simeon, Sargent, Bates: of my own family I have heard nothing. Assure any of them whom you may see of the continuance of my affectionate regard, especially dear Emma. I did not know that it was permitted me to write to you, or I fear she would not have found me so faithful a correspondent on the voyage. As I have heretofore addressed you through her, it is probable that I may be now disposed to address her through you—or, what will be best of all, that we both of us address her in one letter from India. However, you shall decide, my dearest Lydia. I *must* approve your determination, because with that spirit of simple-looking to the Lord which we both endeavour to maintain, we must not doubt that you will be divinely directed. Till I receive an answer to this, my prayers you may be assured will be constantly put up for you that in this affair you may be under an especial guidance, and that in all your ways God may be abundantly glorified by you[181] through Jesus Christ. You say in your letter that*frequently every day* you remember my worthless name before the throne of grace. This instance of extraordinary and undeserved kindness draws my heart toward you with a tenderness which I cannot describe. Dearest Lydia, in the sweet and fond expectation of your being given to me by God, and of the happiness which I humbly hope you yourself might enjoy here, I find a pleasure in breathing out my assurance of ardent love. I have now long loved you most affectionately, and my attachment is more strong, more pure, more heavenly, because I see in you the image of Jesus Christ. I unwillingly conclude, by bidding my beloved Lydia adieu.
H. MARTYN.

Serampore: September 1, 1806.
My dearest Lydia,—With this you will receive the duplicate of the letter I sent you a month ago, by the overland despatch. May it find you prepared to come! All the thoughts and views which I have had of the subject since first addressing you, add tenfold confirmation to my first opinion; and I trust that the blessed God will graciously make it appear that I have been acting under a right direction, by giving the precious gift to me and to the Church in India. I sometimes regret that I had not obtained a promise from you of following me at the time of our last parting at Gurlyn, as I am occasionally apt to be

excessively impatient at the long delay. Many, many months must elapse before I can see you or even hear how you shall determine. The instant your mind is made up you will send a letter by the overland despatch. George will let you know how it is to be prepared, as the Company have given some printed directions. It is a consolation to me during this long suspense, that had I engaged with you before my departure I should not have had such a satisfactory conviction of it being the will of God. The[182] Commander-in-chief is in doubt to which of the three following stations he shall appoint me—Benares, Patna, or Moorshedabad; it will be the last, most probably. This is only two days' journey from Calcutta. I shall take my departure in about six weeks. In the hour that remains, I must endeavour to write to my dear sister Emma, and to Sally. By the fleet which will sail hence in about two months, they will receive longer letters. You will then, I hope, have left England. I am very happy here in preparing for my delightful work, but I should be happier still if I were sufficiently fluent in the language to be actually employed; and happiest of all if my beloved Lydia were at my right hand, counselling and animating me. I am not very willing to end my letter to you; it is difficult not to prolong the enjoyment of speaking, as it were, to one who occupies so much of my sleeping and waking hours; but here, alas! I am aware of danger; and my dear Lydia will, I hope, pray that her unworthy friend may love no creature inordinately.

It will be base in me to depart in heart from a God of such love as I find Him to be. Oh, that I could make some returns for the riches of His love! Swiftly fly the hours of life away, and then we shall be admitted to behold His glory. The ages of darkness are rolling fast away, and shall soon usher in the Gospel period when the whole world shall be filled with His glory. Oh, my beloved sister and friend, dear to me on every account, but dearest of all for having one heart and one soul with me in the cause of Jesus and the love of God, let us pray and rejoice, and rejoice and pray, that God may be glorified, and the dying Saviour see of the travail of His soul. May the God of hope fill us with all joy and peace in believing, that we may both of us abound in hope through the power of the Holy Ghost. Now, my dearest Lydia, I cannot say what I feel—I cannot pour out my soul—I could not if you were here; but I pray that you may love me, if it be the[183] will of God; and I pray that God may make you more and more His child, and give me more and more love for all that is God-like and holy. I remain, with fervent affection,

Yours, in eternal bonds,

H. MARTYN.

TO CHARLES SIMEON[23]

Calcutta: September 1, 1806.

My dearest Brother,—I feel no hesitation about inviting Miss L.G. on her own account, except it be that she should come so far for one who is so utterly unworthy of her. I would rather die than bring one whom I honour so much into a situation of difficulty; but indeed there is no hardship to be encountered. In my absence she might, if she pleased, visit the English ladies who are always to be found at the different stations. The plan about to be adopted by the Baptists is to establish missionary stations in the country; while one missionary makes the circuit of the surrounding country, another shall always be in the way to receive enquiries and to explain. I should think that a zealous woman, acquainted with the language, and especially if assisted by native brethren, might be of use in this way without moving from her house.... Three such men as Carey, Marshman, and Ward, so suited to one another and to their work, are not to be found, I should think, in the whole world.

September 13.—Heard of the arrival of Corrie and Parson at Madras, and of my appointment to Dinapore.

September 15.—Called with Mr. Brown on Mr. Udny, then went up with him to Serampore, and passed much of the afternoon in reading with him a series of newspapers[184] from England. How affecting to think how the fashion of this world passeth away! What should I do without Christ as an everlasting portion! How vain is life, how mournful is death, and what is eternity without Christ! In the evening Marshman and Ward came to us. By endeavouring to recollect myself as before God, I found more comfort, and was enabled to show more propriety in conversation.

September 16.—Passed the day with moonshi in Hindustani and writing sermon. In the evening wrote to Lydia.

September 17.—The blaze of a funeral pile this morning near the pagoda drew my attention. I ran out, but the unfortunate woman had committed herself to the flames before I arrived. The remains of the two bodies were visible. At night, while I was at the missionaries', Mr. Chamberlain arrived from up the country. Just as we rejoiced at the thought of seeing him and his wife, we found she had died in the boat! I do not know when I was so shocked; my soul revolted at everything in this world, which God has so marked with misery—the effect of sin. I felt reluctance to engage in every worldly connection. Marriage seemed terrible, by exposing one to the agonising sight of a wife dying in such circumstances.

September 24.—Went down to Calcutta with Mr. Brown and Corrie, and found letters. My affections of love and joy were so excited by them that it was almost too much for my poor frame. My dearest Lydia's assurances of her love were grateful enough to my heart, but they left somewhat of a sorrowful effect, occasioned I believe chiefly from a fear of her suffering in any degree, and partly from the long time and distance that separate us, and uncertainty if ever we shall be permitted to meet one another in this world. In the evening the Lord gave me near and close and sweet communion with Him on this subject, and enabled me to commit the affair with comfort into His[185] hands. Why did I ever doubt His love? Does He not love us far better than we love one another?

September 25.—Went to Serampore with Mr. Brown and Parson; in the afternoon read with moonshi; enjoyed much of the solemn presence of God the whole day, had many happy seasons in prayer, and felt strengthened for the work of a missionary, which is speedily to begin; blessed be God! My friends are alarmed about the solitariness of my future life, and my tendency to melancholy; but, O my dearest Lord! Thou art with me, Thy rod and Thy staff they comfort me. I go on Thine errand, and I know that Thou art and wilt be with me. How easily canst Thou support and refresh my heart!

TO LYDIA GRENFELL.

Serampore: September 1806.

How earnestly do I long for the arrival of my dearest Lydia! Though it may prove at last no more than a waking dream that I ever expected to receive you in India, the hope is too pleasing not to be cherished till I am forbidden any longer to hope. Till I am assured of the contrary, I shall find a pleasure in addressing you as my own. If you are not to be mine you will pardon me; but my expectations are greatly encouraged by the words you used when we parted at Gurlyn, that I had better *go out* free, implying, as I thought, that you would not be unwilling to follow me if I should see it to be the will of God to make the request. I was rejoiced also to see in your letter that you unite your name with mine when you pray that God would keep us both in the path of duty: from this I infer that you are by no means*determined* to remain separate from me. You will not suppose, my dear Lydia, that I mention these little things to influence your conduct, or to implicate you in an engagement. No, I acknowledge that you are perfectly free, and I have no doubt that you will act as the love and wisdom of our God shall direct. Your[186] heart is far less interested in this business than mine, in all probability; and this on one account I do not regret, as you will be able to see more clearly the directions of God's providence. About a fortnight ago I sent you a letter accompanying the duplicate of the one sent overland in August. If these shall have arrived safe you will perhaps have left England before this reaches it. But if not, let me entreat you to delay not a moment. Yet how will my dear sister Emma be able to part with you, and George—but above all your *mother*? I feel very much for you and for them, but I have no doubt at all about your health and happiness in this country.

The Commander-in-chief has at last appointed me to the station of Dinapore, near Patna, and I shall accordingly take my departure for that place as soon as I can make the necessary preparations. It is not exactly the situation I wished for, though in a temporal point of view it is desirable enough. The air is good, the living cheap, the salary 1,000*l.* a year, and there is a large body of English troops there. But I should have preferred being near Benares, the heart of Hinduism. We rejoice to hear that two other brethren are arrived at Madras on their way to Bengal, sent, I trust, by the Lord to co-operate in overturning the kingdom of Satan in these regions. They are Corrie and Parson, both Bengal chaplains. Their stations will be Benares and Moorshedabad—one on one side of me and the other on the other. There are also now ten Baptist missionaries at Serampore. Surely good is intended for this country.

Captain Wickes, the good old Captain Wickes, who has brought out so many missionaries to India, is now here. He reminds me of Uncle S. I have been just interrupted by the blaze of a funeral pile, within a hundred yards of my pagoda. I ran out, but the wretched woman had consigned herself to the flames before I reached the spot, and I saw only the remains of her and her husband. O Lord,[187] how long shall it be? Oh, I shall have no rest in my spirit till my tongue is loosed to testify against the Devil, and deliver the message of God to these His unhappy bond-slaves. I stammered out something to the wicked Brahmins about the judgments of God upon them for the murder they had just committed, but they said it was an act of her own free-will. Some of the missionaries would have been there, but they are forbidden by the Governor-General to preach to the natives in the British territory. Unless this prohibition is revoked by an order from home it will amount to a total suppression of the mission.

I know of nothing else that will give you a further idea of the state of things here. The two ministers continue to oppose my doctrines with unabated virulence; but they think not that they fight against God. My own heart is at present cold and slothful. Oh, that my soul did burn with love and zeal! Surely were you here I should act with more cheerfulness and activity with so bright a pattern before me. If Corrie brings me a letter from you, and the fleet is not sailed, which, however, is not likely, I shall write to you again. Colonel Sandys will receive a letter from me and Mr. Brown by this fleet. Continue to remember me in your prayers, as a weak brother. I shall always think of you as one to be loved and honoured.

H. MARTYN.

September 26.—Employed as usual in Hindustani; visited Marshman at night. He and Mr. Carey sat with us in the evening. My heart still continuing some degree of watchfulness, but enjoying less sweetness.

October 1.—Reading with moonshi and preparing sermon; found great cause to pray for brotherly love. Preached at night at the mission-church on Eph. ii. 4. Had a very refreshing conversation with Corrie afterwards; we wished it to be for the benefit of two cadets, who supped with us, and I hope it will not be in vain. May the Lord[188] be pleased to make me act with a single eye to His glory. How easy it is to preach about Christ Jesus the Lord, and yet to preach oneself.

None of six letters from Lydia Grenfell have been preserved, but we find in her *Diary* more self-revealing of her heart than could be made to Henry Martyn, and also more severity in judging of herself as in the presence of God.

1806, May 23.—Wrote dear H. I have felt to-day a return of spirits, but have spent them too much in worldly things. I found it a blessed season in prayer, yet I fear whether my satisfaction did not rather arise from being enabled to pray than from any extraordinary communications from above. O Lord, search and try my heart, let not its deceitfulness impose on me.

July 19.—Thought much this week of my dear absent friend.

August 2.—My family's unhappiness preys on my mind—sister burning with anger and resentment against sister, brother against brother, a father against his children. Oh, what a picture! Let me not add to the weight of family sin.

August 4.—Passed a happy day. Read Baxter, and found in doing so my soul raised above. Oh, let me have, blessed Lord, anticipations of this blessedness and foretaste of glory. In Thy presence above I shall be reunited to Thy dear saint, now labouring in Thy vineyard in a distant land. One year is nearly passed since we parted, but scarcely a waking hour, I believe, has he been absent from my mind. In general my remembrance of him is productive of pleasure—that I should possess so large a share of his affection, and be remembered in his prayers, and have an eternity to spend with him, yielding me in turn delightful pleasing meditations; but just now nature[189] grieves that we are no more to meet below; yet, O my blessed Father, I cry, 'Thy will be done, not as I will, but as Thou wilt.'

August 10.—Went to church. My soul was very dull and inanimate throughout the service—the sermon had nothing in it to enliven or instruct. Barren as this place is for other means of grace, I have the Word and leisure to search; I cannot then complain, but of myself there is cause enough. Oh, how is my soul so earthly? why cannot I rise and dwell above? Tied and bound with the chain of sin, fettered and confined, I can only cast a look above. One year is gone since my dear friend left England. The number of our years of separation is so much lessened, and our salvation draws near.

October 19.—My birthday. One-and-thirty years have I existed on this earth, for twenty-five of which all the amount was sin, vanity, and rebellion against God; the last six, though spent differently, yet for every day in them I am persuaded I have sinned in heart, so as justly to merit condemnation of that God in whose mercy I trust.

November 5.—To-day I was reading of David's harp driving away the evil spirit from Saul, and resolved again (the Lord helping me) to try the sweet harp of Jesse's son in my first and last waking thoughts, for sad and disordered are my thoughts upon my friend. The expectation of letters from my dear friend in India by this fleet is almost over, and my mind is rendered anxious about him.

November 25.—My very soul has been cheered by accounts from my dear friend in India, for whom my mind has been greatly anxious. 'Cast thy cares on Me' is a command badly attended to by me.

The formal and first request from Henry Martyn to join him in India reached Lydia Grenfell on March 2, 1807. We learn from his reply in October 1807, from Dinapore,[190] that she had sent a refusal in her mother's name. But, on April 25, the Rev. Charles Simeon called on her with the result which he thus records:

With her mother's leave Miss G. accompanied us to Col. Sandys', when I had much conversation with her about Mr. Martyn's affair. She stated to me all the obstacles to his proposals: first, her health; second, the indelicacy of her going out to India alone on such an errand; third, her former engagement with another person, which had indeed been broken off, and he had actually gone up to London two years ago to be married to another woman, but, as he was unmarried, it seemed an obstacle in her mind; fourth, the certainty that her mother would never consent to it. On these points I observed that I thought the last was the only one that was insurmountable; for that, first, India often agreed best with persons of a delicate constitution—*e.g.* Mr. Martyn himself and Mr. Brown. Second, it is common for ladies to go thither without any previous connection; how much more, therefore, might one go with a connection already formed! Were this the only difficulty, I engaged, with the help of Mr. Grant and Mr. Parry, that she should go under such protection as should obviate all difficulties upon this head. Third, the step taken by the other person had set her at perfect liberty. Fourth, the consent of her mother was indispensable, and as that appeared impossible, the matter might be committed to God in this way. If her mother, of her own accord, should express regret that the connection had been prevented, from an idea of her being irreconcilably averse to it, and that she would not stand in the way of her daughter's wishes, this would be considered as a direction from God in answer to her prayers, and I should instantly be apprised of it by her, in order to communicate to Mr. M. *In this she perfectly agreed.* I told her, however, that I would mention nothing of this to Mr. M., because it would[191] only tend to keep him in painful suspense. Thus the matter is entirely set aside, unless God, by a special interposition of His providence (*i.e.* by taking away her mother, or overruling her mind, contrary to all reasonable expectation, to approve of it), mark His own will concerning it.

We find this account of the crisis in her *Diary*:

1807, March 2.—Passed some peaceful happy days at Tregembo. My return was marked by two events, long to be remembered—seeing John and hearing from H.M. Great has been my distress, but peace is returned, and could I cease from anticipating future evils I should enjoy more. The Lord has been gracious in affording me help, but He made me first feel my weakness, and suffered Satan to harass me. I am called upon now to act a decisive part.

Marazion, March 8.—With David let me say, In the multitude of thoughts within me Thy comforts have refreshed my soul. O Thou! my refuge, my rest, my hiding-place, in every time of sorrow to Thee I fly, and trust in the covert of Thy wings. Thou hast been a shelter for me and a strong tower. I have liberty to pour out my griefs into the bosom of my God, and doing so I am lightened of their burden. The Lord's dealings are singular with me, yet not severe, yea, they are merciful. Twice have I been called on to act[24] ... in a way few are tried in, but the Lord's goodness towards me is so manifest in the first, that I have come to wait in silence and hope the event of this. I am satisfied I have done now what is right, and peace has returned to me; yet there is need of great watchfulness to resist the enemy of souls, who would weaken and depress my soul, bringing to remembrance the affection of my dear friend, and representing my conduct as ungrateful towards him. To-day I have had many distressing feelings on his account, yet in the general I[192] have been looking to things invisible and eternal, and therefore enjoyed peace. I must live more in the contemplation of Christ and heavenly things. Oh, come, fill and satisfy my soul, be my leader and guide, dispose of me as Thou wilt. The pain of writing to him is over, and I feel satisfied I wrote what duty required of me.[25]Now then, return, O my soul, to thy rest.

March 22.—A week of conflict and of mercies is over. May the remembrance of Thy goodness never be forgotten. I bless Thee, O my God, that Thou hast brought me hitherto, and with more reason than David, inquire what am I that Thou shouldest do so?

April 23.—To-day my mind has been painfully affected by the receipt of letters from ——. I found in the presence of my mother I dared not indulge the inclination I feel to mourn; and believing my Heavenly Parent's will to be that I should be careful for nothing, I ought to be equally exerting myself in secret to resist the temptation. How true it is we suffer more in the person of another dear to us than in our own! Lord, I know Thou canst perfectly satisfy him by the consolation of Thy Spirit and communications of Thy grace; Thou canst display the glories of Thy beloved Son to his view, and put gladness into his heart. Oh, support, cheer, and bless him; let Thy left hand be under his head, and Thy right hand embrace him, that he may feel less than his fears suggest. Oh, do Thou powerfully impress our minds with a persuasion of Thy overruling hand in this trial. Let us see it to be Thy will, and be now and ever disposed to bow to it. Uphold me, Jesus, or I fan a prey to distracting thoughts and imagination.

April 24.—The arrival of dear Mr. Simeon has been a cordial to my fainting heart. Lord, do Thou comfort me by him; none but Thyself can give me lasting comfort[193]— instruments are nothing without Thee. Oh, may I now be watchful, for often, through my depraved nature, when unlooked-for deliverance comes, I get careless and light in my frame; then the Lord hides His face, and trouble comes, which no outward circumstances can relieve. I need especial direction from on high. Oh, may my dependence be on the Lord, and I shall not go astray.

April 28.—Went on Saturday with Mr. Simeon and Mr. E. to Helston. Lord, I bless Thy holy name, I adore Thy wonderful unmerited goodness towards such a base, vile creature, that Thou shouldest at this particular season send me counsel and support through the medium of Thy dear servant. I am brought home again in safety, and enjoyed, during my absence, an opportunity of seeing how a Christian lives.

April 29.—The state of my mind lately has led me to fill too much of my *Diary* with expressions of regard for an earthly object, and now I am convinced of the evil of indulging this affection. Oh, may the Lord enable me to mortify it; may this mirror of my heart show me more of love to God and less to anything earthly. This morning was a sad one, and to the present I have to mourn over the barrenness of my soul, its indisposedness to any spiritual exertion. Almost constantly do I remember my dear absent friend; may I do so with less pain.

May 1.—I begin this month in circumstances peculiarly trying, such as I can support only by aid vouchsafed from above, and sought in constant prayer. The Lord is a stronghold in this time of trouble.

May 2.—To-day and yesterday I have found more composure of mind than of late; once indeed the enemy (whose devices I am too ignorant of to meet them as I ought) succeeded in distracting my mind, and excited many sinful passions from the probability that Miss Corrie, who is going to her brother, may be the partner appointed for my dear friend. This continued for a short time only,[194] and I found relief at a throne of grace. It is a

73

subject I must not dwell on—when the trial comes, grace will be given; but at present I have none to meet it; yet have I prayed the Lord to provide him a suitable helpmate. Deceitful is my heart; how little do I know it! O Thou bleeding Saviour, let me hide myself in Thee from deserved wrath, and oh, speak peace once more to my soul.

May 3.—A day of much sinful inquietude. Oh, that I could withdraw my affections! Oh, that I could once more feel I have no desire but after heavenly things! What a chaos has my mind been to-day, even in the house of God and at the throne of grace. I have been, in imagination, conversing with a fellow-creature. Where is thy heart? is a question not now to be answered satisfactorily. Tied and bound with this chain, if for a little time I rise to God, soon I turn from the glories of His face, grieving His Spirit by preferring the ideal presence of my friend—sometimes drawing the scene of his distress, at others the pleasure of his return. Oh, let me not continue thus to walk in the vanity of my mind. Oh, may I find sufficient happiness in the presence of my God here, and live looking to the things not seen, looking to that heavenly country where I shall enjoy in perfection the blessed society and (of?) all I loved below.

May 4.—Passed a day of less conflict, though I have very imperfectly kept my resolution not to indulge vain improbable expectations of the future; yet I have been favoured with a greater freedom from them than yesterday.

May 5.—I have been suddenly to-day seized with a violent depression of spirits and a sadness of heart, hard to be concealed. I have not, as before, fallen into a long train of vain imaginations, drawing scenes improbable and vain, but my soul has lost its spiritual appetite. I am looking forward to distant and uncertain events with anticipations of sorrow and trial impending. O my Lord and my God, come to my relief! |195|

May 9.—Oh, what great troubles and adversities hast Thou showed me, and yet Thou didst turn again and refresh me! The whole of this day has been a dark and exceedingly gloomy season, my mind tossed to and fro like the tempestuous sea. I think the chief cause of my distress arises from a dread of dishonouring the name of the Lord, by appearing to have acted deceitfully in the eyes of my family, and some pride is at the bottom of this (I like not to be thought ill of), and also pain for the disappointment my dear friend will soon know. His situation grieves me infinitely more than my own. I think, for myself, I want nothing more than I find in Thy presence.

May 20.—My chief concern now is lest I should have given too much reason for my dear friend's hoping I might yet be prevailed on to attend to his request, and I feel the restraint stronger than ever, that, having before promised, I am not free to marry. I paint the scene of his return, and, whichever way I take, nothing but misery and guilt seems to await me. Yet oh, I will continue to pray, 'Heal me, and I shall be healed; save me, and I shall be saved.' Thou art my strength and hope, O Lord; though shame is my portion among men. Thou who knowest my heart, Thou wilt not in this condemn me, for oh, Thou knowest these consequences of my regard for Thy dear saint were not intended by me, and that first, when I regarded him otherwise than as a Christian brother, I believed myself free to do so, imagining him I first loved united to another. When I consider this circumstance my mind is relieved of a heavy burden, and yet I must lament the evils that have flown from this mistake. My thoughts have been called since Sunday into the eternal world by the sudden death of a very kind friend, H.C. I have found this event, though the cause of pain, very useful to me at this time.

May 22.—The way Satan takes is made plain to me, and I must resist him in the first pleasing ideas arising|196| from the remembrance of true affection in my dear and ever-esteemed friend. When I yield to these, I am presently lost to all sober thoughts, and plunged soon in the deepest sorrow for the distress it has brought on him; then my conduct towards him and every part of my family is painted in the most horrid colours, till I am nearly distracted. Thus has Satan over and over oppressed me, and relief been afforded my fainting soul through the help of a superior power even than Satan. I must watch and pray, for thus the Lord will bruise Satan under my feet.

August 6.—This season recalls a dear friend to my remembrance. Oh, may he occupy no more of my thoughts and affections than is consistent with the will of God, and pleasing in His sight. May these resignations be manifested by us both.

August 9.—Just two years since I parted from a dear friend and brother, whose memory will ever be cherished by me. Blessed be God! I feel now as if he was the inhabitant of another world, rather than of another part of this earth.

On October 10, 1806, on the close of his preparations for departure to Dinapore, 'at night the missionaries, etc., met us at the pagoda for the purpose of commending me to the grace of God.' 'My soul never yet had such Divine enjoyment. I felt a desire to break from the body, and join the high praises of the saints above.' Next day, in Calcutta, at evening worship at Mr. Myers', 'I found my heaven begun on earth. No work so sweet as that of praying and living wholly to the service of God.' On Sunday, the 12th, 'at night I took my leave of the saints in Calcutta in a sermon on Acts xx. 32. But how very far from being in spirit like the great apostle.' On Monday he went up by land to Barrackpore with Mr. Brown, 'happy in general.' On|197| Tuesday 'Corrie came to me at the pagoda and prayed with me.'

1806, October 15.—Took my leave of the family at Aldeen in morning worship; but I have always found my heart most unable to be tender and solemn when occasions most require it. At eleven I set off in a budgerow with Mr. Brown, Corrie, and Parson. Marshman saw us as we passed the mission-house, and could not help coming aboard. He dined with us, and after going on a little way left us with a prayer. About sunset we landed at the house of the former French governor, and walked four miles through villages to Chandernagore, where we waited at an hotel till the boats came up. With the French host I found a liberty I could not have hoped for in his language, and was so enabled to preach the Gospel to him. There are two Italian monks in this place, who say Mass every day. I wished much to visit the fathers, if there had been time. A person of Calcutta, here for his health, troubled us with his profaneness, but we did not let him go unwarned, nor kept back the counsel of God. At night in the budgerow I prayed with my dear brethren.

October 16.—Rose somewhat dejected, and walked on to Chinsurah, the Dutch settlement, about three miles. There we breakfasted, and dined with Mr. Forsyth, the missionary. We all enjoyed great happiness in the presence and blessing of our God. Mr. Forsyth came on with us from Chinsurah, till we stopped at sunset opposite Bandel, a Portuguese settlement, and then we had Divine service. I prayed and found my heart greatly enlarged. After his departure our conversation was suitable and spiritual. How sweet is prayer to my soul at this time! I seem as if I never could be tired, not only of spiritual joys, but of spiritual employments, since they are now the same.

October 17.—My dear brethren, on account of the bad weather, were obliged to leave me to-day. So we spent|198| the whole morning in a Divine ordinance in which each read a portion of Scripture and all sang and prayed. Mr. Brown's passage, chosen from Joshua i., was very suitable, 'Have I not commanded thee?' Let this be an answer to my fears, O my Lord, and an assurance that I am in Thy work. It was a very affecting season to me. In prayer I was very far from a state of seriousness and affection. Indeed, I have often remarked that I have never yet prayed comfortably with friends when it has been preceded by a chapter of the Revelation. Perhaps because I depend too much on the feelings which the imagery of that book excites, instead of putting myself into the hands of the Spirit, the only author of the prayer of faith. They went away in their boat, and I was left alone for the first time, with none but natives.

FOOTNOTES:

|22|*The Life and Times of Carey, Marshman, and Ward*, London, 1859. *The Life of William Carey* (John Murray), 2nd edition, 1887.

|23|First published (1892) by Rev. H.C.G. Moule from the autograph collection made by Canon Carus, the successor and biographer of Charles Simeon.

|24|A line has been erased by a subsequent writer.

|25|'Her letter was to bid me a last farewell.'—Martyn's *Journal*. This was received November 23.

|199|

CHAPTER VI

DINAPORE AND PATNA, 1807-1809

Until, in 1852 and the ten years following, Lord Dalhousie's railway up the Ganges valley was completed to Allahabad, the usual mode of proceeding up-country from Calcutta was by the house-boat known as the budgerow, which is still common on the many rivers of Bengal where English planters and officials are found. At the rate of twenty-five miles a day the traveller is towed up against stream by the boatmen. When time is no object, and opportunities are sought for reading, shooting, and intercourse with the natives, the voyage is delightful in the cool season. Henry Martyn rejoiced in six weeks of this solitary life—alone yet not alone, and ever about his Father's business. His studies were divided between Hindustani and Sanskrit; he was much occupied in prayer and in the reading of the Greek and Hebrew Scriptures. Morning and evening he spent himself among the people on the banks, and at the ghauts and bazaars of the mighty river, preaching Christ and spreading abroad the New Testament. The dense population and the spiritual darkness, as the panorama of native life moved hourly before his eyes, on river and on land, stirred up the busiest of Christians to be still busier, in spite of his fast-wasting body;[200] 'What a wretched life shall I lead if I do not exert myself from morning till night, in a place where, through whole territories, I seem to be the only light!' His gun supplied him with small game, 'enough to make a change with the curry.'

At Cutwa, one of Carey's mission stations, he had fellowship with Chamberlain, receiving that 'refreshment of spirit which comes from the blessing of God on Christian communion.' 'Tell Marshman,' he wrote, 'with my affectionate remembrance, that I have seriously begun the Sanskrit Grammar.' To Ward he sends a list of errata which he found in a tract in the Persian character. He had his Serampore moonshi with him. At Berhampore, soon to be occupied by Mr. Parson as chaplain, and by the London Missionary Society, he spent some time, for it was the great military station of the old Nawab Nazim's capital, Moorshidabad, which Clive described as wealthier than London, and quite as populous. Henry Martyn at once walked into the hospital, where the surgeon immediately recognised him as an old schoolfellow and townsman. But even with such help he could not induce the men to rise and assemble for Divine service. 'I left three books with them and went away amidst the sneers and titters of the common soldiers. Certainly it is one of the greatest crosses I am called to bear, to take pains to make people hear me. It is such a struggle between a sense of propriety and modesty on the one hand, and a sense of duty on the other, that I find nothing equal to it.' At Rajmahal, like Carey six years before, he met some of the hill tribes—'wrote down from their mouth some of the names of things.'

At Maldah he was in the heart of the little Christian community which, under Charles Grant twenty years[201] before, had proved the salt of Anglo-Indian society, and had made the first attempt with Carey's assistance to open vernacular Christian schools. With Mr. Ellerton, whose wife had witnessed the duel between Warren Hastings and Philip Francis, and who as a widow indeed lived to the Mutiny of 1857 as the friend of Bishop Daniel Wilson, he went to Gomalty, and visited one of the schools. 'The cheerful faces of the little boys, sitting cross-legged on their mats round the floor, much delighted me. While they displayed their power of reading, their fathers, mothers, etc., crowded in numbers round the door and windows.' Here we see the now vast educational system of Bengal in the birth. Not less striking is the contrast, due to the progress of that system on its missionary side, when we find Martyn, in 1806, recording his surprise at the extraordinary fear and unwillingness of the people to take tracts and books. One postmaster, when he found what the booklet was about, returned it with the remark that a person who had his legs in two boats went on his way uncomfortably. Passing Colgong and Monghyr, he 'reached Patna. Walked about the scene of my future ministry with a spirit almost overwhelmed at the sight of the immense multitudes.' On November 26 he arrived at Dinapore—'the multitudes at the water-side prodigious.'

Nowhere, in British India as it was in 1807, could Henry Martyn have found a better training field, at once as chaplain to the troops and missionary to the Mohammedans, than the Patna centre of the great province of Bihar. For fourteen miles, Patna, the Mohammedan city, Bankipore, the British civil station, and Dinapore, the British military station, line the right bank of the Ganges, which is there two miles broad. Patna itself[202]—'the city,' as the word means—was the Buddhist capital to which the Greek ambassador Megasthenes came from Seleukos Nikator, 300 B.C., and the Chinese pilgrim, Hwen T'sang, 637 years A.D. But under the Mogul emperors and down to the present day, Patna has been the focus of the most fanatical sect of Islam. There Meer Kasim murdered sixty Englishmen in 1763; and so little did a century's civilisation affect the place, which Christian missionaries, except Martyn, neglected till recently, that in 1857 it was a centre of the Mutiny, and in 1872 it was the nucleus of Wahabi rebellion. The second city in Bengal next to Calcutta, and the fifth city in all India in inhabitants, Patna with Bankipore and Dinapore commanded an accessible native population of half a million. Such was Henry Martyn's first 'parish' in the East. For the mass of these he opened schools and translated the Word of God; with their learned men he 'disputed' continually, in the spirit of Paul seeking to commend to them the very Christ.

Besides the Company's civil servants in Bankipore whom he never ceased to influence, he was specially charged with the spiritual care of two European regiments, consisting at one time of 1,700 men and 80 officers in various positions. Then and up till 1860, when what was known as 'the White Mutiny' led the Queen's Government to disband the troops, the East India Company had a European force of its own, specially recruited and paid more highly than the royal regiments. The men were generally better educated than the ordinary private of those days, were, indeed, often runaway sons of good families and disreputable adventurers from many countries. As a fighting force they were splendid veterans; in all other respects[203] their history and character as well as his own experience of them on board ship, justified Martyn's language in a letter to Mr. Brown. 'My disdainful and abandoned countrymen among the military; they are impudent children and stiff-hearted, and will receive, I fear, my ministrations, as all the others have done, with scorn. Yet Jesus wept over Jerusalem. Henceforward let me live with Christ alone.' How loving and faithful, if not always tender, his ministry was among them and their native women, and how it gained their respect till it formed a little Church in the army, we shall see.

Having settled down in barrack apartments at 50 rupees a month till he should get a house against the hot season, and having called on the general commanding and others, after the Anglo-Indian fashion, he reported to his longing friends in Aldeen: 'I stand alone;[204] not one voice is heard saying, "I wish you good luck in the name of the Lord." I offered to come over to Bankipore to officiate to them on the Sabbath. They are going to take this into consideration. I have found out two schools in Dinapore. I shall set on foot one or two schools without delay, and by the time the scholars are able to read we can get books ready for them.' In this spirit and by a renewed act of self-dedication he entered on the year 1807:

Seven years have passed away since I was first called of God. Before the conclusion of another seven years, how probable is it that these hands will have mouldered into dust! But be it so: my soul through grace hath received the assurance of eternal life, and I see the days of my[204] pilgrimage shortening without a wish to add to their number. But oh, may I be stirred up to a faithful discharge of my high and awful work; and laying aside, as much as may be, all carnal cares and studies, may I give myself to this 'one thing.' The last has been a year to be remembered by me, because the Lord has brought me safely to India, and permitted me to begin, in one sense, my missionary work. My trials in it have been very few; everything has turned out better than I expected; loving-kindness and tender mercies have attended me at every step: therefore here will I sing His praise. I have been an unprofitable servant, but the Lord hath not cut me off: I have been wayward and perverse, yet He has brought me further on the way to Zion; here, then, with sevenfold gratitude and affection, would I stop and devote myself to the blissful service of my adorable Lord. May He continue His patience, His grace, His direction, His spiritual influences, and I shall at last surely come off conqueror. May He speedily open my mouth, to make known the mysteries of the Gospel, and in great mercy grant that the heathen may receive it and live!

The hostility of the officers and civilians to his message sometimes became scorn, when they saw his efforts to teach and preach to the natives. These were days when the Patna massacre was still remembered. So few baptized Christians knew the power of the Faith which they practically dishonoured, that they had no desire to make it known to others; many even actually resented the preaching of Christ to the people, as both politically dangerous and socially an insult to the ruling race. This feeling has long since disappeared in India at least, though its expression is not unknown in some of the colonies where the land is held by the dark savages. Henry Martyn keenly felt such opposition, and none the less that the natives of the Patna[205] district—especially the Mohammedans—were in their turn hostile to a government which had supplanted them so recently. A few weeks after his arrival we find him writing this in his *Journal*:

1806, December 1.—Early this morning I set off in my palanquin for Patna. Something brought the remembrance of my dear Lydia so powerfully to my mind that I could not cease thinking of her for a moment. I know not when my reflections seemed to turn so fondly towards her; at the same time I scarcely dare to wish her to come to this country. The whole country is manifestly disaffected. I was struck at the anger and contempt with which multitudes of the natives eyed me in my palanquin.

December 2.—On my way back called on Mr. D., the Judge, and Mr. F., at Bankipore. Mr. F.'s conversation with me about the natives was again a great trial to my spirit; but in the multitude of my troubled thoughts I still saw that there is a strong consolation in the hope set before us. Let men do their worst, let me be torn in pieces, and my dear L. torn from me; or let me labour for fifty years amidst scorn, and never seeing one soul converted; still it shall not be worse for my soul in eternity, nor worse for it in time. Though the heathen rage and the English people imagine a vain thing, the Lord Jesus, who controls all events, is my friend, my master, my God, my all. On the Rock of Ages when I feel my foot rest my head is lifted up above all mine enemies round about, and I sing, yea, I will sing praises unto the Lord. If I am not much mistaken, sore trials are awaiting me from without. Yet the time will come when they will be over. Oh, what sweet refuge to the weary soul does the grave appear! There the wicked cease from troubling, and there the weary are at rest. Here every man I meet is an enemy; being an enemy to God, he is an enemy to me also on that account; but he is an enemy too to me because I am an Englishman.|206| Oh, what a place must heaven be, where there are none but friends! England appears almost a heaven upon earth, because there one is not viewed as an unjust intruder; but, oh, the heaven of my God! the general assembly of the first-born, the spirits of the just made perfect, and Jesus! Oh, let me for a little moment labour and suffer reproach!

1807, January 2.—They seem to hate to see me associating at all with the natives, and one gave me a hint a few days ago about taking my exercise on foot. But if our Lord had always travelled about in His palanquin, the poor woman who was healed by touching the hem of His garment might have perished. Happily I am freed from the shackles of custom; and the fear of man, though not extirpated, does not prevail.

January 8.—Pundit was telling me to-day that there was a prophecy in their books that the English should remain one hundred years in India, and that forty years were now elapsed of that period; that there should be a great change, and they should be driven out by a king's son, who should then be born. Telling this to moonshi, he said that about the same time the Mussulmans expected some great events, such as the coming of Dujjel, and the spread of Islam over the earth.

January 29.—The expectation from prophecy is very prevalent hereabouts that the time is coming when all the Hindus will embrace the religion of the English; and the pundit says that in many places they had already begun. About Agra, and Delhi, and Narwa, in the Mahratta dominions, there are many native Christian families.

Henry Martyn's occupation of the Aldeen Pagoda had resulted, after his departure, in the formation, by Brown, Corrie, Parson, and Marmaduke Thompson, the Madras chaplain, of what would now be called a clerical club, with these three objects—to aid the British and Foreign Bible|207|Society, then recently established; to help forward the translation of the Scriptures into the languages of the East; and especially to meet the whole expense of the Sanskrit and Greek Testaments, and to send on to Mr. Brown, for circulation, a quarterly report of the prospects, plans, and actual situation of each member so far as the Church is concerned. Of this Evangelical Anglican Brotherhood Martyn seems to have been the most active member during his brief career. His translations were made for it, in the first instance. 'The Synod', or 'the Associated Clergy,' as he called it at different times, when as yet there was no Bishop of Calcutta, consciously linked him to the fellowship of the Saints, to the Church and the University from which he had come forth. We find him noting seven years after 'the day I left Cambridge: my thoughts frequently recurred with many tender recollections to that beloved seat of my brethren, and again I wandered in spirit amongst the trees on the banks of the Cam.'

The letters from these four chaplains cheered him at Dinapore when he was 'very much depressed in spirits,' and he hastens to write to each, giving this picture of his life:

From a solitary walk on the banks of the river I had just returned to my dreary rooms, and with the reflection that just at this time of the day I could be thankful for a companion, was taking up the flute to remind myself of your social meetings in worship, when your two packages of letters, which had arrived in my absence, were brought to me. For the contents of them, all I can say is, Bless the Lord, O my soul, and all that is within me bless His holy name! The arrival of another dear brother, and the joy you so largely partake of in fellowship with God and with one another, act as a cordial to my soul. They show me what I want to learn, that the Lord God[208] Omnipotent reigneth, and that they that keep the faith of Jesus are those only whom God visits with His strong consolations. I want to keep in view that our God is the God of the whole earth, and that the heathen are given to His exalted Son, the uttermost parts of the earth for a possession.

Continually his love of music breaks forth alike for the worship of God and the association of friendship and affection. His correspondence with Brown was regular, but as that of a son with a father. His letters to Corrie, his old Cambridge junior, are frank and free. His joy was great when Corrie was stationed at the rock-fortress of Chunar, not very far from Dinapore, so that they occasionally met and officiated for each other. But up to this time his chief, his almost fearful human, delight was to think of Lydia by night and by day.

1806, December 10.—A dream last night was so like reality, and the impression after it was so deep upon my spirits, that I must record the date of it. It was about Lydia. I dreamt that she had arrived, but that after some conversation I said to her, 'I know this is a dream; it is too soon after my letter for you to have come.' Alas! it is only a dream; and with this I awoke, and sighed to think that it was indeed only a dream. Perhaps all my hope about her is but a dream! Yet be it so; whatever God shall appoint must be good for us both, and with that I will endeavour to be tranquil and happy, pursuing my way through the wilderness with equal steadiness, whether with or without a companion.

December 14. (Sunday.)—Service performed by an after order, at ten o'clock. The general was present, about twenty officers, and some of their ladies. I preached on the parable of the tares of the field. Much of the rest of the[209] day I was in great distraction, owing to the incessant recurrence of thoughts about Lydia. My impatience and fear respecting her sometimes rose to such a height that I felt almost as at Falmouth, when I was leaving Europe, as I thought to see her no more. But in the evening it pleased the Lord to show me something of the awful nearness of the world of spirits, and the unmeasurable importance of my having my thoughts and cares devoted to my missionary work. Thus I obtained peace. I prayed in sincerity and fervour, that if there were any obstacle in the sight of God, the Lord might never suffer us to meet.

December 21. (Sunday.)—In the evening, after a solemn season of prayer, I received letters from Europe, one from Cousin T., Emma, Lydia, and others. The torrent of vivid affection which passed through my heart at receiving such assurances of regard continued almost without intermission for four hours. Yet, in reflection afterwards, the few words my dearest Lydia wrote turned my joy into tender sympathy with her. Who knows what her heart has suffered! After all, our God is our best portion; and it is true that if we are never permitted to meet, we shall enjoy blissful intercourse for ever in glory.

December 22.—Thinking far too much of dear Lydia all day.

December 23.—Set apart the chief part of this day for prayer, with fasting; but I do not know that my soul got much good. Oh, what need have I to be stirred up by the Spirit of God, to exert myself in prayer! Had no freedom or power in prayer, though some appearance of tenderness. Lydia is a snare to me; I think of her so incessantly, and with such foolish and extravagant fondness, that my heart is drawn away from God. Thought at night, Can that be true love which is other than God would have it? No; that which is lawful is most genuine when regulated by the holy law of God.

December 25.—Preached on 1 Tim. i. 15 to a large[210] congregation. Those who remained at the Sacrament were chiefly ladies, and none of them young men. My heart still entangled with this idolatrous affection, and consequently unhappy. Sometimes I gained deliverance from it for a short time, and was happy in the love of God. How awful the thought, that while perishing millions demand my every thought and care, my mind should be distracted about such an extreme trifle as that of my own comfort! Oh, let me at last have done with it, and the merciful God save me from departing from Him, and committing that horrible crime of forsaking the fountain of living waters, and hewing out to myself broken cisterns.

As the delightful cold season of the Bihar uplands passed all too quickly, and the dry hot winds of Upper India began to scorch its plains, the solitary man began to think it 'impossible I could ever subsist long in such a climate.' From April 1807 his hereditary disease made rapid advances, while he reproached himself for lassitude and comparative idleness, and put additional constraint on himself to work and to pray unceasingly. From this time his *Journal* has frequent records of sickness, of loss of appetite, and of 'pain' in his ministrations, ending in loss of voice altogether for a time. Corrie and Brown and his other correspondents remonstrated, but they were at a distance. He needed a watchful and authoritative nurse such as only a wife could be, and he found only lack of sympathy or active opposition. He lived, as we can now see, as no white man in the tropics in any rank of life should live, from sheer simplicity, unselfishness, and consuming zeal. When the hot winds drove him out of the barracks, the first rainy season flooded his house. At all times and amid the insanitary horrors of an Indian cemetery he had to bury[211] the dead of a large cantonment in a sickly season. His daily visits to the hospital were prolonged, for there he came soul to soul with the sinner, the penitent, and the rejoicing. And all the time he is writing to Corrie and each of his friends, 'I feel anxious for your health.' To marry officers and baptize children he had to make long journeys by palanquin, and expose his wasting body alike to heat and rain. But amid it all his courage never fails, for it is rooted in God; his heart is joyful, for he has the peace that passeth all understanding.

1807, May 18.—Through great mercy my health and strength are supported as by a daily miracle. But oh, the heat! By every device of darkness and tatties I cannot keep the thermometer below 92°, and at night in bed I seem in danger of suffocation. Let me know somewhat more particularly what the heat is, and how you contrive to bear it. The worst bad effect I experience is the utter loss of appetite. I dread the eating time.

July 7.—Heat still so great as to oblige me to abandon my quarters.

July 8.—Went to Bankipore to baptize a child. One of the ladies played some hymn-tunes on my account. If I were provided with proper books much good might be done by these visits, for I meet with general acceptance and deference. In the evening buried a man who had died in the hospital after a short illness. My conscience felt again a conviction of guilt at considering how many precious hours I waste on trifles, and how cold and lukewarm my spirit is when addressing souls.

August 23. (Sunday.)—Preached on Job xix. 25-27: 'I know that my redeemer liveth.' There seemed little or no attention; only one officer there besides Major Young. At Hindustani prayers, the women few, but attentive; again blest with much freedom; at the hospital was seized[212] with such pain from over-exertion of my voice, that I was obliged to leave off and go away.

To Brown he writes: 'The rains try my constitution. I am apt to be troubled with shortness of breath, as at the time I left you. Another rainy reason I must climb some hill and live there; but the Lord is our rock. While there is work which *we* must do, we shall live.' Again in the early Sunday morning of August he dreamed—

That as I was attacked so violently in July, but recovered, at the same time next year I should be attacked again, and carried off by death. This, however, would only be awaking in a better world. If I may but awake up satisfied with Thy likeness, why shall I be afraid? I think I have but one wish to live, which is, that I may do the Lord's work, particularly in the Persian and Hindustani translations; for this I could almost feel emboldened to supplicate, like Hezekiah, for prolongation of life, even after receiving this, which may be a warning.

After six months' experience of his Dinapore-cum-Patna parish, Martyn sent in 'to the Associated Clergy' the first quarterly report of his own spiritual life, and of his work for others.

April 6.—I begin my first communication to my dear and honoured brethren, with thankfully accepting their proposal of becoming a member of their society, and I bless the

God and Father of our Lord Jesus Christ for this new instance of His mercy to His unworthy creature. May His grace and favour be vouchsafed to us, and His Holy Spirit direct all our proceedings, and sanctify our communications to the purposes for which we are united.

On a review of the state of my mind since my arrival at Dinapore, I observe that the graces of joy and love have been at a low ebb. Faith has been chiefly called into|213|exercise, and without a simple dependence on the Divine promises I should still every day sink into fatal despondency. Self-love and unbelief have been suggesting many foolish fears respecting the difficulties of my future work among the heathen. The thought of interrupting a crowd of busy people like those at Patna, whose every day is a market-day, with a message about eternity, without command of language sufficient to explain and defend myself, and so of becoming the scorn of the rabble without doing them good, was offensive to my pride. The manifest disaffection of the people, and the contempt with which they eyed me, confirmed my dread. Added to this the unjust proceedings of many of the principal magistrates hereabout led me to expect future commotions in the country, and that consequently poverty and murder would terminate my career.

'Sufficient for the day is the evil thereof'—'As thy days are so shall thy strength be,' were passages continually brought to my remembrance, and with these at last my mind grew quiet. Our countrymen, when speaking of the natives, said, as they usually do, that they cannot be converted, and if they could they would be worse than they are. Though I have observed before now that the English are not in the way of knowing much about the natives, yet the number of difficulties they mentioned proved another source of discouragement to me. It is surprising how positively they are apt to speak on this subject, from their never acknowledging God in anything: 'Thy judgments are far above out of his sight.' If we labour to the end of our days without seeing one convert, it shall not be worse for us in time, and our reward is the same in eternity. The cause in which we are engaged is the cause of mercy and truth, and therefore, in spite of seeming impossibilities, it must eventually prevail.

I have been also occasionally troubled with infidel thoughts, which originated perhaps from the cavillings of|214| the Mohammedans about the person of Christ; but these have been never suffered to be more than momentary. At such times the awful holiness of the Word of God, and the deep seriousness pervading it, were more refreshing to my heart than the most encouraging promises in it. How despicable must the Koran appear with its mock majesty and paltry precepts to those who can read the Word of God! It must presently sink into contempt when the Scriptures are known.

Sometimes when those fiery darts penetrated more deeply, I found safety only in cleaving to God, as a child clasps to his mother's neck. These things teach me the melancholy truth that the grace of a covenant God can alone keep me from apostasy and ruin.

The European society here consists of the military at the cantonment and the civil servants at Bankipore. The latter neither come into church nor have accepted the offer of my coming to officiate to them. There is, however, no contempt shown, but rather respect. Of the military servants very few officers attend, and of late scarcely any of the married families, but the number of privates, and the families of the merchants, always make up a respectable congregation. They have as yet heard very little of the doctrines of the Gospel. I have in general endeavoured to follow the directions contained in Mr. Milner's letter on this subject, as given in Mr. Brown's paper, No. 4.

At the hospital I have read Doddridge's *Rise and Progress*, and *The Pilgrim's Progress*. As the people objected to extempore preaching at church, I have in compliance with their desires continued to use a book. But on this subject I should be glad of some advice from my brethren.

I think it needless to communicate the plans or heads of any of my sermons, as they have been chiefly on the Parables. It is of more importance to observe that the|215|Word has not gone forth in vain, blessed be God! as it has hitherto seemed to do in most places where I have been called to minister; and this I feel to be an animating testimony of His presence and blessing. I think the commanding officer of the native regiment here and his lady are seeking their salvation in earnest; they now refuse all invitations on the Lord's day, and pass most of that day at least in reading the Word, and at all times discover an inclination to religious conversation. Among the privates, one I have little doubt is truly converted to God, and is a great refreshment to me. He parted at once with his native woman, and allows her a separate maintenance. His conversion has excited much notice and conversation about religion among the rest, and three join him in coming twice a week to my quarters for exposition, singing and prayer.

I visit the English very little, and yet have had sufficient experience of the difficulty of knowing how a minister should converse with his people. I have myself fallen into the worst extreme, and, from fear of making them connect religion with gloom, have been led into such shameful levity and conformity to them as ought to fill me with grief and deep self-abasement.

How repeatedly has guilt been brought upon my conscience in this way! Oh, how will the lost souls with whom I have trifled the hours away look at me in the day of judgment! I hope I am more and more convinced of the wickedness and folly of assuming any other character than that of a minister. I ought to consider that my proper business with the flock over which the Holy Ghost hath made me overseer is the business of another world, and if they will not consider it in the same light, I do not think that I am bound to visit them.

About the middle of last month, the Church service being ready in Hindustani, I submitted to the commanding officer of the European regiment a proposal to perform|216| Divine service regularly for the native women of his regiment, to which he cordially assented. The whole number of women, about 200, attended with great readiness, and have continued to do so. Instead of a sermon, the Psalms, and the appointed lessons, I read in two portions the Gospel of St. Matthew regularly forward, and occasionally make some small attempts at expounding. The conversion of any of such despised people is never likely perhaps to be of any extensive use in regard to the natives at large; but they are a people committed to me by God, and as dear to Him as others; and next in order after the English, they come within the expanding circle of action.

After much trouble and delay, three schools have been established for the native children on Mr. Creighton's plan—one at Dinapore, one at Bankipore, and one at Patna, at the last of which the Persian character is taught as well as the Nagri. The number of children already is about sixty. The other schoolmasters, not liking the introduction of these free schools, spread the report that my intention was to make them Christians, and send them to Europe; in consequence of which the zemindars retracted their promises of land, and the parents refused to send their children; but my schoolmasters very sensibly went to the people, and told them, 'We are men well known among you, and when we are made Christians then do you begin to fear.' So their apprehensions have subsided; but when the book of Parables, which is just finished, is put into their hands, I expect a revival of their fears. My hope is that I shall be able to ingratiate myself a little with the people before that time; but chiefly that a gracious God will not suffer Satan to keep his ground any longer, now that the appointed means are used to dislodge him. But, though these plans should fail, I hope to be strengthened to fight against him all my days. For, from what I feel within and see without, I know enough of him|217| to vow, with my brethren, eternal enmity against him and his cause.

Respecting the state of the natives hereabouts, I believe that the Hindus are lax, for the rich men being few or none, there are few Brahmins and few *tumashas (fêtes)*, and without these idolatry droops. The Mohammedans are numerous and ignorant, but from the best of them I cannot learn that more than three arguments can be offered for their religion, which are— the miracles wrought by Mohammed, those still wrought by his followers, and his challenge in the second chapter of the Koran, about producing a chapter like it, all of which are immediately answered.

If my brethren have any others brought forward to them they will, I hope, mention them; and if they have observed any remark or statement apparently affect a native's mind, they will notice it.

Above all things, *seriousness* in argument with them seems most desirable, for without it they laugh away the clearest proofs. Zeal for making proselytes they are used to, and generally attribute to a false motive; but a tender concern manifested for their souls is certainly new to them, and seemingly produces corresponding seriousness in their minds.

From an officer who had been in the Mahratta service, I learned some time ago that there were large bodies of Christians at Narwa, in the Mahratta dominions, Sardhana, Delhi, Agra, Bettia, Boglipore. To obtain more information respecting them, I sent a circular letter to the missionaries residing at the three latter places, and have received two letters in reply. The padre at Boglipore is a young man just arrived, and his letter contains no information. From the letter of the padre at Agra I subjoin some extracts, premising that my questions were: 1. By whom were you sent? 2. How long has a mission been established in the place of your residence? 3. Do you[218] itinerate, and to what distance? 4. Have you any portion of the MSS. translated, or do you distribute tracts? 5. Do you allow any remains of caste to the baptized? 6. Have you schools? are the masters heathen or Christians? 7. Is there any native preacher or catechist? 8. Number of converts.

In concluding my report, I take the liberty of proposing two questions on which I should be thankful for communications in your next quarterly report.

1. On the manner in which a minister should observe the Sabbath; whether he should make it a point of duty to leave no part of his discourses to prepare on that day? Whether our particular situation in this country, requiring redoubled exertion in those of us at least who are called to the heathen, will justify the introduction of a secular work into the Sabbath, such as translating the Scriptures, etc.?

2. In the commencement of our labours among the heathen, to which model should our preaching be conformed,—to that of John the Baptist and our Saviour, or that of the Apostles? The first mode seems more natural, and if necessary for the Jews, comparatively so enlightened, how much more for the heathen, who have scarcely any notions of morality! On the other hand, the preaching of the cross has in all ages won the most ignorant savages; and the Apostles preached it at once to heathens as ignorant perhaps as these.

Like Marshman and the Serampore missionaries, Henry Martyn kept up a Latin correspondence with the missionaries sent from Rome by the Propaganda to the stations founded by Xavier, and those afterwards established by that saint's nephew in the days of the tolerant Akbar. At the beginning of this century, Anglican, Baptist, and Romanist missionaries all over the East co-operated with[219] each other in translation work and social intercourse. More than once Martyn protected the priest at Patna from the persecution of the military authorities. He planned a visit to their station at Bettia, to the far north, at the foot of the Himalayas. In hospital his ministrations were always offered to the Irish soldiers in the absence of their own priest, and always without any controversial reference. In his *Journal* he is often indignant at the Popish perversion of the doctrines of grace, and in preaching he occasionally set forth the truth, but in pastoral and social intercourse he never failed to show the charity of the Christian scholar and the gentleman.

Major Young, with his wife, was the first of the officers to welcome Martyn's preaching. Soon the men in hospital learned to appreciate his daily visits, and to attend to his earnest reading and talk. A few began to meet with him at his own house regularly, for prayer and the exposition of Holy Scripture. In January, he writes of one Sunday: 'Great attention. I think the Word is not going forth in vain. In the afternoon read at the hospital. The steward I found had been long stationed at Tanjore and knew Schwartz; that Schwartz baptized the natives not by immersion, but by sprinkling, and with godfathers, and read the services both in English and Tamil. Felt much delighted at hearing anything about him. The man told me that the men at the hospital were very attentive and thankful that I came amongst them. Passed the evening with great joy and peace in singing hymns.' In the heat of May he writes:[220] 'Found fifty sick at the hospital, who heard *The Pilgrim's Progress* with great delight. Some men came to-night, but my prayer with them was exceedingly poor and lifeless.'

In these days, thanks to Lord Lawrence and Sir Henry Norman, there is a prayer-hall in every cantonment, ever open for the soldier who seeks quiet communion with God. Then—'Six soldiers came to me to-night. To escape as much as possible the taunts of their wicked companions, they go out of their barracks in opposite directions to come to me. At night a young Scotsman of the European regiment came to me for a hymn-book. He expressed with tears his past wickedness and determination to lead a religious life.' On the other side we have such passages as these: 'What sort of men are these committed to my care? I had given them one more warning about their whoredom and drunkenness, and it's the truth grappling with their consciences that makes them furious.' Of the Company's European regiment he writes to Corrie: 'A more wicked set of men were, I suppose, never seen. The general, the colonel of the 67th, and their own colonel all acknowledge it. At the hospital when I visit their part, some go to a corner and invoke blasphemies upon me because, as they now believe, the man I speak to dies to a certainty.' A young lieutenant of fine abilities he recommended strenuously to go into the ministry.

Although, fifteen years before, Sir John Shore had given orders as to the building of churches at military stations, and Lord Wellesley had set an example of interest in the moral and spiritual welfare of the Company's servants, nothing had been done outside of the three Presidency cities. All that Henry Martyn found provided for him, as chaplain, on his first Sunday at Dinapore, was a long drum, on which he placed the Prayer-book. He was requested not to preach, because the men could not stand so long. He found the men playing at fives on Sunday.[221] All that he soon changed, by an appeal to the general to put a stop to the games on Sunday, and by holding service at first in a barrack, and then in his own house. Before leaving Calcutta he had observed, in a conversation with the Governor-General, on the disgrace of there being no places of worship at the principal subordinate stations; upon which directions were given to prepare plans of building. He wrote to the equally troubled Corrie at Chunar. A year later nothing had been done, and he draws this picture to Corrie: 'From the scandalous disorder in which the Company have left the ecclesiastical part of their affairs, so that we have no place fit, our assemblies are little like worshipping assemblies. No kneeling because no room; no singing, no responses.' At last Sir George Barlow sent an order for an estimate for building a church, but Martyn had left for Cawnpore, only to see a worse state of things there. But the faithfulness of the 'black' chaplains was telling. He writes, on March 14, 1808:

The 67th are now all here. The number of their sick makes the hospital congregation very considerable, so that if I had no natives, translations, etc., to think of, there is call enough for my labours and prayers among all these Europeans. The general at my request has determined to make the whole body of troops attend in three divisions; and yesterday morning the Company's European, and two companies of the King's, came to church in great pomp, with a fine band of music playing. The King's officers, according to their custom, have declared their intention not to call upon the Company's; therefore I mean to call upon them. I believe I told you that 900 of the 67th are Roman Catholics. It seemed an uncommonly splendid Mohurrum here also. Mr. H., an assistant judge lately appointed to Patna, joined the procession in a[222] Hindustani dress, and went about beating his breast, etc. This is a place remarkable for such folly. The old judge, you know, has built a mosque here, and the other judge issued an order that no marriage nor any feasting should be held during the season of Mohammedan grief. A remarkably sensible young man called on me yesterday with the Colonel; they both seem well disposed to religion. I receive many gratifying testimonies to the change apparently taking place among the English in religious matters in India; testimonies, I mean, from the mouths of the people, for I confess I do not observe much myself.

Having translated the Church Service into Hindustani, Henry Martyn was ready publicly to minister to the native women belonging to the soldiers of the Company's European regiment. From such unions, rarely lawful, sprang the now great and important Eurasian community, many of whom have done good service to the Church and the Empire. 'The Colonel approved, but told me that it was my business to find them an order, and not his.'

1807, March 23.—So I issued my command to the Sergeant-Major to give public notice in the barracks that there would be Divine service in the native language on the morrow. The morrow came, and the Lord sent 200 women, to whom I read the whole of the morning service. Instead of the lessons I began Matthew, and ventured to expound a little, and but a little. Yesterday we had a service again, but I think there were not more than 100. To these I opened my mouth rather more boldly, and though there was the appearance of lamentable apathy in the countenances of most of them, there were two or three who understood and trembled at the sermon of John the Baptist. This proceeding of mine is, I believe, generally approved among the English, but the women come, I fear,[223] rather because it is the wish of their masters. The day after attending service they went in flocks to the Mohurrum, and even of those who are baptized, many, I am told, are so addicted to their old heathenism, that they obtain money from their husbands to give to the Brahmins. Our time of Divine service in English is seven in the morning, and in Hindustani two in the afternoon. May the Lord smile on this first attempt at ministration in the native language!

1807, March 23.—A few days ago I went to Bankipore to fulfil my promise of visiting the families there; and amongst the rest called on a poor creature whose black wife has made him apostatise to Mohammedanism and build a mosque. Major Young went with me, and the old man's son-in-law was there. He would not address a single word to me, nor a salutation at parting, because I found an occasion to remind him that the Son of God had suffered in the stead of sinners. The same day I went on to Patna to see how matters stood with respect to the school. Its situation is highly favourable, near an old gate now in the midst of the city, and where three ways meet; neither master nor children were there. The people immediately gathered round me in great numbers, and the crowd thickened so fast, that it was with difficulty I could regain my palanquin. I told them that what they understood by making people Christians was not my intention; I wished the children to be taught to fear God and become good men, and that if, after this declaration, they were still afraid, I could do no more; the fault was not mine, but theirs. My schools have been heard of among the English sooner than I wished or expected. The General observed to me one morning that that school of mine made a very good appearance from the road; 'but,' said he, 'you will make no proselytes.' If that be all the opposition he makes, I shall not much mind.

[224]

A week later he wrote:

March 30.—Sick in body, but rather serious and humble in spirit, and so happy; corrected the Parables for a fair copy. Reading the Koran and Hindustani Ramayuna, and translating Revelation; a German sergeant came with his native woman to have her baptized; I talked with her a good while, in order to instruct her, and found her extraordinarily quick in comprehension.

April 1.—The native woman came again, and I passed a great deal of time in instructing her in the nature of the Gospel; but, alas! till the Lord touch her heart, what can a man do? At night the soldiers came, and we had again a very happy time; how graciously the Lord fulfils His promise of being where two or three are gathered together! The pious soldier grows in faith and love, and spoke of another who wants to join us. They said that the native women accounted it a great honour to be permitted to come to a church and hear the Word of God, and wondered why I should take such trouble for them.

'How shall it ever be possible to convince a Hindu or Brahmin of anything?' wrote Henry Martyn to Corrie after two years' experience in Bengal.

1808, January 4.—Truly, if ever I see a Hindu a real believer in Jesus, I shall see something more nearly approaching the resurrection of a dead body than anything I have yet seen. However, I well remember Mr. Ward's words, 'The common people are angels compared with the Brahmins.' Perhaps the strong man armed, that keeps the goods in peace, shall be dispossessed from these, when the mighty Word of God comes to be ministered by us.

'We shall live to see better days.' For these he prepared his translations of the Word of God. He wished to [225] itinerate among the people, but his military duties kept him to the station. When Mr. Brown made another attempt to get him fixed in the Mission-Church he replied, 'The evangelisation of India is a more important object than preaching to the European inhabitants of Calcutta.' To Corrie he wrote: 'Those sequestered valleys seen from Chunar present an inviting field for missionary labours. A Sikh, making a pilgrimage to Benares, came to me; he was very ignorant, and I do not know whether he understood what I endeavoured to show him about the folly of pilgrimages, the nature of true holiness, and the plan of the Gospel.'

1808, February 12.—Sabat describes so well the character of a missionary that I am ashamed of my great house, and mean to sell it the first opportunity, and take the smallest quarters I can find. Would that the day were come when I might throw off the coat and substitute the jamer; I long for it more and more; and am often very uneasy at being in the neighbourhood of so great a Nineveh without being able to do anything immediately for the salvation of so many perishing souls. What do you think of my standing under a shed somewhere in Patna as the missionaries did in the Lal Bazar? Will the Government interfere? What are your sensations on the late news? I fear the judgments of God on our proud nation, and that, as we have done nothing for the Gospel in India, this vineyard will be let out to others who shall bring the fruits of it in their season. I think the French would not treat Juggernaut with quite so much ceremony as we do.

Above all men in India, at that time and during the next half-century, however, Henry Martyn was a missionary to the Mohammedans. For them he learned and he translated Hindustani, Persian, and Arabic. With their[226] moulvies he conducted controversies; and for years he associated with himself that extraordinary Arab, Sabat, who made life a burden to him.

Sabat and Abdallah, two Arabs of notable pedigree, becoming friends, resolved to travel together. After a visit to Mecca they went to Cabul, where Abdallah entered the service of Zeman Shah, the famous Ameer. There an Armenian lent him the Arabic Bible, he became a Christian, and he fled for his life to Bokhara. Sabat had preceded him there, and at once recognised him on the street. 'I had no pity,' said Sabat afterwards. 'I delivered him up to Morad Shah, the king.' He was offered his life if he would abjure Christ. He refused. Then one of his hands was cut off, and again he was pressed to recant. 'He made no answer, but looked up steadfastly towards heaven, like Stephen, the first martyr, his eyes streaming with tears. He looked at me, but it was with the countenance of forgiveness. His other hand was then cut off. But he never changed, and when he bowed his head to receive the blow of death all Bokhara seemed to say, "What new thing is this?"'

Remorse drove Sabat to long wanderings, in which he came to Madras, where the Government gave him the office of mufti, or expounder of the law of Islam in the civil courts. At Vizagapatam he fell in with a copy of the Arabic New Testament as revised by Solomon Negri, and sent out to India by the Society for Promoting Christian Knowledge in the middle of last century. He compared it with the Koran, the truth fell on him 'like a flood of light,' and he sought baptism in Madras at the hands of the Rev. Dr. Kerr. He was named Nathaniel. He was then twenty-seven years of age.[227]

When the news reached his family in Arabia his brother set out to destroy him, and, disguised as an Asiatic, wounded him with a dagger as he sat in his house at Vizagapatam. He sent him home with letters and gifts to his mother, and then gave himself up to propagate the truth he had once, in his friend Abdallah's person, persecuted to the death. He became one of the translating staff of the Serampore brotherhood, and did good service on the Arabic and Persian Scriptures. Mr. John Marshman, who knew him well, used to describe him as a man of lofty station, of haughty carriage, and with a flowing black beard. Delighted with the simple life and devotion of the missionaries, he dismissed his two Arab servants, and won the affection of all. When Serampore arranged to leave to Henry Martyn the Persian translation of the New Testament, Sabat left them with tears in his eyes for Dinapore. In almost nothing does the saintliness of Martyn appear so complete as in the references in his *Journal* to the pride, the vanity, the malice, the rage of this 'artless child of the desert,' when it became apparent that his knowledge of Persian and Arabic had been over-estimated. The passages are pathetic, and are equalled only by those which, in the closing days of his life, describe the dying missionary's treatment by his Tartar escort. But to the last, Sabat, according to Colonel MacInnes of Penang,[27][228] 'never spoke of Mr. Martyn without the most profound respect, and shed tears of grief whenever he recalled how severely he had tried the patience of this faithful servant of God. He mentioned several anecdotes to show with what extraordinary sweetness Martyn had borne his numerous provocations. "He was less a man," he said, "than an angel from heaven."'

The rest of Sabat's story may at once be told. Moved by rage at the exposure, by the Calcutta moonshis, of the incorrectness of his Arabic, and at the suspicions that his translations were copies from some old version, Sabat apostatised by publishing a virulent attack on Christianity. 'As when Judas acted the traitor, Ananias the liar, and Simon Magus the refined hypocrite, so it was when Sabat daringly departed from the nominal profession of the truth. The righteous sorrowed, the unrighteous triumphed; yet wisdom was justified of her children,' wrote Mr. Sargent. He left Calcutta as a trader for Penang, where he wrote to the local newspaper declaring that he professed Christianity anew, and he entered the service of the fugitive Sultan of Acheen, on the north of Sumatra. Thence, when he was imprisoned by the insurgents, he wrote letters with his own blood to the Penang authorities, declaring that he was in some sense a martyr for Christ. All the private efforts of Colonel MacInnes to obtain his freedom were in vain; he was tied up in a sack and thrown into the sea. In the light of these events we must now read Henry Martyn's *Journal*:

1807, August 24.—To live without sin is what I cannot expect in this world, but to desire to live without it may be the experience of every hour. Thinking to-night of the qualifications of Sabat, I felt the conviction, both in reflection and prayer, of the power of God to make him another St. Paul.

November 10.—The very first day we began to spar. He would come into none of my plans, nor did I approve of his; but I gave way, and by yielding prevailed, for he[229] now does everything I tell him.... Sabat lives and eats with me, and goes to his bungalow at night, so that I hope he has no care on his mind. On Sunday morning he went to church with me. While I was in the vestry a bearer took away his chair from him, saying it was another gentleman's. The Arab took fire and left the church, and when I sent the clerk after him he would not return. He anticipated my expostulations after church, and began to lament that he had *two* dispositions, one old, the other new.

1808, January 11.—Sabat sometimes awakes some of the evil parts of my nature. Finding I have no book of Logic, he wishes to translate one of his compositions, to instruct me in that science. He is much given to contradict, and set people right, and that he does with an air so dogmatical, that I have not seen the like of it since I left Cambridge. He looks on the missionaries at Serampore as so many degrees below him in intellect, that he says he could write so deeply on a text, that not one of them would be able to follow him. So I have challenged him in their name, and to-day he has brought me the first half of his essay or sermon on a text: with some ingenuity, it has the most idle display of school-boy pedantic logic you ever saw. I shall translate it from the Persian, in order to assist him to rectify his errors. He is certainly learned in the learning of the Arabs, and how he has acquired so much in a life so active is strange, but I wish it could be made to sit a little easier on him. I look forward to St. Paul's Epistles, in hopes some good will come to him from them. It is a very happy circumstance that he did not go to preach at his first conversion; he would have entangled himself in metaphysical subjects out of his depth, and probably made shipwreck of his own faith. I have, I think, led him to see that it is dangerous and foolish to attempt to prove the doctrine of the Trinity by reason, as he said at first he was perfectly able to do.[230]

January 30.—Sabat to-day finishes St. Matthew, and will write to you on the occasion. Your letter to him was very kind and suitable, but I think you must not mention his logic to him, except with contempt; for he takes what you say on that head as homage due to his acquirements, and praise to him is brandy to a man in a high fever. He loves as a Christian brother; but as a logician he holds us all in supreme contempt. He assumes all the province of reasoning as his own by right, and decides every question magisterially. He allows Europeans to know a little about Arithmetic and Navigation, but nothing more. Dear man! I smile to observe his pedantry. Never have I seen such an instance of dogmatical pride since I heard Dr. Parr preach his Greek Sermon at St. Mary's, about the τὸ ὄν.

March 7.—Mirza is gone to the Mohurrum to-day: he discovers no signs of approach to the truth. Sabat creates himself enemies in every quarter by his jealous and passionate spirit, particularly among the servants. At his request I have sent away my tailor and bearers, and he is endeavouring to get my other servants turned away; because without any proof he suspects them of having persuaded the bearers not to come into his service. He can now get no bearers nor tailor to serve him. One day this week he came to me, and said that he meant to write to Mr. Brown to remove him from this place, for everything went wrong—the people were all wicked, etc. The immediate cause of this vexation was that some boxes, which he had been making at the expense of 150 rupees, all cracked at the coming on of the hot weather. I concealed my displeasure at his childish fickleness of temper, and discovered no anxiety to retain him, but quietly told him of some of the consequences of removing, so it is gone out of his mind. But Mirza happened to hear all Sabat's querulous harangue, and, in order to vex and disgust him effectually, rode almost into his house, and came in with[231] his shoes. This irritated the Arab; but Mirza's purpose was not answered. Mirza began next day to tell a parcel of lies about Sabat, and to bring proofs of his own learning. The manifest tendency of all this was to make a division between Sabat and me, and to obtain his *salary* and work for himself. Oh, the hypocrisy and wickedness of an Indian! I never saw a more remarkable contrast in two men than in Mirza and Sabat. One is all exterior—the other has no outside at all; one a most consummate man of the world—the other an artless child of the desert.

March 28.—Sabat has been tolerably quiet this week; but think of the keeper of a lunatic, and you see me. A war of words broke out the beginning of last week, but it ended in an honourable peace. After he got home at night he sent a letter, complaining of a high crime and misdemeanour in some servant; I sent him a soothing letter, and the wild beast fell asleep. In all these altercations we take occasion to consider the extent of Christian forbearance, as necessary to be exercised in all the smaller occasions of life, as well as when persecution comes for religion. This he has not been hitherto aware of. One night in prayer I forgot to mention Mr. Brown; so, after I had done, he continued on his knees and went on and prayed in Persian for him. I was much pleased at this.

Did you read Lord Minto's speech, and his commendation of those *learned and pious men*, the missionaries? I have looked upon him ever since as a nursing-father to the Church.

April 11.—It is surprising that a man can be so blinded by vanity as to suppose, as Sabat does, that he is superior to Mirza in Hindustani; yet this he does, and maintains it stoutly. I am tired of combating this opinion, as nothing comes of our arguments but strifes. Another of his odd opinions is, that he is so under the immediate influence and direction of the Spirit, that there will not be one single error in his whole Persian translation. You perceive a little[232] enthusiasm in the character of our brother. As often as he finds himself in any difficulty, he expects a dream to set him right.

April 26.—These Orientals with whom I translate require me to point out the connection between every two sentences, which is often more than I can do. It is curious how accurately they observe all the rules of writing, and yet generally write badly. I can only account for it by supposing that they have been writing too long. From time immemorial they have been authors, without progressive knowledge; and so to produce variety they supply their lack of knowledge by overstraining their imagination; hence their extravagant metaphors and affected way of expressing the commonest things. Sabat, though a real Christian, has not lost a jot of his Arabian pride. He looks upon the Europeans as mushrooms, and seems to regard my pretensions to any learning as we do those of a savage or an ape.

May 31.—Some days Sabat overworked himself and was laid up. He does his utmost. He is increasingly dear to me, as I see more of the meekness and gentleness of Christ in him. Our conflicts I hope are over, and we shall draw very quietly together side by side.

In all this, and much more that followed, or is unrecorded, Henry Martyn was being prepared unconsciously for his formal and unanswered controversies with the learned Mussulmans of Persia. His letters to Corrie tell of his farther experience with his moonshis and the moulvies of Patna, and describe the true spirit of such 'disputings' for the truth.

1807, April 28.—Of what importance is our walk in reference to our ministry, and particularly among the natives. For myself, I never enter into a dispute with them without having reason to reflect that I mar the work[233] for which I contend by the spirit in which I do it. During my absence at Monghyr moonshi went to a learned native for assistance against an answer I had given him to their main argument for the Koran, and he not being able to render it, they mean to have down their leading man from Benares to convince me of the truth of their religion. I wish a spirit of inquiry may be excited, but I lay not much stress upon *clear arguments*; the work of God is seldom wrought in this way. To preach the Gospel, with the Holy Ghost sent down from heaven, is a better way to win souls.

May 4.—I am preparing for the assault of this great Mohammedan Imaum. I have read the Koran and notes twice for this purpose, and even filled whole sheets with objections, remarks, questions, etc.; but, alas! what little hopes have I of doing him or any of them good in this way! Moonshi is in general mute.

October 28.—At night, in a conversation with Mirza accidentally begun, I spoke to him for more than three hours on Christianity and Mohammedanism. He said there was no passage in the Gospel that said no prophet shall come after Christ. I showed him the last verse in Matthew, the passages in Isaiah and Daniel, on the eternity of Christ's kingdom, and proved it from the nature of the way of salvation in the Gospel. I then told him my objections against Mohammedanism, its laws, its defects, its unnecessariness, the unsuitableness of its rewards, and its utter want of support by proof. When he began to mention Mahomet's miracles, I showed him the passages in the 6th and 13th chapters of the Koran, where he disavows the power. Nothing surprised him so much as these passages; he is, poor man, totally indifferent about all religion; he told me that I had produced great doubt in his mind, and that he had no answer to give.

November 21.—My mind violently occupied with thoughts respecting the approaching spread of the Gospel,|234| and my own going to Persia. Sabat's conversation stirs up a great desire in me to go; as by his account all the Mahometan countries are ripe for throwing off the delusion. The gracious Lord will teach me, and make my way plain before my face. Oh, may He keep my soul in peace, and make it indifferent to me whether I die or live, so Christ be magnified by me. I have need to receive this spirit from Him, for I feel at present unwilling to die, as if my own life and labours were necessary for this work, or as if I should be deprived of the bliss of seeing the conversion of the nations. Vain thought! God, who keeps me here awhile, arranges every part of His plans in unerring wisdom, and if I should be cut off in the midst of my plans, I shall still, I trust, through mercy, behold His works in heaven, and be everlastingly happy in the never-ceasing admiration of His works and nature. Every day the disputes with Mirza and Moorad Ali become more interesting. Their doubts of Mahometanism seem to have amounted almost to disbelief. Moorad Ali confessed that they all received their religion, not on conviction, but because it was the way of their fathers; and he said with great earnestness, that if some great Sheikh-ool-Islam, whom he mentioned, could not give an answer, and a satisfactory, rational evidence, of the truth of Islamism, he would renounce it and be baptized. Mirza seemed still more anxious and interested, and speaks of it to me and Sabat continually. In translating 1 Timothy i. 15, I said to them, 'You have in that verse heard the Gospel; your blood will not be required at my hands; you will certainly remember these words at the last day.' This led to a long discussion, at the close of which, when I said that, notwithstanding their endeavours to identify the two religions, there is still so much difference 'that if our word is true you are lost,' they looked at each other almost with consternation, and said 'It is true.' Still the Trinity and the incarnation of Christ afford a plea to the one, and a difficulty to the other.|235|

At another time, when I had, from some passage, hinted to Mirza his danger, he said with great earnestness, 'Sir, why won't you try to save me?' 'Save you?' said I, 'I would lay down my life to save your soul: what can I do?' He wished me to go to Phoolwari, the Mussulman college, and there examine the subject with the most learned of their doctors. I told him I had no objection to go to Phoolwari, but why could not he as well inquire for himself whether there were any evidence for Mohammedanism?

1808, June 14.—Called on Bahir Ali Khan, Dare, and the Italian padre; with Bahir Ali I stayed two hours, conversing in Persian. He began our theological discussion with a question to me, 'How do you reconcile God's absolute power and man's free will?' I pleaded ignorance and inability, but he replied to his own question very fully, and his conclusion seemed to be that God had created evil things for the trial of His creatures. His whole manner, look, authority, and copiousness constantly reminded me of the Dean of Carlisle.|28| I asked him for the proofs of the religion of Mahomet. The first he urged was the eloquence of the Koran. After a long time he conceded that it was, of itself, an insufficient argument. I then brought forward a passage of the Koran containing a sentiment manifestly false; on which he floundered a good deal; but concluded with saying that I must wait till I knew more of logic and Persian before he could explain it to me satisfactorily. On the whole, I was exceedingly pleased with his candour, politeness, and good sense. He said he had nothing to lose by becoming a Christian, and that, if he were once persuaded of the truth, he would change without hesitation. He showed me an Arabic translation of Euclid.

June 15.—Read an account of Turkey. The bad|236| effects of the book were so great that I found instant need of prayer, and I do not know when I have had such divine and animating feelings. Oh, it is Thy Spirit that makes me pant for the skies. It is He that shall make me trample the world and my lusts beneath my feet, and urge my onward course towards the crown of life.

December 5.—Went to Patna to Sabat, and saw several Persians and Arabians. I found that the intended dispute had come to nothing, for that Ali had told Sabat he had been advised by his father not to dispute with him. They behaved with the utmost incivility to him, not giving him a place to sit down, and desiring him at last to go. Sabat rose, and shook his garment against them, and said, 'If you know Mohammedanism to be right, and will not try to convince me, you will have to answer for it at the day of judgment. I have explained to you the Gospel; I am therefore pure from your blood.' He came home and wrote some poetry on the Trinity, and the Apostles, which he recited to me. We called on Mizra Mehdi, a jeweller, who showed us some diamonds, emeralds, and rubies. With an old Arabian there I tried to converse in Arabic. He understood my Arabic, but I could not understand his. They were all full of my praise, but then the pity was that I was a Christian. I challenged them to show what there was wrong in being a Nazarene, but they declined. Afterwards we called on the nabob Moozuffur Ali Khan. The house Sabat lived in was properly an Oriental one; and, as he said, like those in Syria. It reminded me often of the Apostles, and the recollection was often solemnising.

December 6 to 8.—Betrayed more than once into evil temper, which left dreadful remorse of conscience; I cried unto God in secret, but the sense of my sinfulness was overwhelming. It had a humbling effect, however. In prayer with my men I was led more unfeignedly to humble myself even to the dust, and after that I enjoyed, through the sovereign mercy of God, much peace, and a sense of His|237|presence. Languid in my studies; indisposition causing sleepiness. Reading chiefly Persian and a little Greek: Hanway, Waring, and Franklin's Travels into Persia. Haji Khan, a sensible old man from Patna, called two days following, and sat a long time conversing upon religion.

To MRS. DARE, GAYA
Dinapore: May 19, 1808.
Dear Mrs. Dare,|29|—Your letter arrived just in time to save you from some severe animadversions that were preparing for you. I intended to have sent by your young friend some remarks, direct and oblique, on the variableness of the sex, the facility with which promises are made and broken, the pleasures of indolence, and other topics of the like nature,—but your kind epistle disarms me. Soon after you left us, the heat increased to a degree I had never before felt, and made me often think of you with concern. I used to say to Colonel Bradshaw, 'I wonder how Mrs. Dare likes Gya, and its burning hills—I dare say she would be glad to be back again.' Well, I should be glad if we had you here again. I want female society, and among the ladies of Dinapore there is none with whom I have a chance of obtaining a patient hearing when speaking to them on the subject of their most important interest. This, you know, is the state of all but Mrs. Stuart, and it is a state of danger and death. Follow them no more, my dear friend: but now, in the solitude of Gya, learn those lessons of heavenly wisdom, that, when you are brought again into a larger society, you may not yield to the impulse of doing as others do, but, by a life of true seriousness, put them to shame.

I go on much as usual, occupied all day, and laying a|238| weary head on the pillow at night. My health, which you inquire after so kindly, is on the whole good; but I am daily reminded that it is a fragile frame I carry about.

August 23.—I rejoice to find by your letter that you are contented with your lot. Before the time of Horace, and since too, contentment has been observed to be a very rare thing on earth, and I know not how it is to be obtained but by learning in the school of the

Gospel. 'I have *learned*,' said even St. Paul, 'in whatsoever state I am, therewith to be content.' To be a little slanderous for once, I suspect Colonel Bradshaw, our common friend, who will send you a letter by the same sepoy, must have a lecture or two more read to him in this science, as he is far from being perfect in it. He has, you know, all that heart can wish of this world's goods, and yet he is restless; sometimes the society is dull; at other times the blame is laid on the quarters, and he must go out of cantonments. To-day he is going to Gya, to-morrow on the river. Now, I tell him that he need not change his place, but his heart. Let him seek his happiness in God, and he will carry about a paradise in his own bosom. *The wilderness and the solitary place shall be glad for him, and the desert shall rejoice and blossom as the rose.*

September 23.—My dear Mrs. Dare, attend to the call of God; He never speaks more to the heart than by affliction. Such a season as this, so favourable to the commencement of true piety, may never again occur. Hereafter time may have riveted worldly habits on you, and age rendered the heart insensible. Begin now to be melancholy? No—to be seriously happy, to be purely happy, everlastingly happy.

Ever, through the solitude, the suffering, and the toiling of the first twelve months at Dinapore, the thought of Lydia Grenfell, the hope of her union to him, and her help[239] in his agonising for India, runs like a chord of sad music. He thus writes to his cousin, her sister:

Indeed, all my Europe letters this season have brought me such painful news that I almost dread receiving another. Such is the vanity of our expectations. I had been looking out with more than ordinary anxiety for these letters, thinking they would give me some account of Lydia's coming—whereas yours and hers have only wounded me, and my sister's,[30] giving me the distressing tidings of her ill-health, makes my heart bleed. Oh, it is now that I feel the agony of having half the globe intervening between us. Could I but be with her: yet God who heareth prayer will surely supply my place. From Sally I expect neither promptness nor the ability to console her sister. This is the first time Sally has taken up her pen to write to me, and thought an apology necessary for her neglect. Perhaps she has been wrapt up in her dear husband, or her dearer self. I feel very angry with her. But my dear faithful Lydia has more than compensated for all the neglect of my own relations. I believe she has sent me more than all the rest in England put together. If I had not loved her before, her affectionate and constant remembrance of me would win my heart.

You mention the name of your last little one (may she be a follower of her namesake!). It reminds me of what Mr. Brown has lately written to me. He says that Mrs. B. had determined her expected one should be called after me: but, as it proved to be a girl, it was called *Lydia Martyn Brown*, a combination that suggests many reflections to my mind.

And now I ought to begin to write about myself and India: but I fear you are not so interested about me as you used to be: yet the Church of God, I know, is dear to you always! Let me speak of the ministers. The Gospel[240] was preached before the Governor-General by seven different evangelical chaplains in the course of six months. Of these five have associated, agreeing to communicate with each other quarterly reports of their proceedings. They are Mr. Brown at Calcutta, Thompson at Cuddalore, Parson at Berhampore, Corrie at Chunar, and myself here. Corrie and myself, as being most similarly employed, correspond every week. He gives all his attention to the languages, and has his heart wholly towards the heathen. He has set on foot four schools in his neighbourhood, and I four here along the banks of the Ganges, containing 120 boys: he has nearly the same number. The masters are heathens—but they have consented with some reluctance to admit the Christian books. The little book on the Parables in the dialect of Bihar, which I had prepared for them, is now in the press at Serampore; for the present, they read with their own books the Sermon on the Mount. We hope by the help of God to enlarge the plan of the schools very considerably, as soon as we have felt the ground, and can advance boldly.

Respecting my own immediate plans, I am rather in the dark. They wish to engage me as a translator of the Scriptures into Hindustani and Persian, by the help of some learned natives; and if this plan is settled at Calcutta, I shall engage in it without hesitation, as conceiving it to be the most useful way in which I can be employed at present in the Church of God. If not, I hope to begin to itinerate as soon as the rains are over; not that I can hope

91

to be easily understood yet, but by mixing familiarly with the natives I should soon learn. Little permanent good, however, can be done till some of the Scriptures can be put into their hands. On this account I wish to help forward this work as quick as possible, because a chapter will speak plainly in a thousand places at once, while I can speak, and not very plainly, but in one. One advantage attending the delay of public preaching will be that the schools will[241] have a fair run, for the commencement of preaching will be the downfall of the schools. I have my tent ready, and would set out with pleasure to-morrow if the time for this work were come. As there is public service here every Lord's Day, three days' journey is the longest I can take. This may hereafter prove an inconvenience: but the advantages of being a Company's servant are incalculable. A missionary not in the service is liable to be stopped by every subaltern; but there is no man that can touch me. Amongst the Europeans at this station I am not without encouragement. Eight or ten, chiefly corporals or sergeants, come to my quarters Sunday and Wednesday nights for social worship: but it does not appear that more than one are truly converted. The commanding officer of the native battalion and his lady, whom I mentioned in my last, are, I think, increasingly serious—but the fear of man is their snare. Mrs. Young says that, with Lydia to support her, she could face the frown of the world. I had been looking forward with pleasure to the time when she *would* have such support, and rejoiced that Lydia would have so sensible and hopeful a companion.

Dinapore: December, 1807.
My dear Cousin,—Your letter, after so long a silence, was a great relief to me, as it assured me of your undiminished affection; but I regretted you had been so sparing in your consolations on the subject of my late disappointment. Remember, it was to you I used to unbosom all my anxieties, and I still look to you for that sympathising tenderness which no other person perhaps feels for me, or at least can venture to express. How every particular of our conversation in the journey from Redruth to Plymouth Dock returns to my mind! I have reason indeed to remember it—from that time I date my sorrows—we talked too much about Lydia. Her last letter was to bid me a final farewell, so I must not write[242] to her without her permission; she wished she might hear by you that I was happy. I am therefore obliged to say that God has, according to her prayer, kept me in peace, and indeed strengthened me unto all patience and long-suffering with joyfulness. At first, like Jonah, I was more grieved at the loss of my gourd than at the sight of the many perishing Ninevehs all round me; but now my earthly woes and earthly attachments seem to be absorbing in the vast concern of communicating the Gospel to these nations. After this last lesson from God on the vanity of creature love, I feel desirous to be nothing, to have nothing, to ask for nothing, but what He gives. So remarkably and so repeatedly has He baffled my schemes of earthly comfort that I am forced at last to believe His determination to be, that I should live in every sense a stranger and pilgrim on the earth. Lydia allows me not the most distant prospect of ever seeing her; and if indeed the supposed indelicacy of her coming out to me is an obstacle that cannot be got over, it is likely indeed to be a lasting separation: for when shall I ever see it lawful to leave my work here for three years, when every hour is unspeakably precious? I am beginning therefore to form my plans as a person in a state of celibacy, and mean to trouble you no more on what I have been lately writing about so much. However, let me be allowed to make one request; it is that Lydia would at least consider me as she did before, and write as at that time. Perhaps there may be some objection to this request, and therefore I dare not urge it. I say only that by experience I know it will prove an inestimable blessing and comfort to me. If you really wish to have a detailed account of my proceedings, exert your influence in effecting this measure; for you may be sure that I shall be disposed to write to *her* letters long enough, longer than to any other, for this reason among others, that of the three in the world who have most love for me, *i.e.* Sally, Lydia, and yourself, I believe[243] that, notwithstanding all that has happened, the middle one loves most truly. If this conjecture of mine is well-founded, she will be most interested in what befalls me, and I shall write in less fear of tiring. My bodily health, which you require me always to mention, is prodigious, my strength and spirits are in general greater than ever they were, and this under God I ascribe to the susceptibility of my frame,

giving me instant warning of anything that may disorder it. Half-an-hour's exposure to the sun produces an immediate overflow of bile: therefore I take care never to let the sun's rays fall upon my body. Vexation or anxiety has the same effect. For this, faith and prayer for the peace of God are the best remedy.

Since my last letter, written a few months ago in reply to Cousin T., I do not recollect that anything has happened. Dr. Buchanan's last publication on the Christian Institution will give you the most full and interesting accounts of the affairs of our Lord's kingdom in India. The press seems to us all to be the great instrument at present. Preaching by the European Mission here has in no instance that I know of been successful. Everything in our manner, pronunciation, and doctrine is so new and strange, that to instruct them properly *virâ voce* seems to be giving more time to a small body of them than can be conveniently spared from the great mass. Yet, on the other hand, I feel reason to be guarded against the love of carnal ease, which would make me prefer the literary work of translating to that of an itinerant: upon the whole, however, I acquiesce in the work that Dr. B. has assigned me, from conviction. Through the blessing of God I have finished the New Testament in the Perso-Arabic-Hindustani, but it must undergo strict revisal before it can be sent to the press. My assistants in this work were Mirza Mahommed Ali and Moorad Ali, two Mahometans, and I sometimes hope there are convictions in their minds which they will not be able to shake off. They have not much doubt of the [244] falsehood of Mahometanism, and the truth of the Gospel, but they cannot take up the cross.

The arrival of Jawad Sabat, our Arabian brother, at Dinapore, had a great effect upon them.... He is now employed in translating the New Testament into Persian and Arabic, and great will be the benefit to his own soul, that he is called to study the Word of God: the Bible Society at home will, I hope, bear the expense of printing it. This work, whenever it is done properly, will be the downfall of Mahometanism. What do I not owe to the Lord for giving me to take part in a translation? Never did I see such wonders of wisdom and love in the blessed book, as since I have been obliged to study every expression; and it is often a delightful reflection, that even death cannot deprive us of the privilege of studying its mysteries.... I forgot to mention Lydia's profile, which I received. I have now to request her miniature picture, and you must draw on Mr. Simeon, my banker, for the expense.... I need not assure you and Cousin T. of my unceasing regard, nor Lydia of my unalterable attachment. God bless you all, my beloved friends. Pray for me, as I do also for you. Our separation will soon be over.

July 3.—Received two Europe letters—one from Lydia, and the other from Colonel Sandys. The tender emotions of love, and gratitude, and veneration for her, were again powerfully awakened in my mind, so that I could with difficulty think of anything else; yet I found myself drawn nearer to God by the pious remarks of her letter. Nature would have desired more testimonies of her love to me, but grace approved her ardent love to her Lord.

TO CHARLES SIMEON[31]

Danapore (*sic*): January, 1808.

My dearest Friend and Brother,—I must begin my letter with assurances of eternal regard; eternal will it be if I [245] find grace to be faithful.... My expectation of seeing Lydia here is now at an end. I cannot doubt any longer what is the Divine will, and I bow to it. Since I have been led to consider myself as perfectly disengaged from the affairs of this life, my soul has been filled with more ardent desires to spend and be spent in the service of God; and though in truth the world has now little to charm me, I think these desires do not arise from a misanthropic disgust to it.... I never loved, nor ever shall love, human creature as I love her.

Soon after David Brown of Calcutta wrote to Charles Simeon, whom a rumour of Henry Martyn's engagement to Miss Corrie, his friend's sister, had reached: 'How could you imagine that Miss C. would do as well as Miss L.G. for Mr. Martyn? Dear Martyn is married already to three wives, whom, I believe, he would not forsake for all the princesses in the earth—I mean his three translations of the Holy Scriptures.'

To Mrs. Brown at Aldeen, who was his confidante in India, Martyn wrote on July 21:

It appears that the letter by the overland despatch did not reach Lydia. Again, the Sarah Christiana packet, which carried the duplicate, ought to have arrived long before the sailing of these last ships from England, but I see no account of her. It is probable, therefore, that I shall have to wait a considerable time longer in uncertainty; all which is good, because so hath the Lord appointed it.

July 25.—Hard at Arabic grammar all day, after finishing sermon. Sat in the evening a long time at my door, after the great fatigue of the day, to let my mind relax itself, and found a melancholy pleasure in looking back upon the time spent at St. Hilary and Marazion.[246] How the days and years are gone by, as a tale that is told!

At last the blow had fallen.

October 24.—An unhappy day: received at last a letter from Lydia, in which she refuses to come because her mother will not consent to it. Grief and disappointment threw my soul into confusion at first, but gradually as my disorder subsided my eyes were opened, and reason resumed its office. I could not but agree with her that it would not be for the glory of God, nor could we expect His blessing, if she acted in disobedience to her mother. As she has said, 'They that walk in crooked paths shall not find peace;' and if she were to come with an uneasy conscience, what happiness could we either of us expect?

TO LYDIA GRENFELL

Dinapore: October 24, 1807.

My dear Lydia,—Though my heart is bursting with grief and disappointment, I write not to blame you. The rectitude of all your conduct secures you from censure. Permit me calmly to reply to your letter of March 5, which I have this day received.

You condemn yourself for having given me, though unintentionally, encouragement to believe that my attachment was returned. Perhaps you have. I have read your former letters with feelings less sanguine since the receipt of the last, and I am still not surprised at the interpretation I put upon them. But why accuse yourself for having written in this strain? It has not increased my expectations nor consequently embittered my disappointment. When I addressed you in my first letter on the subject, I was not induced to it by any appearances of regard you had expressed, neither at any subsequent period have my hopes of your consent been founded on a belief of your attachment to me. I knew that your conduct would be[247] regulated, not by personal feelings, but by a sense of duty. And therefore you have nothing to blame yourself for on this head.

In your last letter you do not assign among your reasons for refusal a want of regard to me. In that case I could not in decency give you any further trouble. On the contrary, you say that '*present* circumstances seem to you to forbid my indulging expectations.' As this leaves an opening, I presume to address you again; and till the answer arrives must undergo another eighteen months of torturing suspense.

Alas! my rebellious heart—what a tempest agitates me! I knew not that I had made so little progress in a spirit of resignation to the Divine will. I am in my chastisement like a bullock unaccustomed to the yoke, like a wild bull in a net, full of the fury of the Lord, the rebuke of my God. The death of my late most beloved sister almost broke my heart; but I hoped it had softened me and made me willing to suffer. But now my heart is as though destitute of the grace of God, full of misanthropic disgust with the world, and sometimes feeling resentment against yourself and Emma, and Mr. Simeon, and, in short, all whom I love and honour most; sometimes, in pride and anger, resolving to write neither to you nor to any one else again. These are the motions of sin. My love and my better reason draw me to you again.... But now with respect to your mother, I confess that the chief and indeed only difficulty lies here. Considering that she is *your* mother, as I hoped she would be mine, and that her happiness so much depends on you; considering also that I am God's minister, which amidst all the tumults of my soul I dare not forget, I falter in beginning to give advice which may prove contrary to the law of God. God forbid, therefore, that I should say, disobey your parents, where the Divine law does not command you to disobey them; neither do I positively take upon myself to say[248] that this is a case in which the law of God requires you to act in contradiction to them. I would rather suggest to your mother some considerations which justify me in attempting to deprive her of the company of a beloved child.

October 26.—A Sabbath having intervened since the above was written, I find myself more tranquillised by the sacred exercises of the day. One passage of Scripture which you

94

quote has been much on my mind, and I find it very appropriate and decisive,—that we are not to 'make to ourselves crooked paths, which whoso walketh in shall not know peace.' Let me say I must be therefore contented to wait till you feel that the way is clear. But I intended to justify myself to Mrs. Grenfell. Let her not suppose that I would make her or any other of my fellow-creatures miserable, that I might be happy. If there were no reason for your coming here, and the contest were only between Mrs. Grenfell and me, that is, between her happiness and mine, I would urge nothing further, but resign you to her. But I have considered that there are many things that might reconcile her to a separation from you (if indeed a separation is necessary, for if she would come along with you, I should rejoice the more). First, she does not depend on you alone for the comfort of her declining years. She is surrounded by friends. She has a greater number of sons and daughters honourably established in the world than falls to the lot of most parents—all of whom would be happy in having her amongst them. Again, if a person worthy of your hand, and settled in England, were to offer himself, Mrs. Grenfell would not have insuperable objections, though it *did* deprive her of her daughter. Nay, I sometimes think, perhaps arrogantly, that had I myself remained in England, and in possession of a competency, she would not have withheld her consent. Why, then, should my banishment from my native country, in the service of mankind, be a reason with any for inflicting an additional wound, far more painful than a separation from my dearest relatives?|249|

I have no claim upon Mrs. Grenfell in any way, but let her only conceive a son of her own in my circumstances. If she feels it a sacrifice, let her remember that it is a sacrifice made to duty; that your presence here would be of essential service to the Church of God it is superfluous to attempt to prove. If you really believe of yourself as you speak, it is because you were never out of England.

Your mother cannot be so misinformed respecting India and the voyage to it as to be apprehensive on account of the climate or passage, in these days when multitudes of ladies every year, with constitutions as delicate as yours, go to and fro in perfect safety, and a vastly greater majority enjoy their health here than in England. With respect to my means I need add nothing to what was said in my first letter. But, alas! what is my affluence good for now? It never gave me pleasure but when I thought you were to share it with me. Two days ago I was hastening on the alterations in my house and garden, supposing you were at hand; but now every object excites disgust. My wish, upon the whole, is that if you perceive it would be your duty to come to India, were it not for your mother—and of that you cannot doubt—supposing, I mean, that your inclinations are indifferent, then you should make her acquainted with your thoughts, and let us leave it to God how He will determine her mind.

In the meantime, since I am forbidden to hope for the immediate pleasure of seeing you, my next request is for a mutual engagement. My own heart is engaged, I believe, indissolubly.

My reason for making a request which you will account bold is that there can then be no possible objection to our correspondence, especially as I promise not to persuade you to leave your mother.

In the midst of my present sorrow I am constrained to remember yours. Your compassionate heart is pained from having been the cause of suffering to me. But|250|care not for me, dearest Lydia. Next to the bliss of having you with me, my happiness is to know that you are happy. I shall have to groan long, perhaps, with a heavy heart; but if I am not hindered materially by it in the work of God, it will be for the benefit of my soul. You, sister beloved in the Lord, know much of the benefit of affliction. Oh, may I have grace to follow you, though at a humble distance, in the path of patient suffering, in which you have walked so long! Day and night I cease not to pray for you, though I fear my prayers are of little value.

But, as an encouragement to you to pray, I cannot help transcribing a few words from my journal, written at the time you wrote your letter to me (March 7): 'As on the two last days' (you wrote your letter on the 5th), 'felt no desire for a comfortable settlement in the world, scarcely pleasure at the thought of Lydia's coming, except so far as her being sent might be for the good of my soul and assistance in my work. How manifestly is there an omnipresent, all-seeing God, and how sure we may be that prayers for spiritual blessings are heard by our God and Father! Oh, let that endearing name quell every murmur! When I am sent for to different parts of the country to officiate at marriages, I sometimes think, amidst the festivity of the company, Why does all go so easily with them, and so hardly with me? They come together without difficulty, and I am baulked and disconcerted almost every step I take, and condemned to wear away the time in uncertainty. Then I call to mind that to live without chastening is allowed to the spurious offspring, while to suffer is the privilege of the children of God.'

Dearest Lydia, must I conclude? I could prolong my communion with you through many sheets; how many things have I to say to you, which I hoped to have communicated in person. But the more I write and the more I think of you, the more my affection warms, and I should[251] feel it difficult to keep my pen from expressions that might not be acceptable to you.

Farewell! dearest, most beloved Lydia, remember your faithful and ever affectionate, H. MARTYN.

October 25. (Sunday.)—Preached on Isaiah lii. 13 to a large congregation, my mind continually in heaviness, and my health disturbed in consequence. The women still fewer than ever at Hindustani prayer, and, at night, some of the men who were not on duty did not come; all these things are deeply afflicting, and yet my heart is so full of its own griefs, that I mourn not as I ought for the Church of God. I have not a moment's relief from my burdens but after being some time in prayer; afterwards my uneasiness and misery return again.

October 26.—Mirza from Benares arrived to-day; I employed all the day in writing letters to Mr. Brown, Corrie, and Lydia. The last was a sweet and tranquillising employment to me. I felt more submission to the Divine will, and began to be more solicitous about Lydia's peace and happiness than my own. How much has she been called to suffer! These are they that come out of great tribulation.

To REV. DAVID BROWN

Dinapore: October 26, 1807.

My dear Sir,—I have received your two letters of the 14th and 17th; the last contained a letter from Lydia. It is as I feared. She refuses to come because her mother will not give her consent. Sir, you must not wonder at my pale looks when I receive so many hard blows on my heart. Yet a Father's love appoints the trial, and I pray that it may have its intended effect. Yet, if you wish to prolong my existence in this world, make a representation to some persons at home who may influence her friends.[252] Your word will be believed sooner than mine. The extraordinary effect of mental disorder on my bodily frame is unfortunate; trouble brings on disease and disorders the sleep. In this way I am labouring a little now, but not much; in a few days it will pass away again. He that hath delivered and doth deliver, is He in whom we trust that He will yet deliver.

The queen's ware on its way to me can be sold at an outcry or sent to Corrie. I do not want queen's ware or anything else now. My new house and garden, without the person I expected to share it with me, excite disgust.

November 25.—Letters came from Mr. Simeon and Lydia, both of which depressed my spirits exceedingly; though I have been writing for some days past, that I might have it in my power to consider myself free, so as to be able to go to Persia or elsewhere;—yet, now that the wished-for permission is come, I am filled with grief; I cannot bear to part with Lydia, and she seems more necessary to me than my life; yet her letter was to bid me a last farewell. Oh, how have I been crossed from childhood, and yet how little benefit have I received from these chastisements of my God! The Lord now sanctify this, that since the last desire of my heart also is withheld, I may with resignation turn away for ever from the world, and henceforth live forgetful of all but God. With Thee, O my God, there is no disappointment; I shall never have to regret that I loved Thee too well. Thou hast said, 'Delight thyself in the Lord, and He shall give thee the desires of thine heart.'

November 26.—Received a letter from Emma, which again had a tendency to depress my spirits; all the day I could not attain to sweet resignation to God. I seemed to be cut off for ever from happiness in not having Lydia with me.

The receipt of his letter of October 24, 1807, was thus acknowledged, before God, by Lydia Grenfell in her *Diary*:

1808, May 9.—A letter from my dear friend in India (requesting me to come out) reached me. These words form my comfort: 'Be still, and know that I am God.' I see my duty pointed out, and am persuaded, dark as the prospect is, God will appear God in this matter; whether we meet again or not, His great power and goodness will be displayed—it has been in quieting my heart, for oh, the trial is not small of seeing the state of his mind. But I am to be still, and now, O Lord, let Thy love fill my soul, let it be supreme in his breast and mine; there is no void where Thou dwellest, whatever else is wanting.

May 11.—My mind distressed, perplexed, and troubled for my dear friend; much self-reflection for having suffered him to see my regard for him (and what it is), yet the comforts of God's Word return—'Why take ye thought?' said our Lord. Yet to-morrow burdens the present day. Oh, pity and support me to bear the thought of injuring his peace—inquire if the cause is of God.

May 15.—Lord, Thou seest my wanderings—oh, how many, how great! Put my tears into Thy bottle. Yes, my Lord, I can forsake Thee and be content; I turn and turn, restless and miserable, till I am turned to Thee. What a week have I passed! never may such another pass over my head!—my thoughts wholly occupied about my absent friend—distressed for his distress, and full of self-reproaches for all that's past—writing bitter things against myself—my heart alienated dreadfully from God—and the duties I am in the habit of performing all neglected. Oh, should the Lord not awake for me and draw me back, whither should I go? His Word has been my comfort at times, but Satan or conscience (I doubt which) tells me I am in a delusion to take the comfort of God's Word, for I[254] ought to suffer. But am I justified in putting comfort from me? since I no way excuse myself, but am, I trust, humbled for my imprudence in letting my friend know the state of mind towards him, and this is all I have injured him in. I accuse myself, too, for want of candour with my family, and oh, let me not forget the greatest offence of all—not consulting the will and glory of God in indulging and encouraging a regard He seems to frown on. I have to-day found deliverance, and felt some measure of calm reliance. I know there is a particular providence over him and me, but this belief does not lessen my fears of acting wrong—I am as responsible as if all were left to me. What shall I do but say, Because Thou hast been my help, therefore in the shadow of Thy wings will I trust? I fly to Thy power and take shelter in Thy love to sinners. Oh, for a continually bleeding heart, mourning for sin!

June 12.—I have peace in my soul to-day. My remembrance of God's dear saint in India is frequent, but I am still in this affair, and expect to know more of the infinite power, wisdom, and goodness of our God in it and by it than I have heretofore. My prayer for him constantly is that he maybe supported, guided, and made in all things obedient and submissive to the will of his God.

Henry Martyn seems to have written again to Marazion, at this time, a letter which has not been preserved, for Lydia Grenfell thus refers to it:

August 29.—Heard of my absent dear friend by this day's post, and was strangely affected, though the intelligence was satisfactory in every respect. I sought deliverance in prayer, and the Lord spoke peace to my agitated mind, and gave me what I desired—liberty of soul to return to Himself, and the contemplation of heavenly things, though a sadness remained on my spirit. Heard three sermons, for I thought it best to be less alone than[255] usual, lest my thoughts should wander. Found great hardness of heart in the services of the day, but I doubt whether my affections were spiritual or not, though they arose from a longing to be in heaven, and a joyful sense of the certainty that God would bring me there.

September 11.—After some days of darkness and distress, sweet peace and light return, and my soul rests on God as my all-sufficient help. Oh, the idolatrous state of my heart! what painful discoveries are made to me! I see the stream of my affections has been turned from God and on.... An exertion must be made, like cutting off a right hand, in order to give Thee, O Lord, my heart. I must hear neither of nor from the person God has called in His providence to serve Him in a distant country. Oh, to be resolute, knowing by woeful experience the necessity of guarding my thoughts against the remembrance of one, though dear. As I value the presence of my God, I must avoid everything that leads my thoughts to this subject—O Lord, keep me dependent on Thee for grace to do so; Thou hast plainly informed me of Thy will by withholding Thy presence at this time, and Thy Word directed me to lay aside this weight.

October 30.—Thought of my dear friend to-night with tenderness, but entire resignation to Thy will, O our God, in never seeing or hearing from him again; to meet him above is my desire.

December 30.—I reckon among my mercies the Lord's having enabled me to choose a single life, and that my friend in India has been so well reconciled to my determination. That trial was a sore one, and I believe the effects of it will be felt as long as I live. My weak frame could not support the perturbed state of my mind, and the various painful apprehensions that assailed me on his arrival nearly wore me down. But the Lord removed them all by showing me He approved of my choice, and in granting me the tidings of his enjoying peace and|256| happiness in our separation. Every burden now respecting him is removed, and my soul has only to praise the wise and gracious hand which brought me through that thorny path. It was one I made to myself, by ever entering into a correspondence with him, and by expressing too freely my regard.

On March 28, 1809, Martyn wrote to Mr. Brown:

Your letter is just come. The Europe letter is from Lydia. I trembled at the handwriting.... It was only more last words, sent by the advice of Colonel Sandys, lest the non-arrival of the former might keep me in suspense.... I trust that I have done with the entanglements of this world; seldom a day passes but I thank God for the freedom from earthly care which I enjoy.

And so end Henry Martyn's love-letters, marked by a delicacy as well as tenderness of feeling in such contrast to the action of Lydia Grenfell throughout, as to explain the mingled resentment and resignation in which they close. The request for a mutual engagement which would justify correspondence at least seems to have been unheeded for some months, till the news of his serious illness in July 1808 led her again to write to him, as taking the place of his sister who had been removed by death. He was ordered to Cawnpore, and set off in the hot season by Chunar and Ghazipore, writing these last words on April 11, 1809, from Dinapore:

My men seem to be in a more flourishing state than they have yet been. About thirty attend every night. I had a delightful party this week, of six young men, who will, I hope, prove to be true soldiers of Christ. Seldom, even at Cambridge, have I been so much pleased.

FOOTNOTES:

|26|Even in 1889 we find a Patna missionary writing of his work from Bankipore as a centre: 'The people in every village, except those on the Dinapore road, said that no Sahib had ever been in their village before. Sometimes my approach was the cause of considerable alarm.'

|27|*Memoir of the Rev. Thomas Thomason, M.A.,* by Rev. J. Sargent, M.A., 2nd edition, 1834, London.

|28|Rev. Dr. Milner.

|29|The names of Capt. Dare and Mrs. Dare occur in the *Journals and Letters* between February 17 and March 24, 1808, wherein Martyn's relations with them are described just as in this set of letters.

|30|Mrs. Laura Curgenven: born January 1779, died in the year 1807.

|31|See Moule's *Charles Simeon,* p. 201.

|257|

CHAPTER VII
CAWNPORE, 1809-1810

Mrs. Sherwood, known in the first decade of this century as a writer of such Anglo-Indian tales as *Little Henry and his Bearer,* and as a philanthropist who did much for the white and the dark orphans of British soldiers in India, was one of the many who came under the influence of Henry Martyn. This Lichfield girl, whose father had been the playmate of

Samuel Johnson, and who had known Garrick and Dr. Darwin, Hannah More and Maria Edgeworth, had married her cousin, the paymaster of the King's 53rd Regiment of Foot. The regiment was sent to Bengal. On its way up the Hoogli from Calcutta in boats, Mr. Sherwood and his wife were walking after sunset, when they stumbled on 'a small society' of their own men, who met regularly to read their Bibles and to pray, often in old stores, ravines, woods, and other retired places. 'The very existence of any person in the barracks who had the smallest notion of the importance of religion was quite unsuspected by me,' writes Mrs. Sherwood in her Autobiography.[32][258] 'I am not severe when I assert that at that time there really was not one in the higher ranks in the regiment who had courage enough to come forward and say, "I think it right, in this distant land, to do, as it regards religion, what I have been accustomed to do at home."' At Berhampore, the chaplain, Mr. Parson, began that good work in the 53rd which Martyn and Corrie afterwards carried on. When it continued the voyage up the Ganges, after a season, by Dinapore to Cawnpore, Mr. Parson gave the Sherwoods a letter of introduction to Martyn, then about to leave Dinapore. To this fact we owe the fullest and the brightest glimpses that we get of Henry Martyn, from the outside, all through his career. We are enabled to supplement the abasing self-revelation of his nature before God, as recorded in his *Journal*, by the picture of his daily life, drawn by a woman of keen sympathy and some shrewdness.

The moment the boat anchored at Dinapore Mr. Sherwood set out on foot to present his letter. He found the chaplain in the smaller square, at some distance, in a 'sort of church-like abode with little furniture, the rooms wide and high, with many vast doorways, having their green jalousied doors, and long verandahs encompassing two sides of the quarters.'

Mr. Martyn received Mr. Sherwood not as a stranger, but as a brother,—the child of the same father. As the sun was already low, he must needs walk back with him to see me. I perfectly remember the figure of that simple-hearted and holy young man, when he entered our budgerow. He was dressed in white, and looked very pale, which, however, was nothing singular in India; his hair, a light brown, was raised from his forehead, which was a remarkably fine one. His features were not regular, but the expression was so luminous, so intellectual, so affectionate, so beaming with Divine charity, that no one could have looked at his features, and thought of their[259] shape or form,—the out-beaming of his soul would absorb the attention of every observer. There was a very decided air, too, of the gentleman about Mr. Martyn, and a perfection of manners which, from his extreme attention to all minute civilities, might seem almost inconsistent with the general bent of his thoughts to the most serious subjects. He was as remarkable for ease as for cheerfulness, and in these particulars his *Journal* does not give a graphic account of this blessed child of God. I was much pleased at the first sight of Mr. Martyn. I had heard much of him from Mr. Parson; but I had no anticipation of his hereafter becoming so distinguished as he subsequently did. And if I anticipated it little, he, I am sure, anticipated it less; for he was one of the humblest of men.

Mr. Martyn invited us to visit him at his quarters at Dinapore, and we agreed to accept his invitation the next day. Mr. Martyn's house was destitute of every comfort, though he had multitudes of people about him. I had been troubled with a pain in my face, and there was not such a thing as a pillow in the house. I could not find anything to lay my head on at night but a bolster stuffed as hard as a pin-cushion. We had not, as is usual in India, brought our own bedding from the boats. Our kind friend had given us his own room; but I could get no rest during the two nights of my remaining there, from the pain in my face, which was irritated by the bolster; but during each day, however, there was much for the mind to feed upon with delight. After breakfast Mr. Martyn had family prayers, which he commenced by singing a hymn. He had a rich, deep voice, and a fine taste for vocal music. After singing, he read a chapter, explained parts of it, and prayed extempore. Afterwards he withdrew to his studies and translations. The evening was finished with another hymn, Scripture reading, and prayers. The conversion of the natives and the building up of the kingdom of Christ were the great objects for which alone that child of God seemed to exist.[260]

He believed that he saw the glimmering of this day in the exertions then making in Europe for the diffusion of the Scriptures and the sending forth of missionaries. Influenced by the belief that man's ministry was the instrumentality which, by the Holy Spirit, would be made effectual to the work, we found him labouring beyond his strength, and doing all in his power to excite other persons to use the same exertions.

Henry Martyn was one of the very few persons whom I have ever met who appeared never to be drawn away from one leading and prevailing object of interest, and that object was the promotion of religion. He did not appear like one who felt the necessity of contending with the world, and denying himself its delights, but rather as one who was unconscious of the existence of any attractions in the world, or of any delights which were worthy of his notice. When he relaxed from his labours in the presence of his friends, it was to play and laugh like an innocent, happy child, more especially if children were present to play and laugh with him. In my Indian Journal I find this remark: 'Mr. Martyn is one of the most pleasing, mild, and heavenly-minded men, walking in this turbulent world with peace in his mind, and charity in his heart.'

As the regiment was passing Chunar, after a night in 'the polluted air' of Benares, the Sherwoods were met by a boat with fresh bread and vegetables from Corrie. On their arrival at Cawnpore, Mrs. Sherwood at once opened two classes for the 'great boys' and 'elder girls.' Many of the former died in a few years, and not a few of the latter married officers above their own birth. Such were the conditions of military life in India at that time, notwithstanding the Calcutta Orphan Schools which David Brown had first gone out to India to organise; for Henry Lawrence and his noble wife, Honoria, with their Military Orphan Asylums in the hills, belonged to a later generation.[261]

When first ordered to Cawnpore, in the hottest months of 1809, Henry Martyn resolved to apply to the Military Board for permission to delay his departure till the rainy season. But, though even then wasted by consumption and ceaseless toil, and tempted to spend the dreary months with the beloved Corrie at Chunar, as he might well have done under the customary rules, he could not linger when duty called. Had he not resolved to 'burn out' his life? So, deluding himself by the intention to 'stay a little longer to recruit' at Chunar, should he suffer from the heat, he set off in the middle of April in a palanquin by Arrah, afterwards the scene of a heroic defence in the great Mutiny; Buxar, where a battle had been fought not long before, and Ghazipore, seat of the opium manufacture, like Patna. Sabat was sent on in a budgerow, with his wife Ameena and the baggage. This is Martyn's account, to Brown, of the voyage above Chunar:

Cawnpore: May 3, 1809.

I transported myself with such rapidity to this place that I had nearly transported myself out of the world. From Dinapore to Chunar all was well, but from Allahabad to that place I was obliged to travel two days and nights without intermission, the hot winds blowing like fire from a furnace. Two days after my arrival the fever which had been kindling in my blood broke out, and last night I fainted repeatedly. But a gracious God has again interposed to save my life; to-day I feel well again. Where Sabat is I do not know. I have heard nothing of him since leaving Dinapore. Corrie is well, but it is grievous to see him chained to a rock with a few half-dead invalids, when so many stations—amongst others, the one I have left—are destitute....

I do not like this place at all. There is no church, not so much as the fly of a tent; what to do I know not[262] except to address Lord Minto in a private letter. Mr. (Charles) Grant, who is anxious that we should labour principally for the present among the Europeans, ought, I think, to help us with a house. I mean to write to Mr. Simeon about this.

I feel a little uncomfortable at being so much farther removed from Calcutta. At Dinapore I had friends on both sides of me, and correspondence with you was quick: here I seem cut off from the world. Alas! how dependent is my heart upon the creature still. I am ordered to seal up.—Yours affectionately ever,

H. MARTYN.

This is Mrs. Sherwood's description of his arrival:

On May 30 the Rev. Henry Martyn arrived at our bungalow. The former chaplain had proceeded to the presidency, and we were so highly favoured as to have Mr. Martyn appointed in his place. I am not aware whether we expected him, but certainly not at the time when he did appear. It was in the morning, and we were situated as above described, the desert winds blowing like fire without, when we suddenly heard the quick steps of many bearers. Mr. Sherwood ran out to the leeward of the house, and exclaimed, 'Mr. Martyn!' The next moment I saw him leading in that excellent man, and saw our visitor, a moment afterwards, fall down in a fainting fit. He had travelled in a palanquin from Dinapore, and the first part of the way he moved only by night. But between Cawnpore and Allahabad, being a hundred and thirty miles, there is no resting-place, and he was compelled for two days and two nights to journey on in his palanquin, exposed to the raging heat of a fiery wind. He arrived, therefore, quite exhausted, and actually under the influence of fever. There was not another family in Cawnpore except ours to which he could have gone with pleasure; not because any family would have denied shelter to a countryman in such a condition, but, alas! they[263] were only Christians in name. In his fainting state Mr. Martyn could not have retired to the sleeping-room which we caused to be prepared immediately for him, because we had no means of cooling any sleeping-room so thoroughly as we could the hall. We, therefore, had a couch set for him in the hall. There he was laid, and very ill he was for a day or two. The hot winds left us, and we had a close, suffocating calm. Mr. Martyn could not lift his head from the couch. In our bungalow, when shut up as close as it could be, we could not get the thermometer under $96°$, though the punkah was constantly going. When Mr. Martyn got a little better he became very cheerful, and seemed quite happy with us all about him. He commonly lay on his couch in the hall during the morning, with many books near to his hand, and amongst these always a Hebrew Bible and a Greek Testament. Soon, very soon, he began to talk to me of what was passing in his mind, calling to me at my table to tell me his thoughts. He was studying the Hebrew characters, having an idea, which I believe is not a new one, that these characters contain the elements of all things, though I have reason to suppose he could not make them out at all to his satisfaction; but whenever anything occurred to him he must needs make it known to me.

He was much engaged also with another subject, into which I was more capable of entering. It was his opinion that, if the Hindus could be persuaded that all nations are made of one blood, to dwell upon the face of the earth, and if they could be shown how each nation is connected by its descent from the sons and grandsons of Noah with other nations existing upon the globe, it would be a means of breaking down, or at least of loosening, that wall of separation which they have set up between themselves and all other people. With this view Mr. Martyn was endeavouring to trace up the various leading families of the earth to their great progenitors; and so much pleased was I[264] with what he said on this subject, that I immediately committed all I could remember to paper, and founded thereupon a system of historical instruction which I ever afterwards used with my children. Mr. Martyn, like myself at this time, was often perplexed and dismayed at the workings of his own heart, yet, perhaps, not discerning a hundredth part of the depth of the depravity of his own nature, the character of which is summed up in Holy Writ in these two words—'utterly unclean.' He felt this the more strongly because he partook also of that new nature 'which sinneth not.' It was in the workings and actings of that nature that his character shone so pre-eminently as it did amid a dark and unbelieving society, such as was ours then at Cawnpore.

In a very few days he had discerned the sweet qualities of the orphan Annie, and had so encouraged her to come about him that she drew her chair, and her table, and her green box to the vicinity of his couch. She showed him her verses, and consulted him about the adoption of more passages into the number of her favourites. Annie had a particular delight in all the pastoral views given in Scripture of our Saviour and of His Church; and when Mr. Martyn showed her this beautiful passage, 'Feed Thy people with Thy rod, the flock of Thine heritage, which dwell solitarily in the wood, in the midst of Carmel' (Micah vii. 14), she was as pleased with this passage as if she had made some wonderful acquisition. What could have been more beautiful than to see the Senior Wrangler and the almost infant Annie thus conversing together, whilst the elder seemed to be in no ways conscious of any condescension in bringing down his mind to the level of the child's? Such are the beautiful influences of the Divine Spirit, which, whilst they depress the high places of human pride, exalt the lowly valleys.

When Mr. Martyn lost the worst symptoms of his illness he used to sing a great deal. He had an uncommonly|265| fine voice and fine ear; he could sing many fine chants, and a vast variety of hymns and psalms. He would insist upon it that I should sing with him, and he taught me many tunes, all of which were afterwards brought into requisition; and when fatigued himself, he made me sit by his couch and practise these hymns. He would listen to my singing, which was altogether very unscientific, for hours together, and he was constantly requiring me to go on, even when I was tired. The tunes he taught me, no doubt, reminded him of England, and of scenes and friends no longer seen. The more simple the style of singing, the more it probably answered his purpose.

As soon as Mr. Martyn could in any way exert himself, he made acquaintance with some of the pious men of the regiment (the same poor men whom I have mentioned before, who used to meet in ravines, in huts, in woods, and in every wild and secret place they could find, to read, and pray, and sing); and he invited them to come to him in our house, Mr. Sherwood making no objection. The time first fixed was an evening after parade, and in consequence they all appeared at the appointed hour, each carrying their mora (a low seat), and their books tied up in pocket-handkerchiefs. In this very unmilitary fashion they were all met in a body by some officers. It was with some difficulty that Mr. Sherwood could divert the storm of displeasure which had well-nigh burst upon them on the occasion. Had they been all found intoxicated and fighting, they would have created less anger from those who loved not religion. How truly is it said that 'the children of this world are wiser in their generation than the children of light.' Notwithstanding this unfortunate *contretemps*, these poor good men were received by Mr. Martyn in his own apartment; and a most joyful meeting he had with them. We did not join the party, but we heard them singing and praying, and the sound was very sweet. Mr. Martyn then promised them that when he had|266| got a house he would set aside a room for them, where they might come every evening, adding he would meet them himself twice in the week. When these assemblies were sanctioned by our ever kind Colonel Mawby, and all difficulties, in short, overcome, many who had been the most zealous under persecution fell quite away, and never returned. How can we account for these things? Many, however, remained steadfast under evil report as well as good report, and died, as they had lived, in simple and pure faith.

I must not omit another anecdote of Mr. Martyn, which amused us much at the time, after we had recovered the alarm attending it. The salary of a chaplain is large, and Mr. Martyn had not drawn his for so long a time, that the sum amounted perhaps to some hundreds. He was to receive it from the collector at Cawnpore. Accordingly he one morning sent a note for the amount, confiding the note to the care of a common coolie, a porter of low caste, generally a very poor man. This man went off, unknown to Mr. Sherwood and myself, early in the morning. The day passed, the evening came, and no coolie arrived. At length Mr. Martyn said in a quiet voice to us, 'The coolie does not come with my money. I was thinking this morning how rich I should be; and, now, I should not wonder in the least if he has not run off, and taken my treasure with him.' 'What!' we exclaimed, 'surely you have not sent a common coolie for your pay?' 'I have,' he replied. Of course we could not expect that it would ever arrive safe; for it would be paid in silver, and delivered to the man in cotton bags. Soon afterwards, however, it did arrive—a circumstance at which we all greatly marvelled.

Cawnpore, of which Henry Martyn was chaplain for the next two years, till disease drove him from it, was the worst station to which he could have been sent. The district, consisting of clay uplands on the Doab between|267| the Ganges and the Jumna rivers, which unite below at Allahabad, was at that time a comparatively desolate tract, swept by the hot winds, and always the first to suffer from drought. The great famine of 1837 afterwards so destroyed its unhappy peasantry and labourers, that the British Government made its county town one of the two terminals of the great Ganges canal, which the Marquis of Dalhousie opened, and irrigated the district by four branches with their distributing channels. Even then, and to this day, Cawnpore has not ceased to be a repulsive station. Its leather factories and cotton mills do not render it less so, nor the memory of the five massacres of British officers, their wives and children, by the infamous Nana Dhoondoo Panth, which still seems to cover it as with a pall, notwithstanding the gardens and the marble screen inclosing the figure of the Angel of the Resurrection with the palm of victory above the Massacre Well. The people of the town at least have always been disagreeable, from Hindu discontent and Mohammedan sulkiness. The British cantonment used to be at Bilgram, on the opposite bank, in the territory of Oudh. Well might Martyn write of such a station as Cawnpore: 'I do not like this place at all,' although he then enjoyed the social ministrations of the Sherwoods, and was constant in his own service to the Master among British and natives alike, and at his desk in translation work.

The first use which the chaplain made of his pay was this, according to Mrs. Sherwood: 'Being persuaded by some black man, he bought one of the most undesirable houses, to all appearance, which he could have chosen.' But he had chosen wisely for his daily duties of translation and preaching to the natives.[268]

Mr. Martyn's house was a bungalow situated between the Sepoy Parade and the Artillery Barracks, but behind that range of principal bungalows which face the Parade. The approach to the dwelling was called the Compound, along an avenue of palm trees and aloes. A more stiff, funeral avenue can hardly be imagined, unless it might be that one of noted sphynxes which I have read of as the approach to a ruined Egyptian temple. At the end of this avenue were two bungalows, connected by a long passage. These bungalows were low, and the rooms small. The garden was prettily laid out with flowering shrubs and tall trees; in the centre was a wide space, which at some seasons was green, and a *chabootra*, or raised platform of chunam (lime), of great extent, was placed in the middle of this space. A vast number and variety of huts and sheds formed one boundary of the compound; these were concealed by the shrubs. But who would venture to give any account of the heterogeneous population which occupied these buildings? For, besides the usual complement of servants found in and about the houses of persons of a certain rank in India, we must add to Mr. Martyn's household a multitude of pundits, moonshis, schoolmasters, and poor nominal Christians, who hung about him because there was no other to give them a handful of rice for their daily maintenance; and most strange was the murmur which proceeded at times from this ill-assorted and discordant multitude. Mr. Martyn occupied the largest of the two bungalows. He had given up the least to the wife of Sabat, that wild man of the desert whose extraordinary history has made so much noise in the Christian world.

It was a burning evening in June, when after sunset I accompanied Mr. Sherwood to Mr. Martyn's bungalow, and saw for the first time its avenue of palms and aloes. We were conducted to the *chabootra*, where the company was already assembled; there was no lady but myself. This[269] *chabootra* was many feet square, and chairs were set for the guests. A more heterogeneous assembly surely had not often met, and seldom, I believe, were more languages in requisition in so small a party. Besides Mr. Martyn and ourselves, there was no one present who could speak English. But let me introduce each individual separately. Every feature in the large disk of Sabat's face was what we should call exaggerated. His eyebrows were arched, black, and strongly pencilled; his eyes dark and round, and from time to time flashing with unsubdued emotion, and ready to kindle into flame on the most trifling occasion. His nose was high, his mouth wide, his teeth large, and looked white in contrast with his bronzed complexion and fierce black mustachios. He was a large and powerful man, and generally wore a skull-cap of rich shawling, or embroidered silk, with circular flaps of the same hanging over each ear. His large, tawny throat and neck had no other covering than that afforded by his beard, which was black. His attire was a kind of jacket of silk, with long sleeves, fastened by a girclle, or girdle, about his loins, to which was appended a jewelled dirk. He wore loose trousers, and embroidered shoes turned up at the toes. In the cold season he threw over this a wrapper lined with fur, and when it was warmer the fur was changed for silk. When to this costume is added ear-rings, and sometimes a golden chain, the Arab stands before you in his complete state of Oriental dandyism. This son of the desert never sat in a chair without contriving to tuck up his legs under him on the seat, in attitude very like a tailor on his board. The only languages which he was able to speak were Persian, Arabic, and a very little bad Hindustani; but what was wanting in the words of this man was more than made up by the loudness with which he uttered them, for he had a voice like rolling thunder. When it is understood that loud utterance is considered as an ingredient of respect in the East, we cannot suppose that one who had been much in[270] native courts should think it necessary to modulate his voice in the presence of the English Sahib-log.[33][271]

The second of Mr. Martyn's guests, whom I must introduce as being not a whit behind Sabat in his own opinion of himself, was the Padre Julius Cæsar, an Italian monk of the order of the Jesuits, a worthy disciple of Ignatius Loyola. Mr. Martyn had become acquainted with him at Patna, where the Italian priest was not less zealous and active in making proselytes than the Company's chaplain, and probably much more wise and subtle in his movements than the latter. The Jesuit was a handsome young man, and dressed in the complete costume of the monk, with his little skull-cap, his flowing robes, and his cord. The materials, however, of his dress were very rich; his robe was of the finest purple satin, and his cord of twisted silk, and his rosary of costly stones, whilst his air and manner were extremely elegant. He spoke French fluently, and there Mr. Sherwood was at home with him, but his native language was Italian. His conversation with Mr. Martyn was carried on partly in Latin and partly in Italian. A third guest was a learned native of India, in his full and handsome Hindustani costume; and a fourth[272] a little, thin, copper-coloured, half-caste Bengali gentleman, in white nankeen, who spoke only Bengali. Mr. Sherwood made a fifth, in his scarlet and gold uniform; myself, the only lady, was the sixth; and add our host, Mr. Martyn, in his clerical black silk coat, and there is our party. Most assuredly I never listened to such a confusion of tongues before or since. Such a noisy, perplexing Babel can scarcely be imagined. Everyone who had acquired his views of politeness in Eastern society was shouting at the top of his voice, as if he had lost his fellow in a wood; and no less than eight languages were in constant request, viz. English, French, Italian, Arabic, Persian, Hindustani, Bengali, and Latin.

In order to lengthen out the pleasures of the evening, we were scarcely seated before good Mr. Martyn recollected that he had heard me say that I liked a certain sort of little mutton pattie, which the natives made particularly well; so, without thinking how long it might take to make these same patties, he called to a servant to give orders that mutton patties should be added to the supper. I heard the order, but never dreamed that perhaps the mutton might not be in the house. The consequence of this order was that we sat on the *chabootra* till it was quite dark, and till I was utterly weary with the confusion. No one who has not been in or near the tropics can have an idea of the glorious appearance of the heavens in these regions, and the brilliancy of the star-lit nights, at Cawnpore. Mr. Martyn used often to show me the pole-star, just above the line of the horizon; and I have seen the moon, when almost new, looking like a ball of ebony in a silver cup. Who can, therefore, be surprised that the science of astronomy should first have been pursued by the shepherds who watched their flocks by night in the plains of the South? When the mutton patties were ready, I was handed by Mr. Martyn into the hall of the bungalow. Mr. Martyn took the top of the table, and[273] Sabat perched himself on a chair at the bottom. I think it was on this day, when at table, Sabat was telling some of his own adventures to Mr. Martyn, in Persian, which the latter interpreted to Mr. Sherwood and myself, that the wild Arab asserted that there were in Tartary and Arabia many persons converted to Christianity, and that many had given up their lives for the faith. He professed to be himself acquainted with two of these, besides Abdallah. 'One,' he said, 'was a relation of his own.' But he gave but small proof of this man's sincerity. This convert, if such he was, drew the attention of the priests by a total neglect of all forms; and this was the more remarkable on account of the multiplied forms of Islam; for at the wonted hour of prayer a true Mussulman must kneel down and pray in the middle of a street, or between the courses of a feast, nay, even at the moment when perhaps his hands might be reeking with a brother's blood. This relative of Sabat's, however, was, as he remarked, observed to neglect all forms, and he was called before the heads of his tribe, and required to say wherefore he was guilty of this offence. His answer was, 'It is nothing.' He proceeded to express himself as if he doubted the very existence of a God. The seniors of the tribe told him that it would be better for him to be a Christian than an atheist; adding, therefore, 'If you do not believe in our prophet you must be a Christian;' for they wisely accounted that no man but a fool could be without some religion. The man's reply was, that he thought the Christian's a better religion than that of Mahomet; the consequence of which declaration was that they stoned him until he died. The other example which Sabat gave us was of a boy in Baghdad, who was converted by an Armenian, and endeavoured to escape, but was pursued, seized, and offered pardon if he would recant; but he was preserved in steadfastness to the truth, and preferred death to returning to Mahometanism. His life was required of him.[274]

From the time Mr. Martyn left our house he was in the constant habit of supping with us two or three times a week, and he used to come on horseback, with the sais running by his side. He sat his horse as if he were not quite aware that he was on horseback, and he generally wore his coat as if it were falling from his shoulders. When he dismounted, his favourite place was in the verandah, with a book, till we came in from our airing. And when we returned many a sweet and long discourse we had, whilst waiting for our dinner or supper. Mr. Martyn often looked up to the starry heavens, and spoke of those glorious worlds of which we know so little now, but of which we hope to know so much hereafter. Often we turned from the contemplation of these to the consideration of the smallness, and apparent diminutiveness in creation, of our own little globe, and of the exceeding love of the Father, who so cared for its inhabitants that He sent His Son to redeem them.

On the occasion of the baptism of my second Lucy, never can I forget the solemn manner with which Mr. Martyn went through the service, or the beautiful and earnest blessing he implored for my baby, when he took her into his arms after the service was concluded. I still fancy I see that child of God as he looked down tenderly on the gentle babe, and then looked upwards, asking of his God that grace and mercy for the infant which he truly accounted as the only gift which parents ought to desire. This babe, in infancy, had so peculiar a gentleness of aspect, that Mr. Martyn always called her Serena.

Little was spoken of at Mr. Martyn's table but of various plans for advancing the triumphs of Christianity. Among the plans adopted, Mr. Martyn had, first at Dinapore and then at Cawnpore, established one or two schools for children of the natives of the lower caste. His plan was to hire a native schoolmaster, generally a Mussulman, to appoint him a place, and to pay him an anna[275] (1½d.) a head for each boy whom he could induce to attend school. These boys the master was to teach to write and read. It was Mr. Martyn's great aim, and, indeed, the sole end of his exertions, to get Christian books into the school. As no mention was ever made of proselytism, there was never any difficulty found in introducing even portions of the Scripture itself, more especially portions of the Old Testament, to the attention of the children. The books of Moses are always very acceptable to a Mussulman, and Genesis is particularly interesting to the Hindus. Mr. Martyn's first school at Cawnpore was located in a long shed, which was on the side of the cavalry lines. It was the first school of the kind I ever saw. The master sat at one end, like a tailor, on the dusty floor; and along under the shed sat the scholars, a pack of little urchins, with no other clothes on than a skull-cap and a piece of cloth round the loins. These little ones squatted, like their master, in the sand. They had wooden imitations of slates in their hands, on which, having first written their lessons with chalk, they recited them, *à pleine gorge*, as the French would say, being sure to raise their voices on the approach of any European or native of note. Now, Cawnpore is about one of the most dusty places in the world. The Sepoy lines are the most dusty part of Cawnpore; and as the little urchins are always well greased, either with cocoanut oil or, in failure thereof, with rancid mustard oil, whenever there was the slightest breath of air they always looked as if they had been powdered all over with brown powder. But what did this signify? They would have been equally dusty in their own huts. In these schools they were in the way of getting a few ideas; at all events, they often got so far as to be able to copy a verse on their wooden slates. Afterwards they committed to memory what they had written. Who that has ever heard it can forget the sounds of the various notes with which these little people intonated[276] their 'Aleph Zubbur ah—Zair a—Paiche oh,' as they waved backwards and forwards in their recitations? Or who can forget the vacant self-importance of the schoolmaster, who was generally a long-bearded, dry old man, who had no other means of proving his superiority over the scholars but making more noise than even they could do? Such a scene, indeed, could not be forgotten; but would it not require great faith to expect anything green to spring from a soil so dry? But this faith was not wanting to the Christians then in India.

Besides the 53rd Regiment, the Cavalry Corps called in those days the 8th Light Dragoons, and six companies of Artillery, were stationed at Cawnpore. At the first parade service, on May 15, 1809, 'two officers dropped down and some of the men. They wondered how I could go through the fatigue,' wrote their new chaplain, not many days after his nearly fatal palanquin journey from Chunar. His voice even reached the men at the other end of the square which they had formed. Above a hundred men were in hospital, a daily congregation. Every night about a dozen of the soldiers met with him in the house. Not only the men but the officers were privately rebuked by him for swearing. Of the General he writes: 'He has never been very cordial, and now he is likely to be less so; though it was done in the gentlest way, he did not seem to like it. Were it not to become all things to all men in order to save some, I should never trouble them with my company. But how then should I be like Christ? I have been almost the whole morning engaged in a good-humoured dispute with Mrs. P., who, in an instant after my introduction to her, opened all her guns of wit and eloquence against me for attempting to convert the Brahmans.' A little later he writes of a dinner at the brigade-major's with the chief[277] persons of the station: 'I could gain no attention while saying grace; and the moment the ladies withdrew the conversation took such a turn that I was obliged to make a hasty retreat. Oh! the mercy to have escaped their evil ways.'

The year was one of alarms of war, from which the history of our Indian Empire can rarely be free, surrounded as it is by a ring-fence of frontier tribes and often aggressive States. But in those days the great internal conflicts for the consolidation of our power, and the peace and prosperity of peoples exposed to anarchy for centuries, were still being waged. Marathas, Sikhs, and Goorkhas had all to be pacified in 1809. Now the infantry were being sent to the conquest of Bundlekhund and difficult siege of the fortress of Kalinjar, as old as the Mahabharat Epic in which it is mentioned. Now the artillery were under orders to march to Lodiana to check Ranjeet Singh. Now the cavalry were sent off to the, at first, fatal chase of the Goorkhas by Gillespie. Thus it was that their ever-careful chaplain sought to prepare them for the issue:

October 20.—Spoke to my men on preparation for the Lord's Supper, and endeavoured to prepare myself for the ordinance, by considering my former life of sin, and all my unfaithfulness since my call to the Gospel. My heart was, as usual, insensible for a long time, but at last a gracious God made me feel some compunction, and then my feelings were such as I would wish they always were. I resolved at the time that it should be my special labour every day to obtain, and hold fast, this humbling view of my own depravity.

October 22. (Sunday.)—Preached at sunrise to the 53rd, on Acts xxviii. 29. At ten, about sixteen of the regiment, with Mr. and Mrs. Sherwood and Sabat, met in my[278]bungalow, where, after a short discourse on 'Behold the Lamb of God,' we commemorated the death of the Lord. It was the happiest season I have yet had at the Lord's Table, though my peace and pleasure were not unalloyed; the rest of the day I felt weak in body, but calm in mind, and rather spiritual; at night I spoke to the men on Rev. xxii. 2; the number was double; afterwards had some conversation on eternal things, but had reason to groan at the hollow-heartedness and coldness with which I do my best works.

November 18.—At night I took leave of my beloved Church previous to their departure for Bundlekhund with their regiment. I spoke to them from Gen. xxviii: 'I will be with thee in all places whithersoever thou goest,' etc. The poor men were much affected; they gave me their wills and watches.

November 19. (Sunday.)—Preached at sunrise to the dragoons, on John i. 17: 'The law was given by Moses.' At eleven at head-quarters, on Rom. iii. 19.

Nowhere are eucharistic seasons of communion so precious as in exile, and especially in the isolation of a tropical station. Not unfrequently in India, Christian people, far separated from any ordained minister, and about to part from each other, are compelled, by loving obedience to the Lord, to meet thus together. But what joy it must have been to have been ministered to at such times by one of Henry Martyn's consecrated saintliness! Mrs. Sherwood lingers over her description of that Cawnpore service of October 22, 1809—the long inner verandah of the house, where daily prayer was wont to be made, shut in by lofty doors of green lattice-work; the table, with the white cloth and all things requisite, at one end; hassocks on which to kneel, and a high form in front of the table;[279] all 'decent and in good order, according to the forms of the Church of England.' Still there was no church building. His first parade service in the hot winds brought on fever, so that he proposed to ask for the billiard-room, 'which is better than the ball-room,' but in vain. His next service was in the riding-school, but 'the effluvium was such as would please only the knights of the turf. What must the Mohammedans think of us? Well may they call us "dogs," when even in Divine worship we choose to kennel ourselves in such places.' The General delayed to forward to Government the proposal for a church.

Henry Martyn's missionary work among the natives became greatly extended at Cawnpore, as his scrupulous conscience and delicate scholarship allowed him to use in public the colloquial Hindustani, and in conversation the more classical Persian. To Corrie he wrote, five months after his arrival there:

What will friends at home think of Martyn and Corrie? They went out full of zeal, but, behold! what are they doing? Where are their converts? They talked of the banyan-tree before they went out; but now they seem to prefer a snug bungalow to field-preaching. I fear I should look a little silly if I were to go home just at this time; but more because I should not be able to make them understand the state of things than because my conscience condemns me. Brother, what can you do? If you itinerate like a European, you will only frighten the people; if as a native, you will be dead in one year. Yet the latter mode pleases me, and nothing would give me greater pleasure than so to live, with the prospect of being able to hold out a few years.

Again, to an old Cambridge friend:

[280]

November, 1809.—Respecting my heart, about which you ask, I must acknowledge that H. Martyn's heart at Dinapore is the same as H. Martyn's heart at Cambridge. The tenor of my prayer is nearly the same, except on one subject, the conversion of the heathen. At a distance from the scene of action, and trusting too much to the highly-coloured description of missionaries, my heart used to expand with rapture at the hope of seeing thousands of the natives melting under the Word as soon as it should be preached to them. Here I am called to exercise faith—that so it shall one day be. My former feelings on this subject were more agreeable, and at the same time more according with the truth; for if we believe the prophets, the scenes that time shall unfold, 'though surpassing fable, are yet true.' While I write, hope and joy spring up in my mind. Yes, it shall be; yonder stream of Ganges shall one day roll through tracts adorned with Christian churches, and cultivated by Christian husbandmen, and the holy hymn be heard beneath the shade of the tamarind. All things are working together to bring on the day, and my part in the blessed plan, though not at first exactly consonant to my wishes, is, I believe, appointed me by God. To translate the Word of God is a work of more lasting benefit than my preaching would be. But, besides that, I am sorry to say that my strength for public preaching is almost gone. My ministrations among the Europeans at this station have injured my lungs, and I am now obliged to lie by except on the Sabbath days, and once or twice in the week.... However, I am sufficiently aware of my important relations to the natives, and am determined not to strain myself any more for the Europeans. This rainy season has tried my constitution severely. The first attack was with spasms, under which I fainted. The second was a fever, from which a change of air, under God, recovered me. There is something in the air at the close of the rains so unfavourable, that public speaking at that time is a violent strain upon the whole [281] body. Corrie passed down a few weeks ago to receive his sister. We enjoyed much refreshing communion in prayer and conversation on our dear friends at and near Cambridge, and found peculiar pleasure in the minutest circumstances we could recollect about you all.

At Cawnpore, in front of his house, he began his wonderful preaching to the native beggars and ascetics of all kinds, Hindoo *jogees* and Mohammedan *fakeers*, the blind and the deaf, the maimed and the halt, the diseased and the dying, the impostor and the truly needy. These classes had soon found out the sympathetic padre-sahib, and to secure peace he seems to have organised a weekly dole of an anna each or of rice.

He wrote to Corrie:

I feel unhappy, not because I do nothing, but because I am not willing to do my duty. The flesh must be mortified, and I am reluctant to take up the cross. Sabat said to me yesterday, 'Your beggars are come: why do not you preach to them? It is your duty.' I made excuses; but why do not I preach to them? My carnal spirit says that I have been preaching a long time without success to my servants, who are used to my tongue; what can I expect from them—the very dregs of the people? But the true cause is shame: I am afraid of exposing myself to the contempt of Sabat, my servants, and the mob, by attempting to speak in a language which I do not speak well. To-day in prayer, one consideration has been made of some power in overcoming this shameful backwardness:—these people, if I neglect to speak to them, will give me a look at the last day which may fill me with horror. Alas! brother, where is my zeal?

December 17. (Sunday.)—Preached to H.M. Light Dragoons on Rev. iii. 20:[282]'Behold, I stand at the door and knock,' etc. There was great attention. In the afternoon the beggars came, to the number of above four hundred, and, by the help of God, I determined to preach to them, though I felt as if I were leading to execution. I stood upon the *chabootra* in front of which they were collected.

To Corrie he thus described his talks with his 'congregation of the poor':

I went without fear, trusting to myself, and not to the Lord, and accordingly I was put to shame—that is, I did not read half as well as the preceding days. I shuffled and stammered, and indeed I am persuaded that there were many sentences the poor things did not understand at all. I spoke of the dry land, rivers, etc.; here I mentioned Gunga,'a good river,' but there were others as good. God loves Hindus, but does He not love others also? He gave them a good river, but to others as good. All are alike before God. This was received with applause. On the work of the fourth day, 'Thus sun and moon are lamps. Shall I worship a candle in my hand? As a candle in the house, so is the sun in the sky.' Applause from the Mohammedans. There were also hisses, but whether these betokened displeasure against me or the worship of the sun I do not know. I then charged them to worship Gunga and sun and moon no more, but the honour they used to give to them, henceforward to give to God their Maker. Who knows but even this was a blow struck, at least a branch lopped from the tree of heathenism? The number was about 550. You need not be deterred, dear brother, if this simple way of teaching do any good.

Again:

I spoke on the corruption of human nature, 'The Lord saw that every imagination,' etc. In the application I said,[283] 'Hence all outward works are useless while the heart remains in this state. You may wash in Gunga, but the heart is not washed.' Some old men shook their heads, in much the same way as we do when seriously affected with any truth. The number was about seven hundred. The servants told me it was nonsense to give them all rice, as they were not all poor; hundreds of them are working people; among them was a whole row of Brahmins. I spoke to them about the Flood; this was interesting, as they were very attentive, and at the end said, 'Shabash wa wa' (Well said).

Mrs. Sherwood pictures the scene after an almost pathetic fashion:

We went often on the Sunday evenings to hear the addresses of Mr. Martyn to the assembly of mendicants, and we generally stood behind him. On these occasions we had to make our way through a dense crowd, with a temperature often rising above 92°, whilst the sun poured its burning rays upon us through a lurid haze of dust. Frightful were the objects which usually met our eyes in this crowd: so many monstrous and diseased limbs, and hideous faces, were displayed before us, and pushed forward for our inspection, that I have often made my way to the *chabootra*with my eyes shut, whilst Mr. Sherwood led me. On reaching the platform I was surrounded by our own people, and yet even there I scarcely dared to look about me. I still imagine that I hear the calm, distinct, and musical tones of Henry Martyn, as he stood raised above the people, endeavouring, by showing the purity of the Divine law, to convince the unbelievers that by their works they were all condemned; and that this was the case of every man of the offspring of Adam, and they therefore needed a Saviour who was both willing and able to redeem them. From time to time low murmurs and curses would arise in the distance, and then roll forward, till they became so loud as to drown the voice of this pious one, generally concluding with hissings and fierce cries.[284] But when the storm passed away, again might he be heard going on where he had left off, in the same calm, steadfast tone, as if he were incapable of irritation from the interruption. Mr. Martyn himself assisted in giving each person his *pice* (copper) after the address was concluded; and when he withdrew to his bungalow I have seen him drop, almost fainting, on a sofa, for he had, as he often said, even at that time, a slow inflammation burning in his chest, and one which he knew must eventually terminate his existence. In consequence of this he was usually in much pain after any exertion of speaking.

No dreams nor visions excited in the delirium of a raging fever can surpass these realities. These devotees vary in age and appearance: they are young and old, male and female, bloated and wizened, tall and short, athletic and feeble; some clothed with abominable rags; some nearly without clothes; some plastered with mud and cow-dung; others with matted, uncombed locks streaming down to their heels; others with heads bald or scabby, every countenance being hard and fixed, as it were, by the continual indulgence of bad passions, the features having become exaggerated, and the lips blackened with tobacco, or blood-red with the juice of the henna. But these and such as these form only the general mass of the people; there are among them still more distinguished monsters. One little man generally comes in a small cart drawn by a bullock; his body and limbs are so shrivelled as to give, with his black skin and large head, the appearance of a gigantic frog. Another has his arm fixed above his head, the nail of the thumb piercing through the palm of the hand; another, and a very large man, has his ribs and the bones of his face externally traced with white chalk, which, striking the eye in relief above the dark skin, makes him appear, as he approaches, like a moving skeleton. When Mr. Martyn collected these people he was most carefully watched by the British authorities.

[285]

Shall anyone say that the missionary chaplain's eighteen months' work among this mixed multitude of the poor and the dishonest was as vain as he himself, in his humility, feared that it was? 'Greater works' than His own were what the Lord of Glory, who did like service to man in the Syria of that day, promised to His believing followers.

On the wall which enclosed his compound was a kiosk, from which some young Mussulman idlers used to look down on the preacher, as they smoked their hookahs and sipped their sherbet. One Sunday, determined to hear as well as see, that they might the more evidently scoff, they made their way through the crowd, and with the deepest scorn took their place in the very front. They listened in a critical temper, made remarks on what they heard, and returned to the kiosk. But there was one who no longer joined in their jeering. Sheikh Saleh, born at Delhi, Persian and Arabic moonshi of Lucknow, then keeper of the King of Oudh's jewels, was a Mussulman so zealous that he had persuaded his Hindu servant to be circumcised. But he was afterwards horrified by the treachery and the atrocities of his co-religionists in the Rajpoot State of Joudhpore, whither he had gone. He was on his way back to his father at Lucknow when, on a heart thus prepared, there fell the teaching of the English man of God as to the purity of the Divine law and salvation from sin by Jesus Christ.

Eager to learn more of Christianity from its authoritative records, he sought employment on the translating staff of the preacher, through a friend who knew Sabat. He was engaged to copy Persian manuscripts by that not too scrupulous tyrant, without the knowledge of Martyn or any of the English. On receiving the [286] completed Persian New Testament, to have it bound, he read it all, and his conversion by the Spirit of God, its Author, was complete. He determined to attach himself to Martyn, who as yet knew him not personally. He followed him to Calcutta, and applied to him for baptism. After due trial during the next year he was admitted to the Church under the new name of 'Bondman of Christ,' Abdool Massee'h. This was almost the last act of the Rev. David Brown, who since 1775 had spent his life in diffusing Christian knowledge in Bengal. Abdool's conversion caused great excitement in Lucknow. Nor was this all. The new convert was sent to Meerut, when Mr. Parson was chaplain in that great military station, and there he won over the chief physician of the Rajah of Bhurtpore, naming him Taleb Massee'h. After preaching and disputing in Meerut, Abdool visited the Begum Sumroo's principality of Sardhana, where he left Taleb to care for the native Christians. They and the Sherwoods together were the means of calling and preparing several native converts for baptism, all the fruit, direct and indirect, of Henry Martyn's combined translating and preaching of the New Testament at Cawnpore.

Mrs. Sherwood writes:

We were told that Mr. Corrie might perhaps be unable to come as far as Delhi, and the candidates for baptism became so anxious that they set off to meet him on the Delhi road. We soon heard of their meeting from Mr. Corrie himself, and that he was pleased with them. Shortly afterwards our beloved friend appeared, with tents, camels, and elephants, and we had the pleasure of having his largest tent pitched in our compound, for we had not room for all his suite within the house. Then for the next week our house and grounds brought to my mind what I had often fancied of a scene in some high festival in Jerusalem;[287] but ours was an assembly under a fairer, brighter dispensation. 'Here we are,' said Mr. Corrie, 'poor weary pilgrims;' and he applied the names of 'Christian' and 'Mercy' to his wife and an orphan girl who was with them. Dear Mr. Corrie! perhaps there never was a man so universally beloved as he was. Wherever he was known, from the lisping babe who climbed upon his knee to the hoary-headed native, he was regarded as a bright example of Christian charity and humility. On Sunday, January 31, the baptism of all the converts but one took place. Numbers of Europeans from different quarters of the station attended. The little chapel was crowded to overflowing, and most affecting indeed was the sight. Few persons could restrain their tears when Mr. Corrie extended his hand to raise the silver curls which clustered upon the brow of Monghul Das, one of the most sincere of the converts. The ceremony was very affecting, and the convert, who stood by and saw the others baptized, became so uneasy that, when Mr. Corrie set off to return, he followed him. For family reasons this man's baptism had been deferred, as he hoped by so doing to bring others of his family into the Church of God.

How delightfully passed that Sunday!—how sweet was our private intercourse with Mr. Corrie! He brought our children many Hindustani hymns, set to ancient Oriental melodies, which they were to sing at the Hindu services, and we all together sang a hymn, which I find in my Journal designated by this title:

'WE HAVE SEEN HIS STAR IN THE EAST'

In Britain's land of light my mind
To Jesus and His love was blind,
Till, wandering midst the heathen far,
Lo in the East I saw His star.
Oh, should my steps, which distant roam,
Attain once more my native shore,
Better than India's wealth by far,
I'll speak the worth of Bethlehem's star.

[288]There is little merit in the composition of this hymn; but it had a peculiar interest for us at that time, and the sentiment which it professes must ever retain its interest.

Long after this the good seed of the Kingdom, as sown by Henry Martyn, continued to bear fruit, which in its turn propagated itself. In 1816 there came to Corrie in Calcutta, for further instruction, from Bareilly, a young Mohammedan ascetic and teacher who, at seventeen, had abandoned Hinduism, seeking peace of mind. He fell in with Martyn's Hindustani New Testament, and was baptized under the new name of Fuez Massee'h. Under somewhat similar circumstances Noor Massee'h was baptized at Agra. The missionary labours of Martyn at Cawnpore, followed up by Corrie there and at Agra soon after, farther resulted in the baptism there of seventy-one Hindus and Mohammedans, of whom fifty were adults. All of these, save seven, remained steadfast, and many became missionaries in their turn. The career of Abdool Massee'h closed in 1827, after he had been ordained in the Calcutta cathedral by Bishop Heber, who loved him. His last breath was spent in singing the Persian hymn, translated thus:

Beloved Saviour, let not me
In Thy kind heart forgotten be!
Of all that deck the field or bower,
Thou art the sweetest, fairest flower!

Youth's morn has fled, old age comes on.
But sin distracts my soul alone;

Beloved Saviour, let not me
In Thy kind heart forgotten be.

As from Dinapore Martyn sought out the moulvies of Patna, so from Cawnpore he found his way to Lucknow[289] There, after he had baptized a child of the Governor-General's Resident, he met the Nawab Saadut Ali, and his eyes for the first time beheld one who had full power of life and death over his subjects. He visited the moulvies, at the tomb of Asaf-ood-Dowla, who were employed to read the Koran constantly. 'With them I tried my strength, of course, and disputed for an hour; it ended in their referring me for an answer to another.'

Toil such as Martyn's, physical and mental, in successive hot seasons, in such hospitals and barracks as then killed off the British troops and their families, and without a decent church building, would have sacrificed the healthiest in a few years. Corrie had to flee from it, or he would never have lived to be the first and model Bishop of Madras. But such labours, such incessant straining of the voice through throat and lungs, acting on his highly neurotic constitution, and the phthisical frame which he inherited from his mother, became possible to Henry Martyn only because he willed, he agonised, to live till he should give at least the New Testament to the peoples of Arabia and Persia, and to the Mohammedans of India, in their own tongues. We see him in his *Journal*, before God, spiritually spurring the sides of his intent day by day, and running like the noble Arab horse till it drops—its object gained. He had many warnings, and if he had had a wife to see that he obeyed the voice of Providence he might have outlived his hereditary tendency in such a tropical climate as that of India—a fact since proved by experience. He had narrowly escaped death at Dinapore a few months before, and he knew it. But it is well that, far more frequently than the world knows, such cases occur in the missionary fields of the world. The Brainerds and the Martyns, the Pattesons[290] and the Hanningtons, the Keith-Falconers and the Mackays—to mention some of the dead only—have their reward in calling hundreds to fill their places, not less than the Careys and the Livingstones, the Duffs and the Wilsons, the Frenches and the Caldwells. To all who know the tropics, and especially the seasons of India, the dates that follow are eloquent.

1809, May 29.—The East has been long forsaken of God, and depravity in consequence more thoroughly wrought into them. I have been very ill all this week, the disorder appearing in the form of an intermittent. In the night cold sweats, and for about five hours in the day head-ache and vertigo. Last night I took some medicine, and think that I am better, though the time when the fever has generally come on is not yet arrived. But I hardly know how to be thankful enough for this interval of ease.

September 25.—Set out at three in the morning for Currah, and reached it on the 26th in the morning, and married a Miss K. to Mr. R.; the company was very unpleasant, so after passing the night there, I set out and travelled all day and night, and through Divine mercy arrived at home again on the 28th, but excessively fatigued, indeed almost exhausted. At night with the men, my whole desire was to lie low in the dust. 'Thou hast left thy first love,' on which I spoke, was an awful call to me, and I trust in God I shall ever feel it so.

November 19.—Received a letter from Mr. Simeon, mentioning Sarah's illness; consumption has seized her, as it did my mother and sister, and will carry her off as it did them, and now I am the only one left. Oh, my dear Corrie, though I know you are well prepared, how does nature bleed at the thought of a beloved sister's drooping and dying! Yet still to see those whom I love go before me, without so much as a doubt of their going to glory, will,[291] I hope, soothe my sorrow. How soon shall I follow? I know it must be soon. The paleness and fatigue I exhibit after every season of preaching show plainly that death is settled in my lungs.

1810, April 9.—From the labours of yesterday, added to constant conversation and disagreement with visitors to-day, I was quite exhausted, and my chest in pain.

April 10.—My lungs still so disordered that I could not meet my men at night.

April 15. (Sunday.)—Preached to the Dragoons on the parable of the pounds. At the General's on Luke xxii 22. With the native congregation I strained myself greatly in order to be heard, and to this I attribute the injury I did myself to-day. Attempted the usual service with my men at night, but after speaking to them from a passage in Scripture, was obliged to leave them before prayer.

April 16.—Imprudently joined in conversation with some dear Christian friends to-night, and talked a great deal; the pain in the chest in consequence returned.

May 12.—This evening thrown with great violence from my horse: while he was in full gallop, the saddle came off, but I received no other injury but contusion. Thus a gracious Providence preserves me in life. But for His kindness I had been now dragging out a wretched existence in pain, and my blessed work interrupted for years perhaps.

Henry Martyn was too absorbed in the higher life at all times to be trusted in riding or driving. Mrs. Sherwood writes:

I often went out with him in his gig, when he used to call either for me or Miss Corrie, and whoever went with him went at the peril of their lives. He never looked where he was driving, but went dashing through thick and thin, being always occupied in reading Hindustani by word of mouth, or discussing some text of Scripture. I certainly[292] never expected to have survived a lesson he gave me in his gig, in the midst of the plain at Cawnpore, on the pronunciation of one of the Persian letters.

All through his Cawnpore life, also, the wail of disappointed love breaks from time to time. On Christmas day, 1809, he received, through David Brown as usual, a letter 'from Lydia, containing a second refusal; so now I have done.' On March 23, 1810, Mr. Steven's letter reached him, reporting the death of his last sister. 'She was my dear counsellor and guide for a long time in the Christian way. I have not a relation left to whom I feel bound by ties of Christian fellowship, and I am resolved to form no new connection of a worldly nature, so that I may henceforward hope to live entirely, as a man of another world.' Meanwhile he has received Lydia Grenfell's sisterly offer, to which he thus replies in the first of eleven letters, to one who had sunk the lover in the Christian friend, as was possible to two hearts so far separated and never to meet again in this world. But she was still his 'dearest.'

TO LYDIA GRENFELL.

Cawnpore: March 30, 1810.

Since you kindly bid me, my beloved friend, consider you in the place of that dear sister whom it has pleased God in His wisdom to take from me, I gratefully accept the offer of a correspondence, which it has ever been the anxious wish of my heart to establish. Your kindness is the more acceptable, because it is shown in the day of affliction. Though I had heard of my dearest sister's illness some months before I received the account of her death, and though the nature of her disorder was such as left me not a ray of hope, so that I was mercifully prepared for the event, still the certainty of it fills me with anguish. It is not that she has left me, for I never ex[293]pected to see her more on earth. I have no doubt of meeting her in heaven, but I cannot bear to think of the pangs of dissolution she underwent, which have been unfortunately detailed to me with too much particularity. Would I had never heard them, or could efface them from my remembrance. But oh, may I learn what the Lord is teaching me by these repeated strokes! May I learn meekness and resignation. May the world always appear as vain as it does now, and my own continuance in it as short and uncertain. How frightful is the desolation which Death makes, and how appalling his visits when he enters one's family. I would rather never have been born than be born and die, were it not for Jesus, the Prince of life, the Resurrection and the Life. How inexpressibly precious is this Saviour when eternity seems near! I hope often to communicate with you on these subjects, and in return for your kind and consolatory letters to send you, from time to time, accounts of myself and my proceedings. Through you I can hear of all my friends in the West. When I first heard of the loss I was likely to suffer, and began to reflect on my own friendless situation, you were much in my thoughts, whether you would be silent on this occasion or no? whether you would persist in your resolution? Friends indeed I have, and brethren, blessed be God! but two brothers[34] cannot supply the place of one sister. When month after month passed away, and no letter came from you, I almost abandoned the hope of ever hearing from you again. It only remained to wait the result of my last application through Emma. You have kindly anticipated my request, and, I need scarcely add, are more endeared to me than ever.

Of your illness, my dearest Lydia, I had heard nothing, and it was well for me that I did not.—Yours most affectionately,

H. MARTYN.

[294]

To David Brown he wrote, 'My long-lost Lydia consents to write to me again;' and in three weeks he thus addresses to Lydia herself again a letter of exquisite tenderness:

TO LYDIA GRENFELL.

Cawnpore: April 19, 1810.

I begin my correspondence with my beloved Lydia, not without a fear of its being soon to end. Shall I venture to tell you that our family complaint has again made its appearance in me, with more unpleasant symptoms than it has ever yet done? However, God, who two years ago redeemed my life from destruction, may again, for His Church's sake, interpose for my deliverance. Though, alas! what am I that my place should not instantly be supplied with far more efficient instruments? The symptoms I mentioned are chiefly a pain in the chest, occasioned, I suppose, by over-exertion the two last Sundays, and incapacitating me at present from all public duty, and even from conversation. You were mistaken in supposing that my former illness originated from study. Study never makes me ill—scarcely ever fatigues me—but my lungs! death is seated there; it is speaking that kills me. May it give others life! 'Death worketh in us, but life in you.' Nature intended me, as I should judge from the structure of my frame, for chamber-council, not for a pleader at the Bar. But the call of Jesus Christ bids me cry aloud and spare not. As His minister, I am a debtor both to the Greek and the barbarian. How can I be silent when I have both ever before me, and my debt not paid? You would suggest that energies more restrained will eventually be more efficient. I am aware of this, and mean to act upon this principle in future, if the resolution is not formed too late. But you know how apt we are to outstep the bounds of prudence when there is no kind of monitor at hand to warn us of the consequences.[295]

Had I been favoured with the one I wanted, I might not now have had occasion to mourn. You smile at my allusion, at least I hope so, for I am hardly in earnest. I have long since ceased to repine at the decree that keeps us as far asunder as the east is from the west, and yet am far from regretting that I ever knew you. The remembrance of you calls forth the exercise of delightful affections, and has kept me from many a snare. How wise and good is our God in all His dealings with His children! Had I yielded to the suggestions of flesh and blood, and remained in England, as I should have done, without the effectual working of His power, I should without doubt have sunk with my sisters into an early grave. Whereas here, to say the least, I may live a few years, so as to accomplish a very important work. His keeping you from me appears also, at this season of bodily infirmity, to be occasion of thankfulness. Death, I think, would be a less welcome visitor to me, if he came to take me from a wife, and that wife were you. Now, if I die, I die unnoticed, involving none in calamity. Oh, that I could trust Him for all that is to come, and love Him with that perfect love which casteth out fear; for, to say the truth, my confidence is sometimes shaken. To appear before the Judge of quick and dead is a much more awful thought in sickness than in health. Yet I dare not doubt the all-sufficiency of Jesus Christ, nor can I, with the utmost ingenuity of unbelief, resist the reasonings of St. Paul, all whose reasons seem to be drawn up on purpose to work into the mind the persuasion that God will glorify Himself by the salvation of sinners through Jesus Christ. I wish I could more enter into the meaning of this 'chosen vessel.' He seems to move in a world by himself, and sometimes to utter the unspeakable words such as my natural understanding discerneth not; and when I turn to commentators I find that I have passed out of the spiritual to the material world, and have got amongst men like myself. But soon,[296] as he says, we shall no longer see as in a glass, by reflected rays, but see as we are seen, and know as we are known.

April 25.—After another interval I resume my pen. Through the mercy of God I am again quite well, but my mind is a good deal distressed at Sabat's conduct. I forbear writing what I think, in the hope that my fears may prove groundless; but indeed the children of the East are adepts in deceit. Their duplicity appears to me so disgusting at this moment, that I can only find relief from my growing misanthropy by remembering Him who is the faithful and true Witness; in whom all the promises of God are 'yea and amen'; and by turning to the faithful in Europe—children that will not lie. Where shall we find sincerity in a native of the East? Yesterday I dined in a private way with ——. After one year's inspection of me they begin to lose their dread and venture to invite me. Our conversation was occasionally religious, but topics of this nature are so new to fashionable people, and those upon which they have thought so much less than on any other, that often from the shame of having nothing to say they pass to other subjects where they can be more at home. I was asked after dinner if I liked music. On my professing to be an admirer of harmony, cantos were performed and songs sung. After a time I inquired if they had no sacred music. It was now recollected that they had some of Handel's, but it could not be found. A promise, however, was made that next time I came it should be produced. Instead of it the 145th Psalm-tune was played, but none of the ladies could recollect enough of the tune to sing it. I observed that all our talents and powers should be consecrated to the service of Him who gave them. To this no reply was made, but the reproof was felt. I asked the lady of the house if she read poetry, and then proceeded to mention Cowper, whose poems, it seems, were in the library; but the lady had never heard of the book. This was produced, and I read[297] some passages. Poor people! here a little and there a little is a rule to be observed in speaking to them.

April 26.—From speaking to my men last night, and again to-day conversing long with some natives, my chest is again in pain, so much so that I can hardly speak. Well, now I am taught, and will take more care in future. My sheet being full, I must bid you adieu. The Lord ever bless and keep you. Believe me to be with the truest affection,—Yours ever,

H. MARTYN.

TO REV. T.M. HITCHINS, PLYMOUTH DOCK

Cawnpore: October 10, 1809.

My dearest Brother,—I am again disappointed in receiving no letter from you. The last intelligence from the West of England is Lydia's letter of July 8, 1808. Colonel Sandys has long since ceased to write to me, and I have no other correspondent. It is very affecting to me to be thus considered as dead by almost all my natural relations and early connections; and at this time, when I am led to think of you and the family to which you are united, and have been reading all your letters over, I feel that I could dip my pen deep in melancholy; for, strange as it may seem to you, I love so true, that though it is now the fifth year since I parted from the object of my affection, she is as dear to me as ever; yet, on the other hand, I find my present freedom such a privilege that I would not lose it for hardly any consideration. It is the impossibility of compassing every wish, that I suppose is the cause of any uneasiness that I feel. I know not how to express my thoughts respecting Lydia better than in Martial's words—*Nec tecum possum vivere nec sine te.* However, these are not my general sentiments; it pleases God to cause me to eat my meat with gladness, praising God. Almost always I am without carefulness, as indeed it would be to my shame if I were not.[298]

My kindest remembrances attend my dearest sisters, Emma and Lydia, as they well know. You two are such bad correspondents that on this ground I prefer another petition for the renewal of Lydia's correspondence,—she need not suspect anything now, nor her friends. I have no idea that I should trouble her upon the old subject, even if I were settled in England—for oh, this vain world! *quid habet commodi? quid non potius laboris?*

But I never expect to see England more, nor do I expect that though all obstacles should be removed, she would ever become mine unless I came for her, and I now do not wonder at it, though I did before. If any one of my sisters had had such a proposal made to them, I would never have consented to their going, so you may see the affair is ended between us. My wish is that she would be scribe for you all, and I promise on my part to send you through her an ample detail *of all my* proceedings; also she need not imagine that I may form another attachment—in which case she might suppose a correspondence with an unmarried lady might be productive of difficulties,—for after one disappointment I am not likely to try my chance again, and if I do I will give her the earliest intelligence of it, with the same frankness with which I have always dealt (with her).

Meanwhile, on the silent shores of South Cornwall, Lydia Grenfell was thus remembering him before God:

1809, March 30.—My dear friend in India much upon my heart lately, chiefly in desires that the work of God may prosper in his hands, and that he may become more and more devoted to the Lord. I seem, as to the future, to have attained what a year or two since I prayed much for—to regard him absent as in another state of existence, and my affection is holy, pure, and spiritual for this dear saint of God; when it is otherwise, it is owing to my looking back. Recollections sometimes intrude, and I welcome|299| them, alas, and act over again the past—but Lord, Thy holy, blessed will be done—cheerfully, thankfully I say this.

Tregembo, July 11.—I have suffered from levity of spirit, and lost thereby the enjoyment of God. How good then is it in the Lord to employ means in His providence to recall His wanderer to Himself and happiness! Such mercy belongeth unto God—and this His care over me I will record as a testimony against myself, if I forsake Him again and lose that sweet seriousness of mind, so essential to my peace and safety. Though I have never (perhaps for many hours in a day) ceased to remember my dear friend in India, it has not of late been in a way but as I might love and think of him in heaven. Why is it then that the intelligence of his probable nearness to that blessed abode should distress me? yet it did, and does so still. It is this intelligence which has, I hope, taught that my late excessive cheerfulness was dangerous to my soul, in weakening my hold of better and calmer joys. I was directed, I think, to the thirty-sixth Psalm for what I wanted on this occasion, as I was once before to the sixty-first, and I have found it most wonderfully cheering to my heart. The Lord, as 'the preserver of man and beast,' caused me to exercise dependence on Him respecting the result of my friend's illness. Then the description of the Divine perfections drew back my wandering heart, I hope to God. The declaration of those who trust in God being abundantly satisfied with the fatness of His house, taught me where real enjoyment alone will be found; but the concluding part opened in a peculiarly sweet way to my mind: 'Thou shalt make them drink of the river of Thy pleasures.'

October 23.—I am under some painful forebodings respecting my dear absent friend, and know not how to act. I am strongly impelled to write to him, now that he is in affliction and perhaps sickness himself—yet I dread|300| departing from the plain path of duty. 'O Lord, direct me,' is my cry. I hope my desire is to do Thy will, and only Thy will. I have given him up to Thee—oh, let me do so sincerely, and trust in Thy fatherly care.

1810, January 1.—Felt the necessity of beginning this year with prayer for preserving grace. Prayed with some sense of my own weakness and dependence on God—with a conviction of much sin and hope in His mercy through Jesus Christ. Oh, to be Thine, Lord, in heart and life this year! Had a remembrance of those most dear to me in prayer, and found it very sweet to commend them to God, especially my friend in India—perhaps not now in India, but in heaven. Oh, to join him at last in Thy blissful presence!

January 24.—Heard yesterday of the marriage of Mr. John—what a mercy to me do I feel it!—a load gone off my mind, for every evil I heard of his committing I feared I might have been the cause of, by my conduct ten years since—I rejoice in this event for his sake and my own.

February 6.—Heard at last of the safety of my friend in India, and wrote to him— many fears on my mind as to its propriety, and great deadness of soul in doing it—yet ere I concluded I felt comforted from the thought of the nearness of eternity, and the certainty that then, without any fear of doing wrong, I should again enjoy communion with him.

February 24.—Many sad presages of evil concerning my absent friend, yet I am enabled to leave all to God—only now I pray, if consistent with His will, his life may be spared, and as a means of it, that God may incline him to return again to this land. I never did before dare to ask this, believing the cause of God would be more advanced by his remaining in India; but now I pray, without fear of doing wrong or opposing the will of God, for his return.

March 5.—I am sensible of a very remarkable change in the desires of my soul before God, respecting my absent|301| friend. I with freedom and peace now pray continually that he may be restored to his friends and country; before, I never dared to ask anything but that the Lord would order this as His wisdom saw fit, and thought it not a subject for prayer. His injured health causes me to believe that India is not the place for his labours—and, oh, that his mind may be rightly influenced and the Lord's will done, whether it be his remaining there or returning.

April 23.—Wrote to India.

November 30.—Heard yesterday, and again to-day, from India.[135] The illness of my friend fills me with apprehensions on his account, and I seemed called on to prepare for hearing of his removal. I wish to place before my eyes the blessedness of the change to him, and, though agitated and sad, I can bear to think of our never more beholding each other in this world. This indeed has long been my expectation, and that he should have left the toils of mortality for the joys of heaven should, on his account, fill me with praise—yet my heart cannot rise with thankfulness. I seem stupefied, insensible to any feeling but that of anxiety to hear again and know the truth, and that my heart could joy in God at all times; but alas! all is cold there! Oh, return, blessed Spirit of life and peace.

1811, March 28.—Heard from my dearest friend in India.[136] Rose early. Found my spirit engaged in prayer, but was far ... otherwise in reading. Such dulness and inattention as ought deeply to abase me, vanity and a desire to appear of importance in the school, beset me.

Corrie had been ordered from his narrow parish of Chunar to the wider field of Agra, and on his way up was directed to remain at Cawnpore to help his friend, whose physical exhaustion was too apparent even to the most[302] careless officer. Among those influenced by both was one of the surgeons, Dr. Govan,[37] who was spared, at St. Andrews, till after the Mutiny of 1857, when in an unpublished lecture to its Literary and Philosophical Society, he thus alluded to these workers in Cawnpore:

The Hukeem and the missionary hear native opinion spoken out with much greater freedom than the political agent, the judge, or commandant. 'Were there many more of the *Sahibean Ungez* (the English gentlemen) in character like the Padre Sahibs (Corrie and Martyn), Christianity would make more progress here,' was the unvaried testimony of the natives in their favour.... I cannot help mentioning the results of various conversations I had with two natives of Eastern rank and family employed by the Venerable Mr. Corrie, afterwards Bishop of Madras, and the Rev. Henry Martyn, in Scripture translation, and whose assistance I had used in the study of the languages, as they quite coincide with much which I had the opportunity of hearing among men of still higher position in the native educated community, when attached to the staff of the Governor-General: 'By the decrees of God,' said the Mohammedan noble, 'and the ubiquity of their fleets, armaments, and commerce, it appears plainly that the European nations have become the arbiters of the destinies of the nations of Asia. Yet this seems to us strange in the followers of Him who taught that His true disciples must be ready to give their cloaks also to him who took from them their coats.' To which I had no better reply than this, that the progress of events in the world's history seems to us to give evidence that undoubtedly a Divine message had been sent, both to governments and their subjects, to which, at their peril, both must give attention.[303] But that, as a question of public national policy, it seemed generally admitted and understood that the civil rulers of no nation, Christian, Mohammedan, or Heathen, were laid under an obligation, by their individual beliefs, to allow a country, unable to govern itself by reason of its interminable divisions and subjects of deadly internal strife, to be occupied and made use of by their European or other enemies, as a means for their own injury or destruction, for any criminal or sinful acts, done in the building up of a nation or government. I may add that I never heard a native of India attempt directly to impugn the perfect justice of the British possession of India on this ground. 'The Padre Sahib has put the subject in its true light' (said the same Mohammedan authority) 'when he said that Christianity had higher objects in view, in its influence on human character, than to enforce absolute rules about meats and drinks; for should he even induce me (which is unlikely) to become more of a Christian than I am, believing, as I do, in the authority of the Old Testament prophets, and in Jesus Christ as a prophet sent by God, he will never persuade me to look upon many articles of diet used by Christians with anything but the most intense disgust and abhorrence, and he will assuredly find it the same with most of these idolatrous Hindus.'

We return to Martyn's *Journal* and *Correspondence*:

July 8. (Sunday.)—Corrie preached to the 53rd a funeral sermon on the death of one of their captains. In the afternoon I spoke to the natives on the first commandment, with greater fluency than I have yet found. My thoughts to-day very much towards Lydia; I began even to be reconciled to the idea of going to England for her.[304] 'Many are the thoughts of a man's heart, but the counsel of the Lord, that shall stand.'

TO LYDIA GRENFELL.

Cawnpore: August 14, 1810.

With what delight do I sit down to begin a letter to my beloved Lydia! Yours of February 5, which I received a few days ago, was written, I conceive, in considerable embarrassment. You thought it possible it might find me married, or about to be so. Let me begin, therefore, with assuring you, with more truth than Gehazi did his master, 'Thy servant went no whither:' my heart has not strayed from Marazion, or Gurlyn, or wherever you are. Five long years have passed, and I am still faithful. Happy would it be if I could say that I had been equally true to my profession of love for Him who is fairer than ten thousand, and altogether lovely. Yet to the praise of His grace let me recollect that twice five years have passed away since I began to know Him, and I am still not gone from Him. On the contrary, time and experience have endeared the Lord to me more and more, so that I feel less inclination, and see less reason for leaving Him. What is there, alas! in the world, were it even everlasting?

I rejoice at the accounts you give me of your continued good health and labours of love. Though you are not so usefully employed as you might be in India, yet as that must not be, I contemplate with delight your exertions at the other end of the world. May you be instrumental in bringing many sons and daughters to glory. What is become of St. Hilary and its fairy scenes? When I think of Malachy, and the old man, and your sister, and Josepha, etc., how some are dead, and the rest dispersed, and their place occupied by strangers, it seems all like a dream.

August 15.—It is only little intervals of time that I can find for writing; my visitors, about whom I shall write presently, taking up much of my leisure from necessary duty. Here follow some extracts from my *Journal....*[305]

Here my *Journal* must close. I do not know whether you understand from it how we go on. I must endeavour to give you a clearer idea of it.

We all live here in bungalows, or thatched houses, on a piece of ground enclosed. Next to mine is the church, not yet opened for public worship, but which we make use of at night with the men of the 53rd. Corrie lives with me, and Miss Corrie with the Sherwoods. We usually rise at daybreak, and breakfast at six. Immediately after breakfast we pray together, after which I translate into Arabic with Sabat, who lives in a small bungalow on my ground. We dine at twelve, and sit recreating ourselves with talking a little about dear friends in England. In the afternoon, I translate with Mirza Fitrut into Hindustani, and Corrie employs himself in teaching some native Christian boys whom he is educating with great care, in hopes of their being fit for the office of catechist. I have also a school on my premises, for natives; but it is not well attended. There are not above sixteen Hindu boys in it at present: half of them read the Book of Genesis. At sunset we ride or drive, and then meet at the church, where we often raise the song of praise, with as much joy, through the grace and presence of our Lord, as you do in England. At ten we are all asleep. Thus we go on. To the hardships of missionaries we are strangers, yet not averse, I trust, to encounter them when we are called. My work at present is evidently to translate; hereafter I may itinerate. Dear Corrie, I fear, never will, he always suffers from moving about in the daytime. But I should have said something about my health, as I find my death was reported at Cambridge. I thank God I am perfectly well, though not very strong in my lungs; they do not seem affected yet, but I cannot speak long without uneasiness. From the nature of my complaint, if it deserves the name, it is evident that England is the last place I should go to. I should go home only to find a grave. How shall I[306] therefore ever see you more on this side of eternity? Well! be it so, since such is the will of God: we shall meet, through grace, in the realms of bliss.

I am truly sorry to see my paper fail. Write as often as possible, every three months at least. Tell me where you go, and whom you see and what you read.

August 17.—I am sorry to conclude with saying that my yesterday's boasted health proved a mistake; I was seized with violent sickness in the night, but to-day am better. Continue to pray for me, and believe me to be, your ever affectionate,

H. MARTYN.

September 22.—Was walking with Lydia; both much affected, and speaking on the things dearest to us both. I awoke, and behold it was a dream. My mind remained very solemn and pensive; shed some tears; the clock struck three, and the moon was riding near her highest noon; all was silence and solemnity, and I thought with some pain of the sixteen thousand miles between us. But good is the will of the Lord, if I see her no more.

TO LYDIA GRENFELL

From the Ganges: October 6, 1810.

My dearest Lydia,—Though I have had no letter from you very lately, nor have anything particular to say, yet having been days on the water without a person to speak to, tired also with reading and thinking, I mean to indulge myself with a little of what is always agreeable to me, and sometimes good for me; for as my affection for you has something sacred in it, being founded on, or at least cemented by, an union of spirit in the Lord Jesus; so my separation also from you produced a deadness to the world, at least for a time, which leaves a solemn impression as often as I think of it. Add to this, that as I must not indulge the hope of ever seeing you again in this world, I[307] cannot think of you without thinking also of that world where we shall meet. You mention in one of your letters my coming to England, as that which may eventually prove a duty. You ought to have added, that in case I do come, you will consider it a duty not to let me come away again without you. But I am not likely to put you to the trial. Useless as I am here, I often think I should be still more so at home. Though my voice fails me, I can translate and converse. At home I should be nothing without being able to lift my voice on high. I have just left my station, Cawnpore, in order to be silent six months. I have no cough, or any kind of consumption, except that reading prayers, or preaching, or a slight cold, brings on pain in the chest. I am advised therefore to recruit my strength by rest. So I am come forth, with my face towards Calcutta, with an ulterior view to the sea. Nothing happened at Cawnpore, after I wrote to you in September but I must look to my *Journal.*

I think of having my portrait taken in Calcutta, as I promised Mr. Simeon five years ago. Sabat's picture would also be a curiosity. Yesterday I carried Col. Wood to dine with me, at the Nabob Bahir Ali's. Sabat was there. The Colonel, who had been reading by the way the account of his conversion, in the Asiatic and East Society Report, which I had given him, eyed him with no great complacency, and observed in French, that Sabat might not understand him, 'Il a l'air d'un sauvage.' Sabat's countenance is indeed terrible; noble when he is pleased, but with the look of an assassin when he is out of humour. I have had more opportunities of knowing Sabat than any man has had, and I cannot regard him with that interest which the 'Star in the East' is calculated to excite in most people. Buchanan says, I wrote (to whom I do not know) in terms of admiration and affection about him. Affection I do feel for him, but admiration, if I did once feel it, I am not conscious of it at present. I tremble for everything[308] our dear friends publish about our doings in India, lest shame come to us and them.

Calcutta, November 5.—A sheet full, like the preceding, I had written, but the moment it is necessary to send off my letter I cannot find it. That it does not go on to you is of little consequence, but into whose hands may it have fallen? It is this that grieves me. It was the continuance of my *Journal* to Calcutta, where I arrived the last day in October. Constant conversation with dear friends here has brought on the pain in the chest again, so that I do not attempt to preach. In two or three weeks I shall embark for the Gulf of Persia, where, if I live, I shall solace myself in my hours of solitude with writing to you.

Farewell, beloved friend; pray for me, as you do, I am sure, and doubt not of an unceasing interest in the heart and prayers of your ever affectionate,

H. MARTYN.

Ordered away on six months' sick leave, Henry Martyn had the joy of once at least ministering to his soldier flock in the 'new church,' which he had induced the authorities to form out of an ordinary bungalow. Daily and fondly had he watched the preparations, reporting to Brown: 'My church is almost ready for the organ and the bell.' On Sunday, September 16, he had written:

'Rain prevented me from having any service in public; the natives not being able to sit upon the grass, I could not preach to them.'

On Sunday, September 30, he thus took farewell of his different congregations:

Corrie preached to the Dragoons, at nine the new church was opened. There was a considerable congregation, and I preached on, 'In all places where I record my name, I will come unto thee and bless thee.' I felt something of[309] thankfulness and joy, and our dear friends the same. The Sherwoods and Miss Corrie stayed with us the rest of the day. In the afternoon I preached the Gospel to the natives for the first time, giving them a short account of the life, death, miracles, manner of teaching, death and resurrection of Jesus, then the doctrines of His religion, and concluded with exhorting them to believe in Him, and taking them to record that I had declared to them the glad tidings that had come to us, and that if they rejected it I was clear from their blood, and thus I bid them farewell.

Mrs. Sherwood thus describes the scene:

On the Sunday before Mr. Martyn left the church was opened, and the bell sounded for the first time over this land of darkness. The church was crowded, and there was the band of our regiment to lead the singing and the chanting. Sergeant Clarke—our Sergeant Clarke—had been appointed as clerk; and there he sat under the desk in due form, in his red coat, and went through his duty with all due correctness. The Rev. Daniel Corrie read prayers, and Mr. Martyn preached. That was a day never to be forgotten. Those only who have been for some years in a place where there never has been public worship can have any idea of the fearful effect of its absence, especially among the mass of the people, who, of course, are unregenerate. Every prescribed form of public worship certainly has a tendency to become nothing more than a form, yet even a form may awaken reflection, and any state is better than that of perfect deadness. From his first arrival at the station Mr. Martyn had been labouring to effect the purpose which he then saw completed; namely, the opening of a place of worship. He was permitted to see it, to address the congregation once, and then he was summoned to depart. How often, how very often, are human beings called away, perhaps from this world, at the moment they have been enabled to bring to bear some favourite object.[310] Blessed are those whose object has been such a one as that of Henry Martyn. Alas! he was known to be, even then, in a most dangerous state of health, either burnt within by slow inflammation, which gave a flush to his cheek, or pale as death from weakness and lassitude.

On this occasion the bright glow prevailed—a brilliant light shone from his eyes—he was filled with hope and joy; he saw the dawn of better things, he thought, at Cawnpore, and most eloquent, earnest, and affectionate was his address to the congregation. Our usual party accompanied him back to his bungalow, where, being arrived, he sank, as was often his way, nearly fainting, on a sofa in the hall. Soon, however, he revived a little, and called us all about him to sing. It was then that we sang to him that sweet hymn which thus begins:

O God, our help in ages past,
Our hope for years to come,
Our shelter from the stormy blast,
And our eternal home.

We all dined early together, and then returned with our little ones to enjoy some rest and quiet; but when the sun began to descend to the horizon we again went over to Mr. Martyn's bungalow, to hear his *last* address to the *fakeers*. It was one of those sickly, hazy, burning evenings, which I have before described, and the scene was precisely such a one as I have recounted above. Mr. Martyn nearly fainted again after this effort, and when he got to his house, with his friends about him, he told us that he was afraid he had not been the means of doing the smallest good to any one of the strange people whom he had thus so often addressed. He did not even then know of the impression he had been enabled to make, on one of these occasions, on Sheikh Saleh. On the Monday our beloved friend went to his boats, which lay at the Ghaut, nearest the bungalow; but in the cool of the evening, how[311]ever, whilst Miss Corrie and myself were taking the air in our tonjons, he came

119

after us on horseback. There was a gentle sadness in his aspect as he accompanied me home; and Miss Corrie came also. Once again we all supped together, and united in one last hymn. We were all low, very, very low; we could never expect to behold again that face which we then saw—to hear again that voice, or to be again elevated and instructed by that conversation. It was impossible to hope that he would survive the fatigue of such a journey as he meditated. Often and often, when thinking of him, have these verses, so frequently sung by him, come to my mind:

E'er since by faith I saw the stream
Thy flowing wounds supply,
Redeeming love has been my theme,
And shall be till I die.
Then, in a nobler, sweeter song,
I'll sing Thy power to save,
When this poor lisping, stammering tongue
Is silent in the grave.

Henry Martyn's continued to be the military church of Cawnpore till 1857, when it was destroyed in the Mutiny. Its place has been taken by a Memorial Church which visibly proclaims forgiveness and peace on the never-to-be forgotten site of Wheeler's entrenchment—consecrated ground indeed!

On October 1 he left Cawnpore, 'after a parting prayer with my dearest brother Corrie,'[138] to whom he wrote from Allahabad:

[312]

Thus far we are come in safety; but my spirits tell me that I have parted with friends. Your pale face as it appeared on Monday morning is still before my eyes, and will not let me be easy till you tell me you are strong and prudent. The first night there blew a wind so bleak and cold, through and through my boat and bed, that I rose, as I expected, with a pain in the breast, which has not quite left me, but will, I hope, to-night, when I shall take measures for expelling it. There is a gate not paid for yet belonging to the churchyard, may you always go through it in faith and return through it with praise. You are now in prayer with our men. The Lord be with you, and be always with you, dearest brother.

Ministering to all who needed his services, in preaching, baptizing, and marrying, on his way down the great Ganges, at Benares, at Ghazipore, where he met with 'the remains' of his old 67th regiment, at Bhagulpore, and at Bandel, where he called on the Roman Catholics, on November 12 he at last came to Aldeen.

[313]

Children jumping, shouting, and convoying me in troops to the house. They are a lovely family indeed, and I do not know when I have felt so delighted as at family worship last night. To-day Mr. Brown and myself have been consulting at the Pagoda.

After four years' absence he seemed a dying man to his Serampore and Calcutta friends, Brown, Thomason, Udny, and Colonel Young of Dinapore memory. But he was ever cheerful, and he preached every Sunday for five weeks, though in his *Journal* we find this on November 21:

Caught a cold, and kept awake much of the night by a cough. From this day perhaps I may date my decay. Nature shrinks from dissolution, and conscience trembles at the thought of a judgment to come. But I try to rejoice in God through our Lord Jesus Christ.

November 25. (Sunday.)—Preached at the old church, on 'While Paul reasoned of righteousness,' etc. The Governor-General, Lord Minto, was present, desiring, as was supposed, to abolish the distinction which had been made between the two churches. One passage in my sermon appeared to some personal, and on reconsideration I thought it so myself, and was excessively distressed at having given causeless offence, and perhaps preventing much good. Lord! pardon a blind creature. How much mischief may I do through mere thoughtlessness!

December 2.—Preached at eight, on 'Grace reigns,' and was favoured with strength of body and joy of heart in proclaiming the glorious truth.

December 25.—Preached, with much comfort to myself, on 'God so loved the world that He gave His only begotten Son,' etc. Mr. Brown on 'Let your light so shine before men,' etc. The whole sum collected about seven thousand rupees. At night Mr. Thomason on[314] 'Through the tender mercy of our God, whereby the dayspring from on high hath visited us.' This day how many of those who love the Lord Jesus Christ in sincerity are rejoicing in His birth. My dear Lydia remembers me.

December 31.—Had a long dispute with Marshman, which brought on pain in the chest.

He opened the year 1811 by preaching for the new Calcutta Auxiliary of the British and Foreign Bible Society his published sermon on Christian India and the Bible, to be read in the light of his own translation work hereafter. He thus on the same day committed himself to the future in the spirit of St. Paul:

1811.—The weakness which has come upon me in the course of the last year, if it should not give an entire new turn to my life, is likely to be productive of events in the course of the present year which I little expected, or at least did not expect so soon. I now pass from India to Arabia, not knowing what things shall befall me there; but assured that an ever-faithful God and Saviour will be with me in all places whithersoever I go. May He guide and protect me, and after prospering me in the thing whereunto I go, bring me back again to my delightful work in India. It would be a painful thought indeed, to suppose myself about to return no more. Having succeeded, apparently, through His blessing, in the Hindustani New Testament, I feel much encouraged, and could wish to be spared in order to finish the Bible.

FOOTNOTES:

[32] *The Life of Mrs. Sherwood* (chiefly autobiographical), edited by her Daughter. London, 1854.

[33] 'He was at that time married to his seventh wife; that is, according to his own account. Ameena was a pretty young woman, though particularly dark for a purdah-walla, or one, according to the Eastern custom, who is supposed always to sit behind a purdah, or curtain. She occupied the smaller bungalow, which adjoined the larger by a long, covered passage. Our children often went to see her whilst they were at Mr. Martyn's, and I paid her one formal visit. I found her seated on the ground, encircled by cushions within gauze mosquito-curtains, stretched by ropes from the four corners of the hall. In the daytime these curtains were twisted and knotted over her head, and towards the night they were let down around her, and thus she slept where she had sat all day. She had one or two women in constant attendance upon her, though her husband was a mere subordinate. These Eastern women have little idea of using the needle, and very few are taught any other feminine accomplishment. Music and literature, dancing and singing, are known only to the Nautch or dancing-girls by profession. Hence, nothing on earth can be imagined to be more monotonous than the lives of women in the East; such, I mean, as are not compelled to servile labour. They sit on their cushions behind their curtains from day to day, from month to month, with no other occupation than that of having their hair dressed, and their nails and eyelids stained, and no other amusement than hearing the *gup*, or gossip of the place where they may happen to be; nor is any gossip too low or too frivolous to be unacceptable. The visits of our children and nurses were very acceptable to Ameena, and she took much and tender notice of the baby. She lived on miserable terms with her husband, and hated him most cordially. She was a Mussulman, and he was very anxious to make her a Christian, to which she constantly showed strong opposition. At length, however, she terminated the controversy in the following extraordinary manner: "Pray, will you have the goodness to inform me where Christians go after death?" "To heaven and to their Saviour," replied Sabat. "And where do Mahometans go?" she asked. "To hell and the devil," answered the fierce Arab. "You," said the meek wife, "will go to heaven, of course, as being a Christian." "Certainly," replied Sabat. "Well, then," she said, "I will continue to be a Mussulman, because I should prefer hell and the devil without you, to heaven itself in your presence." This anecdote was told to Mr. Martyn by Sabat himself, as a proof of the hardened spirit of his wife.

'Ameena was, by the Arab's own account, his seventh wife. He had some wonderful story to tell of each of his former marriages; but that which he related of his sixth wife exceeded all the rest in the marvellous and the romantic. He told this tale at Mr. Martyn's table one evening, whilst we were at supper, during the week we lived in the house. He spoke in Persian, and Mr. Martyn interpreted what he said, and it was this he narrated: It was on some occasion, he said, in which Fortune had played him one of her worst tricks, and reduced him to a state of the most abject poverty, that he happened to arrive one night at a certain city, which was the capital of some rajah, or petty king—Sabat called this person a king. It seemed he arrived at a crisis in which the king's only daughter had given her father some terrible offence, and in order to be revenged upon her, the father issued his commands that she should be compelled to take for her husband the first stranger who arrived in the town after sunset. This man happened to be our Arab; he was accordingly seized and subjected to the processes of bathing and anointing with precious oil. He was then magnificently dressed, introduced into the royal hall, and duly married to the princess, who proved not only to be fair as the houris, but to be quite prepared to love the husband whom Fortune had sent her. He lived with her, he pretended, I know not how many years, and they were perfectly happy until the princess died, and he lost the favour of his majesty. I think that Sabat laid the scene of this adventure in or near Agra. But this could hardly be. That such things have been in the East—that is, that royal parents have taken such means of avenging themselves on offending daughters—is quite certain; but I cannot venture to assert that Sabat was telling the truth when he made himself the hero of the tale.'

[34]Corrie and Brown.

[35]By letters written March 30 and April 19, 1810, from Cawnpore.

[36]By letter written August 14, 1810.

[37]On leaving the station Henry Martyn presented his French New Testament to Dr. Govan, a little morocco-bound volume which his son prizes as an heirloom.

[38]We have these reminiscences of Henry Martyn's Cawnpore from Bishop Corrie, when, as Archdeacon of Calcutta, he again visited it. In 1824 he writes: 'I arrived at this station on the day fourteen years after sainted Martyn had dedicated the church. The house he occupied stands close by. The view of the place and the remembrance of what had passed greatly affected me.... I had to assist in administering the sacrament, and well it was, on the whole, that none present could enter into my feelings, or I should have been overcome.' Again: 'How would it have rejoiced the heart of Martyn could he have had the chief authorities associated, by order of Government, to assist him in the work of education; and how gladly would he have made himself their servant in the work for Jesus' sake! One poor blind man who lives in an outhouse of Martyn's, and received a small monthly sum from him, often comes to our house, and affords a mournful pleasure in reminding me of some little occurrence of those times. A wealthy native too, who lived next door to us, sent his nephew to express to me the pleasure he derived from his acquaintance with Martyn. These are all the traces I have found of that "excellent one of the earth" at the station.'

In 1833 Corrie was again at Cawnpore, which had two chaplains then, and thus wrote: 'October 6.—I attended Divine service at the church bungalow, and stood up once more in Martyn's pulpit. The place is a little enlarged. The remembrance of Martyn and the Sherwoods, and Mary (his sister), with the occupations of that period, came powerfully to my recollection, and I could not prevent the tears from flowing. A sense of the forgiving love of God, with the prospect of all joining in thankful adoration in the realms of bliss, greatly preponderates.'

[315]

CHAPTER VIII

FROM CALCUTTA TO CEYLON, BOMBAY, AND ARABIA

Two motives made Henry Martyn eager to leave India for a time, and to cease the strain on his fast-ebbing strength, caused by incessant preaching and speaking: he desired to prolong his life, but to prolong it only till he should give the Mohammedans of Arabia and Persia the Word of God in their own tongues. After his first, almost fatal, attack at Dinapore, Corrie, who had gone to help him in his duties, wrote to 'the Patriarch,' as they called Mr. Brown, at Aldeen: 'He wishes to be spared on account of the translations, but with great earnestness said, "I wish to have my whole soul swallowed up in the will of God."' Two years after, Corrie wrote to England from Cawnpore: 'He is going to try sea air. May God render it effectual to his restoration. His life is beyond all price to us. You know

122

what a profound scholar he is, and all his acquirements are dedicated to the service of Christ. If ever man, since St. Paul, could use these words, he may, *One thing I do*. But the length of his life will depend on his desisting from public duties.' To Martyn himself, when at last he had left Cawnpore, Corrie wrote: 'If you will not take rest, dear brother, come away back;' informing him, at the same time, that he had returned to a Colonel, whom he had married, 1,600 rupees, he and Martyn having resolved to decline all fees for marrying and burying in India, where[316] such were a stumbling-block in the way of morality and religion, constituted as Anglo-Indian society was at that time.

When he was leaving Cawnpore, Henry Martyn was about to destroy what he called 'a number of memorandums.' These afterwards proved to be his *Journals* from January 1803 to 1811, some of which were written in Latin, and some in Greek, for greater secrecy. Corrie remonstrated with him, and persuaded him to seal them up and leave them in his hands. Lord Minto, the Governor-General, and General Hewett, the Commander-in-chief, after receiving a statement of Martyn's object, gave their sanction to his spending his sick-leave in Persia and Syria. At first the only ship he could find bound for Bombay, *en route* to the Persian Gulf, was one of the native buggalows which carried the coasting trade in the days before the British India Steam Navigation Company had begun to develop the commerce of the Indian Ocean all along East Africa, Southern Asia, the Spice Islands, and Australasia. But he wrote to Corrie:

The captain of the ship after many excuses has at last refused to take me, on the ground that I might try to convert the Arab sailors, and so cause a mutiny in the ship. So I am quite out of heart, and more than half disposed to go to the right about, and come back to Cawnpore.

His uncompromising earnestness as a witness for Christ was well known. Fortunately, a month after, the Honourable Mountstuart Elphinstone 'was proceeding to take the residency of Poona,' and Martyn secured a passage in the same ship, the Hummoody, an Arab coaster belonging to[317] a Muscat merchant, and manned by his Abyssinian slave as Nakhoda.

His last message to Calcutta, on the evening of the first Sunday of the year 1811, was on *The one thing needful*. Next morning he quietly went on board Mr. Elphinstone's pinnace 'without taking leave of my two dear friends in Calcutta.' As they dropped down the Hoogli, anchoring for two nights in its treacherous waters, his henceforth brief entries in his *Journal* are these: '8th. Conversation with Mr. Elphinstone, and disputes with his Persian moulvi, left me weak and in pain. 9th. Reached the ship at Saugur, and began to try my strength with the Arab sailors.' He found that the country-born captain, Kinsay, had been brought up by Schwartz, and he obtained from him much information regarding the habits and the rule of the Lutheran apostle of Southern India. This is new:

It was said that Schwartz had a warning given him of his death. One clear moonlight night he saw a light, and heard a voice which said to him, 'Follow me.' He got up and went to the door; here the vision vanished. The next day he sent for Dr. Anderson and said, 'An old tree must fall.' On the doctor's perceiving there was nothing the matter with him, Schwartz asked him whether he observed any disorder in his intellect; to which the doctor replied, 'No.' He and General Floyd (now in Ireland), another friend of Schwartz, came and stayed with him. The next fifteen days he was continually engaged in devotion, and attended no more to the school: on the last day he died in his chair.

Henry Martyn was well fitted by culture and training to appreciate the society of such statesmen and thinkers as[318] Mountstuart Elphinstone, Sir John Malcolm, Sir James Mackintosh, and Jonathan Duncan, who in their turn delighted in his society during the next five weeks. Of the first he wrote to Corrie: 'His agreeable manners and classical acquirements made me think myself fortunate indeed in having such a companion, and I found his company the most agreeable circumstance in my voyage.' They walked together in the cinnamon groves of Ceylon, when the ship touched at Colombo; together they talked of the work of Xavier as they skirted Cape Comorin, and observed Portuguese churches every two or three miles, with a row of huts on each side. 'Perhaps,' he wrote in his *Journal*, 'many of these poor people, with all the incumbrances of Popery, are moving towards the kingdom of heaven.' Together the two visited old Goa, the ecclesiastical capital, its convents and churches. The year after their visit the Goa Inquisition, one of the cruellest of its branches since its foundation, was suppressed. Henry Martyn's letters to Lydia Grenfell best describe his experiences and impressions:

TO LYDIA GRENFELL

At Sea, Coast of Malabar: February 4, 1811.

The last letter I wrote to you, my dearest Lydia, was dated November 1810. I continued in Calcutta to the end of the year, preaching once a week, and reading the Word in some happy little companies, with whom I enjoyed that sweet communion which all in this vale of tears have reason to be thankful for, but especially those whose lot is cast in a heathen land. On New-year's day, at Mr. Brown's urgent request, I preached a sermon for the Bible Society, recommending an immediate attention to the state of the native Christians. At the time I left Calcutta they talked[319] of forming an auxiliary society. Leaving Calcutta was so much like leaving England, that I went on board my boat without giving them notice, and so escaped the pain of bidding them farewell. In two days I met my ship at the mouth of the river, and we put to sea immediately. Our ship is commanded by a pupil of Schwartz, and manned by Arabians, Abyssinians, and others. One of my fellow-passengers is Mr. Elphinstone, who was lately ambassador at the court of the King of Cabul, and is now going to be resident at Poona, the capital of the Mahratta empire. So the group is rather interesting, and I am happy to say not averse to religious instruction; I mean the Europeans. As for the Asiatics, they are in language, customs, and religion, as far removed from us as if they were inhabitants of another planet. I speak a little Arabic sometimes to the sailors, but their contempt of the Gospel, and attachment to their own superstition, make their conversion appear impossible. How stupendous that power which can make these people the followers of the Lamb, when they so nearly resemble Satan in pride and wickedness! The first part of the voyage I was without employment, and almost without thought, suffering as usual so much from sea sickness, that I had not spirits to do anything but sit upon the poop, surveying the wide waste of waters blue. This continued all down the Bay of Bengal. At length in the neighbourhood of Ceylon we found smooth water, and came to an anchor off Colombo, the principal station in the island. The captain having proposed to his passengers that they should go ashore and refresh themselves with a walk in the cinnamon gardens, Mr. Elphinstone and myself availed ourselves of the offer, and went off to inhale the cinnamon breeze. The walk was delightful. The huts of the natives, who are (in that neighbourhood at least) most of them Protestants, are built in thick groves of cocoanut-tree, with openings here and there, discovering the sea. Everything bore the appearance of contentment. I[320] contemplated them with delight, and was almost glad that I could not speak with them, lest further acquaintance should have dissipated the pleasing ideas their appearance gave birth to. In the gardens I cut off a piece of the bark for you. It will not be so fragrant as that which is properly prepared; but it will not have lost its fine smell, I hope, when it reaches you.

At Captain Rodney's, the Chief Secretary to Government, we met a good part of the European society of Colombo. The party was like most mixed parties in England, where much is said that need not be remembered. The next day we stretched across the Gulf of Manaar, and soon came in sight of Cape Comorin, the great promontory of India. At a distance the green waves seemed to wash the foot of the mountain, but on a nearer approach little churches were seen, apparently on the beach, with a row of little huts on each side. Was it these maritime situations that recalled to my mind Perran church and town in the way to Gurlyn; or that my thoughts wander too often on the beach to the east of Lamorran? You do not tell me whether you ever walk there, and imagine the billows that break at your feet to have made their way from India. But why should I wish to know? Had I observed silence on that day and thenceforward, I should have spared you much trouble, and myself much pain. Yet I am far from regretting that I spoke, since I am persuaded that all things will work together for good. I sometimes try to put such a number of things together as shall produce the greatest happiness possible, and I find that even in imagination I cannot satisfy myself. I set myself to see what is that 'good for the sons of men, which they should do under heaven all the days of their life,' and I find that paradise is not here. Many things are delightful, some things are almost all one could wish; but yet in all beauty there is deformity, in the most perfect something wanting, and there is no hope of its ever being otherwise.[321] 'That which is crooked cannot be made straight, and that which is wanting cannot be numbered.' So that the expectation of happiness on earth seems chimerical to the last degree. In my schemes of happiness I place myself of course with you, blessed with great success in the ministry, and seeing all India turning to the Lord. Yet it is evident that with these joys there would be mingled many sorrows. The care of all the churches was a burden to the mighty mind of St. Paul. As for what we should be together, I judge of it from our friends. Are they quite beyond the vexations of common life? I think not—still I do not say that it is a question whether they gained or lost by marrying. Their affections will live when ours (I should rather say mine) are dead. Perhaps it may not be the effect of celibacy; but I certainly begin to feel a wonderful indifference to all but myself. From so seldom seeing a creature that cares for me, and never one that depends at all upon me, I begin to look round upon men with reciprocal apathy. It sometimes calls itself deadness to the world, but I much fear that it is deadness of heart. I am exempt from worldly cares myself, and therefore do not feel for others. Having got out of the stream into still water, I go round and round in my own little circle. This supposed deterioration you will ascribe to my humility; therefore I add that Mr. Brown could not help remarking the difference between what I am and what I was, and observed on seeing my picture, which was taken at Calcutta for Mr. Simeon, and is thought a striking likeness, that it was not Martyn that arrived in India, but Martyn the recluse.

February 10.—To-day my affections seem to have revived a little. I have been often deceived in times past, and erroneously called animal spirits joy in the Holy Ghost. Yet I trust that I can say with truth, 'To them who believe, He is precious!' Yes, Thou art precious to my soul, my transport and my trust. No thought now is so sweet as that which those words suggest[322]—'*In Christ.*' Our destinies thus inseparably united with those of the Son of God, what is too great to be expected? All things are yours, for ye are Christ's! We may ask what we will, and it shall be given to us. Now, why do I ever lose sight of Him, or fancy myself without Him, or try to do anything without Him? Break off a branch from a tree, and how long will it be before it withers? To-day, my beloved sister, I rejoice in you before the Lord, I rejoice in you as a member of the mystic body, I pray that your prayers for one who is unworthy of your remembrance may be heard, and bring down tenfold blessings on yourself. How good is the Lord in giving me grace to rejoice with His chosen all over the earth; even with those who are at this moment going up with the voice of joy and praise, to tread His courts and sing His praise. There is not an object about me but is depressing. Yet my heart expands with delight at the presence of a gracious God, and the assurance that my separation from His people is only temporary.

On the 7th we landed at Goa, the capital of the Portuguese possessions in the East. I reckoned much on my visit to Goa, expecting, from its being the residence of the archbishop and many ecclesiastics, that I should obtain such information about the Christians in India as would render it superfluous to make inquiries elsewhere, but I was much disappointed. Perhaps it was owing to our being accompanied by several officers, English and Portuguese, that the archbishop and his principal agents would not be seen; but so it was, that I scarcely met with a man who could make himself intelligible. We are shown what strangers are usually shown, the churches and monasteries, but I wanted to contemplate man, the only thing on earth almost that possesses any interest for me. I beheld the stupendous magnificence of their noble churches without emotion, except to regret that the Gospel was not preached in them. In one of the monasteries we saw the tomb of Francis Xavier, the Apostle of India, most richly ornamented, as[323] well as the room in which it stands, with paintings and figures in bronze, done in Italy. The friar who showed us the tomb, happening to speak of the grace of God in the heart, without which, said he, as he held the sacramental wafer, the body of Christ profits nothing. I began a conversation with him, which, however, came to nothing.

We visited among many other places the convent of nuns. After a long altercation with the lady porter we were admitted to the antechamber, in which was the grate, a window with iron bars, behind which the poor prisoners make their appearance. While my companions were purchasing their trinkets I was employed in examining their countenances, which I did with great attention. In what possible way, thought I, can you support existence, if you do not find your happiness in God? They all looked ill and discontented, those at least whose countenances expressed anything. One sat by reading, as if nothing were going on. I asked to see the book, and it was handed through the grate. Finding that it was a Latin prayer-book, I wrote in Latin something about the love of the world, which seclusion from it would not remove. The Inquisition is still existing at Goa. We were not admitted as far as Dr. Buchanan was, to the Hall of Examination, and that because he printed something against the inquisitors which came to their knowledge. The priest in waiting acknowledged that they had some prisoners within the walls, and defended the practice of imprisoning and chastising offenders, on the ground of its being conformed to the custom of the Primitive Church. We were told that when the officers of the Inquisition touch an individual, and beckon him away, he dares not resist; if he does not come out again, no one must ask about him; if he does, he must not tell what was done to him.

 February 18.—(Bombay.) Thus far I am brought in safety. On this day I complete my thirtieth year.[324] 'Here I raise my Ebenezer; Hither by Thy help I'm come.' 27th. It is sweet to reflect that we shall at last reach our home. I am here amongst men who are indeed aliens to the commonwealth of Israel and without God in the world. I hear many of those amongst whom I live bring idle objections against religion, such as I have answered a hundred times. How insensible are men of the world to all that God is doing! How unconscious of His purposes concerning His Church! How incapable, seemingly, of comprehending the existence of it! I feel the meaning of St. Paul's words—'Hath abounded toward us in all wisdom and prudence, having made known unto us the mystery of His will, that He would gather in one all things in Christ.' Well! let us bless the Lord. 'All thy children shall be taught of the Lord, and great shall be the peace of thy children.' In a few days I expect to sail for the Gulf of Persia in one of the Company's sloops of war.

 Farewell, my beloved Lydia, and believe me to be ever yours most affectionately,
 H. MARTYN.

 All through the voyage, in the Bay of Bengal and the Indian Ocean, the scholar was busy with his books, the Hebrew Old Testament, 'reading Turkish grammar, Niebuhr's *Arabia*, making extracts from Maracci's *Refutation of the Koran*, in general reading the Word of God with pleasure.'

 February 10. (Sunday.)—Somewhat of a happy Sabbath; I enjoyed communion with the saints, though far removed from them; service morning and night in the cabin.

 January 14 to 17.—When sitting on the poop Mr. Elphinstone kindly entertained me with information about India, the politics of which he has had such opportunities of making himself acquainted with. The Afghans, to whom he went as ambassador, to negotiate a treaty of alliance in case of invasion by the French, possess a tract of country considerably larger than Great Britain, using[325] the Persian and Pushtu languages. Their chief tribe is the Doorani, from which the king is elected. Shah Zeman was dethroned by his half-brother Mahmood, governor of Herat, who put out his eyes. Shah Zeman's younger brother Shoujjah took up arms, and after several defeats established himself for a time. He was on the throne when Mr. Elphinstone visited him, but since that Mahmood has begun to dispute the sovereignty with him. Mr. Elphinstone has been with Holkar and Sindia a good deal. Holkar he described as a little spitfire, his general, Meer Khan, possessed abilities; Sindia none; the Rajah of Berar the most politic of the native powers, though the Nizam the most powerful; the influence of residents at Nagpoor and Hyderabad very small.

 February 17.—Mostly employed in writing the Arabic tract, also in reading the Koran; a book of geography in Arabic, and *Jami Abbasi* in Persian.

 I would that all should adore, but especially that I myself should lie prostrate. As for self, contemptible self, I feel myself saying, let it be forgotten for ever; henceforth let Christ live, let Christ reign, let Him be glorified for ever.

 February 18.—Came to anchor at Bombay. This day I finish the 30th year of my unprofitable life, an age in which Brainerd had finished his course. He gained about a hundred savages to the Gospel; I can scarcely number the twentieth part. If I cannot act, and rejoice, and love with the ardour some did, oh, let me at least be holy, and sober, and wise. I am now at the age at which the Saviour of men began His ministry, and at which John the

Baptist called a nation to repentance. Let me now think for myself and act with energy. Hitherto I have made my youth and insignificance an excuse for sloth and imbecility: now let me have a character, and act boldly for God.

February 19.—Went on shore. Waited on the Governor, and was kindly accommodated with a room at the Government House.

[326]

The Governor was the good Jonathan Duncan, in the last year of his long administration and of his benevolent life. In the first decade of the nineteenth century Bombay was a comparatively little place, but the leaders of its English society were all remarkable men. In the short time, even then, Bombay had become the political and social centre of all the Asiatics and Africans, from Higher Asia, the Persian Gulf, and Arabia, to Abyssinia, Zanzibar, and the Comoro Isles; especially had it then begun to be what every generation since has made it more and more, the best centre from which to direct a Christian mission to the Mohammedans. With Poona, it is the capital of the most subtle and unimpressionable class, the Marathi Brahmans, and it is the point from which most widely to influence the Parsees. But as a base of operations against Islam it has never yet been fully used or appreciated. The late Hon. Ion Keith-Falconer preferred Aden, or the neighbouring village of Sheikh Othman, the British door into Arabia, of which he took possession for the Master by there laying down his life in the ripeness of his years, his scholarship, and his prosperity. But even in Arabia such work may be directed from Bombay. The city, like its harbour for commerce, stands without a rival as a missionary and civilising focus. Henry Martyn spent his weeks there in mastering the needs of its varied races and religionists, Jewish and Arabic, Persian and Brahman, talking with representative men of all the cults, and striving to influence them. He kept steadily in view his duty to the Mohammedans, writing his Arabic tract, and consulting as to his Persian translation of the Scriptures. It was not given to him to remain there. Dr. Taylor, whom he had joined with Brown and the Serampore Brotherhood at Aldeen in com[327]mending to God, was hard at work on the Malayalim New Testament, and he often visited the press to see the sacred work in progress. It was to be the life task of the Scottish Dr. John Wilson, twenty years after, to use Bombay as the missionary key of the peoples who border the Indian Ocean.

The friend of Mountstuart Elphinstone and guest of the Governor, Henry Martyn was welcomed by the literary society of the city, which at that time was unrivalled in the East. It is fortunate that we thus obtain an impartial estimate of his personal character and scholarship from such men as Elphinstone, Mackintosh, and Malcolm. In their journals and letters, written with all the frankness of private friendship, we see the consistent and ever-watchful saint, but at the same time the lively talker, the brilliant scholar, and, above all, the genial companion and even merry comrade. Since he had left Cambridge Henry Martyn had not enjoyed society like this, able to appreciate his many-sided gifts, and to call forth his natural joyfulness. In Bombay we see him at his best all round as man, scholar, saint, and missionary.

In Sir T.E. Colebrooke's Life of that most eminent Indian statesman who twice refused the crown of the Governor-General,[391] we find Mountstuart Elphinstone writing thus to his friend Strachey:[328]'We have in Mr. Martyn an excellent scholar, and one of the mildest, cheerfullest, and pleasantest men I ever saw. He is extremely religious, and disputes about the faith with the Nakhoda, but talks on all subjects, sacred and profane, and makes others laugh as heartily as he could do if he were an infidel. We have people who speak twenty-five languages (not apiece) in the ship.' Again, in his Journal of July 10, 1811, Elphinstone has this entry: 'Mr. Martyn has proved a far better companion than I reckoned on, though my expectations were high. His zeal is unabated, but it is not troublesome, and he does not press disputes and investigate creeds. He is familiar with Greek and Latin, understands French and Italian, speaks Persian and Arabic, has translated the Scriptures into Hindustani, and is translating the Old Testament from Hebrew. He was an eminent mathematician even at Cambridge, and, what is of more consequence, he is a man of good sense and taste, and simple in his manners and character, and cheerful in his conversation.' He who, in the close intimacy of shipboard life in the tropics, could win that eulogy from a critic so lofty and so experienced, must have been at once more human and more perfect than his secret *Journal,* taken alone, has led its readers to believe possible.

Sir John Malcolm, fresh from his second mission to Persia, was writing his great *History of Persia* in the quiet of Parell and Malabar Hill, with the help of the invaluable criticism of Sir James Mackintosh, whom he described to his brother Gilbert as 'a very extraordinary man.' Malcolm introduced Mackintosh and Elphinstone to each other, and Elphinstone lost not a day in taking Martyn to call on the Recorder. Although the distinguished Scots Highlander, who had become the admiring friend of Robert Hall when they were fellow students at Aberdeen University, was in full sympathy with missionary enthusiasm, and condemned the intolerance of the East India Company,[329][40] Martyn and he did not at first 'cotton' to each other. The former wrote thus of him:

1811, February 22.—Talked a good deal with the Governor about my intended journey.

February 23.—Went with him to his residence in the country, and at night met a large party, amongst whom were Sir J. Mackintosh and General Malcolm: with Sir James I had some conversation on different subjects; he was by no means equal to my expectations.

Mackintosh's account of their first interview was this:

February 24. (Sunday.)—Elphinstone introduced me to a young clergyman called Martyn, come round from Bengal on his way to Bussora, partly for health and partly to improve his Arabic, as he is translating the Scriptures into that language. He seems to be a mild and benevolent enthusiast—a sort of character with which I am always half in love. We had the novelty of grace before and after dinner, all the company standing.

Again, a week after:

March 1.—Mr. Martyn, the saint from Calcutta, called here. He is a man of acuteness and learning; his meekness is excessive, and gives a disagreeable impression of effort to conceal the passions of human nature.

Both had the Celtic fire, but Sir James Mackintosh had not lived with Sabat. Another month passed, and the two were learning to appreciate each other.

Padre Martyn, the saint, dined here in the evening; it was a very considerably more pleasant evening than usual; he is a mild and ingenious man. We had two or three hours' good discussion on grammar and metaphysics.

[330]

Henry Martyn's growing appreciation of Mackintosh is seen in this later passage in his *Journal:*

1811, March 1.—Called on Sir J. Mackintosh, and found his conversation, as it is generally said to be, very instructive and entertaining. He thought that the world would be soon Europeanised, in order that the Gospel might spread over the world. He observed that caste was broken down in Egypt, and the Oriental world made Greek by the successors of Alexander, in order to make way for the religion of Christ. He thought that little was to be apprehended, and little hoped for, from the exertions of missionaries. Called at General Malcolm's, and though I did not find him at home, was very well rewarded for my trouble in getting to his house, by the company of Mr. ——, lately from R. Dined at Farish's with a party of some very amiable and well-behaved young men. What a remarkable difference between the old inhabitants of India and the new-comers. This is owing to the number of religious families in England.

March 4.—Dined at General Malcolm's, who gave me a Chaldee missal. Captain Stewart, who had accompanied him as his secretary into Persia, gave me much information about the learned men of Ispahan.

March 8.—Spent the first part of the day at General Malcolm's, who gave me letters of introduction and some queries respecting the wandering tribes of Persia.

The reference to young Mr. Farish, is to one who afterwards became interim Governor of Bombay, and the friend of John Wilson, and who, because he taught a class in the Sunday School that used to meet in the Town Hall, was for the time an object of suspicion and attack by the Parsees and Hindus, on the baptism of Dhanjibhai Naoroji, the first Parsee to put on Christ.[41]

[331]

128

On Malcolm, according to Sir John Kaye, his biographer,[42] the young Christian hero appears to have made a more favourable impression than on Mackintosh. Perhaps the habitual cheerfulness of his manner communicated itself to the 'saint from Calcutta,' of whom he wrote to Sir Gore Ouseley, the British ambassador, that he was likely to add to the hilarity of his party.

He requested me to give him a line to the Governor of Bushire, which I did, as well as one to Mahomed Nebbee Khan. But I warned him not to move from Bushire without your previous sanction. His intention is, I believe, to go by Shiraz, Ispahan, and Kermanshah to Baghdad, and to endeavour on that route to discover some ancient copies of the Gospel, which he and many other saints are persuaded lie hid in the mountains of Persia. Mr. Martyn also expects to improve himself as an Oriental scholar; he is already an excellent one. His knowledge of Arabic is superior to that of any Englishman in India. He is altogether a very learned and cheerful man, but a great enthusiast in his holy calling. He has, however, assured me, and begged I would mention it to you, that he has no thought of preaching to the Persians, or of entering into any theological controversies, but means to confine himself to two objects—a research after old Gospels, and the endeavour to qualify himself for giving a correct version of the Scriptures into Arabic and Persian, on the plan proposed by the Bible Society.

I have not hesitated to tell him that I thought you would require that he should act with great caution, and not allow his zeal to run away with him. He declares he will not, and he is a man of that character that I must believe. I am satisfied that if you ever see him, you will be pleased with him. He will give you grace before and[332]after dinner, and admonish such of your party as take the Lord's name in vain; but his good sense and great learning will delight you, whilst his constant cheerfulness will add to the hilarity of your party.

In such social intercourse in the evening, in constant interviews and discussions with Jews and Mohammedans, Parsees and Hindus, during the day, and in frequent preaching for the chaplains, the weeks passed all too rapidly. A ropemaker who had just arrived from London called on him. 'He understood from my preaching that he might open his heart to me. We conversed and prayed together.' Against this and the communion with young Farish and his fellows, we must set the action of those whom he thus describes in a letter to Corrie:

1811, February 26.—Peacefully preaching the Word of life to a people daily edified is the nearest approach to heaven below. But to move from place to place, hurried away without having time to do good, is vexatious to the spirit as well as harassing to the body. Hearing last Saturday that some sons of Belial, members of the Bapre Hunt,[43] intended to have a great race the following day, I informed Mr. Duncan, at whose house I was staying, and recommended the interference of the secular arm. He accordingly sent to forbid it. The messengers of the Bapre Hunt were exceedingly exasperated; some came to church expecting to hear a sermon against hunting, but I merely preached to them on 'the one thing needful.' Finding nothing to lay hold of, they had the race on Monday, and ran *Hypocrite* against*Martha* and *Mary.*

[333]

His last message to India, from the 'faithful saying' of 1 Timothy i. 15, was misunderstood and resented, as his first sermon in Calcutta had been in similar circumstances.

March 24. (Sunday).—Speaking on the evidence of its truth, I mentioned its constant efficacy in collecting the multitude, and commanding their attention, which moral discourses never did. This was considered as a reflection on the ministers of Bombay, which distressed me not a little.

Henry Martyn was granted a passage to Arabia and Persia in the Benares, Captain Sealey, one of the ships of the old Indian Navy, ordered to cruise along with the Prince of Wales in the Persian Gulf. At that time the danger was considerable. For a century the Joasmi Arabs, of 'the pirate coast' of Oman, had been the terror of the Persian Gulf and the Indian Ocean, driving off even the early Portuguese, and confining the Persians, then invulnerable by land, to their own shores. The Wahabee puritans of Islam having mastered them, they added to their own bloodthirsty love of plunder and the slave-trade the fanaticism of Mohammed-ibn-Abdul-Wahab, the 'bestower of blessings,' as the name signifies. The East India Company tolerated them, retaining two or three ships of war in the Gulf for the protection of the factories at Gombroon, Bushire, and Busrah. But, in an evil moment, in the year 1797, the Joasmi pirates dared to seize a British vessel. From that hour their fate was sealed, though the process of clearing the southern coast of Asia of pirates and slavers ended only with the accession of Queen Victoria, in the year when Aden was added to the empire. In 1809-10 the Bombay Government expedition, under[334] Commodore John Wainwright, captured their stronghold of Ras-ul-Khymah, delivered our feudatory of Muscat from their terrorism, and gave the Gulf peace for ten years. The two ships of war which conveyed the chaplain missionary with his message of peace to Eastern Arabia and Persia were sent to complete the work of the Wainwright expedition,[44] which had been summoned by Lord Minto to the conquest of Java. Henry Martyn acted as chaplain to the forty-five sailors and twelve artillerymen who formed the European part of the crew of the Benares. After two days at Muscat he tells the story of his voyage:

TO LYDIA GRENFELL.

Muscat: April 22, 1811.

My dearest Lydia,—I am now in Arabia Felix: to judge from the aspect of the country it has little pretensions to the name, unless burning barren rocks convey an idea of felicity; but perhaps as there is a promise in reserve for the sons of Joktan, their land may one day be blest indeed.

We sailed from Bombay on Lady-day; and on the morning of Easter saw the land of Mekran in Persia. After another week's sail across the mouth of the Gulf, we arrived here, and expect to proceed up the Gulf to Bushire, as soon as we have taken in our water. You will be happy to learn that the murderous pirates against whom we were sent, having received notice of our approach, are all got out of the way, so that I am no longer liable to be shot in a battle, or to decapitation after it, if it be lawful to judge from appearances. These pestilent Ishmaelites indeed, whose hand is against every man's, will escape, and the community suffer, but that selfish friendship of which you once[335] confessed yourself guilty, will think only of the preservation of a friend. This last marine excursion has been the pleasantest I ever made, as I have been able to pursue my studies with less interruption than when ashore. My little congregation of forty or fifty Europeans does not try my strength on Sundays; and my two companions are men who read their Bible every day. In addition to all these comforts, I have to bless God for having kept me more than usually free from the sorrowful mind. We must not always say with Watts, 'The sorrows of the mind be banished from the place;' but if freedom from trouble be offered us, we may choose it rather. I do not know anything more delightful than to meet with a Christian brother, where only strangers and foreigners were expected. This pleasure I enjoyed just before leaving Bombay; a ropemaker who had just come from England, understood from my sermon that I was one he might speak to, so he came and opened his heart, and we rejoiced together. In this ship I find another of the household of faith. In another ship which accompanies us there are two Armenians who do nothing but read the Testament. One of them will I hope accompany me to Shiraz in Persia, which is his native country.

We are likely to be detained here some days, but the ship that will carry our letters to India sails immediately, so that I can send but one letter to England, and one to Calcutta. When will our correspondence be established? I have been trying to effect it these six years, and it is only yet in train. Why there was no letter from you in those dated June and July 1810, I cannot conjecture, except that you had not received any of mine, and would write no more. But I am not yet without hopes that a letter in the beloved hand will yet overtake me somewhere. My kindest and most affectionate remembrances to all the Western circle. Is it because he is your brother that I love George so much? or because he is the last come into the[336]number? The angels love and wait upon the righteous who need no repentance; but there is joy whenever another heir of salvation is born into the family. Read Eph. i. I cannot wish you all these spiritual blessings, since they already are all yours; but I pray that we may have the spirit of wisdom and knowledge to know that they are ours. It is a chapter I keep in mind every day in prayer. We cannot believe too much or hope too much. Happy our eyes that they see, and our ears that they hear.

As it may be a year or more before I shall be back, you may direct one letter after receiving this, if it be not of a very old date, to Bombay, all after to Bengal, as usual. Believe me to be ever, my dearest Lydia, your most affectionate,

H. MARTYN.

April 22.—Landed at Muscat with Lockett and walked through the bazaar; we wished to ascend one of the hills in the neighbourhood, but on the native guards expressing disapprobation, we desisted.

We turn to her *Diary* for the corresponding passage.

1812, February 1.—Heard yesterday from,[451] and wrote to-day to, India. My conviction of being declining in spiritual life is deeper and deeper. I would stop and pause at what is before me. It is no particular outward sin, but an inward loss I mourn.

Every word of Henry Martyn's *Journal* regarding Arabia is precious, alike in the light of his attempt to give its people the Word of God in their own tongue, and of the long delayed and too brief efforts of his successors, Ion Keith-Falconer in Yemen in 1887, and Bishop French in[337]Muscat in 1891. To David Brown, all unknowing of his death, he wrote on April 23:

I left India on Lady-day, looked at Persia on Easter Sunday, and seven days after found myself in Arabia Felix. In a small cove, surrounded by bare rocks, heated through, out of the reach of air as well as wind, lies the good ship Benares, in the great cabin of which, stretched on a couch, lie I. But though weak I am well—relaxed but not disordered. Praise to His grace who fulfils to me a promise which I have scarcely a right to claim—'I am with thee, and will keep thee in all places whither thou goest.'

Last night I went ashore for the first time with Captain Lockett; we walked through the bazaar and up the hill, but saw nothing but what was Indian or worse. The Imam or Sultan is about thirty miles off, fighting, it is said, for his kingdom, with the Wahabees.

You will be happy to learn that the pirates whom we were to scourge are got out of our way, so that I may now hope to get safe through the Gulf without being made to witness the bloody scenes of war.

April 24.—Went with one English party and two Armenians and an Arab who served as guard and guide, to see a remarkable pass about a mile from the town, and a garden planted by a Hindu in a little valley beyond. There was nothing to see, only the little bit of green in this wilderness seemed to the Arab a great curiosity. I conversed a good deal with him, but particularly with his African slave, who was very intelligent about religion. The latter knew as much about his religion as most mountaineers, and withal was so interested, that he would not cease from his argument till I left the shore.

To Corrie he wrote on the same day:

The Imam of Muscat murdered his uncle, and sits on the throne in the place of his elder brother, who is here a[338] cipher. Last night the Captain went ashore to a council of state, to consider the relations subsisting between the Government of Bombay and these mighty chieftains. I attended as interpreter. The Company's agent is an old Hindu who could not get off his bed. An old man in whom pride and stupidity seemed to contend for empire sat opposite to him. This was the Wazeer. Between them sat I, opposite to me the Captain. The Wazeer uttered something in Arabic, not one word of which could I understand. The old Hindu explained in Persian, for he has almost forgot his Hindi, and I to the Captain in English. We are all impatient to get away from this place.

To the last he was busy with his Arabic translation of Scripture. The ships of war crossed and recrossed the Gulf from shore to shore, surveying its coasts and islands in the heat of May, tempered by a north-wester which tossed them about. On May 6 he wrote in his *Journal*:

Much cast down through a sinful propensity, which I little thought was in me at all, till occasion manifested its existence.

On the 19th:

Preached to the ship's company on John iii. 3. My thoughts so much on Lydia, whose old letter I had been reading the day before, that I had a sense of guilt for having neglected the proper duties of the day.

May 20.—We have now a fair wind, carrying us gently to Bushire.

May 22.—Finished the syllabus of Ecclesiastical History which I have been making all the voyage, and extracts from Mosheim concerning the Eastern Church.

On May 21, 1811, Henry Martyn at last reached Persian soil.[339]

Landed at Bushire this morning in good health; how unceasing are the mercies of the Lord; blessed be His goodness; may He still preserve me from danger, and, above all, make my journey a source of future good to this kingdom of Persia, into which I am now come. We were hospitably received by the acting Resident. In the evening I walked out by the sea-side to recollect myself, to review the past, and look forward to the future.

Suffering the will of God is as necessary a part of spiritual discipline as doing, and much more trying.

But he landed still with the desire 'to go to Arabia circuitously by way of Persia,' a course which he declared to be rendered necessary by the advanced state of the season. The people of Arabia were first in his heart.

FOOTNOTES:

[39]In two volumes (John Murray), 1884, see p. 231, vol. i.

[40]*Memoirs*, edited by his son, second edition, London (Moxon), 1836. See vol. ii. pp. 86, 268.

[41]*The Life of John Wilson, D.D., F.R.S.* (John Murray), 2nd edit., p. 137.

[42]*Life and Correspondence*, vol. ii. p. 65 (Smith, Elder & Co.), 1856.

[43]*Bap re* = 'O Father!' the exclamation of Hindus when in surprise or grief; hence a noise or row; hence a Bobbery-pack or hunt is the Anglo-Indian for a pack of hounds of different breeds, or no breed, wherewith young officers hunt jackals or the like. See the late Colonel Sir Henry Yule's *Hobson-Jobson, or Anglo-Indian Glossary* (John Murray), 1886.

[44]C.R. Low's *History of the Indian Navy*, chapter x. vol. i. (Richard Bentley), 1877.

[45]By letter written April 22 or June 23, 1811.

[340]

CHAPTER IX

IN PERSIA—BUSHIRE AND SHIRAZ, 1811

The Persia to whose seven millions of people Henry Martyn was the first in modern times to carry the good-news of God, was just the size of the India of his day. The Mohammedan majority of its scattered inhabitants, in cities, in villages, and wandering over its plains and deserts, had never been, and are not yet, as Shi'ahs, rigid members of Islam, fanatically aggressive against all others, like the orthodox Soonnis. After the apparent extinction of the cult of Zoroaster and the flight of the surviving remnant of Parsees to India, the successive ruling dynasties were liberal and tolerant in their treatment of Christians compared with other Moslem powers; more liberal than Christian Russia is to the Jews and the non-'orthodox' sects. When those cultured and enterprising brothers, Sir Anthony and Sir Thomas Sherley,[46] went from Oxford to the court of Persia, then in all its magnificence under Shah Abbas the Great, two centuries before Henry Martyn, that Shah sent one back as Persian envoy to the Christian powers of Europe, to establish an alliance for the destruction of the Turks. Shah Abbas made over Gombroon to them, calling it by his own name, Bunder Abbas,[341] which it still retains, and his Majesty's grant used such language as this: 'Our absolute commandment, will, and pleasure is that our countries and dominions shall be from this day open to all Christian people *and to their religion*.... Because of the amitie now ioyned with the princes that professe Christ, I do give this patent for all Christian merchants,' etc. Only the intolerance of the Portuguese, who, under Albuquerque, took the island of Ormuz, and so dominated the Persian Gulf till driven out by the English, led this great Asiatic monarch to except the power which Prince Henry the Navigator alone redeems from historical contempt to the present day.

The Suffavian dynasty gave place to the Afghan, and that to the short-lived but wide-spreading empire of Nadir Kooli Khan, from Delhi to the Oxus River and the Caspian Sea. Out of half a century's bloody revolutions, such as formed the normal course of the annals of Asia till Great Britain pushed its 'Peace' up from the Southern Ocean, Aga Mohammed Khan, of the Kajar clan, founded the present dynasty in 1795. His still greater nephew succeeded on his death three years after. Futteh Ali Shah became for the next thirty-eight years the close friend of the British Crown and the East India Company. Shah-in-Shah, or king of the four kings of Afghanistan, Georgia, Koordistan, and Arabistan, the ruler of Persia had now incorporated Arabistan in his own dominion, and had lost Afghanistan. But he still claimed the allegiance of the two subject-sovereigns of Georgia and Koordistan. His uncle had avenged on the people, and especially the beautiful women of Georgia, the transfer of the country by its Wali to the Russian Catherine II. Placed in the commanding centre of Western Asia, Futteh Ali almost[342] immediately found himself the object of eager competition by the representatives of the Christian powers at Teheran. His revenue was estimated by so competent an authority as Sir John Malcolm at nearly six millions sterling. The crown jewels, chief of them the Sea of Light, or Derya-i-Noor, a diamond weighing 178 carats, were then the most valuable collection in the world; for though the Koh-i-Noor had remained with the Afghans, whence through the Sikhs it came to a greater Shah-in-Shah, the Queen-Empress of Great Britain, he still possessed not a little of Nadir's plunder of Delhi.

Sir Robert Ker Porter describes him about the time when Martyn reached his capital, as 'one blaze of jewels,' at the New Year festival of Norooz. On his head was a lofty tiara of three elevations, 'entirely composed of thickly-set diamonds, pearls, rubies, and emeralds, so exquisitely disposed as to form a mixture of the most beautiful colours in the brilliant light reflected from its surface. Several black feathers, like the heron plume, were intermixed with the resplendent aigrettes of this truly imperial diadem, whose bending points were furnished with pear-formed pearls of an immense size. The vesture was of gold tissue nearly covered with a similar disposition of jewelry; and crossing the shoulders were two strings of pearls, probably the largest in the world. But for splendour nothing could exceed the broad bracelets round his arms and the belt which encircled his waist; they actually blazed like fire when the rays of the sun met them. The throne was of pure white marble raised a few steps from the ground, and carpeted with shawls and cloth of gold. While the Great King was approaching his throne, the whole assembly continued bowing their heads to the ground till he had[343] taken his place. In the midst of solemn stillness, while all eyes were fixed on the bright object before them, which sat indeed as radiant and immovable as the image of Mithras itself, a sort of volley of words bursting at one impulse from the mouths of the mollahs and astrologers, made me start, and interrupted my gaze. This strange oratory was a kind of heraldic enumeration of the Great King's titles, dominions, and glorious acts. There was a pause, and then his Majesty spoke. The effect was even more startling than the sudden bursting forth of the mollahs; for this was like a voice from the tombs—so deep, so hollow, and, at the same time, so penetratingly loud.'[*]

That was the man to whose feet the French Emperor Napoleon and the Tsar Alexander, King George III. and the greatest Governor-General of the East India Company, the Marquess Wellesley, sent special embassies; the man from whom they sought secret treaties, lavishing on his courtiers more than royal gifts. To arrest the march of the Afghan invader, who a few years before had reached Lahore on his way to set up again at Delhi the house of Timour, and in order to foil the secret embassy sent by Napoleon, who had resolved to give England its death-blow through India, a young Scotsman, Captain Malcolm, was deputed to Teheran in 1801, following up a native envoy who had been most successful just before. This soldier diplomatist, who was afterwards to help Henry Martyn to a very different success, 'bribed like a king,' and returned with two treaties, political and commercial, but still more with the knowledge which fitted him to write his classic history,[344] and make his second ambassage. For England failed to carry out the first so far as to help the Shah against Russia, and from that hour Persia has seen province after province overwhelmed by the wave from the north.

Taking alarm a second time, just before and after the Peace of Tilsit, both the Crown and the Company appointed plenipotentiaries to Teheran. It was Lord Minto's wise policy to protect our Indian empire 'by binding the Western Frontier States in a chain of friendly alliance.' Hence the Governor-General's four missions, to Sindh, to Lahore, to Cabul, and again to Persia under Sir John Malcolm. Sir Harford Jones appeared as ambassador from the Crown after Malcolm had left Teheran, and took advantage of a change in the political situation to secure the preliminary treaty of 1809, which renewed the pledge of its predecessor to assist the Shah with troops or a subsidy if any European forces should invade his territories. In a modified form this became the definitive treaty of March 14, 1812 (further altered in that of 1814), to arrange which Sir Gore Ouseley was sent out, superseding both Malcolm and Jones.[48][345] Sir Gore Ouseley became Henry[345] Martyn's friend. Commended by Sir John Malcolm to his personal friends among the Persians, and officially encouraged by the British plenipotentiary, the Bengal chaplain seeking health had all the facilities secured to him that were possible to pursue the God-given mission of the apostle of Christ to the peoples of Persia and Arabia.

The strong and wise rule of Futteh Ali Shah kept Persia itself at peace, but he could not get the better of Russian intrigue and attack, even with the friendly offices of the British Government. Up till Martyn's arrival these vast regions had been wrested from the Shah-in-Shah: Georgia, Mingrelia, Daghistan, Sherwan, Karabagh, and Talish. During his presence in the country the negotiations with Russia were going on, which ended in 1813 in the Treaty of Gulistan, surrendering to the Tsar all he had taken, and apparently stopping his advance by a line of demarcation. But as its exact direction had to be settled by commissioners Russia has ever since continued steadily to strip Persia of its northern lands, and only the presence of the British Navy has kept it as yet out of the Persian Gulf.[49]

Such were the historical and political conditions amid which the missionary chaplain of India became a resident in the cities, and a traveller through the villages of Persia and Turkey at the age of thirty. He went there as the friend of Malcolm Sahib, whose gracious dignity and lavish gifts had made him a hero among the officials and many of the people of Persia. He went with letters of introduction[346] from the Governor-General of India and the Governor of Bombay to the new British ambassador, who had lived at Lucknow, and must have known well of his work in the neighbouring station of Cawnpore. He went with the reputation of a man of God in the Oriental sense, and of a scholar who knew the sacred books of Mohammedans and Christians alike, and who sought the good of the people. The Armenian colonies at Calcutta and Bombay had commended him to the many members of their Church in Persia.

Bushire, or Abu Shahr, at which he began his mission to Persia, is the port of that province of Fars from which the whole empire takes its name. Its mixed Persian and Arab population, now numbering some fifteen thousand, its insanitary position on a spit of sand almost surrounded by the sea, and the filthy narrow streets hardly redeemed by the Char Burj or citadel, and the British Residency, do not attract the visitor, and he soon learns that the humid heat of its climate in summer is more insupportable than that even of the Red Sea. From Reshire, close by, in the Anglo-Persian War of 1856-7, General Havelock shelled the town when he pitched the camp of the force to the south of its gate. Henry Martyn was there in the worst season of May and June, when the thermometer rises to 100° in the shade, and sometimes 106°. He became the guest of an English merchant and his Armenian wife, and was received by the Armenians as a priest of great sanctity. His *Journal* describes his receptions and daily occupations.

1811, May 23.—Rode out with a party in the evening, or rather in the afternoon, for the heat of the sun made me ill.

May 24.—The Governor called on us; also the Armenian priest. Received an answer from the ambas[347]sador, Sir Gore Ouseley, to a letter I sent him from Muscat.

May 25.—In the evening called with the two Captains, the Resident, and the Captain of his guard, on the Governor. In consequence of a letter I brought for him from General Malcolm, he was very particular in his attentions, seated me on his own seat, and then sat by my side apart from the rest. I observed that a Christian was not allowed to enter a mosque; he said, 'No,—do you wish to hear the prayers?' I said, 'No, but the preaching, if there is any;' he said there were no preachers except at Yezd.

May 26. (Sunday.)—The Europeans assembled for Divine service, which was performed at the Resident's. I preached on 1 Cor. xv.: 'For He must reign till He hath put all enemies under His feet,' etc. In the evening I went, at the padre's request, to the Armenian church. There was the same disagreeable succession of unmeaning ceremonies and noisy chants as at Bombay. I was introduced within the rails, and at the time of incense I was censed, as the padre afterwards desired me to observe, four times, whereas the laity have the honour done them but once. I asked the old man what was meant by burning incense. He said it was in imitation of the Wise Men of the East, who offered incense to Christ. I told him, Why then do you not offer myrrh and gold? To this he made no reply. Walking afterwards with him by the sea-side, I tried to get into a conversation suitable to our profession as ministers, speaking particularly of the importance of the charge entrusted to us. Nothing could be more vapid and mean than his remarks.

May 27.—Very ill, from head-ache and overpowering sleepiness, arising, as I suppose, from a stroke of the sun. As often as I attempted to read, I fell asleep, and awoke in weakness and pain. How easily may existence be embittered; still I will say, 'Not my will, but Thine be done.' In the evening a Jewish goldsmith called with a fine boy,[348] who read the Hebrew fluently. Grief has marked the countenance of the Eastern Jews in a way that makes them indescribably interesting. I could have wept while looking at them. O Lord, how long? Will Thine anger burn for ever?—is not justice yet satisfied? This afflicted people are as much oppressed in Persia as ever. Their women are not allowed to veil, as all others are required to do; hence, if there be one more than ordinarily beautiful, she is soon known, and a khan or the king sends for her, makes her a Mahometan, and puts her into the harem. As soon as he is tired, she is given to another, and then to another, till she becomes the property of the most menial servant; such is the degradation to which the daughters of Israel are subjected.

May 28.—Through the infinite and unmerited goodness of God I am again restored, and able to do something in the way of reading. The Resident gave us some account this evening of the moral state of Persia. It is enough to make one shudder. If God rained down fire upon Sodom and Gomorrah, how is it that this nation is not blotted out from under heaven? I do not remember to have heard such things of the Hindus, except the Sikhs; they seem to rival the Mahometans.

For personal comfort and freedom from insult or attack, Henry Martyn, when in Bushire, ordered the usual wardrobe of a Persian gentleman. He had suffered his beard and moustachios to vegetate undisturbed since leaving India, as he wrote to Corrie. In conical Astrakhan cap, baggy blue trousers, red boots, and light chintz tunic and *chogha* or flowing coat, mounted on a riding pony, and followed by his Armenian servant on a mule, with another mule for his baggage, he set out on May 30, 1811, for Shiraz. His companion was a British officer. The party formed a large caravan with some thirty horses and mules,[349] carrying goods to the ambassador. They marched by night, in the comparative coolness of 100°, to which the thermometer fell from the noonday heat of 126°, when they lay panting in their tents protected from the scorching dry wind by heavy clothing. The journey of some 170 miles occupied the first nine days of June. After ninety miles over a hot sandy plain the traveller rises, by four rocky *kotuls* or inclines, so steep as to be called ladders, over the spurs of the Zagros range into a cooler region at Kaziroon, on the central plateau of Iran, and then passes through the most delightful valleys, wooded or clad with verdure, to the capital, Shiraz, surrounded by gardens and by cemeteries.

May 30.—Our Persian dresses being ready, we set off this evening for Shiraz. Our kafila consisted of about thirty horses and mules; some carrying things to the ambassador, the rest for our servants and luggage; the animal for my use was a yaboo or riding pony, a mule for my trunks, and one for my servant Zechariah, an Armenian of Ispahan. It was a fine moonlight night, about ten o'clock, when we marched out of the gate of Bushire, and began to make our way over the plain. Mr. B., who accompanied me a little way, soon returned. Captain T. went on, intending to accompany us to Shiraz. This was the first time we had any of us put off the European, and the novelty of our situation supplied us with many subjects for conversation for about two hours. When we began to flag and grow sleepy, and the kafila was pretty quiet, one of the muleteers on foot began to sing: he sang with a voice so plaintive that it was impossible not to have one's attention arrested. At the end of the first tune he paused, and nothing was heard but the tinkling of the bells attached to the necks of the mules; every voice was hushed. The first line was enough for me, and I dare say it set many others thinking of their absent friends.[350]'Without thee my heart can attach itself to none.' It is what I have often felt on setting out on a journey. The friends left behind so absorb the thoughts, that the things by the wayside are seen without interest, and the conversation of strangers is insipid. But perhaps the first line, as well as the rest, is only a promise of fidelity, though I did not take it in that sense when I first heard it. The following is perhaps the true translation:

Think not that e'er my heart can dwell
Contented far from thee;
How can the fresh-caught nightingale
Enjoy tranquillity?

Forsake not then thy friend for aught
That slanderous tongues can say;
The heart that fixes where it ought,
No power can rend away.

Thus we went on, and as often as the kafila by their dulness and sleepiness seemed to require it, or perhaps to keep himself awake, he entertained the company and himself with a song. We met two or three other kafilas taking advantage of the night to get on. My loquacious servant Zachary took care to ask every one whence they came, and by that means sometimes got an answer which raised a laugh against him.

June 1.—At sunrise we came to our ground at Ahmeda, six parasangs, and pitched our little tent under a tree: it was the only shelter we could get. At first the heat was not greater than we had felt it in India, but it soon became so intense as to be quite alarming. When the thermometer was above 112°, fever heat, I began to lose my strength fast; at last it became quite intolerable. I wrapped myself up in a blanket and all the warm covering I could get, to defend myself from the external air; by which means the moisture was kept a little longer upon the body, and not so speedily evaporated as when the skin was exposed;|351| one of my companions followed my example, and found the benefit of it. But the thermometer still rising, and the moisture of the body being quite exhausted, I grew restless, and thought I should have lost my senses. The thermometer at last stood at 126°: in this state I composed myself, and concluded that though I might hold out a day or two, death was inevitable. Captain T., who sat it out, continued to tell the hour, and height of the thermometer; and with what pleasure did we hear of its sinking to 120°, 118°, etc. At last the fierce sun retired, and I crept out, more dead than alive. It was then a difficulty how I could proceed on my journey: for besides the immediate effects of the heat, I had no opportunity of making up for the last night's want of sleep, and had eaten nothing. However, while they were loading the mules, I got an hour's sleep, and set out, the muleteers leading my horse, and Zechariah, my servant, an Armenian, of Ispahan, doing all in his power to encourage me. The cool air of the night restored me wonderfully, so that I arrived at our next *munzil* with no other derangement than that occasioned by want of sleep. Expecting another such day as the former, we began to make preparation the instant we arrived on the ground. I got a tattie made of the branches of the date-tree, and a Persian peasant to water it; by this means the thermometer did not rise higher than 114°. But what completely secured me from the heat was a large wet towel, which I wrapped round my head and body, muffling up the lower part in clothes. How could I but be grateful to a gracious Providence, for giving me so simple a defence against what I am persuaded would have destroyed my life that day! We took care not to go without nourishment, as we had done: the neighbouring village supplied us with curds and milk. At sunset, rising up to go out, a scorpion fell upon my clothes; not seeing where it fell, I did not know what it was; but Captain T., pointing it out, gave the alarm, and I struck it off, and he|352| killed it. The night before we found a black scorpion in our tent; this made us rather uneasy; so that though the kafila did not start till midnight, we got no sleep, fearing we might be visited by another scorpion.

June 2.—We arrived at the foot of the mountains, at a place where we seemed to have discovered one of Nature's ulcers. A strong suffocating smell of naphtha announced something more than ordinarily foul in the neighbourhood. We saw a river:—what flowed in it, it seemed difficult to say, whether it were water or green oil; it scarcely moved, and the stones which it laved it left of a greyish colour, as if its foul touch had given them the leprosy. Our place of encampment this day was a grove of date-trees, where the atmosphere, at sunrise, was ten times hotter than the ambient air. I threw myself down on the burning ground, and slept; when the tent came up I awoke, as usual, in a burning fever. All this day I had recourse to the wet towel, which kept me alive, but would allow of no sleep. It was a sorrowful Sabbath; but Captain T. read a few hymns, in which I found great consolation. At nine in the evening we decamped. The ground and air were so insufferably hot, that I could not travel without a wet towel round my face and neck. This night, for the first time, we began to ascend the mountains. The road often passed so close to the edge of the tremendous precipices, that one false step of the horse would have plunged his rider into inevitable destruction. In such circumstances I found it useless to attempt guiding the animal, and therefore gave him the rein. These poor animals are so used to journeys of this sort, that they generally step sure. There was nothing to mark the road but the rocks being a little more worn in one place than in another. Sometimes my horse, which led the way, as being the muleteer's, stopped, as if to consider about the way: for myself, I could not guess, at such times, where the road lay, but he always found it. The sublime scenery would have impressed me much, in[353] other circumstances; but my sleepiness and fatigue rendered me insensible to everything around me. At last we emerged *superas ad auras*, not on the top of a mountain to go down again, but to a plain, or upper world. At the pass, where a cleft in the mountain admitted us into the plain, was a station of Rahdars. While they were examining the muleteer's passports, etc., time was given for the rest of the kafila to come up, and I got a little sleep for a few minutes.

June 4.—We rode briskly over the plain, breathing a purer air, and soon came in sight of a fair edifice, built by the king of the country for the refreshment of pilgrims. In this caravanserai we took our abode for the day. It was more calculated for Eastern than European travellers, having no means of keeping out the air and light. We found the thermometer at 110°. At the passes we met a man travelling down to Bushire with a load of ice, which he willingly disposed of to us. The next night we ascended another range of mountains, and passed over a plain, where the cold was so piercing that with all the clothes we could muster we were shivering. At the end of this plain we entered a dark valley, contained by two ranges of hills converging one to another. The muleteer gave notice that he saw robbers. It proved to be a false alarm; but the place was fitted to be a retreat for robbers; there being on each side caves and fastnesses from which they might have killed every man of us. After ascending another mountain, we descended by a very long and circuitous route into an extensive valley, where we were exposed to the sun till eight o'clock. Whether from the sun or from continued want of sleep, I could not, on my arrival at Kaziroon, compose myself to sleep; there seemed to be a fire within my head, my skin like a cinder, and the pulse violent. Through the day it was again too hot to sleep; though the place we occupied was a sort of summer-house in a garden of cypress-trees, exceedingly well fitted up with mats and coloured glass. Had the kafila gone on[354] that night, I could not have accompanied it; but it halted there a day, by which means I got a sort of night's rest, though I awoke twenty times to dip my burning hand in water. Though Kaziroon is the second greatest town in Fars, we could get nothing but bread, milk, and eggs, and those with difficulty. The Governor, who is under great obligations to the English, heard of our arrival, but sent no message.

June 5.—At ten we left Kaziroon and ascended a mountain: we then descended from it on the other side into a beautiful valley, where the opening dawn discovered to us ripe fields of wheat and barley, with the green oak here and there in the midst of it. We were reminded of an autumnal morning in England. Thermometer 62°.

June 6.—Half-way up the Peergan Mountain we found a caravanserai. There being no village in the neighbourhood, we had brought supplies from Kaziroon. My servant Zachary got a fall from his mule this morning, which much bruised him; he looked very sorrowful, and had lost much of his garrulity.

June 7.—Left the caravanserai at one this morning, and continued to ascend. The hours we were permitted to rest, the mosquitoes had effectually prevented me from using, so that I never felt more miserable and disordered; the cold was very severe; for fear of falling off, from sleep and numbness, I walked a good part of the way. We pitched our tent in the vale of Dustarjan, near a crystal stream, on the banks of which we observed the clover and golden cup: the whole valley was one green field, in which large herds of cattle were browsing. The temperature was about that of spring in England. Here a few hours' sleep recovered me in some degree from the stupidity in which I had been for some days. I awoke with a light heart, and said:|355| 'He knoweth our frame, and remembereth that we are but dust. He redeemeth our life from destruction, and crowneth us with loving kindness and tender mercies. He maketh us to lie down in the green pastures, and leadeth us beside the still waters.' And when we leave this vale of tears, there is 'no more sorrow, nor sighing, nor any more pain.' 'The sun shall not light upon thee, nor any heat; but the Lamb shall lead thee to living fountains of waters.'

June 8.—Went on to a caravanserai, three parasangs, where we passed the day. At night set out upon our last march for Shiraz. Sleepiness, my old companion and enemy, again overtook me. I was in perpetual danger of falling off my horse, till at last I pushed on to a considerable distance beyond the kafila, planted my back against a wall, and slept I know not how long, till the good muleteer came up and gently waked me.

June 9. (Sunday.)—By daylight we found ourselves in the plain of Shiraz. We went to the halting-place outside the walls of the city, but found it occupied; however, after some further delay, we were admitted with our servants into another; as for the kafila, we saw no more of it. The ambassador, Sir Gore Ouseley, was encamped near us; Sir William and Major D'Arcy, and Dr. Sharp, called on us, but I did not see the two first, being asleep at the time. In the evening we dined with his excellency, who gave us a general invitation to his table. Returned to our garden, where we slept.

June 10.—Went this morning to Jaffir Ali Khan's, to whom we had letters from General Malcolm, and with whom we are to take up our abode. After the long and tedious ceremony of coffee and *kaleans* (pipes), breakfast made its appearance on two large trays: curry, pilaws, various sweets cooled with snow and perfumed with rose-water, were served in great profusion in china plates and basins, a few wooden spoons beautifully carved; but being in a Persian dress, and on the ground, I thought it high time to throw off the European, and so ate with my hands. After breakfast Jaffir took me to a summer-house in his|356| garden, where his brother-in-law met us, for the purpose of a conversazione. From something I had thrown out at breakfast about Sabat, and accident, he was curious to know what were our opinions on these subjects. He then began to explain his own sentiments on Soofi-ism, of which it appeared he was a passionate admirer.

June 11.—Breakfasted at Anius with some of the Embassy, and went with them afterwards to a glass-house and pottery. Afterwards called on Mr. Morier, secretary to the Embassy, Major D'Arcy, and Sir W. Ouseley. Our host, Jaffir Ali Khan, gave us a good deal of information this evening, about this country and government. He used to sit for hours with the king at Teheran telling him about India and the English.

June 12.—Employed about *Journal*, writing letters, reading *Gulistan*, but excessively indolent. In the morning I enjoyed much comfort in prayer. What a privilege to have a God to go to, in such a place, and in such company. To read and pray at leisure seemed like coming home after being long abroad. Psalm lxxxix. was a rich repast to me. Why is it not always thus with me?

At Shiraz Henry Martyn was in the very heart of old Persia, to which the eldest son of Shem had given his name, Elam. One of the greatest of the Shahs, Kareem Khan, made Shiraz his capital, instead of the not distant Persepolis, which also Martyn visited. The founder of the present dynasty levelled its walls and desolated its gardens, but the city of the six gates still dominates the fine valley which no tyrant could destroy, and has still a pleasing appearance, though its Dewan Khana has been stripped of the royal pillars to adorn the palace of the new capital of Teheran. Even Timour respected Shiraz; when red with the blood of Ispahan, he sent for Hafiz, and asked how the poet dared to dispose of the Tartar's richest cities, Bokhara|357| and Samarcand, for the mole on his lady's cheek. 'Can the gifts of Hafiz ever impoverish Timour?' was the answer; and Shiraz was spared. Kareem Khan long after built mausoleums over the dust of the Anacreon of Persia, and over that of Sadi, its Socrates in verse, as Sir Robert Ker Porter well describes the author of the *Gulistan*, which was Martyn's daily companion at this time.

SHIRAZ

We have an account of Shiraz[50] and the people of Persia, written six years before Martyn's visit, by Edward Scott Waring, Esq., of the Bengal Civil Establishment, who, led by ill-health and curiosity, followed the same route by Bushire and Kaziroon to the city. He is sceptical as to those splendours which formed the theme of Hafiz, and describes the city as[358] 'worth seeing, but not worth going to see.' The tomb of the poet[51] the Hafizieh garden he found to be of white marble, on which two of his odes were very beautifully cut; a few durweshes daily visited the spot and chanted his verses. Mr. George N. Curzon, M.P.,[52] the latest visitor, contrasts the grave of Hafiz with that of his contemporary Dante, at Ravenna. Sadi's grave was then quite neglected; no one had carved on it the beautiful epitaph (paraphrased by Dryden) which he wrote for himself on the *Bostan*: 'O passenger! who walkest over my grave, think of the virtuous persons who have gone before me. What has Sadi to apprehend from being turned into dust? he was but earth when alive. He will not continue dust long, for the winds will scatter him over the whole universe.' Yet as long as the garden of knowledge has blossomed not a nightingale has warbled so sweetly in it. It would be strange if such a nightingale should die, and not a rose grow upon its grave. Sir Robert Ker Porter, twelve years later, found both spots alike neglected. One poet had written of the garden where Hafiz was buried,[359] 'Paradise does not boast such lovely banks as those of Rocknabeel, nor such groves as the high-scented fragrance of the bowers of Mosella.' Another now sadly writes, 'Though the bowers of love grew on its banks, and the sweet song of Hafiz kept time with the nightingale and the rose, the summer is past and all things are changed.'

Six years after Henry Martyn's residence in Shiraz, Sir Robert Ker Porter entered the city, which to him, as to every Christian or even English-speaking man, became thenceforth more identified with this century's apostle to the Persians than with even Hafiz and Sadi. 'Faint with sickness and fatigue,' he writes,[53][360] 'I felt a momentary reviving pleasure in the sight of a hospitable city, and the cheerful beauty of the view. As I drew near, the image of my exemplary countryman, Henry Martyn, rose in my thoughts, seeming to sanctify the shelter to which I was hastening. He had approached Shiraz much about the same season of the year, A.D. 1811, and like myself was gasping for life under the double pressure of an inward fire and outward burning sun. He dwelt there nearly a year, and on leaving its walls the apostle of Christianity found no cause for shaking off the dust of his feet against the Mohammedan city. The inhabitants had received, cherished and listened to him; and he departed thence amidst the blessings and tears of many a Persian friend. Through his means the Gospel had then found its way into Persia, and, as it appears to have been sown in kindly hearts, the gradual effect hereafter may be like the harvest to the seedling. But, whatever be the issue, the liberality with which his doctrines were permitted to have been discussed, and the hospitality with which their promulgation was received by the learned, the nobles, and persons of all ranks, cannot but reflect lasting honour on the Government, and command our respect for the people at large. Besides, to a person who thinks at all on these subjects, the circumstances of the first correct Persian translation of the Holy Scriptures being made at Shiraz, and thence put into the royal hands and disseminated through the empire, cannot but give an almost prophetic emphasis to the transaction, as arising from the very native country, Persia Proper, of the founder of the empire who first bade the temple of Jerusalem be rebuilt, who returned her sons from captivity, and who was called by name to the Divine commission.'

As the guest of Jaffir Ali Khan, now in his house in Shiraz, and now in his orange summer garden, Henry Martyn gave himself up to the two absorbing duties of making a new translation of the New Testament into Persian, assisted by his host's brother-in-law, Mirza Seyd Ali Khan, and of receiving and, in the Pauline sense, disputing with the learned Mohammedans of the city and neighbourhood. But all through his inner life, sanctified by his spiritual experience and intensifying that, there continued to run the love of Lydia Grenfell.

TO LYDIA GRENFELL.

Shiraz: June 23, 1811.

How continually I think of you, and indeed converse with you, it is impossible to say. But on the Lord's day in particular, I find you much in my thoughts, because it is on that day that I look abroad, and take a view of the universal church, of which I observe that the saints in England form the most conspicuous part. On that day, too, I indulge myself with a view of the past, and look over again those happy days, when, in company with those[361] I loved, I went up to the house of God with a voice of praise. How then should I fail to remember her who, of all that are dear to me, is the dearest? It is true that I cannot look back upon many days, nor even many hours passed with you—would they had been more—but we have insensibly become more acquainted with each other, so that, on my part at least, it may be said that separation has brought us nearer to one another. It was a momentary interview, but the love is lasting, everlasting. Whether we ever meet again or not, I am sure that you will continue to feel an interest in all that befalls me.

After the death of my dear sister, you bid me consider that I had one sister left while you remained; and you cannot imagine how consolatory to my mind this assurance is. To know that there is one who is willing to think of me, and has leisure to do so, is soothing to a degree that none can know but those who have, like me, lost all their relations.

I sent you a letter from Muscat, in Arabia, which I hope you received; for if not, report will again erase my name from the catalogue of the living, as I sent no other to Europe. Let me here say with praise to our ever-gracious Heavenly Father, that I am in perfect health; of my spirits I cannot say much; I fancy they would be better were 'the beloved Persis' by my side. This name, which I once gave you, occurs to me at this moment, I suppose, because I am in Persia, entrenched in one of its valleys, separated from Indian friends by chains of mountains and a roaring sea, among a people depraved beyond all belief, in the power of a tyrant guilty of every species of atrocity. Imagine a pale person seated on a Persian carpet, in a room without table or chair, with a pair of formidable moustachios, and habited as a Persian, and you see me.

June 26.—Here I expect to remain six months. The reason is this: I found on my arrival here, that our attempts[362] at Persian translation in India were good for nothing; at the same time they proposed, with my assistance, to make a new translation. It was an offer I could not refuse, as they speak the purest dialect of the Persian. My host is a man of rank, his name Jaffir Ali Khan, who tries to make the period of my captivity as agreeable as possible. His wife—for he has but one—never appears; parties of young ladies come to see her, but though they stay days in the house, he dare not go into the room where they are. Without intending a compliment to your sex, I must say that the society here, from the exclusion of females, is as dull as it can well be. Perhaps, however, to a stranger like myself, the most social circles would be insipid. I am visited by all the great and the learned; the former come out of respect to my country, the latter to my profession. The conversation with the latter is always upon religion, and it would be strange indeed, if with the armour of truth on the right hand and on the left, I were not able to combat with success the upholders of such a system of absurdity and sin. As the Persians are a far more unprejudiced and inquisitive people than the Indians, and do not stand quite so much in awe of an Englishman as the timid natives of Hindustan, I hope they will learn something from me; the hope of this reconciles me to the necessity imposed on me of staying here; about the translation I dare not be sanguine. The prevailing opinion concerning me is, that I have repaired to Shiraz in order to become a Mussulman. Others, more sagacious, say that I shall bring from India some more, under pretence of making them Mussulmans, but in reality to seize the place. They do not seem to have thought of my wish to have them converted to my religion; they have been so long accustomed to remain without proselytes to their own. I shall probably have very little to write about for some months to come, and therefore I reserve the extracts of my *Journal* since I last wrote to you for some other oppor[363]tunity; besides that, the ambassador, with whose despatches this will go, is just leaving Shiraz.

July 2.—The Mohammedans now come in such numbers to visit me, that I am obliged, for the sake of my translation-work, to decline seeing them. To-day one of the apostate sons of Israel was brought by a party of them, to prove the Divine mission of Mohammed from the Hebrew Scriptures, but with all his sophistry he proved nothing. I can almost say with St. Paul, I feel continual pity in my heart for them, and love them for their fathers' sake, and find a pleasure in praying for them. While speaking of the return of the Jews to Jerusalem, I observed that the 'Gospel of the kingdom must first be preached in all the world, and then shall the end come.' He replied with a sneer, 'And this event, I suppose you mean to say, is beginning to take place by your bringing the Gospel to Persia.'

July 5.—I am so incessantly occupied with visitors and my work, that I have hardly a moment for myself. I have more and more reason to rejoice at my being sent here; there is such an extraordinary stir about religion throughout the city, that some good must come of it. I sometimes sigh for a little Christian communion, yet even from these Mohammedans I hear remarks that do me good. To-day, for instance, my assistant observed, 'How He loved those twelve persons!' 'Yes,' said I, 'and not those twelve only, but all those who shall believe in Him, as He said, "I pray not for them alone, but for all them who shall believe on me through their word."' Even the enemy is constrained to wonder at the love of Christ. Shall not the object of it say, What manner of love is this? I have learned that I may get letters from England much sooner than by way of India. Be so good as to direct to me, to the care of Sir Gore Ouseley, Bart., Ambassador at Teheran, care of J. Morier, Esq., Constantinople, care of G. Moon, Esq., Malta. I have seen Europe newspapers of[364]only four months' date, so that I am delightfully near you. May we live near one another in the unity of the Spirit, having one Lord, one hope, one God and Father. In your prayers for me pray that utterance may be given me that I may open my mouth boldly, to make known the mysteries of the Gospel. I often envy my Persian hearers the freedom and eloquence with which they speak to me. Were I but possessed of their powers, I sometimes think that I should win them all; but the work is God's, and the faith of His people does not stand in the wisdom of men, but in the power of God. Remember me as usual with the most unfeigned affection to all my dear friends. This is now the seventh letter I send you without having received an answer. Farewell!

Yours ever most affectionately,

H. MARTYN.

Shiraz: September 8, 1811.

A courier on his way to the capital affords me the unexpected pleasure of addressing my most beloved friend. It is now six months since I left India, and in all that time I have not heard from thence. The dear friends there, happy in each other's society, do not enough call to mind my forlorn condition. Here I am still, beset by cavilling infidels, and making very little progress in my translation, and half disposed to give it up and come away. My kind host, to relieve the tedium of being always within a walled town, pitched a tent for me in a garden a little distance, and there I lived amidst clusters of grapes, by the side of a clear stream; but nothing compensates for the loss of the excellent of the earth. It is my business, however, as you will say, and ought to be my effort, to make saints, where I cannot find them. I do use the means in a certain way, but frigid reasoning with men of perverse minds seldom brings men to Christ. However, as they require it, I reason, and accordingly challenged them to prove the[365] Divine mission of their prophet. In consequence of this, a learned Arabic treatise was written by one who was considered as the most able man, and put into my hands; copies of it were also given to the college and the learned. The writer of it said that if I could give a satisfactory answer to it he would become a Christian, and at all events would make my reply as public as I pleased. I did answer it, and after some faint efforts on his part to defend himself, he acknowledged the force of my arguments, but was afraid to let them be generally known. He then began to inquire about the Gospel, but was not satisfied with my statement. He required me to prove from the very beginning the Divine mission of Moses, as well as of Christ; the truth of the Scriptures, etc. With very little hope that any good will come of it, I am now employed in drawing out the evidences of the truth; but oh! that I could converse and reason, and plead with power from on high. How powerless are the best-directed arguments till the Holy Ghost renders them effectual.

A few days ago I was just on the eve of my departure for Ispahan, as I thought, and my translator had consented to accompany me as far as Baghdad, but just as we were setting out, news came that the Persians and Turks were fighting thereabouts, and that the road was in consequence impassable. I do not know what the Lord's purpose may be in keeping me here, but I trust it will be for the furtherance of the Gospel of Christ, and in that belief I abide contentedly.

My last letter to you was dated July. I desired you to direct to me at Teheran. As it is uncertain whether I shall pass anywhere near there, you had better direct to the care of S. Morier, Esq., Constantinople, and I can easily get your letters from thence.

I am happy to say that I am quite well, indeed, never better; no returns of pain in the chest since I left India. May I soon receive the welcome news that you also are|366|well, and prospering even as your soul prospers. I read your letters incessantly, and try to find out something new, as I generally do, but I begin to look with pain at the distant date of the last. I cannot tell what to think, but I cast all my care upon Him who hath already done wonders for me, and am sure that, come what will, it shall be good, it shall be best. How sweet the privilege that we may lie as little children before Him! I find that my wisdom is folly and my care useless, so that I try to live on from day to day, happy in His love and care. May that God who hath loved us, and given us everlasting consolation and good hope through grace, bless, love, and keep my ever-dearest friend; and dwelling in the secret place of the Most High, and abiding under the shadow of the Almighty, may she enjoy that sweet tranquillity which the world cannot disturb. Dearest Lydia! pray for me, and believe me to be ever most faithfully and affectionately yours,

H. MARTYN.

Shiraz: October 21, 1811.

It is, I think, about a month since I wrote to you, and so little has occurred since that I find scarcely anything in my *Journal*, and nothing worth transcribing. This state of inactivity is becoming very irksome to me. I cannot get these Persians to work, and while they are idle I am sitting here to no purpose. Sabat's laziness used to provoke me excessively, but Persians I find are as torpid as Arabs when their salary does not depend on their exertions, and both very inferior to the feeble Indian, whom they affect to despise. My translator comes about sunrise, corrects a little, and is off, and I see no more of him for the day. Meanwhile I sit fretting, or should do so, as I did at first, were it not for a blessed employment which so beguiles the tediousness of the day that I hardly perceive it passing. It is the study of the Psalms in the Hebrew. I have long|367| had it in contemplation, in the assurance, from the number of flat and obscure passages that occur in the translations, that the original has not been hitherto perfectly understood. I am delighted to find that many of the most unmeaning verses in the version turn out, on close examination, to contain a direct reference to the Lord our Saviour. The testimony of Jesus is indeed the spirit of prophecy. He is never lost sight of. Let them touch what subject they will, they must always let fall something about Him. Such should we be, looking always to Him. I have often attempted the 84th Psalm, endeared to me on many accounts as you know, but have not yet succeeded. The glorious 16th Psalm I hope I have mastered. I write with the ardour of a student communicating his discoveries and describing his difficulties to a fellow student.

I think of you incessantly, too much, I fear, sometimes; yet the recollection of you is generally attended with an exercise of resignation to His will. In prayer I often feel what you described five years ago as having felt—a particular pleasure in viewing you as with me before the Lord, and entreating our common Father to bless both His children. When I sit and muse my spirit flies away to you, and attends you at Gurlyn, Penzance, Plymouth Dock, and sometimes with your brother in London. If you acknowledge a kindred feeling still, we are not separated; our spirits have met and blended. I still continue without intelligence from India; since last January I have heard nothing of any one person whom I love. My consolation is that the Lord has you all under His care, and is carrying on His work in the world by your means, and that when I emerge I shall find that some progress is made in India especially, the country I now regard as my own. Persia is in many respects a ripe field for the harvest. Vast numbers secretly hate and despise the superstition imposed on them, and as many of them as have heard the Gospel approve it, but they dare not hazard their lives for the|368| name of the Lord Jesus. I am sometimes asked whether the external appearance of Mohammedanism might not be retained with Christianity, and whether I could not baptize them without their believing in the Divinity of Christ. I tell them, No.

Though I have complained above of the inactivity of my translation, I have reason to bless the Lord that He thus supplies Gibeonites for the help of His true Israel. They are employed in a work of the importance of which they are unconscious, and are making provision for future Persian saints, whose time is, I suppose, now near. Roll back, ye crowded years, your thick array! Let the long, long period of darkness and sin at last give way to the brighter hours of light and liberty, which wait on the wings of the Sun of Righteousness. Perhaps we witness the dawn of the day of glory, and if not, the desire that we feel, that Jesus may be glorified, and the nations acknowledge His sway, is the earnest of the Spirit, that when He shall appear we shall also appear with Him in glory. Kind love to all the saints who are waiting His coming.

Yours, with true affection, my ever dearest Lydia,

H. MARTYN.

It is now determined that we leave Shiraz in a week, and as the road through Persia is impassable through the commotions which are always disturbing some part or other of this unhappy country, I must go back to Bushire.

My scribe finished the New Testament; in correcting we are no further than the 13th of Acts.

October 24 to 26.—Resumed my Hebrew studies; on the two first days translated the eight first Psalms into Persian, the last all day long thinking about the word Higgaion in the 9th Psalm.

October 27 to 29.—Finished Psalm xii. Reading the 5th of St. Matthew to Zachariah my servant. Felt awfully convinced of guilt; how fearlessly do I give way to causeless anger, speaking contemptuously of men, as if I had never read this chapter. The Lord deliver me from all my wickedness, and write His holy law upon my heart, that I may walk circumspectly before Him all the remaining days of my life.

November 1.—Everything was prepared for our journey to Baghdad by the Persian Gulf, and a large party of Shiraz ladies, chiefly of Mirza Seid Ali's family, had determined to accompany us, partly from a wish to visit the tombs, and partly to have the company of their relations a little longer. But a letter arriving with the intelligence that Bagdhad was all in confusion, our kafila separated, and I resolved to go on through Persia to Armenia, and so to Syria. But the season was too far advanced for me to think of traversing the regions of Caucasus just then, so I made up my mind to winter at Shiraz.

FOOTNOTES:

[46] *The Three Brothers, or the Travels and Adventures of Sir Anthony, Sir Robert, and Sir Thomas Sherley in Persia, Russia, Turkey, Spain, &c.,* London, 1825.

[47] *Travels in Georgia, Persia, Armenia, Ancient Babylonia, &c.,* by Sir Robert Ker Porter, 2 vols., London, 1821.

[48] Mr. J.C. Marshman, C.S.I., who lived through the history of India, from Wellesley to Lord Lawrence, and personally knew almost all its distinguished men, writes in his invaluable History: 'The good sense of Sir Harford and Colonel Malcolm gradually smoothed down all asperities, and it was not long before they agreed to unite their efforts to battle the intrigues and the cupidity of the court. Colonel Malcolm was received with open arms by the king, who considered him the first of Englishmen. "What induced you," said he at the first interview, "to hasten away from Shiraz without seeing my son?" "How could I," replied the Colonel with his ever ready tact, "after having been warmed by the sunshine of your Majesty's favour, be satisfied with the mere reflection of that refulgence in the person of your son?" "Mashalla!" exclaimed the monarch, "Malcolm Sahib is himself again." ... Sir Gore Ouseley had acquired the confidence of Lord Wellesley by the great talents he exhibited when in a private station at the court of Lucknow, and upon his recommendation was appointed to Teheran as the representative of the King of England.' The two embassies cost the East India Company 380,000*l.*

[49] Sir C.U. Aitchison's *Collection of Treaties, Engagements, and Sunnuds relating to India and Neighbouring Countries,* 2nd edition, vol. vi. Calcutta, 1876.

[50] *A Tour to Sheeraz by the route of Karroon and Feerozabad,* London, 1807.

[51] In two splendid volumes, printed by native hands under the sanction of the Government at Calcutta, in 1891, Lieutenant-Colonel H. Wilberforce Clarke published an English prose translation of *The Divan, written in the Fourteenth Century,* by Khwaja Shamshu-d-

Din Muhammad-i-Hafiz. The work is described in the *Quarterly Review* of January 1892, by a writer who thus begins: 'About two miles north-west of Shiraz, in the garden called Mosella which is, being interpreted, "the place of prayer," lies, beneath the shadow of cypress-trees, one of which he is said to have planted with his own hand, Shems-Edden Mohammed, surnamed Hafiz, or "the steadfast in Scripture," poet, recluse, and mystic.... No other Persian has equalled him in fame—not Sadi, whose monument, now in ruins, may be visited near his own; nor Firdusi, nor Jami. Near the garden tomb is laid open the book of well nigh seven hundred poems which he wrote. According to Sir Gore Ouseley, who turned over its pages in 1811, it is a volume abounding in bright and delicate colour, with illuminated miniatures, and the lovely tints of the Persian caligraphy.'

[52]*Persia and the Persian Question*, 2 vols. (Longmans), 1892.

[53]*Travels*, vol. i. pp. 687-8.

[370]

CHAPTER X
IN PERSIA—CONTROVERSIES WITH MOHAMMEDANS, SOOFIS, AND JEWS

Henry Martyn's first week in Persia was enough to lead him to use such language as this: 'If God rained down fire upon Sodom and Gomorrah, how is it that this nation is not blotted out from under heaven? I do not remember to have heard such things of the Hindus, except the Sikhs; they seem to rival the Mohammedans.' The experienced Bengal civilian, Mr. E. Scott Waring, had thus summed up his impressions: 'The generality of Persians are sunk in the lowest state of profligacy and infamy, and they seldom hesitate alluding to crimes which are abhorred and detested in every civilised country in the universe. Their virtues consist in being most excellent companions, and in saying this we say everything which can be advanced in their favour. The same argument cannot be advanced for them which has been urged in favour of the Greeks, for they have laws which stigmatise the crimes they commit.' Every generation seems to have departed farther and farther from the character of the hero-king, Cyrus. At the present time, after two visits to Europe by their Shah, the governing class, the priestly[371] order of Moojtahids, and the people seem to be more hopelessly corrupt than ever.[54]

So early as the twelfth century the astronomer-poet of Persia, Omar Khayyam, of Naishapur, in his few hundred tetrastichs of exquisite verse which have ever since won the admiration of the world, struck the note of dreary scepticism and epicurean sensuality, as the Roman Lucretius had done. His age was one of spiritual darkness, when men felt their misery, and all the more that they saw no means of relieving it. The purer creed of Zoroaster had been stamped down but not rooted out by the illiterate Arab hordes of Mohammed. A cultured Aryan race could not accept submissively the ignorant fanaticism of the Semitic sons of the desert. The Arabs destroyed or drove out ultimately to India the fire-worshippers who had courage to prefer their faith to the Koran; the mass of the people and their leaders worked out the superficial Mohammedanism identified with the name and the sufferings of Ali. The new national religion became more and more a falsehood, alike misrepresenting the moral facts and the character and claims of God, and not really believed in by the general conscience. The few who from time to time arose endowed with spiritual fervour or poetic fire, found no vent through the popular religion, and no satisfaction for the aching void of the heart. The loftier natures ran by an inevitable law of the human mind either into such self-indulgent despairing scepticism as Omar Khayyam's, or into the sensual mysticism of Sadi, Jami, and Hafiz, of the whole tribe of ascetic enthusiasts and impostors, the Soofis, fakeers, and durweshes, who fill the world of Islam, from[372] the mosques on the Bosporus to the secret chambers of Persia and Oudh. To all such we may use one of the few rare tetrastichs which Omar Khayyam was compelled by his higher nature to write:[55]

O heart! wert thou pure from the body's dust,
Thou shouldest soar naked spirit above the sky;
Highest heaven is thy native seat—for shame, for shame,
That thou shouldest stoop to dwell in a city of clay!

We must remember all this when we come to the disputations of Henry Martyn with the doctors of Shiraz and Persia. They, and some fifteen millions out of the hundred and eighty millions of Islam in the world, are Shi'ahs, or 'followers' of Ali, whom, as Mohammed's first cousin and son-in-law, they accept as his first legitimate imam, kaliph, or successor; while they treat the *de facto* kaliphs of the Soonni Muslims—Abu Bakr, Omar, and Othman—as usurpers. The Persians are in reality more tolerant of the Christians, the Jews, and even the Majusi (Magi), or fire-worshippers, all of whom are people of the Book who have received an inspired revelation, than of their Soonni co-religionists. The people—though not of course their ruler, who is of Turkish origin—are more tolerant of new sects, such as that of Babism, and even their spiritual guides or the more respectable among these are in expectation of a new leader, the twelfth, the Imam-al-Mahdi, who has once before been manifested, and has long been waiting secretly for the final consummation.

We must also realise the extent to which Soofi-ism had saturated the upper classes and the Moojtahid order, who sought out Henry Martyn, and even recognised in|373| him the Divine drunkenness, so that they always treated him and spoke of him as a *merdi khodai*, a man of God. The first Soofi—a name taken either from the word for the woollen dress of the Asiatic or from that for purity—was Ali, according to the Shi'ahs; but this form of philosophical mysticism, often attended by carnal excesses through which its devotees express themselves, is rather Hindu in its origin. The deepest thought of the Asiatic, without the revelation of Jesus Christ, is for Brahman and Buddhist, Sikh and Soofi, Hindu and Mohammedan, this absorption into the Divine Essence, so as to lose all personality and individual consciousness. That Essence may be the sum total of all things—the materialistic side; or the spirit underlying matter, the idealistic side, but the loss of individuality is the ultimate aim. But such absorption can be finally reached only by works—asceticism, pilgrimage, almsgiving, meditation—and by cycles of trans-migrations to sublimate the soul for unconsciousness of all that is objective, and of self itself. Hafiz is as full of wine and women in his poems as Anacreon or the worst of the Latin erotic poets; but the Soofis, who revel in his verses, maintain that they 'profess eager desire with no carnal affection, and circulate the cup, but no material goblet, since all things are spiritual in their sect; all is mystery within mystery.'

What Henry Martyn learned to find, in even his brief experience of the Aryan Shi'ahs, to whom he offered the love of Christ and through the Son a personal union with the Father, is best expressed in this description by the most recent skilled writer on the people, before referred to:

Persia is the one purely Mohammedan country which, in the process of a national revolt against the rigid hide|374|-bound orthodoxy of Islam, has only succeeded in wrapping more closely round its national and political life the encircling folds of that 'manteau commode, sous lequel s'abrite, en se cachant à peine, tout le passé.' Under the extravagances and fanaticism of the Shi'ah heresy, the old Zoroastrian faith lives on, transformed into an outward conformity to the forms of the Moslem creed, and the product is that grotesque confusion of faith and fanaticism, mysticism and immorality, rationalism and superstition, which is the despair and astonishment of all who have looked beneath the surface of ordinary everyday life in Persia. Soofi-ism, with its profound mysticism and godless doctrine, has found a congenial home in Persia, often, indeed, blossoming into beautiful literary form such as is found in the *Rubaiyāt* of Omar Khayyam, or in the delightful pages of the *Gulistan* of Sheikh Sadi, or in the poems of Hafiz.

Soofi-ism is the illegitimate offspring of scepticism and fanaticism. It is tersely described by one Persian writer as 'a sensual plunging into the abyss of darkness'; by another as 'a deadly abomination'; and by a third as 'the part of one who goes raving mad with unlawful lusts.' Nevertheless, as Professor Kuenen has well observed, the true Soofi is a Moslem no more.

All Martyn's experience among the Wahabees of Patna and the Shi'ahs of Lucknow had fitted him for the discussions which were almost forced upon him in Persia, for he went there to translate the New Testament afresh. But he had, in his reading, sought to prepare himself for the Mohammedan controversy. When coasting round India, he made this entry in his *Journal*|375| '*1811, January 28.*—Making extracts from Maracci's *Refutation of Koran*. Felt much false shame at being obliged to confess my ignorance of many things which I ought to have known.' Soofi-ism met him the day after he reached Shiraz, on the first visit of Seyd Ali, brother-in-law of his host, Jaffir Ali Khan. Thus:

June 10.—He spoke so indistinctly, and with such volubility, that I did not well comprehend him, but gathered from his discourse that we are all parts of the Deity. I observed that we had not these opinions in Europe, but understood that they were parts of the Brahmanic system. On my asking him for the foundation of his opinions, he said the first argument he was prepared to bring forward was this: God exists, man also exists, but existence is not twofold, therefore God and man are of the same nature. The minor I disputed: he defended it with many words. I replied by objecting the consequences, Is there no difference between right and wrong? There appeared a difference, he said, to us, but before God it was nothing. The waves of the sea are so many aspects and forms, but it is still but one and the same water. In the outset he spoke with great contempt of all revelation. 'You know,' said he, 'that in the law and Koran, etc., it is said, God *created heaven* and the*earth,*' etc. Reverting to this, I asked whether these opinions were agreeable to what the prophets had spoken. Perceiving me to be not quite philosophical enough for him, he pretended some little reverence for them, spoke of them as good men, etc., but added that there was no evidence for their truth but what was traditionary. I asked whether there was anything unreasonable in God's making a revelation of His will. He said, No. Whether a miracle for that purpose was not necessary, at least useful, and therefore credible? He granted it. Was not evidence from testimony rational evidence? Yes. Have you then rational evidence for the religion of Mohammed? He said the division of the moon was generally brought forward, but he saw no sufficient evidence for believing it; he mentioned the Koran with[376]some hesitation, as if conscious that it would not stand as a miracle. I said eloquence depended upon opinion; it was no miracle for any but Arabs, and that some one may yet rise up and write better. He allowed the force of the objection, and said the Persians were very far from thinking the eloquence of the Koran miraculous, however the Arabs might think so. The last observation he made was, that it was impossible not to think well of one by whose example and instructions others had become great and good; though therefore little was known of Mohammed, he must have been something to have formed such men as Ali. Here the conversation ceased. I told them in the course of our conversation that, according to our histories, the law and Gospel had been translated into Persian before the time of Mohammed. He said they were not to be found, because Omar in his ignorant zeal had probably destroyed them. He spoke with great contempt of the 'Arab asses.'

June 13.—Seyd Ali breakfasted with us. Looking at one of the plates in Hutton's*Mathematical Dictionary,* where there was a figure of a fountain produced by the rarefaction of the air, he inquired into the principle of it, which I explained; he disputed the principle, and argued for the exploded idea that nature abhors a vacuum. We soon got upon religion again. I showed him some verses in the Koran in which Mohammed disclaims the power of working miracles. He could not reply. We talked again on the evidence of testimony. The oldest book written by a Mohammedan was the sermons of Ali. Allowing these sermons to be really his, I objected to his testimony for Mohammed, because he was interested in the support of that religion. I asked him the meaning of a contested passage; he gave the usual explanation; but as soon as the servants were gone he turned round and said, 'It is only to make a rhyme.' This conversation seemed to be attended with good. Our amiable host, Jaffir Ali, Mirza Jan, and Seyd[377] Ali seemed to be delighted with my arguments against Mohammedanism, and did not at last evince a wish to defend it. In the evening Jaffir Ali came and talked most agreeably on religious subjects, respecting the obvious tendency of piety and impiety, and the end to which they would lead in a future world. One of his remarks was, 'If I am in love with any one, I shall dream of her at night; her image will meet me in my sleep. Now death is but a sleep; if therefore I love God, or Christ, when I fall asleep in death I shall meet Him, so also if I love Satan or his works.' He could wish, he said, if he had not a wife and children, to go and live on the top of a mountain, so disgusted was he with the world and its concerns. I told him this was the first suggestion in the minds of devotees in all religions, but that in reality it was not the way to escape the pollution of the world, because a man's wicked heart will go with him to the top of a mountain. It is the grace of God changing the heart which will alone raise us above the world. Christ commands His people to 'abide in Him'; this is the secret source of fruitfulness, without which they are as branches cut off from the tree. He asked whether there was no mention of a prophet's coming after Christ. I said, No. 'Why then,' said he, 'was any mention made of Ahmed in the Koran?' He said, 'One day an English gentleman said to me, "I believe that Christ was no better than myself." "Why then," said I, "you are worse than a Mohammedan."'

June 24.—Went early this morning to the Jewish synagogue with Jaffir Ali Khan. At the sight of a Mohammedan of such rank, the chief person stopped the service and came to the door to bring us in. He then showed us the little room where the copies of the law were kept. He said there were no old ones but at Baghdad and Jerusalem; he had a printed copy with the Targum, printed at Leghorn. The only European letters in it were the words 'con approbazione,' of which he was anxious to know the [378] meaning. The congregation consisted chiefly of little boys, most of whom had the Psalter. I felt much distressed that the worship of the God of Israel was not there, and therefore I did not ask many questions. When he found I could read Hebrew, he was very curious to know who I might be, and asked my name. I told him Abdool Museeh, in hopes that he would ask more, but he did not, setting me down, I suppose, as a Mohammedan.

June 25.—Every day I hear stories of these bloody Tartars. They allow no Christian, not even a Soonni, to enter their country, except in very particular cases, such as merchants with a pass; but never allow one to return to Persia if they catch him. They argue, 'If we suffer this creature to go back, he will become the father of other infidels, and thus infidelity will spread: so, for the sake of God and His prophet, let us kill him.' About 150 years ago the men of Bokhara made an insidious attempt to obtain a confession from the people of Mushed that they were Shi'ahs. Their moulvies begged to know what evidence they had for the Khaliphat of Ali. But the men of Mushed, aware of their purpose, said, 'We Shi'ahs! no, we acknowledge thee for friends.' But the moollahs of Bokhara were not satisfied with this confession, and three of them deliberated together on what ought to be done. One said: 'It is all hypocrisy; they must be killed.' The other said: 'No, if all be killed we shall kill some Soonnis.' The third said: 'If any can prove that their ancestors have ever been Soonnis they shall be saved, but not else.' Another rejoined that, from being so long with Shi'ahs, their faith could not be pure, and so it was better to kill them. To this another agreed, observing that though it was no sin before men to let them live, he who spared them must be answerable for it to God. When the three bloody inquisitors had determined on the destruction of the Shi'ah city, they gave the signal, and 150,000 Tartars marched down and put all to the sword. [379]

June 26.—We were to-day, according to our expectation, just about setting off for Ispahan, when, Mirza Ibrahim returning, gave us information that the Tartars and Koords had made an irruption into Persia, and that the whole Persian army was on its march to Kermanshah to meet them. Thus our road is impassable. I wrote instantly to the ambassador, to know what he would advise, and the minister sent off an express with it. Mirza Ibrahim, after reading my answer, had nothing to reply, but made such a remark as I did not expect from a man of his character, namely, that *he* was sufficiently satisfied the Koran was a miracle, though he had failed to convince me. Thus my labour is lost, except it be with the Lord. I have now lost all hope of ever convincing Mohammedans by argument. The most rational, learned, unprejudiced, charitable men confessedly in the whole town cannot escape from the delusion. I know not what to do but to pray for them. I had some warm conversation with Seyd Ali on his infidelity. I asked him what he wanted. Was there any one thing on earth, of the same antiquity, as well attested as the miracles, etc., of Christianity? He confessed not, but he did not know the reason he could not believe: perhaps it was levity and the love of the world, or the power of Satan, but he had no faith at all. He could not believe even in a future state. He asked at the end, 'Why all this earnestness?' I said, 'For fear you should remain in hell for ever.' He was affected, and said no more.

June 27.—The Prime Minister sent me, as a present, four mules-load of melons from Kaziroon. Seyd Ali reading the 2nd chapter of St. Matthew, where the star is said to go before the wise men, asked: 'Then what do you say to that, after what you were proving yesterday about the stars?' I said:[380] 'It was not necessary to suppose it was one of those heavenly bodies; any meteor that had the appearance of a star was sufficient for the purpose, and equally miraculous.' 'Then why call it a star?' 'Because the magi called it so, for this account was undoubtedly received from them. Philosophers still talk of a falling star, though every one knows that it is not a star.'

September 2 to 6.—At Mirza Ibrahim's request we are employed in making out a proof of the Divine mission of Moses and Jesus. He fancies that my arguments against Mohammedanism are equally applicable against these two, and that as I triumphed when acting on the offensive, I shall be as weak as he when I act on the defensive.

September 7 to 11.—Employed much the same; daily disputes with Jaffir Ali Khan about the Trinity; if they may be called disputes in which I bring forward no arguments, but calmly refer them to the Holy Scriptures. They distress and perplex themselves without measure, and I enjoy a peace, as respects these matters, which passeth understanding. There is no passage that so frequently occurs to me now as this: 'They shall be all taught of God, and great shall be the peace of thy children.' I have this testimony that I have been taught of God.

1812, January 19.—Aga Baba coming in while we were translating, Mirza Seyd Ali told him he had been all the day decrying the law. It is a favourite tenet of the Soofis, that we should be subject to no law. Aga Baba said that if Christ, while He removed the old law, had also forborne to bring in His new way, He would have done still better. I was surprised as well as shocked at such a remark from him, but said nothing. The poor man, not knowing how to exist without amusement, then turned to a game at chess. How pitiable is the state of fallen man! Wretched, and yet he will not listen to any proposals of relief; stupidly ignorant, yet too wise to submit to learn anything from God. I have often wondered to see how the merest dunce thinks himself qualified to condemn and ridicule revealed religion. These Soofis pretend too to be latitudinarians, assigning idolaters the same rank as others in nearness to God, yet they have all in their turn spoken contemptuously[381] of the Gospel. Perhaps because it is so decisively exclusive. I begin now to have some notion of Soofi-ism. The principle is this: Notwithstanding the good and evil, pleasure and pain that is in the world, God is not affected by it. He is perfectly happy with it all; if therefore we can become like God we shall also be perfectly happy in every possible condition. This, therefore, is salvation.

January 21.—Aga Boozong, the most magisterial of the Soofis, stayed most of the day with Mirza Seyd Ali and Jaffir Ali Khan in my room. His speech as usual—all things are only so many forms of God; paint as many figures as you will on a wall, it is still but the same wall. Tired of constantly hearing this same vapid truism, I asked him, 'What then? With the reality of things we have nothing to do, as we know nothing about them.' These forms, if he will have it that they are but forms, affect us with pleasure and pain, just as if they were more real. He said we were at present in a dream; in a dream we think visionary things real—when we wake we discover the delusion. I asked him how did he know but that this dream might continue for ever. But he was not at all disposed to answer objections, and was rather vexed at my proposing them. So I let him alone to dissent as he pleased. Mirza Seyd Ali read him some verses of St. Paul, which he condescended to praise, but in such a way as to be more offensive to me than if he had treated it with contempt. He repeated again how much he was pleased with the sentiments of Paul, as if his being pleased with them would be a matter of exultation to me. He said they were excellent precepts for the people of the world. The parts Mirza Seyd Ali read were Titus iii. and Hebrews viii. On the latter Mirza Seyd Ali observed that he (Paul) had not written ill, but something like a good reasoner. Thus they sit in judgment on God's Word, never dreaming that they are to be judged by it. On the contrary, they regard the best parts, as they call them, as approaching only[382]towards the heights of Soofi-ism. Aga Boozong finally observed that as for the Gospels he had not seen much in them, but the Epistles he was persuaded would make the book soon well known. There is another circumstance that gained Paul importance in the eyes of Mirza Seyd Ali, which is, that he speaks of Mark and Luke as his servants.

January 24.—Found Seyd Ali rather serious this evening. He said he did not know what to do to have his mind made up about religion. Of all the religions Christ's was the best, but whether to prefer this to Soofi-ism he could not tell. In these doubts he was tossed to and fro, and is often kept awake the whole night in tears. He and his brother talk together on these things till they are almost crazed. Before he was engaged in this work of translation, he says, he used to read about two or three hours a day; now he can do nothing else; has no inclination for anything else, and feels unhappy if he does not correct his daily portion. His late employment has given a new turn to his thoughts as well as to those of his friends; they had not the most distant conception of the contents of the New Testament. He says his Soofi friends are exceedingly anxious to see the Epistles, from the accounts he gives of them, and also he is sure that almost the whole of Shiraz are so sensible of the load of unmeaning ceremonies in which their religion consists, that they will rejoice to see or hear of anything like freedom, and that they would be more willing to embrace Christ than the Soofis, who, after taking so much pains to be independent of all law, would think it degrading to submit themselves to any law again, however light.

February 4.—Mirza Seyd Ali, who has been enjoying himself in idleness and dissipation these two days instead of translating, returned full of evil and opposition to the Gospel. While translating 2 Peter iii., 'Scoffers ... saying, Where is the promise of his coming?' he began to ask 'Well, they are in the right; where are any of His promises fulfilled?' I said the heathen nations have been given to|383| Christ for an inheritance. He said No; it might be more truly said that they are given to Mohammed, for what are the Christian nations compared with Arabia, Persia, India, Tartary, etc.? I set in opposition all Europe, Russia, Armenia, and the Christians in the Mohammedan countries. He added, at one time when the Abbasides carried their arms to Spain, the Christian name was almost extinct. I rejoined, however, that he was not yet come to the end of things, that Mohammedanism was in itself rather a species of heretical Christianity, for many professing Christians denied the Divinity of our Lord, and treated the Atonement as a fable. 'They do right,' said he; 'it is contrary to reason that one person should be an atonement for all the rest. How do you prove it? it is nowhere said in the Gospels. Christ said He was sent only to the lost sheep of the house of Israel.' I urged the authority of the Apostles, founded upon His word, 'Whatsoever ye shall bind on earth shall be bound in heaven, and whatsoever ye shall loose on earth,' etc. 'Why, what are we to think of them,' said he, 'when we see Paul and Barnabas quarrelling; Peter acting the hypocrite, sometimes eating with the Gentiles, and then withdrawing from fear; and again, all the Apostles, not knowing what to do about the circumcision of the Gentiles, and disputing among themselves about it?' I answered, 'The infirmities of the Apostles have nothing to do with their authority. It is not everything they do that we are commanded to imitate, nor everything they might say in private, if we knew it, that we are obliged to attend to, but the commands they leave for the Church; and here there is no difference among them. As for the discussions about circumcision, it does not at all appear that the Apostles themselves were divided in their opinions about it; the difficulty seems to have been started by those believers who had been Pharisees.' 'Can you give me a proof,' said he,|384| 'of Christianity, that I may either believe, or be left without excuse if I do not believe—a proof like that of one of the theorems of Euclid?' I said it is not to be expected, but enough may be shown to leave every man inexcusable. 'Well,' said he, 'though this is only probability, I shall be glad of that.' 'As soon as our Testament is finished,' I replied, 'we will, if you please, set about our third treatise, in which, if I fail to convince you, I can at least state the reasons why I believed.' 'You had better,' said he, 'begin with Soofi-ism, and show that that is absurd'—meaning, I suppose, that I should premise something about the *necessity* of revelation. After a little pause, 'I suppose,' said he, 'you think it sinful to sport with the characters of those holy men?' I said I had no objection to hear all their objections and sentiments, but I could not bear anything spoken disrespectfully of the Lord Jesus; 'and yet there is not one of your Soofis,' I added, 'but has said something against Him. Even your master, Mirza Abul Kasim, though he knows nothing of the Gospel or law, and has not even seen them, presumed to say that Moses, Christ, Mohammed, etc., were all alike. I did not act in this way. In India I made every inquiry, both about Hinduism and Mohammedanism. I read the Koran through twice. On my first arrival here I made it my business to ask for your proofs, so that if I condemned and rejected it, it was not without consideration. Your master, therefore, spoke rather precipitately.' He did not attempt to defend him, but said, 'You never heard *me* speak lightly of Jesus.' 'No; there is something so awfully pure about Him that nothing is to be said.'

March 18.—Sat a good part of the day with Abul Kasim, the Soofi sage, Mirza Seyd Ali, and Aga Mohammed Hasan, who begins to be a disciple of the old man's. On my expressing a wish to see the Indian book, it was proposed to send for it, which they did, and then read it aloud. The stoicism of it I controverted, and said that the entire annihilation of the passions, which the stupid Brahman described as perfection, was absurd. On my continuing to[385] treat other parts of the book with contempt, the old man was a little roused, and said that this was the way that pleased them, and my way pleased me. That thus God provided something for the tastes of all, and as the master of a feast provides a great variety, some eat *pilao*, others prefer *kubab*, etc. On my again remarking afterwards how useless all these descriptions of perfection were, since no rules were given for attaining it, the old man asked what in my opinion was the way. I said we all agreed in one point, namely, that union with God was perfection; that in order to that we must receive the Spirit of God, which Spirit was promised on condition of believing in Jesus. There was a good deal of disputing about Jesus, His being exclusively the visible God. Nothing came of it apparently, but that Mirza Seyd Ali afterwards said, 'There is no getting at anything like truth or certainty. We know nothing at all; you are in the right, who simply believe because Jesus had said so.'

March 22.—These two days I have been thinking from morning to night about the Incarnation; considering if I could represent it in such a way as to obviate in any degree the prejudices of the Mohammedans; not that I wished to make it appear altogether agreeable to reason, but I wanted to give a consistent account of the nature and uses of this doctrine, as they are found in the different parts of the Holy Scriptures. One thing implied another to such an extent that I thought necessarily of the nature of life, death, spirit, soul, animal nature, state of separate spirits, personality, the person of Christ, etc., that I was quite worn out with fruitless thought. Towards evening Carapiet with another Armenian came and conversed on several points of theology, such as whether the fire of hell were literally fire or only remorse, whether the Spirit proceeded from the Father and the Son, or from the Father only, and how we are to reconcile those two texts, that 'for every idle word that men shall speak,' etc., with the promises of salvation[386] through faith? Happening to speak in praise of some person who practised needless austerities, I tried to make him understand that this was not the way of the Gospel. He urged these texts—'Blessed are they that mourn,' 'Blessed are ye that weep now,' etc. While we were discussing this point, Mohammed Jaffir, who on a former occasion had conversed with me a good deal about the Gospel, came in. I told him the question before us was an important one, namely, how the love of sin was to be got out of the heart. The Armenian proceeded, 'If I wish to go to a dancing or drinking, I must deny myself.' Whether he meant to say that this was sufficient I do not know, but the Mohammedan understanding him so, replied that he had read yesterday in the Gospel, 'that whosoever looketh upon a woman,' etc., from which he inferred that obedience of the heart was requisite. This he expressed with such propriety and gracefulness, that, added to the circumstance of his having been reading the Gospel, I was quite delighted, and thought with pleasure of the day when the Gospel should be preached by Persians. After the Armenians were gone we considered the doctrines of the Soofis a little. Finding me not much averse to what he thought some of their most exceptionable tenets, such as union with God, he brought this argument: 'You will allow that God cannot bind, compel, command Himself.' 'No, He cannot.' 'Well, if we are one with God, we cannot be subject to any of His laws.' I replied: 'Our union with God is such an union as exists between the members of a body. Notwithstanding the union of the hand with the heart and head, it is still subject to the influence and control of the ruling power in the person.' We had a great deal of conversation afterwards on the Incarnation. All his Mohammedan prejudices revolted. 'Sir, what do you talk of? the self-existent become contained in space, and suffer need!' I told him that it was the manhood of Christ that suffered need, and as for the essence of the Deity, if he would tell[387] me anything about it, where or how it was, I would tell him how the Godhead was in Christ. After an effort or two he found that every term he used implied our frightful doctrine, namely, personality, locality, etc. This is a thought that is now much in my mind—

that it is so ordered that, since men never can speak of God but through the medium of language, which is all material, nor think of God but through the medium of material objects, they do unwillingly come to God through the Word, and think of God by means of an Incarnation.

March 28.—The same person came again, and we talked incessantly for four hours upon the evidences of the two religions, the Trinity, Incarnation, etc., until I was quite exhausted, and felt the pain in my breast which I used to have in India.

April 7.—Observing a party of ten or a dozen poor Jews with their priest in the garden, I attacked them, and disputed a little with the Levite on Psalms ii., xvi. and xxiv. They were utterly unacquainted with Jesus, and were surprised at what I told them of His Resurrection and Ascension. The priest abruptly broke off the conversation, told me he would call and talk with me in my room, and carried away his flock. Reading afterwards the story of Joseph and his brethren, I was much struck with the exact correspondence between the type and antitype. Jesus will at last make Himself known to His brethren, and then they will find that they have been unknowingly worshipping Him while worshipping the Lord of Hosts, the God of Israel.

April 8.—The Prince dining to-day at a house on the side of a hill, which commands a view of the town, issued an order for all the inhabitants to exhibit fireworks for his amusement, or at least to make bonfires on the roofs of their houses, under penalty of five tomans in case of neglect. Accordingly fire was flaming in all directions, enough to have laid any city in Europe in ashes. One man fell off a roof and was killed, and two others in the same way were[388] so hurt that their lives were despaired of, and a woman lost an eye by the stick of a sky-rocket.

July 9.—Made an extraordinary effort, and as a Tartar was going off instantly to Constantinople, wrote letters to Mr. Grant for permission to come to England, and to Mr. Simeon and Lydia, informing them of it; but I have scarcely the remotest expectation of seeing it, except by looking at the Almighty power of God.

Dined at night at the ambassador's, who said he was determined to give every possible *éclat* to my book, by presenting it himself to the King. My fever never ceased to rage till the 21st, during all which time every effort was made to subdue it, till I had lost all my strength and almost all my reason. They now administer bark, and it may please God to bless the tonics; but I seem too far gone, and can only say, 'Having a desire to depart and be with Christ, which is far better.'

TO REV. D. CORRIE

Shiraz: September 12, 1811.

Dearest Brother,—I can hardly conceive, or at least am not willing to believe, that you would forget me six successive months; I conclude, therefore, that you must have written, though I have not seen your handwriting since I left Calcutta.

The Persian translation goes on but slowly. I and my translator have been engaged in a controversy with his uncle, which has left us little leisure for anything else. As there is nothing at all in this dull place to take the attention of the people, no trade, manufactures, or news, every event at all novel is interesting to them. You may conceive, therefore, what a strong sensation was produced by the stab I aimed at the vitals of Mohammed. Before five people had seen what I wrote, defences of Islam swarmed into ephemeral being from all the moulvi maggots of the[389] place, but the more judicious men were ashamed to let me see them. One moollah, called Aga Akbar, was determined to distinguish himself. He wrote with great acrimony on the margin of my pamphlet, but passion had blinded his reason, so that he smote the wind. One day I was on a visit of ceremony to the Prime Minister, and sitting in great state by his side, fifty visitors in the same hall, and five hundred clients without, when who should make his appearance but my tetric adversary, the said Aga Akbar, who came for the express purpose of presenting the Minister with a piece he had composed in defence of the prophet, and then sitting down told me he should present me with a copy that day. 'There are four answers,' said he, 'to your objection against his using the sword.' 'Very well,' said I, 'I shall be glad to see them, though I made no such objection.' Eager to display his attainments in all branches of science, he proceeded to call in question the truth of our European philosophy, and commanded me to show that the earth moved, and not the sun. I told him that in matters of religion, where the salvation of men was concerned, I would give up nothing to them, but as for points in philosophy they might have it all their own way. This was not what he wanted; so after looking at the Minister, to know if it was not a breach of good manners to dispute at such a time, and finding that there was nothing contrary to custom, but that, on the contrary, he rather expected an answer, I began, but soon found that he could comprehend nothing without diagrams. A moonshi in waiting was ordered to produce his implements, so there was I, drawing figures, while hundreds of men were looking on in silence.

But all my trouble was in vain—the moollah knew nothing whatever of mathematics, and therefore could not understand my proofs. The Persians are far more curious and clever than the Indians. Wherever I go they ask me questions in philosophy, and are astonished that I do not[390] know everything. One asked me the reason of the properties of the magnet. I told him I knew nothing about it. 'But what do your learned men say?' '*They* know nothing about it.' This he did not at all credit.

I do not find myself improving in Persian; indeed, I take no pains to speak it well, not perceiving it to be of much consequence. India is the land where we can act at present with most effect. It is true that the Persians are more susceptible, but the terrors of an inquisition are always hanging over them. I can now conceive no greater happiness than to be settled for life in India, superintending native schools, as we did at Patna and Chunar. To preach so as to be readily understood by the poor is a difficulty that appears to me almost insuperable, besides that grown-up people are seldom converted. However, why should we despair? If I live to see India again, I shall set to and learn Hindi in order to preach. The day may come when even our word may be with the Holy Ghost and with power. It is now almost a year since I left Cawnpore, and my journey is but beginning: when shall I ever get back again? I am often tempted to get away from this prison, but again I recollect that some years hence I shall say: 'When I was at Shiraz why did not I get the New Testament done? What difference would a few months have made?' In August I passed some days at a vineyard, about a parasang from the city, where my host pitched a tent for me, but it was so cold at night that I was glad to get back to the city again. Though I occupy a room in his house, I provide for myself. Victuals are cheap enough, especially fruit; the grapes, pears, and water-melons are delicious; indeed, such a country for fruit I had no conception of. I have a fine horse which I bought for less than a hundred rupees, on which I ride every morning round the walls. My vain servant, Zechariah, anxious that his master should appear like an ameer, furnished him (*i.e.* the horse) with a saddle, or rather a pillion, which[391] fairly covers his whole back; it has all the colours of the rainbow, but yellow is predominant, and from it hang down four large tassels, also yellow. But all my finery does not defend me from the boys. Some cry out, 'Ho, Russ!' others cry out, 'Feringhi!' One day a brickbat was flung at me, and hit me in the hip with such force that I felt it quite a providential escape. Most of the day I am about the translation, sometimes, at a leisure hour, trying at Isaiah, in order to get help from the Persian Jews. My Hebrew reveries have quite disappeared, merely for want of leisure. I forgot to say that I have been to visit the ruins of Persepolis, but this, with many other things, must be reserved for a hot afternoon at Cawnpore.

What would I give for a few lines from you, to say how the men come on, and whether their numbers are increasing, whether you meet the Sherwoods at the evening repast, as when I was there! My kindest love to them, your sister, and all that love us in the truth. May the grace of the Lord Jesus Christ be with your spirit, and with your faithful and affectionate brother,

H. MARTYN.

The Secretary to the British Embassy to Persia, and afterwards himself Minister Plenipotentiary to its Court, Mr. James Morier, has given us a notable sketch of Henry Martyn as a controversialist for Christ, and of the impression that he made on the officials, priests, and people of all classes. As the author of the *Adventures of Hajji Baba of Ispahan* and other life-like tales of the East, and as an accomplished traveller, the father of the present Ambassador to St. Petersburg is the first authority on such a subject. In his *Second Journey through Persia, Armenia, and Asia Minor to Constantinople*[56] he thus writes:

[392]

The Persians, who were struck with his humility, his patience and resignation, called him a *merdi khodai*, a man of God, and indeed every action of his life seemed to be bent towards the one object of advancing the interest of the Christian religion. When he was living at Shiraz, employed in his translation, he neither sought nor shunned the society of the natives, many of whom constantly drew him into arguments about religion, with the intention of persuading him of the truth and excellence of theirs. His answers were such as to stimulate them to further arguments, and in spite of their pride the principal moollahs, who had heard of his reputation, paid him the first visit, and endeavoured in every way to entangle him in his talk. At length he thought that the best mode of silencing them was by writing a reply to the arguments which they brought against our belief and in favour of their own. His tract was circulated through different parts of Persia, and was sent from hand to hand to be answered. At length it made its way to the King's court, and a moollah of high consideration, who resided at Hamadan, and who was esteemed one of the best controversialists in the country, was ordered to answer it. After the lapse of more than a year he did answer it, but such were the strong positions taken by Mr. Martyn that the Persians themselves were ashamed of the futility of their own attempts to break them down: for, after they had sent their answer to the ambassador, they requested that it might be returned to them again, as another answer was preparing to be given. Such answer has never yet been given; and we may infer from this circumstance that if, in addition to the Scriptures, some plain treatises of the evidences of Christianity, accompanied by strictures upon the falseness of the doctrines of Mohammed, were translated into Persian and disseminated throughout that country, very favourable effects would be produced. Mr. Martyn caused a copy of his translation to be beautifully written, and to be presented by the ambassador to the King, who was pleased to receive[393] it very graciously. A copy of it was made by Mirza Baba, a Persian who gave us lessons in the Persian language, and he said that many of his countrymen asked his permission to take Mr. Martyn's translation to their homes, where they kept it for several days, and expressed themselves much edified by its contents. But whilst he was employed in copying it, moollahs (the Persian scribes) used frequently to sit with him and revile him for undertaking such a work. On reading the passage where our Saviour is called 'the Lamb of God,' they scorned and ridiculed the simile, as if exulting in the superior designation of Ali, who is called *Sheer* Khodai, the Lion of God. Mirza Baba observed to them: 'The lion is an unclean beast; it preys upon carcases, and you are not allowed to wear its skin because it is impure; it is destructive, fierce, and man's enemy. The lamb, on the contrary, is in every way *halal* or lawful. You eat its flesh, you wear its skin on your head, it does no harm, and is an animal beloved. Whether is it best, then, to say the Lamb of God, or the Lion of God?'

Henry Martyn had not been two months in Shiraz when, as his attendant expressed it, he became the town-talk. The populace believed that he had come to declare himself a Mussulman, and would then bring five thousand men to the city and take possession of it. Dissatisfied with their own government, many Mohammedans began to desire English rule, such as was making India peaceful and prosperous, and as was supposed to enrich all who enjoyed it. Jewish perverts to Islam crowded to the garden, where at all times, even on Sunday, the saintly visitor was accessible. Armenians spoke to him with a freedom they dared not show in conversation with others. From Baghdad to Busrah, and from Bushire to Ispahan and even[394] Etchmiatzin, visitors crowded to talk with the wonderful scholar and holy man. Thus on July 6 he was presented by Sir Gore Ouseley to the Governor, Prince Abbas Mirza.

Early this morning I went with the ambassador and his suite to court, wearing, agreeably to custom, a pair of red cloth stockings, with green high-heeled shoes. When we entered the great court of the palace a hundred fountains began to play. The prince appeared at the opposite side, in his talar, or hall of audience, seated on the ground. Here our first bow was made. When we came in sight of him we bowed a second time, and entered the room. He did not rise, nor take notice of any but the ambassador, with whom he conversed at the distance of the breadth of the room. Two of his ministers stood in front of the hall outside; the ambassador's mihmander, and the master of the ceremonies, within at the door. We sat down in order, in a line with the ambassador, with our hats on. I never saw a more sweet and engaging countenance than the prince's; there was such an appearance of good nature and humility in all his demeanour, that I could scarcely bring myself to believe that he would be guilty of anything cruel or tyrannical.

Mahommed Shareef Khan, one of the most renowned of the Persian generals, having served the present royal family for four generations, called to see me, out of respect to General Malcolm. An Armenian priest also, on his way from Busrah to Ispahan; he was as ignorant as the rest of his brethren. To my surprise I found that he was of the Latin Church, and read the service in Latin, though he confessed he knew nothing about the language.

The first of Henry Martyn's public controversies with the Shi'ah doctors, as distinguished from the almost daily discussions already described in his *Journal*, took place in the house of the Moojtahid of Shiraz on July 15, 1811.[395] The doctrine of Jesus, represented by such a follower, was beginning so to tell on Shi'ahs and Soofis, ever eager for something new, that the interference of the first authority of Islam in all Persia became necessary. Higher than all other Mohammedan divines, especially among the Shi'ahs, are the three or four Moojtahids.[57] They must be saintly, learned, and aloof from worldly ambition. In Persia each acts as an informal and final court of appeal; he alone dares to temper the tyranny of the Shah by his influence; his house is a sanctuary for the oppressed; the city of his habitation is often saved from violence by his presence. This is the position and the pretension of the man who, having first ascertained that the English man of God did not want demonstration, but admitted that the prophets had been sent, invited him to dinner, preliminary to a conflict. Martyn has left this description of the scene:

About eight o'clock at night we went, and after passing along many an avenue we entered a fine court, where was a pond, and, by the side of it, a platform eight feet high, covered with carpets. Here sat the Moojtahid in state, with a considerable number of his learned friends—among the rest, I perceived the Jew. One was at his prayers. I was never more disgusted at the mockery of this kind of prayer. He went through the evolutions with great exactness, and pretended to be unmoved at the noise and chit-chat of persons on each side of him. The Professor seated Seyd Ali on his right hand, and me on his left. Everything around bore the appearance of opulence and ease, and the swarthy obesity of the little personage himself led me to suppose that he had paid more attention to cooking than to science. But when he began to speak, I saw reason enough for his being so much admired. The[396] substance of his speech was flimsy enough; but he spoke with uncommon fluency and clearness, and with a manner confident and imposing. He talked for a full hour about the soul; its being distinct from the body; superior to the brutes, etc.; about God; His unity, invisibility, and other obvious and acknowledged truths. After this followed another discourse. At length, after clearing his way for miles around, he said that philosophers had proved that a single being could produce but a single being; that the first thing God had created was *Wisdom*, a being perfectly one with Him; after that, the souls of men, and the seventh heaven; and so on till He produced matter, which is merely passive. He illustrated the theory by comparing all being to a circle; at one extremity of the diameter is God, at the opposite extremity of the diameter is matter, than which nothing in the world is meaner. Rising from thence, the highest stage of matter is connected with the lowest stage of vegetation; the highest of the vegetable world with the lowest of the animal; and so on, till we approach the point from which all proceeded. 'But,' said he, 'you will observe that, next to God, something ought to be which is equal to God; for since it is equally near, it possesses equal dignity. What this is philosophers are not agreed upon. You,' said he, 'say it is Christ; but we, that it is the Spirit of the Prophets. All this is what the philosophers have proved, independently of any particular religion.' I rather imagined that it was the invention of some ancient Oriental Christian, to make the doctrine of the Trinity appear more reasonable. There were a hundred things in the Professor's harangue that might have been excepted against, as mere dreams, supported by no evidence; but I had no inclination to call in question dogmas on the truth or falsehood of which nothing in religion depended.

He was speaking at one time about the angels, and asserted that man was superior to them, and that no[397] being greater than man could be created. Here the Jew reminded me of a passage in the Bible, quoting something in Hebrew. I was a little surprised, and was just about to ask where he found anything in the Bible to support such a doctrine, when the

Moojtahid, not thinking it worth while to pay any attention to what the Jew said, continued his discourse. At last the Jew grew impatient, and finding an opportunity of speaking, said to me, 'Why do not you speak? Why do not you bring forward your objections?' The Professor, at the close of one of his long speeches, said to me, 'You see how much there is to be said on these subjects; several visits will be necessary; we must come to the point by degrees.' Perceiving how much he dreaded a close discussion, I did not mean to hurry him, but let him talk on, not expecting we should have anything about Muhammadanism the first night. But, at the instigation of the Jew, I said, 'Sir, you see that Abdoolghunee is anxious that you should say something about Islam.' He was much displeased at being brought so prematurely to the weak point, but could not decline accepting so direct a challenge. 'Well,' said he to me, 'I must ask you a few questions. Why do you believe in Christ?' I replied, 'That is not the question. I am at liberty to say that I do not believe in any religion; that I am a plain man seeking the way of salvation; that it was, moreover, quite unnecessary to prove the truth of Christ to Muhammadans, because they allowed it.' 'No such thing,' said he; 'the Jesus we acknowledge is He who was a prophet, a mere servant of God, and one who bore testimony to Muhammad; not your Jesus, whom you call God,' said he, with a contemptuous smile. He then enumerated the persons who had spoken of the miracles of Muhammad, and told a long story about Salmon the Persian, who had come to Muhammad. I asked whether this Salmon had written an account of the miracles he had seen. He confessed that he had not. 'Nor,' said I,[398]'have you a single witness to the miracles of Muhammad.' He then tried to show that, though they had not, there was still sufficient evidence. 'For,' said he, 'suppose five hundred persons should say that they heard some particular thing of a hundred persons who were with Muhammad, would that be sufficient evidence or not?' 'Whether it be or not,' said I, 'you have no such evidence as that, nor anything like it; but if you have, as they are something like witnesses, we must proceed to examine them and see whether their testimony deserves credit.'

After this the Koran was mentioned; but as the company began to thin, and the great man had not a sufficient audience before whom to display his eloquence, the dispute was not so brisk. He did not indeed seem to think it worth while to notice my objections. He mentioned a well-known sentence in the Koran as being inimitable. I produced another sentence, and begged to know why it was inferior to the Koranic one. He declined saying why, under pretence that it required such a knowledge of rhetoric in order to understand his proofs as I probably did not possess. A scholar afterwards came to Seyd Ali, with twenty reasons for preferring Muhammad's sentence to mine.

It was midnight when dinner, or rather supper, was brought in: it was a sullen meal. The great man was silent, and I was sleepy. Seyd Ali, however, had not had enough. While burying his hand in the dish of the Professor, he softly mentioned some more of my objections. He was so vexed that he scarcely answered anything; but after supper told a very long story, all reflecting upon me. He described a grand assembly of Christians, Jews, Guebres, and Sabeans (for they generally do us the honour of stringing us with the other three), before Imam Ruza. The Christians were of course defeated and silenced. It was a remark of the Imam's, in which the Professor acquiesced, that[399] 'it is quite useless for Muhammadans and Christians to argue together, as they had different languages and different histories.' To the last I said nothing; but to the former replied by relating the fable of the lion and man, which amused Seyd Ali so much that he laughed out before the great man, and all the way home.

The intervention of the Moojtahid only added to the sensation excited among all classes by the saintly Feringhi. The Shi'ah doctors had their second corrective almost ready. They resolved to check the spirit of inquiry by issuing, eleven days after the Moojtahid's attempt, a defence of Muhammadanism by Mirza Ibrahim, described as 'the preceptor of all the moollas.'[558] The event has an interest of its own, apart from Henry Martyn, in the light of a famous controversy which preceded it, and of spiritually fruitful discussions which followed it, all in India. Before Henry Martyn in this field of Christian apologetic was the Portuguese Jesuit, Hieronymo Xavier, and after him were the Scots missionary, John Wilson of Bombay, and the German agent of the Church Missionary Society, C.G. Pfander.

Among the representatives of all religions whom the tolerant Akbar invited to his court at Agra, that out of their teaching he might form an eclectic cult of his own, was Jerome, the nephew of the famous Francis Xavier, then at Goa. For Akbar P. Hieronymo Xavier wrote in Persian two histories, *Christi* and *S. Petri.* To his successor, the Emperor Jahangir, in whose suite he was the first European who visited Kashmir, H. Xavier in the year 1609 dedicated his third Persian book, entitled *A Mirror showing the Truth,* in which the doctrines of the Christian religion are discussed, the mysteries of the Gospel explained, and the vanity of|400| (all) other religions is to be seen. He has been pronounced by a good authority[59] a man of considerable ability and energy, but one who trusted more to his own ingenuity than to the plain and unsophisticated declarations of the Holy Scriptures. Ludovicus de Dieu, the Dutch scholar, who translated his two first works into Latin, most fairly describes each on the title-page as 'multis modis contaminata.' Twelve years after, to the third or controversial treatise of P.H. Xavier an answer was published by 'the most mean of those who stand in need of the mercy of a bounteous God, Ahmed ibn Zaín Elábidín Elálooi,' under a title thus translated, *The Divine Rays in refutation of Christian Error.* To this a rejoinder in Latin appeared at Rome in 1631, from the pen of Philip Guadagnoli, Arabic Professor in the Propaganda College there. He calls it *Apologia pro Christiana Religione.* If we except Raimund Lull's two spiritual treatises and *Ars Major,* and Pocock's Arabic translation of the *De Veritate Religionis Christianæ,* which Grotius wrote as a text-book for the Dutch missionaries in the East Indies, Henry Martyn's was the first attempt of Reformed Christendom to carry the pure doctrine of Jesus Christ to the Asiatic races whom the corruptions of Judaism and the Eastern Churches had blinded into accepting the Koran and all its consequences.

Mirza Ibrahim's Arabic challenge to the Christian scholar is pronounced by so competent and fair an authority as Sir William Muir[60] as made by a man of talent|401| and acuteness, and remarkable for its freedom from violent and virulent remarks.

This argument chiefly concerns the subject of miracles, which he accommodates to the Koran. He defines a miracle as an effect exceeding common experience, accompanied by a prophetic claim and a challenge to produce the like; and he holds that it may be produced by particular experience—that is, it may be confined to any single art, but must be attested by the evidence and confession of those best skilled in that art. Thus he assumes the miracles of Moses and Jesus to belong respectively to the arts of magic and physic, which had severally reached perfection in the times of these prophets; the evidence of the magicians is hence deemed sufficient for the miracles of Moses, and that of the physicians for those of Jesus; but had these miracles occurred in any other age than that in which those arts flourished, their proof would have been imperfect, and the miracles consequently not binding. This extraordinary doctrine—which Henry Martyn shows to be founded upon an inadequate knowledge of history—he proceeds to apply to the Koran, and proves entirely to his own satisfaction that it fulfils all the required conditions. This miracle belonged to the science of eloquence, and in that science the Arabs were perfect adepts. The Koran was accompanied by a challenge, and when they accordingly professed their inability to produce an equal, their evidence, like that of the magicians' and physicians', became universally binding. He likewise dilates upon the superior and perpetual nature of the Koran as an intellectual and a *lasting* miracle, which will remain unaltered when all others are forgotten. He touches slightly on Mohammed's other miracles, and asserts the insufficiency of proof (except through the Koran) for those of all former prophets.

To this, which was accompanied by a treatise on the|402| miracles of Mohammed by Aga Akbar, Henry Martyn wrote a reply in three parts. In what spirit he conducted the controversy, and what influence through him the Spirit of Christ had on some of the Shi'ahs and Soofis, this extract from his *Journal* unconsciously testifies:

1811, September 12 to 15. (Sunday.)—Finished what I had to say on the evidences of religion, and translated it into Persian. Aga Akbar sent me his treatise by one of his disciples. Aga Baba, his brother, but a very different person from him, called; he spoke without disguise of his dislike to Mohammedanism and good-will to Christianity. For his attachment to Mirza Abel, Kasim, his brother, sets him down as an infidel. Mirza Ibrahim is still in doubt, and thinks that he may be a Christian, and be saved without renouncing

156

Mohammedanism; asks his nephew what is requisite to observe; he said, Baptism and the Lord's Supper. 'Well,' said he, 'what harm is there in doing that?' At another time Seyd Ali asked me, after a dispute, whether I would baptize any one who did not believe in the Divinity of Christ? I said, No. While translating Acts ii. and iii., especially where it is said all who believed had one heart and one mind, and had all things in common, he was much affected, and contrasted the beginning of Christianity with that of Mohammedanism, where they began their career with murdering men and robbing caravans; and oh, said he, 'that I were sure the Holy Spirit would be given to me! I would become a Christian at once.' Alas! both his faith and mine are very weak. Even if he were to desire baptism I should tremble to give it. He spake in a very pleasing way on other parts of the Gospel, and seems to have been particularly taken with the idea of a new birth. The state of a new-born child gives him the most striking view of that simplicity which he considers as the height of wisdom. Simplicity is that to which he aspires, he says, above all[403] things. He was once proud of his knowledge, and vain of his superiority to others, but he found that fancied knowledge set him at a greater distance from happiness than anything else.

Martyn's first reply in Persian to Mirza Ibrahim thus begins: 'The Christian Minister thanks the celebrated Professor of Islamism for the favour he has done him in writing an answer to his inquiries, but confesses that, after reading it, a few doubts occurred to him, on account of which, and not for the mere purpose of dispute, he has taken upon himself to write the following pages.' The reply is signed, 'The Christian Minister, Henry Martyn.' One Mirza Mahommed Ruza published in 1813, the year after Martyn's death, a very prolix rejoinder. It is unworthy of lengthened notice, according to Sir William Muir, who thus summarises and comments on the defence made by the Christian scholar:

Henry Martyn's first tract refers chiefly to the subject of miracles: he asserts that, to be conclusive, a miracle must exceed *universal* experience; that the testimony and opinion of the Arabs is therefore insufficient, besides being that of a party concerned; that, were the Koran allowed to be inimitable, that would not prove it to be a miracle; and that its being an *intellectual* miracle is not a virtue, but, by making it generally inappreciable, a defect. He concludes by denying the proof of Mohammed's other miracles, in which two requisites are wanting: viz., their being recorded at or near the time of their occurrence, and the narrators being under no constraint.

The second tract directly attacks Mohammed's mission, by alleging the debasing nature of some of the contents and precepts of the Koran, holds good works and repentance to be insufficient for salvation, and opens the subject of the true atonement as prefigured in types, fulfilled in[404] Christ, and made public by the spread of Christianity which is mentioned as itself a convincing miracle.

The last tract commences with an attack on the absurdities of Soofi-ism, and proceeds to show that the love of God and union with Him cannot be obtained by contemplation, but only by a practical manifestation of His goodness towards us, accompanied by an assurance of our safety; and that this is fulfilled in Christianity not by the amalgamation of the soul with the Deity, but by the pouring out of God's Spirit upon His children, and by the obedience and atonement of Christ. Vicarious suffering is then defended by analogy, the truth of the Mosaic and Christian miracles is upheld, and the whole argument closes with proving the authenticity of the Christian annals by their coincidence with profane history.

Sir William Muir agrees in the opinion of Professor Lee that, situated as Mr. Martyn was in Persia, with a short tract on the Mohammedan religion before him, and his health precarious, the course which he took was perhaps the only one practicable. Sir William adds: 'In pursuing his argument Henry Martyn has displayed great wisdom and skill, and his reasoning appears to be in general perfectly conclusive; in a few instances, however, he has perhaps not taken up the most advantageous ground.'

The appeal of the Christian defender of the faith, at the close of his second part, on the incarnation and atonement, is marked by a loving courtesy:[641]

It is now the prayer of the humble Henry Martyn that these things may be considered with impartiality. If they become the means of procuring conviction, let not the fear of death or punishment operate for a moment to the contrary, but let this conviction have its legitimate effect;|405| for the world, we know, passes away like the wind of the desert. But if what has here been stated do not produce conviction, my prayer is that God Himself may instruct you; that as hitherto ye have held what you believed to be the truth, ye may now become teachers of that which is really so; and that He may grant you to be the means of bringing others to the knowledge of the same, through Jesus Christ, who has loved us and washed us in His own blood, to whom be the power and the glory for ever and ever. Amen.

1811, July 26.—Mirza Ibrahim declared publicly before all his disciples, 'that if I really confuted his arguments, he should be bound in conscience to become a Christian.' Alas! from such a declaration I have little hope. His general good character for uprightness and unbounded kindness to the poor would be a much stronger reason with me for believing that he may perhaps be a Cornelius.

August 2.—Much against his will Mirza Ibrahim was obliged to go to his brother, who is governor of some town thirty-eight parasangs off. To the last moment he continued talking with his nephew on the subject of his book, and begged that, in case of his detention, my reply might be sent to him.

August 7.—My friends talked, as usual, much about what they call Divine love; but I do not very well comprehend what they mean. They love not the holy God, but the god of their own imagination—a god who will let them do as they please. I often remind Seyd Ali of one defect in his system, which is, that there is no one to stand between his sins and God. Knowing what I allude to, he says, 'Well, if the death of Christ intervene, no harm; Soofi-ism can admit this too.'

August 14.—Returned to the city in a fever, which continued all the next day until the evening!

August 15.—Jani Khan, in rank corresponding to one of our Scottish dukes, as he is the head of all the military|406| tribes of Persia, and chief of his own tribe, which consists of twenty thousand families, called on Jaffir Ali Khan with a message from the king. He asked me a great number of questions, and disputed a little. 'I suppose,' said he, 'you consider us all as infidels!' 'Yes,' replied I, 'the whole of you.' He was mightily pleased with my frankness, and mentioned it when he was going away.

August 22.—The copyist having shown my answer to Moodurris, called Moolla Akbar, he wrote on the margin with great acrimony but little sense. Seyd Ali having shown his remarks in some companies, they begged him not to show them to me, for fear I should disgrace them all through the folly of one man.

August 23.—Ruza Kooli Mirza, the great-grandson of Nadir Shah and Aga Mahommed Hasan, called. The prince's nephew, hearing of my attack on Muhammad, observed that the proper answer to it was the sword; but the prince confessed that he began to have his doubts. On his inquiring what were the laws of Christianity—meaning the number of times of prayer, the different washings, &c.—I said that we had two commandments: 'Thou shalt love the Lord thy God with all thy heart, and all thy soul, and all thy strength; and thy neighbour as thyself.' He asked, 'What could be better?' and continued praising them.

The Moolla Aga Mahommed Hasan, himself a Moodurris, and a very sensible, candid man, asked a good deal about the European philosophy, particularly what we did in metaphysics; for instance, 'how, or in what sense, the body of Christ ascended into heaven?' He talked of free-will and fate, and reasoned high, and at last reconciled them according to the doctrines of the Soofis by saying, that 'as all being is an emanation of the Deity, the will of every being is only the will of the Deity, so that therefore, in fact, free-will and fate are the same.' He has nothing to find fault with in Christianity, except the Divinity of|407| Christ. It is this doctrine that exposes me to the contempt of the learned Mahometans, in whom it is difficult to say whether pride or ignorance predominates. Their sneers are more difficult to bear than the brick-bats which the boys sometimes throw at me; however, both are an honour of which I am not worthy. How many times in the day have I occasion to repeat the words:

If on my face, for Thy dear name,
Shame and reproaches be,

158

All hail, reproach, and welcome, shame,
If Thou remember me.

The more they wish me to give up this one point—the Divinity of Christ—the more I seem to feel the necessity of it, and rejoice and glory in it. Indeed, I trust I would sooner give up my life than surrender it.

In the evening we went to pay a long-promised visit to Mirza Abulkasim, one of the most renowned Soofis in all Persia. We found several persons sitting in an open court, in which a few greens and flowers were placed; the master was in a corner. He was a very fresh-looking old man with a silver beard. I was surprised to observe the downcast and sorrowful looks of the assembly, and still more at the silence which reigned. After sitting some time in expectation, and being not at all disposed to waste my time in sitting there, I said softly to Seyd Ali, 'What is this?' He said, 'It is the custom here to think much and speak little.' 'May I ask the master a question?' said I. With some hesitation he consented to let me; so I begged Jaffir Ali to inquire, 'Which is the way to be happy?'

This he did in his own manner; he began by observing that 'there was a great deal of misery in the world, and that the learned shared as largely in it as the rest; that I wished therefore to know what we must do to escape it.' The master replied that[408]'for his part he did not know, but that it was usually said that the subjugation of the passions was the shortest way to happiness.' After a considerable pause I ventured to ask, 'What were his feelings at the prospect of death—hope, or fear, or neither?' 'Neither,' said he, and that 'pleasure and pain were both alike.' I then perceived that the Stoics were Greek Soofis. I asked 'whether he had attained this apathy.' He said, 'No.' 'Why do you think it attainable?' He could not tell. 'Why do you think that pleasure and pain are not the same?' said Seyd Ali, taking his master's part. 'Because,' said I, 'I have the evidence of my senses for it. And you also act as if there was a difference. Why do you eat, but that you fear pain?' These silent sages sat unmoved.

One of the disciples is the son of the Moojtahid who, greatly to the vexation of his father, is entirely devoted to the Soofi doctor. He attended his kalean (pipe) with the utmost humility. On observing the pensive countenance of the young man, and knowing something of his history from Seyd Ali, how he had left all to find happiness in the contemplation of God, I longed to make known the glad tidings of a Saviour, and thanked God on coming away, that I was not left ignorant of the Gospel. I could not help being a little pleasant on Seyd Ali afterwards, for his admiration of this silent instructor. 'There you sit,' said I, 'immersed in thought, full of anxiety and care, and will not take the trouble to ask whether God has said anything or not. No: that is too easy and direct a way of coming at the truth. I compare you to spiders, who weave their house of defence out of their own bowels; or to a set of people who are groping for a light in broad day.'

August 26.—Waited this morning on Mahommed Nubbee Khan, late ambassador at Calcutta, and now prime minister of Fars. There were a vast number of clients in his court, with whom he transacted business while chatting with us. Amongst the others who came and sat with us, was my tetric adversary—Aga Akbar, who came for the very purpose of presenting the minister with a little book[409] he had written in answer to mine. After presenting it in due form, he sat down, and told me he meant to bring me a copy that day—a promise which he did not perform, through Seyd Ali's persuasion, who told him it was a performance that would do him no credit.

August 29.—Mirza Ibrahim begins to inquire about the Gospel. The objections he made were such as these: How sins could be atoned for before they were committed? Whether, as Jesus died for all men, all would necessarily be saved? If faith be the condition of salvation, would wicked Christians be saved, provided they believe? I was pleased to see from the nature of the objections that he was considering the subject. To this last objection, I remarked that to those who felt themselves sinners, and came to God for mercy, through Christ, God would give His Holy Spirit, which would progressively sanctify them in heart and life.

August 30.—Mirza Ibrahim praises my answer, especially the first part.

It was on the sacred rock of Behistun, on the western frontiers of Media, on the high road eastward from Babylonia, that Darius Hystaspes, founder of the civil policy of ancient

Persia, carved the wonderful cuneiform inscriptions which made that rock the charter of Achæmenian royalty. At Persepolis only the platform, the pillared colonnade, and the palace seem to have been built by him; the other buildings, with commemorative legends, were erected by Xerxes and Artaxerxes Ochus. Lassen, Westergaard, and our own Sir Henry Rawlinson,[62] did not decipher these inscriptions for some twenty years after Martyn's visit. How deaf had Ormuzd proved all through[410] the centuries to the prayer which Darius the king cut on a huge slab, twenty-six feet in length and six in height, in the southern wall of the great platform at Persepolis: 'Let not war, nor slavery, nor decrepitude, nor lies obtain power over this province.' Henry Martyn thus wrote of his visit:

After traversing these celebrated ruins, I must say that I felt a little disappointed: they did not at all answer my expectation. The architecture of the ancient Persians seems to me much more akin to that of their clumsy neighbours the Indians, than to that of the Greeks. I saw no appearance of grand design anywhere. The chapiters of the columns were almost as long as the shafts:—though they are not so represented in Niebuhr's plate;—and the mean little passages into the square court, or room, or whatever it was, make it very evident that the taste of the Orientals was the same three thousand years ago as it is now. But it was impossible not to recollect that here Alexander and his Greeks passed and repassed; here they sat and sung, and revelled; now all is in silence, generation on generation lie mingled with the dust of their mouldering edifices:

Alike the busy and the gay,
But flutter in life's busy day,
In fortune's varying colours drest.

As soon as we recrossed the Araxes, the escort begged me to point out the Keblah to them, as they wanted to pray. After setting their faces towards Mecca, as nearly as I could, I went and sat down on the margin near the bridge, where the water, falling over some fragments of the bridge under the arches, produced a roar, which, contrasted with the stillness all around, had a grand effect. Here I thought again of the multitudes who had once pursued their labours and pleasures on its banks. Twenty-one centuries have passed away since they lived; how short, in compari[411]son, must be the remainder of my days. What a momentary duration is the life of man! *Labitur et labetur in omne volubilis ævum*, may be affirmed of the river; but men pass away as soon as they begin to exist. Well, let the moments pass:

They'll waft us sooner o'er
This life's tempestuous sea,
And land us on the peaceful shore
Of blest eternity.

The true character of Martyn's Mohammedan and Soofi controversialists comes out in the fast of Ramazan, the ninth month of the lunar year, when from dawn to sunset of each day a strict fast is observed, most trying to the temper, and from sunset to dawn excess is too naturally the rule, especially, as in this case, when Ramazan falls on the long hot days of summer. Of this month the traditions declare that the doors of heaven are opened and the doors of hell shut, while the devils are chained. At this time the miracle play of Hasan and Husain[63] is acted in the native theatres from night to night. In scene xxxi. are enacted the conversion and murder of an English ambassador. Dean Stanley used to tell that Henry Martyn, horrified at the English oaths put into the mouth of the Persian who represented the ambassador in the tragedy, took him and taught him to repeat the Lord's Prayer instead.

September 20.—First day of the fast of Ramazan. All the family had been up in the night, to take an unseasonable meal, in order to fortify themselves for the abstinence of the day. It was curious to observe the effects of the fast in the house. The master was scolding and beating his servants; they equally peevish and insolent, and the[412] beggars more than ordinarily importunate and clamorous. At noon, all the city went to the grand mosque. My host came back with an account of new vexations there. He was chatting with a friend, near the door, when a great preacher, Hajji Mirza, arrived, with hundreds of followers. 'Why do you not say your prayers?' said the new-comers to the two friends. 'We have finished,' said they. 'Well,' said the other, 'if you cannot pray a second time with us, you had better move out of the way.' Rather than join such turbulent zealots they retired. The reason of this unceremonious address was, that these loving disciples had a desire to pray all in a row with their master, which, it seems, is the custom. There is no public service in the mosque; every man here prays for himself.

Coming out of the mosque some servants of the prince, for their amusement, pushed a person against a poor man's stall, on which were some things for sale, a few European and Indian articles, also some valuable Warsaw plates, which were thrown down and broken. The servants went off without making compensation. No kazi will hear a complaint against the prince's servants.

Hajji Mahommed Hasan preaches every day during the Ramazan. He takes a verse from the Koran, or more frequently tells stories about the Imams. If the ritual of the Christian Churches, their good forms and everything they have, is a mere shadow without a Divine influence attend on them, what must all this Mahometan stuff be? and yet how impossible is it to convince the people of the world, whether Christian or Mahometan, that what they call religion is merely an invention of their own, having no connection with God and His kingdom! This subject has been much on my mind of late. How senseless the zeal of Churchmen against dissenters, and of dissenters against the Church! The kingdom of God is neither meat nor drink, nor anything perishable; but righteousness, and peace, and joy in the Holy Ghost.[413]

Mirza Ibrahim never goes to the mosque, but he is so much respected that nothing is said: they conclude that he is employed in devotion at home. Some of his disciples said to Seyd Ali, before him: 'Now the Ramazan is come, you should read the Koran and leave the Gospel.' 'No,' said his uncle, 'he is employed in a good work: let him go on with it.' The old man continues to inquire with interest about the Gospel, and is impatient for his nephew to explain the evidences of Christianity, which I have drawn up.

September 22. (Sunday.)—My friends returned from the mosque, full of indignation at what they had witnessed there. The former governor of Bushire complained to the vizier, in the mosque, that some of his servants had treated him brutally. The vizier, instead of attending to his complaint, ordered them to do their work a second time; which they did, kicking and beating him with their slippers, in the most ignominious way, before all the mosque. This unhappy people groan under the tyranny of their governors; yet nothing subdues or tames them. Happy Europe! how has God favoured the sons of Japheth, by causing them to embrace the Gospel. How dignified are all the nations of Europe compared with this nation! Yet the people are clever and intelligent, and more calculated to become great and powerful than any of the nations of the East, had they a good government and the Christian religion.

September 29.—The Soofi, son of the Moojtahid, with some others, came to see me. For fifteen years he was a devout Mahometan; visited the sacred places, and said many prayers. Finding no benefit from austerities he threw up Mahommedanism altogether, and attached himself to the Soofi master. I asked him what his object was, all that time? He said, he did not know, but he was unhappy. I began to explain to him the Gospel; but he cavilled at it as much as any bigoted Mahommedan could do, and would not hear of there being any distinction[414] between Creator and creature. In the midst of our conversation, the sun went down, and the company vanished for the purpose of taking an immediate repast.

Mirza Seyd Ali seems sometimes coming round to Christianity against Soofi-ism. The Soofis believe in no prophet, and do not consider Moses to be equal to Mirza Abulkasim. 'Could they be brought,' Seyd Ali says, 'to believe that there has been a prophet, they would embrace Christianity.' And what would be gained by such converts? 'Thy people shall be willing in the day of Thy power.' It will be an afflicted and poor people that shall call upon the name of the Lord, and such the Soofis are not: professing themselves to be wise, they have become fools.

October 7.—I was surprised by a visit from the great Soofi doctor, who, while most of the people were asleep, came to me for some wine. I plied him with questions innumerable; but he returned nothing but incoherent answers, and sometimes no answer at all. Having laid aside his turban, he put on his night-cap, and soon fell asleep upon the carpet. Whilst he lay there his disciples came, but would not believe, when I told them who was there, till they came and saw the sage asleep. When he awoke, they came in, and seated themselves at the greatest possible distance, and were all as still as if in a church. The real state of this man seems to be despair, and it will be well if it do not end in madness. I preached to him the kingdom of God: mentioning particularly how I had found peace from the Son of God and the Spirit of God; through the first, forgiveness; through the second, sanctification. He said it was good, but said it with the same unconcern with which he admits all manner of things, however contradictory. Poor soul! he is sadly bewildered.

As a Persian scholar and controversialist Henry Martyn found a worthy successor in the German, and afterwards[415] Church Missionary Society's missionary, C.G. Pfander, D.D. When for some twelve years stationed at Shushy Fort, on the Russian border of Georgia, he frequently visited Baghdad and travelled through Persia by Ispahan and Teheran. In 1836 the intolerant Russian Government expelled all foreign missionaries from its territories, and Dr. Pfander joined the Church Mission at Agra. In 1835 he first published at Shushy, in Persian, his famous *Mizan ul Haqq*, or *Balance of Truth*. A Hindustani translation was lithographed at Mirzapore in 1843, and Mr. R.H. Weakley, missionary at Constantinople, made an English translation, which was published by the Church Missionary Society in 1867. This, as yet, greatest of works which state the general argument for Christianity and against Islam, was followed by the *Miftah ul Asrar*, in proof of the Divinity of Christ and the doctrine of the Trinity, and by the *Tarik ul Hyat*, or the nature of sin and the way of salvation, of both of which Hindustani translations appeared. In his little English *Remarks on the Nature of Muhammadanism*,[64] as shown in the *Traditions*, Dr. Pfander quotes from Martyn's *Controversy*. By these writings and the personal controversy in India, Dr. Pfander, following Henry Martyn, was the means of winning to Christ, in tolerant British India, many Mohammedan moulvies like him who is now the Rev. Imad-ud-din, D.D.[65]

Henry Martyn's description of the Persian is no less[416] applicable to the Indian Mohammedan, in the opinion of Sir William Muir; 'he is a compound of ignorance and bigotry, and all access to the one is hedged up by the other.' The Koran and the whole system of Islam are based on partial truths, plagiarised from Scripture to an extent sufficient to feed the pride of those who hold them. But beyond these corruptions of Judaism and Christianity, for which the dead Eastern Churches of Mohammed's time and since are responsible, Persians, Turks, Arabs, Afghans, and Hindustan Muhammadans know nothing either of history or Christian Divinity. All controversy, from P.H. Xavier's time to Martyn's, Wilson's, and Pfander's, shows that the key of the position is not the doctrine of the Trinity, as the Shi'ah Moojtahids of Shiraz and Lucknow and the Soonnis everywhere make it, but the genuineness and integrity of the Scriptures, by which the truth of the whole Christian faith will follow, the Trinity included. The Bible, in Hindustani, Persian, and Arabic, with its self-evidencing power, is the weapon which Henry Martyn was busied in forging.

FOOTNOTES:

[54]See article in the *Spectator* for August 17, 1889, by a writer who had recently returned from Persia.

[55]See article on the poet in the *Calcutta Review* for March 1858 (by Professor E.B. Cowell, L.L.D., Cambridge).

[56]London, 1818, pp. 223-4.

[57]Literally, 'one who strives' to attain the highest degree of Mussulman learning.

[58]Persian form of maulvi, the Arabic for a learned man. The word is said to mean 'filled' with knowledge, from *mala*, to fill.

[59]The Rev. S. Lee, D.D., Professor of Arabic in the University of Cambridge for many years, in his *Controversial Tracts on Christianity and Mohammedanism* by the late Rev. Henry Martyn, B.D., and some of the most eminent writers of Persia (1824).

[60]*The Calcutta Review*, No. VIII. vol. iv. Art. VI. 'The Mahommedan Controversy,' pp. 418-76, Calcutta, 1845.

[61]As translated from the Persian by Professor Lee.

[62]Sir Henry, then Major, H.C. Rawlinson, C.B., visited Persepolis in 1835. The *Journals* of the Royal Asiatic Society for 1846-9 publish his copies of the inscription of Behistun and Persepolis and his translations.

[63]See the Play as collected from oral tradition by the late Sir Lewis Pelly, in two volumes, 1879.

[64]Second edition published by the Church Missionary Society in 1858.

'Some of our most eminent Native Christians are converts from Mohammedanism. We may particularly mention the Rev. Jani Ali, B.A.; the Rev. Imad-ud-din, D.D.; the Rev. Imam Shah; the Rev. Mian Sadiq; the Rev. Yakub Ali; Maulavi Safdar Ali, a high Government official; Abdullah Athim, also a high official, now retired, and an honorary lay evangelist.'—*Church Missionary Society's Intelligencer* in 1888.

|417|

CHAPTER XI

IN PERSIA—TRANSLATING THE SCRIPTURES

Great as saint and notable as scholar, in the twelve years of his young life from Senior Wrangler to martyr at thirty-one years of age, the highest title of Henry Martyn to everlasting remembrance is that he gave the Persians in their own tongue the Testament of the one Lord and Saviour Jesus Christ, and the Hebrew Psalms. By that work, the fruit of which every successive century will reveal till the consummation of the ages, he unconsciously wrote his name beside those of the greatest missionaries in the history of the Church of Christ, the sacred scholars who were the first to give the master races of Asia and Africa, of Europe and America, the Word of God in their vernaculars. Let us write the golden list, which for modern Africa and Oceania also we might inscribe in letters of silver,|66| were not most of the translators still living and perfecting their at first tentative efforts, which time must try:

|418|

A.D.		
350	ULFILAS	Gothic (Teut
368	FRUMENTIUS and EDESIUS (Brothers)	Ethiopic
385	HIERONYMUS (Jerome)	Latin
410	MESROBES (Miesrob)	Armenian
861	C. CYRILLUS and METHODIUS (Brothers)	Slavonic (Bul
1380	WICLIF (Bede in 735)	English
1516	ERASMUS (new translation)	Latin
1534	LUTHER (translation from Latin of Erasmus)	German
1661	JOHN ELIOT (first Bible printed in America)	Moheecan
1777	FABRICIUS (Ziegenbalg & Schultze first 1714)	Tamul
1801	WILLIAM CAREY (O.T. in 1802-9)	Bengali, &c.

15	18	HENRY MARTYN	Pe
16	18	HENRY MARTYN (Sabat's N.T. version)	Ar
22	18	JOSHUA MARSHMAN (Morrison & Milne 1823)	Ch
32	18	ADONIRAM JUDSON (O.T. 1834)	Bu
65	18	VAN DYCK	Ar

It was David Brown who was wont to call the Bible 'The Great Missionary which would speak in all tongues the wonderful works of God.'

From first to last and above all Henry Martyn was a philologist. His school and college honours sprang from the root of all linguistic studies, Greek and Latin, in which he was twice appointed public examiner in his college and the University of Cambridge. For the uncritical time in which he lived, and the generations which followed his to the present, he was an enthusiastic and accomplished Hebraist. No young scholar in the first quarter of the nineteenth century was so well equipped for translating the Bible by a knowledge of its two original languages. True, he was the Senior Wrangler of the year 1801, but to him the honour was a 'shadow,' because the mathematical sciences could do nothing for him as a translator and preacher of the words of righteousness, compared with the linguistic. Only once, when the rapture of his holy work had carried him away to the borderland of a dark[419] metaphysical theology, did he record the passing regret that he had abandoned the rationalistic ground of mathematical certainty. His devotion to the study of the languages which interpret and apply to the races of India, Arabia, and Persia, the books of the Christian Revelation, was so absorbing as to shorten his career. Like Carey, he never knew an idle moment, even when on shipboard, and he jealously guarded his time from correspondence, other than that with Lydia Grenfell, Brown and Corrie, that he might live to finish the Hindustani, Persian, and Arabic New Testaments at least. The spiritual motive it was, the desire to win every man to Christ, that urged his unresting course, and in the sacred toil he had the reflex joy of being himself won nearer and nearer by the Spirit.

What do I not owe to the Lord for permitting me to take part in a translation of His Word? Never did I see such wonder, and wisdom, and love in that blessed book as since I have been obliged to study every expression. All day on the translation, employed a good while at night in considering a difficult passage, and being much enlightened respecting it, I went to bed full of astonishment at the wonders of God's Word. Never before did I see anything of the beauty of the language and the importance of the thoughts as I do now. I felt happy that I should never be finally separated from the contemplation of them, or of the things concerning which they are written. Knowledge shall vanish away, but it shall be because perfection has come.

On the other hand, he was ever on the watch against the deadening influence of routine or one-sided study.[420] 'So constantly engaged with outward works of translation of languages that I fear my inward man has declined in spirituality.'

Canon Edmonds expresses the experience of the present writer in the remark,[671] that to read Martyn's *Journal* with the single object of noticing this point is to discover another Martyn, not a saint only, but a grammarian. 'He read grammars as other men read novels, and to him they were more entertaining than novels.' So early as September 28, 1804, in Cambridge we find him at prayer after dinner, before visiting Wall's Lane, and then on his return finishing the Bengali Grammar which he had begun the day before. 'I am anxious to get Carey's Bengali New Testament,' which could not long have reached London. Five days after, Thomas à Kempis, followed by hymns and the writing of a sermon, seemed but the preliminary to his Hindustani as well as Bengali studies. 'Engaged all the rest of the morning by Gilchrist's Hindustani Dictionary. After dinner began Halhed's Bengali Grammar, for I found that the other grammar I had been reading was only for the corrupted Hindustani.' The first traces of his Persian and Arabic studies have an interest all their own:

1804, June 27.—A funeral and calls of friends took up my time till eleven; afterwards *read Persian*, and made some calculations in trigonometry, in order to be familiar with the use of logarithms.

November 23.—Through shortness of time I was about to omit my morning portion of Scripture, yet after some deliberation conscience prevailed, and I enjoyed a solemn seriousness in learning 'mem' in the 119th Psalm. Wasted much time afterwards in looking over *an Arabic grammar*.

When fairly at work in Dinapore he wrote almost daily such passages in his *Journal* as these:

[421]

1807, August 25.—Translating the Epistles; reading Arabic grammar and Persian. 27 to 29.—Studies in Persian and Arabic the same. Delight in them, particularly the latter, so great, that I have been obliged to pray continually that they may not be a snare to me.... 31st.—Resumed the Arabic with an eagerness which I found it necessary to check. Began some extracts from Cashefi which Mr. Gladwin sent me, and thus the day passed rapidly away. Alas! how much more readily does the understanding do its work than the heart.

On reaching Calcutta in 1806 Martyn found this to be the position of the Bible translation work. Carey's early labours had led to the formation of the other English and Scottish Missionary Societies at the close of the last century. By 1803 his experience and that of his colleagues had enabled them, with the encouragement of Brown and Buchanan, to formulate a magnificent plan for translating the Bible into all the languages of the far East. The Marquis Wellesley, though Governor-General, approved, and his College at Fort William, with its staff of learned men, including Carey himself and many Asiatics, had become a school of interpreters. In 1804, after all this, the British and Foreign Bible Society was founded, under the ex-Governor-General, Lord Teignmouth, as its first president. That Society, leaving India to the Serampore Brotherhood, at once directed its attention to the three hundred millions of Chinese, who also could be reached only through the East India Company. But, until six years after, when Dr. Marshman made the first reliable translation of the Bible into the language, in its Mandarin dialect, there was no Chinese translation save an anonymous MS. of a large portion of the New Testament in the British[422] Museum, probably of Roman Catholic origin. At that time the infant Society did not see its way to spend two thousand guineas in producing an edition of a thousand copies of a work about which the few experts differed. So, while giving grants to the Serampore translators, it invited the opinions, as to the formation of a corresponding committee in Calcutta, of George Udny, who had by that time become Member of Council, and the Rev. Messrs. Brown, Buchanan, Carey, Ward, and Marshman. The Serampore plan and its rapid execution had been communicated to all the principal civil and military officials, who, after Lord Wellesley's tolerant and reverent action, subscribed liberally to carry it out, and the Society continued its grants. But when in 1807, under Lord Minto, the anti-Christian reaction set in, caused by a groundless panic as to the Vellore Mutiny, and the Fort William College was reduced, Dr. Buchanan proposed to found 'The Christian Institution,' the Society preferred its original plan of a corresponding committee, which was formed in August 1809.

Martyn had not waited one hour for this. Almost from the day of landing at the capital he was engaged in Hindustani translation, and in studious preparation for his projected Persian and Arabic Bibles. In the brotherly intercourse at Aldeen with the Serampore missionaries it was arranged to leave these three languages entirely to him, under the direction of Mr. Brown. Part of the Society's annual grant to India and Ceylon of a thousand pounds a year was assigned to pay his assistants, Mirza Fitrut, the Persian, and Nathanael Sabat, the Arabian, and to print the results. The Corresponding Committee caused an annual sermon to be preached in Calcutta, to rouse public intelligence and help. On the first day of 1810[423] Mr. Brown preached it in the old church, in the interest chiefly of the thousands of native Christians who had been baptized in Tanjor and Tinnevelli, both

Reformed and Romanist, and needed copies of the Tamul Bible. Such was the result of this appeal, headed by the Commander-in-chief, General Hewett, with the sum of 2,000 Sicca-rupees (250*l.*), that the committee resolved on establishing a 'Bibliotheca Biblica,' combining a Bible Repository and a Translation Library. The Scottish poet and friend of Sir Walter Scott, Dr. Leyden, was foremost in the enterprise, and took charge of work in the languages of Siam and the Spice Islands, as well as in the Pushtu of Afghanistan.

On the first day of 1811 it fell to the Rev. Henry Martyn to preach the second annual sermon.[68] His appeal was for not only the growing native Church of India, but more particularly for the whole number of nominal Christians, of all sects, in India and Ceylon, whom he estimated at 900,000.[69] In 1881 the Government census returned these, in the Greater India of our day but without Ceylon, as upwards of 2,000,000, and in 1891 as 2,280,549. Martyn's figures included 342,000 of the Singhalese, whom the Dutch had compelled by secular considerations outwardly to conform. The sermon, on Galatians vi. 10, was published at the time, and it appears as the last in the volume of *Twenty Sermons by the late Rev. Henry Martyn, B.D.*,[70] first printed at Calcutta with this passage in the preface:[424] 'The desire to know how such a man preached is natural and unavoidable.... His manner in the pulpit was distinguished by a holy solemnity, always suited to the high message which he was delivering, and accompanied by an unction which made its way to the hearts of his audience. With this was combined a fidelity at once forcible by its justice and intrepidity, and penetrating by its affection. There was, in short, a power of holy love and disinterested earnestness in his addresses which commended itself to every man's conscience in the sight of God.'

Addressing the well-paid servants of the East India Company in Calcutta, and its prosperous merchants and shopkeepers, the preacher said: 'Do we not blush at the offers of assistance from home ... where all that is raised may be employed with such effect in benefiting the other three quarters of the globe? Asia must be our care; or, if not Asia, *India* at least must look to none but us. Honour calls as well as duty.' He then continued:

Prove to our friends and the world that the Mother Country need never be ashamed of her sons in India. What a splendid spectacle does she present! Standing firm amidst the overthrow of the nations, and spreading wide the shadow of her wings for the protection of all, she finds herself at leisure, amidst the tumult of war, to form benevolent projects for the best interests of mankind. Her generals and admirals have caused the thunder of her power to be heard throughout the south; now her ministers of religion perform their part, and endeavour to fulfil the high destinies of Heaven in favour of their country. They called on their fellow-citizens to cheer the desponding nations with the Book of the promises of Eternal Life, and thus afford them that consolation from the prospect of a happier world, which they have little expectation of finding amidst the disasters and calamities of this. The summons was obeyed. As fast as the nature of the undertaking became[425] understood, and was perceived to be clearly distinct from all party business and visionary project, great numbers of all ranks in society, and of all persuasions in religion, joined with one heart and one soul, and began to impart freely to all men that which, next to the Saviour, is God's best gift to man....

Shall every town and hamlet in England engage in the glorious cause, and the mighty Empire of India do nothing? Will not our wealth and dignity be our disgrace if we do not employ it for God and our fellow-creatures? What plan could be proposed, so little open to objections, and so becoming our national character and religion, so simple and practicable, yet so extensively beneficial, as that of giving the Word of God to the Christian part of our native subjects?... Despise not their inferiority, nor reproach them for their errors; they cannot get a BIBLE to read; had they been blessed with your advantages, they would have been perhaps more worthy of your respect.

The brief decade of Henry Martyn's working life fell at a time when the science of Comparative Philology was as yet unborn, but the materials were almost ready for generalisation. Sir William Jones, and still more his successor as a scholar—Henry Thomas Colebrooke—had used their opportunities in India well. The Bengal Asiatic Society, in its *Asiatic Researches*, was laboriously piling up facts and speculations. These awaited only the flash of hardworking genius to evolve the order and the laws which have made Comparative Grammar the most fruitful of the historical and psychological sciences. It might have been Martyn's, had he lived to reach England, to manifest that genius. His Asiatic career was contemporary with the most fruitful part of Colebrooke's. He toiled and he speculated, as he mastered the grammar and much of the[426] vocabulary of the great classical and vernacular languages which made him a seven-tongued man. But his divine motive led him to grope for the philological solvent through the imperfect Semitic. The Germans, Schlegel and Bopp, found it rather, and later, in the richer Aryan or Indo-European family, in Sanskrit and old Persian.

His longing to give the Arabs the Scriptures in their purity intensified his devotion to the study of Hebrew; had he lived to give himself to the Persian, he might have anticipated the German critics who used, at second-hand, the materials that he and Colebrooke, and other servants of the East India Company, were annually accumulating. Nor did his Hebraism lead him, at the beginning of the century, to that fertile criticism of the text and the literary origin of the books of the Old Testament which, at the end of the century, is beginning to make the inspired historians and the prophets, the psalmists and the moralists of the old Jews live anew for the modern Church. But how true has proved his prediction to Corrie in the year 1809:

I think that when the construction of Hebrew is fully understood, all the scholars in the world will turn to it with avidity, in order to understand other languages, and then the Word of God will be studied universally.

Again in 1810:

I sit for hours alone contemplating this mysterious language. If light does not break upon me at last it will be a great loss of time, as I never read Arabic or Persian. I have no heart to do it; I cannot condescend any longer to tread in the paths of ignorant and lying grammarians. I sometimes say in my vain heart I will make a deep cut in the mine of philology, or I will do nothing; but you[427] shall hear no more of Scriptural philology till I make some notable discoveries.

Again in 1811, when at Bombay:

Chiefly employed on the Arabic tract, writing letters to Europe, and my Hebrew speculations. The last encroached so much on my time and thoughts that I lost two nights' sleep, and consequently the most of two days, without learning more than I did the first hour.

Happening to think this evening on the nature of language more curiously and deeply than I have yet done, I got bewildered, and fancied I saw some grounds for the opinions of those who deny the existence of matter.... Oh, what folly to be wise where ignorance is bliss!... The further I push my inquiries the more I am distressed. It must be now my prayer, not 'Lord, let me obtain the knowledge which I think would be so useful,' but 'Oh, teach me just as much as Thou seest good for me.' Compared with metaphysics, physics and mathematics appear with a kind and friendly aspect, because they seem to be within the limits in which man can move without danger, but on the other I find myself adrift. Synthesis is the work of God alone.

Henry Martyn's first practical work was in Hindustani. His position in Dinapore and Patna, the capital of Bihar with its Hindi dialects, his duties to the native wives and families of the soldiers whom he taught and exhorted, his preaching to the Hindus and discussions with the Mohammedans, all led him to prepare three works—(1) portions of the *Book of Common Prayer*, which Corrie finished and published seventeen years after his death; (2) a *Commentary on the Parables*, in 1807; (3) the *Four Gospels* in 1809, and in 1810 the whole *New Testament*. Let us look at him in his spiritual and scholarly workshop.[428]

1807, January 18. (Sunday.)—Preached on Numbers xxiii. 19: a serious attention from all. Most of the European tradesmen were present with their families; my soul enjoyed sweet peace and heavenly-mindedness for some time afterwards. The thought suddenly struck me to-day, how easy it would be to translate the chief part of the Church Service for the use of the soldiers' wives, and women and children, and so have the service in Hindustani, by which a door would be opened to the heathen. This thought took such hold of me, that after in vain endeavouring to fix my thoughts on anything else, I sat down in the evening, and translated to the end of the *Te Deum*. But my conscience was not satisfied that this was a Sabbath employment, and I lost the sensible sweetness of the Divine presence. However, by leaving it off, and passing the rest of the evening in reading and singing hymns, I found comfort and joy. Oh, how shall I praise my Lord, that here in this solitude, with people enough indeed, but without any like-minded, I yet enjoy fellowship with all those who in every place call upon the name of our Lord Jesus Christ. I see myself travelling on with them, and I hope I shall worship with them in His courts above.

January 19.—Passed the morning with the moonshi and pundit, dictating to the former a few ideas for the explanation of the Parable of the Rich Fool. When I came to say that there was no eating and drinking, etc., in heaven, but only the pleasures of God's presence and holiness; and that, therefore, we must acquire a taste for such pleasures, the Mussulman was unwilling to write, but the Brahman was pleased, and said that all this was in the Puranas. Afterwards went on with the translation of the Liturgy.

March 23. (To Brown.)—It is with no small delight that I find the day arrived for my writing to my very dear brother. Many thanks for your two letters, and for all the consolation contained in them, and many thanks to our Lord and|429| Saviour, who has given me such a help where I once expected to struggle on alone all my days. Concerning the character in the Nagri papers you have sent me I have to say, it is perfectly the same as the one used here, and I can read it easily; and the difference in both the dialects from the one here is so trifling, that I have not the smallest doubt of the Parables being understood at Benares and Bettia (a Roman Catholic village), and consequently through a vast tract of country. A more important inference is, that in whatever dialect of the Hindustani the translation of the Scriptures shall be made, it will be generally understood. The little book of Parables is at last finished, through the blessing of God. I cannot say I am very well pleased with it on the reperusal; but yet containing, as it does, such large portions of the Word of God, I ought not to doubt of its accomplishing that which He pleaseth.

July 13.—Mr. Ward has also sent me a long and learned letter. He is going to print the Parables without delay for me, and the modern Hindustani version of them for themselves. He says, 'The enmity of the natives to the Gospel is indeed very great, but on this point the lower orders are angels compared with the moonshis and pundits. I believe the man you took from Serampore has his heart as full of this poison as most. The fear of loss of caste among the poor is a greater obstacle than their enmity. Our strait waistcoat makes our arms ache.'

December 29.—Translating from Hebrew into Hindustani in the morning. Wrote to Mr. Udny. Read Arabic and Persian as usual with Sabat. We had some conversation on this subject, whether we might not expect the Holy Spirit would endue us with extraordinary powers in the acquisition of languages, if we could pray for it only with a desire to be useful to the Church of God, and not with a wish for our own glory. There seemed to be no reason|430| against such an expectation. I sometimes pray for the gifts of the spirit, but infinitely greater is the necessity to pray for grace, as I know by the sorrowful experience of my deceitfully corrupt heart.

1808, January 7.—As much of my time as was not employed for the Europeans has been devoted chiefly to translating the Epistles into Hindustani. This work is finished after a certain manner. But Sabat does not allow me to form a very high idea of the style in which it is executed. But if the work should fail—which, however, I am far from expecting—my labour will have been richly repaid by the profit and pleasure derived from considering the Word of God in the original with more attention than I had ever done.

March 31.—I am at present employed in the toilsome work of going through the Syriac Gospels, and writing out the names, in order to ascertain their orthography if possible, and correcting with Mirza the Epistles. This last work is incredibly difficult in Hindustani, and will be nearly as much so in Persian, but very easy and elegant in Arabic.

June 1 to 4.—Employed incessantly in reading the Persian of St. Matthew to Sabat. Met with the Italian padre, Julius, with whom I conversed in French.

June 6.—Going on with the Persian Gospel, visiting the hospital, and with the men at night. My spirit refreshed and revived by every night's ministration to them. Sent the Persian of Matthew to Mr. Brown for the press, and went on with the remainder of the Hindustani of St. Matthew. I have not felt such trials of my temper for many months as to-day. The General declared he was an enemy to my design in translating the Scriptures. My poor harassed soul looked at last to God, and cast its burden of sin at the foot of the cross. Towards evening I found rest and peace. A son-in-law of the Qasi ool Qoorrat, of Patna, a very learned man, called on me. I|431|put to him several questions about Mohammedanism, which confused him; and as he seemed a grave, honest man, they may produce lasting doubts.

1809, September 24.—Began with Mirza Fitrut the correction of the Hindustani Gospels: *Quod felix faustumque sit.* Began with my men a course of lectures from the beginning of the Bible.

September 25 to 28.—Revising Arabic version of Romans; going on in correction of Hindustani; preparing report of progress in translating for Bible Society. Reading occasionally Menishi's *Turkish Grammar.*

Completed in 1810, Martyn's Hindustani New Testament for Mohammedans was passing through the Serampore press when the great fire of March 11, 1812, destroyed all the sheets save the first thirteen chapters of Matthew's Gospel, and melted the fount of Persian type. The Corresponding Committee of the British and Foreign Bible Society, for which it had been prepared, put it to press the second time at Serampore, from finer type, and it appeared in 1814 in an edition of 2,000 copies, on English paper. The demand for portions for immediate use was such that 3,000 copies of the Gospels and Acts, on Patna paper, had been previously struck off. The longing translator—who had once written, 'Oh, may I have the bliss of soon seeing the New Testament in Hindustani and Persian!'—had then been two years dead, but verily his works followed him. Such was the reputation of the version that it was read in the native schools at Agra and elsewhere; while an edition of 2,000 copies in the Deva-Nagri character, for Hindus, appeared in 1817, and was used up till a Hindi version was prepared from it by Mr. Bowley, the zealous agent of the Church Missionary Society at Chunar, by divesting it|432| of the Persian and Arabic terms. Bishop Corrie's revision of this work and portions of the Old Testament were circulated in many editions and extending numbers, in the Kaithi character also, among the millions of Hindus who speak the most widespread of Indian languages with many dialects. The Bible Society in London welcomed Martyn's work, of which Professor Lee prepared a large edition. Learning that the lamented scholar had done some work on the Old Testament in Hindustani, and had taught Mirza Fitrut Hebrew, to enable that able moonshi to carry on the translation from the original, the Society first published Genesis in Hindustani, under Professor Lee's care, in 1817, and then issued a revision of the rough draft of the entire version of the Old Testament, by Bishop Corrie and Mr. Thomason. In 1843 Mr. Schürmann, of the London Missionary Society, and Mr. Justice Hawkins, an elder of the Free Church of Scotland and an accomplished Bengal civilian, issued a uniform revision of the Old and New Testaments in the Arabic and Roman characters, in the course of which Mr. Schürmann 'saw reason to revert in a great measure to the translation of Henry Martyn, especially in the latter half of the version.'[71]Of the different translations of the Bible into Hindustani, the Oordoo or 'camp' language understood by the sixty millions of Mussulmans in India, this criticism is just: 'the idiomatic and faithful version of Henry Martyn still maintains its ground, although, from the lofty elegance of its style, it is better understood by educated than by illiterate Mohammedans.'[72]

In the first generation, from 1814 to 1847, after the|433| appearance of Henry Martyn's work, sixteen editions[73] of the Hindustani New Testament were published and sent into circulation among the then fifty millions of Mussulmans in India. Before Martyn's work was printed, he and Corrie used to dictate to inquirers translations of Bible passages suited to their needs. When Corrie was at Chunar, he tells us, because 'there was not at that time any translation of the Scriptures to put into his hands, a native Roman Catholic took down the translated texts on loose pieces of paper.' Years after, Mr. Wilkinson, of Gorakpore, was called to visit the man on his death-bed, and found him so well acquainted with Scripture that he asked an explanation. 'The poor man produced the loose slips of paper on which he had written my translations,' says Corrie. 'On these, it appeared, his soul had fed through life, and through them he died such a death that Mr. Wilkinson entertained no doubt of his having passed into glory.' In the forty years since the sixteen editions made the Word of God known to thousands of India Mussulmans, the Oordoo Bible has caused the Word to grow mightily, and in many cases to prevail.

The entire Bible in Hindustani was again revised, by Dr. R.C. Mather, after many years' experience in Benares and Mirzapore, and was published, in both the Arabic and Roman characters, in 1869, after continuous labour for more than six years. He stumbled, in the library of the British and Foreign Bible Society, on sixteen manuscript volumes of a Hindustani translation of nearly the whole Old Testament, beginning with Martyn's Genesis. The folios were interleaved, and on the blank pages were thousands of[434] notes in English. At the end of the Pentateuch the copyist records that 'the above has been completed, by order of Paymaster Sherwood, for the Rev. Daniel Corrie, by me, Mákhdum Buksh.' The copy seems to have been the accomplished Thomason's, and to have been deposited in the library by his widow after his death at Port Louis, Mauritius. This practically complete translation of the Old Testament had been lost for forty years. The eulogy passed by Thomason on Martyn's Hindustani New Testament, that it 'will last as a model of elegant writing as well as of faithful translation,' is pronounced by Dr. Mather,[74] after all that time, as, 'in the main, just; the work has lasted and continued to be acceptable, and will perhaps always continue to be useful. All subsequent translators have, as a matter of course, proceeded upon it as a work of excellent skill and learning, and rigid fidelity.'

The modern Arabic translation of the New Testament, by Martyn and Sabat, was not printed (in Calcutta) till 1816, and the translation of the Old Testament was continued under the supervision of Mr. Thomason, who became virtually Martyn's literary executor, and whose labours as Oriental translator and editor hurried him, like his friend, to a premature death. Both had the same biographer—the good Sargent, Rector of Lavington. As Thomason toiled at the Arabic, Persian, and Hindustani editions, he wrote: 'I am filled with astonishment at the opening scenes of usefulness. Send us labourers—send us faithful laborious labourers!'[75] Martyn's Arabic New Testament,[435] produced with the assistance of an undoubtedly learned Arab, as conceited and of temper as intolerable as Sabat, did its work among the 'learned and fastidious' Mohammedans for whom chiefly it was prepared. Professor Lee issued a second edition in London, and Mr. Thomason a third in Calcutta. In common with the old translations, made for the land in which St. Paul began the first missionary work, and reproduced in various Polyglot Bibles, it has been superseded by the wonderfully perfect and altogether beautiful Arabic Bible (Beirut) of Dr. Eli Smith and Dr. Van Dyck, on which these American scholars, assisted by learned natives of Syria and Cairo, were occupied for nearly thirty years. In the Beirut Arabic Scriptures, Henry Martyn's troubled life with Sabat found early and luxuriant fruit. How wisely and humbly the missionary chaplain of the East India Company estimated his own, and especially his Arabic, translations, and how at the same time he longed to live that he might do in 1812-20 what Eli Smith and Van Dyck did in 1837-65, may be seen from these early letters and journals:

TO THE REV. DAVID BROWN, CALCUTTA

Cawnpore: June 11, 1810.

Dearest Sir,—The excessive heat, by depriving me of my rest at night, keeps me between sleeping and waking all day. This is one reason why I have been remiss in answering your letters. It must not, however, be concealed that the man Daniel Corrie has kept me so long talking that I have had no time for writing since his arrival.

Your idea about presenting splendid copies of the Scriptures to native great men has often struck me, but my counsel is, not to do it with the first edition. I have too little faith in the instruments to believe that the first editions[436] will be excellent; and if they should be found defective, we cannot after once presenting the great men with one book, repeat the thing.

Before the second edition of the Arabic, what say you to my carrying the first with me to Arabia, having under the other arm the Persian, to be examined at Shiraz or Teheran? By the time they are both ready I shall have nearly finished my seven years, and may go on furlough.

I am glad to find you promising to give yourself wholly to your plans. I always tremble lest Mrs. Brown should order you home; but I must not suspect her, she has the soul of a missionary. If you go soon we shall all droop and die. Your Polyglot speculations are fine, but Polyglots are Biblical luxuries, intended for the gratification of men of two tongues or more. We must first feed those that have but one, especially as single tongues are growing upon us so fast.

June 12.—To-day I have requested the Commander of the forces to detain D. Corrie here to assist me; he said he did not like to make innovations, but would keep him here for two or three months. This will be a great relief to my labouring chest, for I am still far from being out of the fear of consumption. Tell me that you have prayed for me.

Yours, etc.

H.M.

August 22.—I want silence and diversion, a little dog to play with; or what would be best of all, a dear little child, such as Fanny was when I left her. Perhaps you could learn when the ships usually sail for Mocha. I have set my heart upon going there; I could be there and back in six months.

September 8.—Your tide rolls on with terrifying rapidity, at least I tremble while committing myself to it. You look to me, and I to Sabat; and Sabat I look upon as the staff of Egypt. May I prove mistaken! All, however, does not depend upon him. If my life is spared, there is no[437] reason why the Arabic should not be done in Arabia, and the Persian in Persia, as well as the Indian in India. I hope your Shalome has not left you. I promise myself great advantage in reading Hebrew and Syriac with him.

September 9.—Yours of the 27th ult. is a heart-breaking business. Though I share so deeply in Sabat's disgrace, I feel more for you than myself, but I can give you no comfort except by saying, 'It is well that it was in thine heart.' Your letter will give a new turn to my life. Henceforward I have done with India. Arabia shall hide me till I come forth with an approved New Testament in Arabic. I do not ask your advice, because I have made up my mind, but shall just wait your answer to this, and come down to you instantly. I have been calculating upon the means of support, and find that I shall have wherewithal to live. Besides, the Lord will provide. Before Him I have spread this affair, and do not feel that I shall be acting contrary to His will.... Will Government let me go away for three years before the time of my furlough arrives? If not, I must quit the service, and I cannot devote my life to a more important work than that of preparing the Arabic Bible.

Herewith you will receive the first seven chapters in Persian and Hindustani, though I suppose you have ceased to wish for them. The Persian will only prove that Sabat is not the man for it. I have protested against many things in it, but instead of sending you my objections I inclose a critique by Mirza, who must remain unknown. I am somewhat inclined to think the Arabic not quite so hopeless. Sabat is confident, and eager to meet his opponents. His version of the Romans was certainly not from the old one, because he translated it all before my face from the English; but then, as I hinted long ago, he is inaccurate and not to be depended upon. He entirely approves of my going to Busrah with his translations, and the old one, confident that the decision there will be in his favour. Dear Sir, take measures for transmitting me with the least[438] possible delay; detain me not, for the King's business requires haste.

The King sent His eager servant to Persia, and did not give him the desire of his heart to enter Arabia. Truly he hastened so unrestingly that the Spirit of God led him to complete the Persian New Testament, and then carried him away from the many tongues of mortal men, which as they sprang from disunion, so they are to 'cease' in the one speech of the multitudes of every nation and kindred and tribe and tongue who sing the new song.

The following letter to Charles Simeon, the original of which was presented by his biographer, Canon Carus, to Canon Moor, who permits it to be published here for the first time, fitly introduces Henry Martyn's translation used in Persia. Simeon received it on January 21, 1812, and thus wrote of it to Thomason:

From whom, think you, did I receive a letter yesterday? From our beloved Martyn in Persia. He begins to find his strength improve, and he is 'disputing daily' with the learned, who, he says, are extremely subtile. They are not a little afraid of him, and are going to write a book on the evidences of their religion. The evidences of Mohammedanism! A fine comparison they will make with those of Christianity. Oh, that God may endue our brother with wisdom and strength to execute all that is in his heart. He is desirous of spending two years in Persia, and is willing to sacrifice his salary if the East India Company will not give him leave. I am going in an hour to Mr. Grant to consult him, and shall call on Mr. Astell if Mr. Grant thinks it expedient.[439]

TO REV. C. SIMEON

Shiraz: July 8, 1811.

My dearest Friend and Brother,—My last letter to you was from Bombay. I sailed thence on March 25, in the Company's corvette, the Benares. As the ship was manned principally by Europeans, I had a good deal to do during the voyage, but through the mercy of our Heavenly Father I was so far from suffering that I rather gained strength, and am now apparently as well as ever I was. On Easter day we made the coast of Mekran, in Persia, and on the Sunday following landed at Muscat, in Arabia. Here I met with an African slave, who tried hard to persuade me that I was in the wrong and he in the right. The dispute ended in his asking for an Arabic Testament, which I gave him. We were about a month in the Persian Gulf, generally in sight of land. At last, on May 22, I was set down at Bushire, in Persia, and was kindly received by the English Resident. One day I went to the Armenian church, at the request of the priest, not expecting to see anything like Christian worship, and accordingly I did not. The Word of God was read, indeed, but in such a way that no man could have understood it. After church he desired me to notice that he had censed me *four* times because I was a priest. This will give you an idea of their excessive childishness. I took occasion from his remark to speak about the priest's office, and the awful importance of it. Nothing can be conceived more vapid and inane than his observations.

As soon as my Persian dress was ready, I set off for the interior in a kafila, or small caravan, consisting chiefly of mules, and after a very fatiguing journey of ten days over the mountains, during which time the difference in the thermometer by day and night was often sixty degrees, I arrived at this place about a month ago.[440]

I had no intention of making any stay here, but I found, on my producing Sabat's Persian translation, that I must sit down with native Persians to begin the work once more. The fault found with Sabat's work is that he uses words not only so difficult as to be unintelligible to the generality, but such as never were in use in the Persian.

When it is considered that the issue of all disputes with the Mohammedans is a reference to the Scriptures, and that the Persian and Arabic are known all over the Mohammedan world, it will be evident that we ought to spare no pains in obtaining good versions in these languages. Hence I look upon my staying here for a time as a duty paramount to every other, and I trust that the Government in India will look upon it in the same light. If they should stop my pay, it would not alter my purpose in the least, but it would be an inconvenience. I should be happy, therefore, if the Court of Directors would sanction my residence in these parts for a year or two. No one who has been in Persia will imagine that I am here for my own pleasure. India is a paradise to it. All is poverty and desolation without, and within I have no comfort but in my God. I am in the midst of enemies, who argue against the truth, sometimes with uncommon subtlety. But I pray for the fulfilment of the Lord's promise, and I am assured that He will be with me and give me a mouth and a wisdom, which all my adversaries shall not be able to gainsay or resist. I am sometimes asked whether I am not afraid to speak so boldly against the Mohammedan religion. I tell them if I say or do anything against the laws I am not unwilling to suffer, but if I say nothing but what naturally comes in the course of argument—it is an argument too which you yourselves began—why should I fear? You know the power of the English too well to suppose that they would let any violence be offered to me with impunity.

The English ambassador, Sir Gore Ouseley, whom I[441] met here on his way to Tabreez, carried me with him to the court of the prince, who, though tributary to his father, is a sovereign prince in Elam, as the S. Scriptures call the province of Fars. He has also recommended me to the prince's favourite minister, so that I am in no danger. But there is certainly a great stir among the learned, and every effort is made to support their cause. They have now persuaded the father of all the moollas to write a book in Arabic on the evidences of the Mohammedan religion, a book which is to silence me for ever. I rather suppose that the more their cause is examined the worse it will appear.

I have had no news from India these four months, so I can say nothing of our friends there. Let your next letters be sent not to India, but direct to Persia, in this way: Rev. H.M., care of Sir Gore Ouseley, Bart., Ambassador Extraordinary, etc., *Teheran*; care of S. Morier, Esq., *Constantinople*; care of George Moore, Esq., *Malta*. My kindest love to all your dear people, Messrs. Bowman and Goodall, Farish, Port, Phillips, etc. I hope they continue to remember me once a week in their prayers; to the *four godly professors*;[76] to your young men though to me unknown, and especially to your brother. Believe me to be yours ever most affectionately,

H. MARTYN.

1812, January 1 to 8.—Spared by mercy to see the beginning of another year. The last has been in some respects a memorable year; transported in safety to Shiraz, I have been led, by the particular providence of God, to undertake a work the idea of which never entered my mind till my arrival here, but which has gone on without material interruption and is now nearly finished. To all appearance the present year will be more perilous than any I have seen, but if I live to complete the Persian New Testament, my life after that will be of less importance.[442] But whether life or death be mine, may Christ be magnified in me. If He has work for me to do, I cannot die.

He had just before written this pathetic letter, of exquisite friendliness:

TO THE REV. D. CORRIE

Shiraz: December 12, 1811.

Dearest Brother,—Your letters of January 28 and April 22 have just reached me. After being a whole year without any tidings of you, you may conceive how much they have tended to revive my spirits. Indeed, I know not how to be sufficiently thankful to our God and Father for giving me a brother who is indeed a brother to my soul, and thus follows me with affectionate prayers wherever I go, and more than supplies my place to the precious flock over whom the Holy Ghost hath made us overseers. There is only one thing in your letters that makes me uneasy, and that is, the oppression you complain of in the hot weather. As you will have to pass another hot season at Cawnpore, and I do not know how many more, I must again urge you to spare yourself. I am endeavouring to learn the true use of time in a new way, by placing myself in idea twenty or thirty years in advance, and then considering how I ought to have managed twenty or thirty years ago. In racing violently for a year or two, and then breaking down? In this way I have reasoned myself into contentment about staying so long at Shiraz. I thought at first, what will the Government in India think of my being away so long, or what will my friends think? Shall I not appear to all a wandering shepherd, leaving the flock and running about for my own pleasure! But placing myself twenty years on in time, I say, Why could not I stay at Shiraz long enough to get a New Testament done there, even if I had been detained there on that account three or six years? What work of equal importance can ever come from me? So[443] that now I am resolved to wait here till the New Testament is finished, though I incur the displeasure of Government, or even be dismissed the service. I have been many times on the eve of my departure, as my translator promised to accompany me to Baghdad, but that city being in great confusion he is afraid to trust himself there; so I resolved to go westward through the north of Persia, but found it impossible, on account of the snow which blocks up the roads in winter, to proceed till spring. Here I am therefore, for three months more; our Testament will be finished, please God, in six weeks. I go on as usual, riding round the walls in the morning, and singing hymns at night over my milk and water, for tea I have none, though I much want it. I am with you in spirit almost every evening, and feel a bliss I cannot describe in being one with the dear saints of God all over the earth, through one Lord and one Spirit.

They continued throwing stones at me every day, till happening one day to tell Jaffir Ali Khan, my host, how one as big as my fist had hit me in the back, he wrote to the Governor, who sent an order to all the gates, that if any one insulted me he should be bastinadoed, and the next day came himself in state to pay me a visit. These measures have had the desired effect; they now call me the Feringhi Nabob, and very civilly offer me the kalean; but indeed the Persian commonalty are very brutes; the Soofis declare themselves unable to account for the fierceness of their countrymen, except it be from the influence of

Islam. After speaking in my praise one of them added 'and there are the Hindus too (who have brought the guns), when I saw their gentleness I was quite charmed with them; but as for our Iranees, they delight in nothing but tormenting their fellow creatures.' These Soofis are quite the Methodists of the East. They delight in everything Christian, except in being exclusive. They consider that all will finally return to God, from whom they[444]emanated, or rather of whom they are only different forms. The doctrine of the Trinity they admired, but not the atonement, because the Mohammedans, they say, consider Imam Husain as also crucified for the sins of men; and to everything Mohammedan they have a particular aversion. Yet withal they conform externally. From these, however, you will perceive the first Persian Church will be formed, judging after the manner of men. The employment of my leisure hours is translating the Psalms into Persian. What will poor Fitrut do when he gets to the poetical books? Job, I hope, you have let him pass over. The Books of Solomon are also in a very sorry condition in the English. The Prophets are all much easier, and consequently better done. I hear there is a man at Yezd that has fallen into the same way of thinking as myself about the letters, and professes to have found out all the arts and sciences from them. I should be glad to compare notes with him. It is now time for me to bid you good night. We have had ice on the pools some time, but no snow yet. They build their houses without chimneys, so if we want a fire we must take the smoke along with it. I prefer wrapping myself in my sheepskin.

Your accounts of the progress of the kingdom of God among you are truly refreshing. Tell dear H. and the men of both regiments that I salute them much in the Lord, and make mention of them in my prayers. May I continue to hear thus of their state, and if I am spared to see them again, may we make it evident that we have grown in grace. Affectionate remembrances to your sister and Sherwoods; I hope they continue to prosecute their labours of love. Remember me to the people of Cawnpore who inquire, etc. Why have not I mentioned Col. P.? It is not because he is not in my heart, for there is hardly a man in the world whom I love and honour more. My most Christian salutations to him.[445]

May the grace of the Lord Jesus Christ be with your spirit, dearest brother. Yours affectionately,

H. MARTYN.

Martyn's Cambridge Persian studies were continued for practical Hindustani purposes at Dinapore, in 1809, and the following incident unconsciously lights up his Persian scholarship at that date. Writing to the impatient David Brown at Aldeen, from Patna, on March 28, he says:

You chide me for not trusting my Hindustani to the press. Last week we began the correction of it; present, a Sayyid of Delhi, a poet of Lucknow, three or four literates of Patna, and Baba Ali in the chair; Sabat and myself assessors.

I was amazed and mortified at observing that reference was had to the Persian for every verse, in order to understand the Hindustani. It was, however, a consolation to find that from the Persian they caught the meaning of it instantly, always expressing their admiration of the plainness of their translation.

But when the Persian translation of the four Gospels was printed at Serampore, nearly two years after, Martyn himself was dissatisfied with it. His Cawnpore and especially Lucknow experience had developed him in Persian style, and led him to see that in Persia itself only could the great work be done of translating the Word of God into a language spoken and read from Calcutta and Patna to Damascus and Tabreez.

When Henry Martyn did the noblest achievement of his life, the production of the Persian New Testament, he unknowingly linked himself with the greatest of the Greek Fathers, near whose dust his own was about to be laid. Until the Eastern Church ceased to be aggressive—that is, missionary—Persia, like Central Asia up to China itself,[446] promised to be all Christian. Islam, a corrupted mixture of Judaism and Christianity, took its place. Persia sent a bishop to the Council of Nicæa in 325, and the great Constantine wrote a letter to King Sapor, recommending to his protection the Christian Churches in his empire.[447] Chrysostom (347-407), in his second homily on John, incidentally tells us that 'the Persians, having translated the doctrines of the Gospel into their own tongue, had learned, though barbarians, the true philosophy.' In his homily on the memorial of Mary he puts the Persians first, and our British forefathers last, in this remarkable passage: 'The Persians, the Indians, Scythians, Thracians, Sarmatians, the race of the Moors, and the inhabitants of the British Isles, celebrate a deed performed in a private family in Judea by a woman that had been a sinner.' The isles of Britain, Claudius Buchanan well remarks, then last, are now the first to restore this memorial to the Persians as well as to other Mohammedan nations. Even so late as 1740 the tyrant Nadir Shah, inquiring as to Jesus Christ, asked for a Persian copy of the Gospels, and had presented to him the combined work of an ignorant Romish priest and some Mohammedan moollas, which excited his ridicule. The traveller, Jonas Hanway, tells us that when Henry Martyn saw this production he exclaimed that he did not wonder at Nadir's contempt of it.

Martyn arrived in Shiraz on June 11, 1811; in a week he began his Persian translation of the New Testament, and in February 1812 he completed the happy toil, carried on amidst disputations with Soofis and Shi'ahs, Jews and[447] Christians of the Oriental rites, while consumption wasted his body. His 'leisure' he spent in translating the Hebrew Psalter. Let us look at him, in that South Persian summer and winter and summer again, now in the city of Shiraz, now driven by the sultry heat to the garden of roses and orange-trees outside the walls near the tomb of Hafiz. The Christian poet has pictured the scene—Alford, when Dean of Canterbury in 1851. Twenty years after, he himself was laid in the churchyard of the mother church of England, St. Martin's, under this inscription—'Diversorium Viatoris Hierosolymam Proficiscentis':

HENRY MARTYN AT SHIRAZ

I

A vision of the bright Shiraz, of Persian bards the theme:
The vine with bunches laden hangs o'er the crystal stream;
The nightingale all day her notes in rosy thickets trills,
And the brooding heat-mist faintly lies along the distant hills.

II

About the plain are scattered wide, in many a crumbling heap,
The fanes of other days, and tombs where Iran's poets sleep:
And in the midst, like burnished gems, in noonday light repose
The minarets of bright Shiraz—the City of the Rose.

III

One group beside the river bank in rapt discourse are seen,
Where hangs the golden orange on its boughs of purest green;
Their words are sweet and low, and their looks are lit with joy,
Some holy blessing seems to rest on them and their employ.

IV

The pale-faced Frank among them sits: what brought him from afar?
Nor bears he bales of merchandise, nor teaches skill in war;
One pearl alone he brings with him,—the Book of life and death;
One warfare only teaches he—to fight the fight of faith.
[448]

V

And Iran's sons are round him, and one with solemn tone
Tells how the Lord of Glory was rejected by His own;
Tells, from the wondrous Gospel, of the Trial and the Doom,
The words Divine of Love and Might—the Scourge, the Cross, the Tomb.

VI

Far sweeter to the stranger's ear those Eastern accents sound
Than music of the nightingale that fills the air around:
Lovelier than balmiest odours sent from gardens of the rose,
The fragrance from the contrite soul and chastened lip that flows.

VII

The nightingales have ceased to sing, the roses' leaves are shed,
The Frank's pale face in Tokat's field hath mouldered with the dead:

Alone and all unfriended, midst his Master's work he fell,
With none to bathe his fevered brow, with none his tale to tell.
    VIII
But still those sweet and solemn tones about him sound in bliss,
And fragrance from those flowers of God for evermore is his:
For his the meed, by grace, of those who, rich in zeal and love,
Turn many unto righteousness, and shine as stars above.

This was the beginning of the Persian New Testament:

To REV. DAVID BROWN

Shiraz: June 24, 1811.

Dearest Sir,—I believe I told you that the advanced state of the season rendered it necessary to go to Arabia circuitously by way of Persia. Behold me therefore in the Athens of Fars, the haunt of the Persian man. Beneath are the ashes of Hafiz and Sadi; above, green gardens and running waters, roses and nightingales. Does Mr. Bird envy my lot? Let him solace himself with Aldeen. How gladly would I give him Shiraz for Aldeen; how often|449| while toiling through this miserable country have I sighed for Aldeen! If I am ever permitted to see India again nothing but dire necessity, or the imperious call of duty, will ever induce me to travel again. One thing is good here, the fruit; we have apples and apricots, plums, nectarines, greengages and cherries, all of which are served up with ice and snow. When I have said this for Shiraz I have said all.

But to have done with what grows out of the soil, let us come to the men. The Persians are, like ourselves, immortal; their language had passed a long way beyond the limits of Iran. The men of Shiraz propose to translate the New Testament with me. Can I refuse to stay? After much deliberation I have determined to remain here six months. It is sorely against my will, but I feel it to be a duty. From all that I can collect there appears no probability of our ever having a good translation made out of Persia. At Bombay I showed Moolla Firoz, the most learned man there, the three Persian translations, viz. the Polyglot, and Sabat's two. He disapproved of them all. At Bushire, which is in Persia, the man of the greatest name was Sayyid Hosein. Of the three he liked Sabat's Persian best, but said it seemed written by an Indian. On my arrival at this place I produced my specimens once more. Sabat's Persian was much ridiculed; sarcastic remarks were made on the fondness for fine words so remarkable in the Indians, who seemed to think that hard words made fine writing. His Persic also was presently thrown aside, and to my no small surprise the old despised Polyglot was not only spoken of as superior to the rest, but it was asked, What fault is found in this?—this is the language we speak. The king has also signified that it is his wish that as little Arabic as possible may be employed in the papers presented to him. So that simple Persian is likely to become more and more fashionable. This is a change favourable certainly to our glorious cause. To the|450| poor the Gospel will be preached. We began our work with the Gospel of St. John, and five chapters are put out of hand. It is likely to be the simplest thing imaginable; and I dare say the pedantic Arab will turn up his nose at it; but what the men of Shiraz approve who can gainsay? Let Sabat confine himself to the Arabic, and he will accomplish a great work. The forementioned Sayyid Hosein of Bushire is an Arab. I showed him Erpenius's Arabic Testament, the Christian Knowledge Society, Sabat's, and the Polyglot. After rejecting all but Sabat's, he said this is good, very good, and then read off the 5th of Matthew in a fine style, giving it unqualified commendation as he went along. On my proposing to him to give a specimen of what he thought the best Persian style, he consented; but, said he, give me this to translate from, laying his hand on Sabat's Arabic. At Muscat an Arab officer who had attended us as guard and guide one day when we walked into the country, came on board with his slave to take leave of us. The slave, who had argued with me very strenuously in favour of his religion, reminded me of a promise I had made him of giving him the Gospel. On my producing an Arabic New Testament, he seized it and began to read away upon deck, but presently stopped, and said it was not fine Arabic. However, he carried off the book.

In eight months the Persian translation of the New Testament was done. The *Journal*, during that period, from July 1811 to February 1812, as the sacred task went on, reveals the Holy Spirit moving the hearts of the translator's Mohammedan assistant and Soofi disputants by 'the things of Christ,' while it shows His servant bearing witness, by the account of his own conversion, to His power to save and to make holy.

[451]

December 12.—Letters at last from India. Mirza Sayyid Ali was curious to know in what way we corresponded, and made me read Mr. Brown's letter to me, and mine to Corrie. He took care to let his friends know that we wrote nothing about our own affairs: it was all about translations and the cause of Christ. With this he was delighted.

December 16.—In translating 2 Cor. i. 22, 'Who hath given the earnest of the Spirit in our hearts,' he was much struck when it was explained to him. 'Oh, that I had it,' said he; 'have you received it?' I told him that, as I had no doubt of my acceptance through Christ, I concluded that I had. Once before, on the words, 'Who are saved?' he expressed his surprise at the confidence with which Christians spoke of salvation. On 1 Cor. xv. he observed, that the doctrine of the resurrection of the body was unreasonable; but that as the Mohammedans understood it, it was impossible; on which account the Soofis rejected it.

Christmas Day.—I made a great feast for the Russians and Armenians; and, at Jaffir Ali Khan's request, invited the Soofi master, with his disciples. I hoped there would be some conversation on the occasion of our meeting, and, indeed, Mirza Sayyid Ali did make some attempts, and explained to the old man the meaning of the Lord's Supper; but the sage maintaining his usual silence, the subject was dropped. I expressed my satisfaction at seeing them assembled on such an occasion, and my hope that they would remember the day in succeeding years, and that though they would never see me again in the succeeding years, they would not forget that I had brought them the Gospel. The old man coldly replied that 'God would guide those whom He chose.' Most of the time they continued was before dinner; the moment that was despatched, they rose and went away. The custom is, to sit five or six hours before dinner, and at great men's houses singers attend.

December 31.—The accounts of the desolations of war[452] during the last year, which I have been reading in some Indian newspapers, make the world appear more gloomy than ever. How many souls hurried into eternity unprepared! How many thousands of widows and orphans left to mourn! But admire, my soul, the matchless power of God, that out of this ruin He has prepared for Himself an inheritance. At last the scene shall change, and I shall find myself in a world where all is love.

1812.—The last has been in some respects a memorable year. I have been led, by what I have reason to consider as the particular providence of God, to this place; and have undertaken an important work, which has gone on without material interruption, and is now nearly finished. I like to find myself employed usefully, in a way I did not expect or foresee, especially if my own will is in any degree crossed by the work unexpectedly assigned me, as there is then reason to believe that God is acting. The present year will probably be a perilous one, but my life is of little consequence, whether I live to finish the Persian New Testament or do not. I look back with pity and shame upon my former self, and on the importance I then attached to my life and labours. The more I see of my own works the more I am ashamed of them. Coarseness and clumsiness mar all the works of man. I am sick when I look at man and his wisdom and his doings, and am relieved only by reflecting that we have a city whose builder and maker is God. The least of His works it is refreshing to look at. A dried leaf or a straw makes me feel myself in good company: complacency and admiration take place of disgust.

I compared with pain our Persian translation with the original; to say nothing of the precision and elegance of the sacred text, its perspicuity is that which sets at defiance all attempts to equal it.

January 16.—Mirza Sayyid Ali told me accidentally to-day of a distich made by his friend Mirza Koochut,[453] at Teheran, in honour of a victory gained by Prince Abbas Mirza over the Russians. The sentiment was, that he had killed so many of the Christians, that Christ, from the fourth heaven, took hold of Mahomet's skirt to entreat him to desist. I was cut to the soul at this blasphemy. In prayer I could think of nothing else but that great day when the Son of God shall come in the clouds of heaven, taking vengeance on them that know not God, and convincing men of all their hard speeches which they have spoken against Him.

177

Mirza Sayyid Ali perceived that I was considerably disordered, and was sorry for having repeated the verse, but asked what it was that was so offensive. I told him that 'I could not endure existence if Jesus was not glorified; it would be hell to me if He were to be always thus dishonoured.' He was astonished, and again asked why. 'If anyone pluck out your eyes,' I replied, 'there is no saying *why* you feel pain; it is feeling. It is because I am one with Christ that I am thus dreadfully wounded.' On his again apologising, I told him that 'I rejoiced at what had happened, inasmuch as it made me feel nearer the Lord than ever. It is when the head or heart is struck, that every member feels its membership.' This conversation took place while we were translating. In the evening he mentioned the circumstance of a young man's being murdered—a fine athletic youth, whom I had often seen in the garden. Some acquaintance of his in a slight quarrel had plunged a dagger in his breast. Observing me look sorrowful, he asked why. 'Because,' said I, 'he was cut off in his sins, and had no time to repent.' 'It was just in that way,' said he, 'that I should like to die; not dragging out a miserable existence on a sick-bed, but transported at once into another state.' I observed that 'it was not desirable to be hurried into the immediate presence of God.' 'Do you think,' said he, 'that there is any difference in the presence of God here or there?' 'Indeed I do,' said I.|454|'Here we see through a glass darkly; but there, face to face.' He then entered into some metaphysical Soofi disputation about the identity of sin and holiness, heaven and hell: to all which I made no reply.

January 18.—Aga Ali of Media came: and with him and Mirza Ali I had a long and warm discussion about the essentials of Christianity. The Mede, seeing us at work upon the Epistles, said, 'he should be glad to read them; as for the Gospels they were nothing but tales, which were of no use to him; for instance,' said he, 'if Christ raised four hundred dead to life, what is that to me?' I said, 'it certainly was of importance, for His work furnished a reason for our depending upon His words.' 'What did He say,' asked he, 'that was not known before? the love of God, humility—who does not know these things?' 'Were these things,' said I, 'known before Christ, either among Greeks or Romans, with all their philosophy?' They avowed that the Hindu book *Juh* contained precepts of this kind. I questioned its antiquity; 'but however that may be,' I added, 'Christ came not to *teach* so much as to *die*; the truths I spoke of as confirmed by His miracles were those relating to His person, such as, "Come unto Me, all ye that labour and are heavy laden, and I will give you rest." Here Mirza Sayyid Ali told him that I had professed to have no doubt of my salvation. He asked what I meant. I told him, 'that though sin still remained, I was assured that it should not regain dominion; and that I should never come into condemnation, but was accepted in the Beloved.' Not a little surprised, he asked Mirza Sayyid Ali whether he comprehended this. 'No,' said he, 'nor Mirza Ibrahim, to whom I mentioned it.' The Mede again turning to me asked, 'How do you know this? how do you know you have experienced the second birth?' 'Because,' said I, 'we have the Spirit of the Father; what He wishes we wish; what He hates we hate.' Here he began to be a little more calm and less contentious, and mildly asked[455] how I had obtained this peace of mind: 'Was it merely these books?' said he, taking up some of our sheets. I told him, 'These books, with prayer.' 'What was the beginning of it,' said he, 'the society of some friends?' I related to him my religious history, the substance of which was, that I took my Bible before God in prayer, and prayed for forgiveness through Christ, assurance of it through His Spirit, and grace to obey His commandments. They then both asked whether the same benefit would be conferred on them. 'Yes,' said I, 'for so the Apostles preached, that all who were baptized in His name should receive the gift of the Holy Ghost.' 'Can you assure me,' said Mirza Sayyid Ali, 'that the Spirit will be given to me? if so, I will be baptized immediately.' 'Who am I that I should be surety?' I replied; 'I bring you this message from God, that he who, despairing of himself, rests for righteousness on the Son of God, shall receive the gift of the Holy Ghost; and to this I can add my testimony, if that be worth anything, that I have found the promise fulfilled in myself. But if after baptism you should not find it so in you, accuse not the Gospel of falsehood. It is possible that your faith might not be sincere; indeed, so fully am I persuaded that you do not believe on the Son of God, that if you were to entreat ever so earnestly for baptism I should not dare to administer it at this time, when you have shown so many signs of an unhumbled heart.' 'What! would you have me believe,' said he, 'as a child?'

'Yes,' said I. 'True,' said he, 'I think that is the only way.' Aga Ali said no more, except, 'Certainly he is a good man!'

January 23.—Put on my English dress, and went to the Vizier's, to see part of the tragedy of Husain's death,[78] which they contrive to spin out so as to make it last the first ten days of the Mohurrum. All the apparatus consisted of a few boards for a stage, two tables and[456] a pulpit, under an immense awning, in the court where the company were assembled. The *dramatis personæ* were two; the daughter of Husain, whose part was performed by a boy, and a messenger; they both read their parts. Every now and then loud sobs were heard all over the court. After this several feats of activity were exhibited; the Vizier sat with the moollas. I was appointed to a seat where indeed I saw as much as I wanted, but which, I afterwards perceived, was not the place of honour. As I trust I am far enough from desiring the chief seats in the synagogues, there was nothing in this that could offend me; but I do not think it right to let him have another opportunity of showing a slight to my country in my person.

January 24.—Found Sayyid Ali rather serious this evening. He said he did not know what to do to have his mind made up about religion. Of all the religions Christ's was the best; but whether to prefer this to Soofi-ism he could not tell. In these doubts he is tossed to and fro, and is often kept awake the whole night in tears. He and his brother talk together on these things till they are almost crazed. Before he was engaged in this work of translation, he says he used to read about two or three hours a day, now he can do nothing else; has no inclination for anything else, and feels unhappy if he does not correct his daily portion. His late employment has given a new turn to his thoughts as well as to those of his friends; they had not the most distant conception of the contents of the New Testament. He says his Soofi friends are exceedingly anxious to see the Epistles, from the accounts he gives of them, and also he is sure that almost the whole of Shiraz are so sensible of the load of unmeaning ceremonies in which their religion consists, that they will rejoice to see or hear of anything like freedom, and that they would be more willing to embrace Christ than the Soofis, who, after taking so much pains to be independent of all law, would[457] think it degrading to submit themselves to any law again, however light.

February 2.—From what I suffer in this city, I can understand the feelings of Lot. The face of the poor Russian appears to me like the face of an angel, because he does not tell lies. Heaven will be heaven because there will not be one liar there. The Word of God is more precious to me at this time than I ever remember it to have been; and of all the promises in it, none is more sweet to me than this—'He shall reign till He hath put all enemies under His feet.'

February 3.—A packet arrived from India without a single letter for me. It was some disappointment to me: but let me be satisfied with my God, and if I cannot have the comfort of hearing from my friends, let me return with thankfulness to His Word, which is a treasure of which none envy me the possession, and where I can find what will more than compensate for the loss of earthly enjoyments. Resignation to the will of God is a lesson which I must learn, and which I trust He is teaching me.

February 9.—Aga Boozong came. After much conversation, he said, 'Prove to me, from the beginning, that Christianity is the way: how will you proceed? what do you say must be done?' 'If you would not believe a person who wrought a miracle before you,' said I, 'I have nothing to say; I cannot proceed a step.' 'I will grant you,' said Sayyid Ali, 'that Christ was the Son of God, and more than that.' 'That you despair of yourself, and are willing to trust in Him alone for salvation?' 'Yes.' 'And are ready to confess Christ before men, and act conformably to His Word?' 'Yes: what else must I do?' 'Be baptized in the name of Christ.' 'And what shall I gain?' 'The gift of the Holy Ghost. The end of faith is salvation in the world to come; but even here you shall have the Spirit to purify your heart, and to give you the assurance of everlasting happiness.' Thus Aga Boozong had an[458]opportunity of hearing those strange things from my own mouth, of which he had been told by his disciple the Mede. 'You can say too,' said he, 'that you have received the Spirit?' I told them I believed I had; 'for, notwithstanding all my sins, the bent of my heart was to God in a way it never was before; and that, according to my present feeling, I could not be happy if God was

179

not glorified, and if I had not the enjoyment of His presence, for which I felt that I was now educating.' Aga Boozong shed tears.

After this came Aga Ali, the Mede, to hear, as he said, some of the sentences of Paul. Mirza Sayyid Ali had told them, 'that if they had read nothing but the Gospels, they knew nothing of the religion of Christ.' The sheet I happened to have by me was the one containing the fourth, fifth, and sixth chapters of the Second Epistle to the Corinthians, which Aga Ali read out.

At this time the company had increased considerably. I desired Aga Ali to notice particularly the latter part of the fifth chapter, 'God was in Christ, reconciling the world unto Himself.' He then read it a second time, but they saw not its glory; however, they spoke in high terms of the pith and solidity of Paul's sentences. They were evidently on the watch for anything that tallied with their own sentiments. Upon the passage, 'Always bearing about in the body the dying of the Lord Jesus,' the Mede observed, 'Do you not see that Jesus was in Paul, and that Paul was only another name for Jesus?' And the text, 'Whether we be beside ourselves, it is to God; and whether we be sober, it is for your sakes,' they interpreted thus: 'We are absorbed in the contemplation of God, and when we recover, it is to instruct you.'

Walking afterwards with Mirza Sayyid Ali, he told me how much one of my remarks had affected him, namely, that he had no humility. He had been talking about simplicity and humility as characteristic of the Soofis. 'Humility!' I said to him,[459] 'if you were humble, you would not dispute in this manner; you would be like a child.' He did not open his mouth afterwards, but to say, 'True; I have no humility.' In evident distress, he observed, 'The truth is, we are in a state of compound ignorance—ignorant, yet ignorant of our ignorance.'

February 18.—While walking in the garden, in some disorder from vexation, two Mussulman Jews came up and asked me what would become of them in another world. The Mahometans were right in their way, they supposed, and we in ours, but what must they expect? After rectifying their mistake as to the Mahometans, I mentioned two or three reasons for believing that we are right: such as their dispersion, and the cessation of sacrifices immediately on the appearance of Jesus. 'True, true,' they said, with great feeling and seriousness; indeed, they seemed disposed to yield assent to anything I said. They confessed they had become Mahometans only on compulsion, and that Abdoolghuni wished to go to Baghdad, thinking he might throw off the mask there with safety, but they asked what I thought. I said that the Governor was a Mahometan. 'Did I think Syria safer?' 'The safest place in the East,' I said, 'was India.' Feelings of pity for God's ancient people, and having the awful importance of eternal things impressed on my mind by the seriousness of their inquiries as to what would become of them, relieved me from the pressure of my comparatively insignificant distresses. I, a poor Gentile, blest, honoured, and loved; secured for ever by the everlasting covenant, whilst the children of the kingdom are still lying in outer darkness! Well does it become me to be thankful!

This is my birthday, on which I complete my thirty-first year. The Persian New Testament has been begun, and I may say finished in it, as only the last eight chapters of the Revelation remain. Such a painful year I never passed, owing to the privations I have been called to on the one hand, and the spectacle before me of human[460] depravity on the other. But I hope that I have not come to this seat of Satan in vain. The Word of God has found its way into Persia, and it is not in Satan's power to oppose its progress if the Lord hath sent it.

A week after, on February 24, 1812, Henry Martyn corrected the last page of the New Testament in Persian. As we read his words of thanksgiving to the Lord and his invocation of the Holy Spirit, in the already darkening light of his approaching end, before the beatific vision promised by the Master to the pure in heart, and the blessed companionship with Himself guaranteed to every true servant, we recall the Scottish Columba, whose last act was to transcribe the eleventh verse of the thirty-fourth Psalm, and the English Bede, who died when translating the ninth verse of the sixth chapter of St. John's Gospel.

I have many mercies for which to thank the Lord, and this is not the least. Now may that Spirit who gave the Word, and called me, I trust, to be an interpreter of it, graciously and powerfully apply it to the hearts of sinners, even to the gathering an elect people from amongst the long-estranged Persians!

FOOTNOTES:

|66|'That list, in which Martyn holds a conspicuous place, has grown long of late years, till we are half tempted to forget that the share our age has taken and is taking in the work of translating and distributing the Scriptures, links on to that of those who could remember men who had seen the Lord.' Canon Edmonds' *Sermon*, preached in the Cathedral Church of Truro, October 16, 1890 (Exeter).

|67|*The Churchman* for September 1889, p. 635.

|68|See p. 314.

|69|Evidently taken in detail from Adam's *Religious World Displayed*.

|70|Fourth edition, London, 1822.

|71|*Fortieth Report of the British and Foreign Bible Society*, p. 97.

|72|*The Bible of Every Land* (Bagster), 1848.

|73|See *Contributions Towards a History of Biblical Translations in India*. Calcutta and London (Dalton), 1854.

|74|*Monograph on Hindustani Versions of the Old and New Testaments*, by the Rev. R.C. Mather, LL.D. (without date).

|75|*The Life of Rev. T.T. Thomason, M.A.*, by the late Rev. J. Sargent, M.A., second edition, Seeley's, 1834.

|76|Dr. Milner, Dr. Rumsden, Dr. Jowett, Mr. Farish (Charles Simeon's writing).

|77|*Christian Researches in Asia, with Notices of the Translation of the Scriptures into the Oriental Languages*, by the Rev. Claudius Buchanan, D.D., 10th edition, London, 1814.

|78|See *The Miracle Play of Hasan and Husain*, collected from Oral Tradition, by Sir Lewis Pelly, two vols. 1879.

[461]

CHAPTER XII

SHIRAZ TO TABREEZ—THE PERSIAN NEW TESTAMENT

The next three months were spent, still in Shiraz, in the preparation of copies of the precious Persian MS. of the New Testament, and in very close spiritual intercourse with the company of inquirers whom neither fanaticism, conceit, nor, in some cases, a previously immoral life, had prevented from reverencing the teaching of the man of God. Jaffir Ali Khan's garden became to such a holy place, as the Persian spring passed into the heat of summer. There the privileged translator, Mirza Sayyid Ali; Aga Baba, the Mede; Aga Boozong, vizier of Prince Abbas Mirza, and 'most magisterial of the Soofis;' Mirza Ibrahim, the controversialist leader; Sheikh Abulhassan, and many a moolla to whom he testified that Christ was the Creator and Saviour, gathered round him as he read, 'at their request,' the Old Testament histories. 'Their attention to the Word, and their love and attention to me, seemed to increase as the time of my departure approached. Aga Baba, who had been reading St. Matthew, related very circumstantially to the company the particulars of the death of Christ. The bed of roses on which we sat, and the notes of the nightingales warbling around us, were not so sweet to me as this discourse from the Persian.'

[462]

Telling Mirza Sayyid Ali one day that I wished to return to the city in the evening, to be alone and at leisure for prayer, he said with seriousness, 'Though a man had no other religious society I suppose he might, with the aid of the Bible, live alone with God?' This solitude will, in one respect, be his own state soon;—may he find it the medium of God's gracious communications to his soul! He asked in what way God ought to be addressed: I told him as a Father, with respectful love; and added some other exhortations on the subject of prayer.

May 11.—Aga Baba came to bid me farewell, which he did in the best and most solemn way, by asking, as a final question, 'whether, independently of external evidences, I had any internal proofs of the doctrine of Christ?' I answered, 'Yes, undoubtedly: the change from what I once was is a sufficient evidence to me.' At last he took his leave, in great sorrow, and what is better, apparently in great solicitude about his soul.

The rest of the day I continued with Mirza Sayyid Ali, giving him instructions what to do with the New Testament in case of my decease, and exhorting him, as far as his confession allowed me, to stand fast. He had made many a good resolution respecting his besetting sins. I hope, as well as pray, that some lasting effects may be seen at Shiraz from the Word of God left among them

For the Shah and for the heir-apparent, Prince Abbas Mirza, two copies of the Persian New Testament were specially written out in the perfect caligraphy which the Persians love, and carefully corrected with the translator's own hand. That he might himself present them, especially the former, he left Shiraz on May 11, 1812, after a year's residence in the country. The whole length of the great Persian plateau had to be traversed, by Ispahan to Teheran, thence to the royal camp at Sultania, and finally to Tabreez, where was Sir Gore Ouseley, the British ambassador, through[463] whom alone the English man of God could be introduced to the royal presence. He was accompanied by Mr. Canning, an English clergyman.

The journey occupied eight weeks, and proved to be one of extreme hardship, which rapidly developed Henry Martyn's disease. At one time his life was in danger, in spite of the letters which he carried from General Malcolm's friend, and now his own, Jaffir Ali Khan, to the Persian prime minister at Teheran. Mrs. Bishop's experience of travel by the same road[79] at a more favourable season, over the 'great mud land' to which centuries of misrule have changed the populous paradise of Darius, enables us to imagine what the brief record of the *Journal* only half reveals seventy years ago. The old village which the founder of the Kajar dynasty enlarged into Teheran, straggles within eleven miles of walls in the most depressed part of an uninteresting waste. Save for the exterior of the Shah's palace, and those of some of his ministers, the suburb with the European legations, and now the large and handsome buildings of the American Presbyterian Mission, it is unworthy of being a capital city. Eager to present the sacred volume while life was left to him, Henry Martyn hurried away to find Mirza Shufi, the premier, and the Shah, who were in camp a night's journey off at Karach.

May 13.—Remained all day at the caravanserai, correcting the Prince's copy.

May 14.—Continued our journey through two ridges of mountains to Imanzadu: no cultivation to be seen anywhere, nor scarcely any natural vegetable production, except[464] the broom and hawthorn. The weather was rather tempestuous, with cold gusts of wind and rain. We were visited by people who came to be cured of their distempers.

May 16.—We found a hoar frost, and ice on the pools. The excessive cold at this place is accounted for by its being the highest land between the Persian Gulf and the Caspian Sea. The baggage not having come up, we were obliged to pass another day in this uncomfortable neighbourhood, where nothing was to be procured for ourselves or our horses, the scarcity of rain this year having left the ground destitute of verdure, and the poor people of the village near us having nothing to sell.

May 21.—Finished the revision of the Prince's copy. At eleven at night we started for Ispahan, where we arrived soon after sunrise on the 22nd, and were accommodated in one of the king's palaces. Found my old Shiraz scribe here, and corrected with him the Prince's copy.

May 23.—Called on the Armenian bishops at Julfa, and met Matteus. He is certainly vastly superior to any Armenian I have yet seen. We next went to the Italian missionary, Joseph Carabiciate, a native of Aleppo, but educated at Rome. He spoke Latin very sprightly, considering his age, which was sixty-six, but discovered no sort of inclination to talk about religion. Until lately he had been supported by the Propaganda; but weary at last of exercising his functions without remuneration, and even without the necessary provision, he talked of returning to Aleppo.

May 24. (Sunday.)—Went early this morning to the Armenian church attached to the episcopal residence. Within the rails were two out of the four bishops, and other ecclesiastics, but in the body of the church only three people. Most of the Armenians at Julfa, which is now reduced to five hundred houses, attended at their re[465]spective parish churches, of which there are twelve, served by twenty priests. After their pageantry was over, and we were satisfied with processions, ringing of bells, waving of colours, and other ceremonies, which were so numerous as entirely to remove all semblance of spiritual worship, we were condemned to witness a repetition of the same mockery at the Italian's church, at his request. I could not stand it out, but those who did observed that the priest ate

182

and drank all the consecrated elements himself, and gave none to the few poor women who composed his congregation, and who, the Armenian said, had been hired for the occasion.

Before returning to Ispahan we sat a short time in the garden with the bishops. They, poor things, had nothing to say, and could scarcely speak Persian; so that all the conversation was between me and Matteus. At my request he brought what he had of the Holy Scriptures in Persian and Arabic. They were Wheloi's Persian Gospels, and an Arabic version of the Gospels printed at Rome. I tried in vain to bring him to any profitable discussion; with more sense than his brethren, he is not more advanced in spiritual knowledge. Returned much disappointed. Julfa had formerly twenty bishops and about one hundred clergy, with twenty-four churches.

June 2.—Soon after midnight we mounted our horses. It was a mild moonlight night and a nightingale filled the whole valley with his notes. Our way was along lanes, over which the wood on each side formed a canopy, and a murmuring rivulet accompanied us till it was lost in a lake. At daylight we emerged into the plain of Kashan, which seems to be a part of the great Salt Desert. On our arrival at the king's garden, where we intended to put up, we were at first refused admittance, but an application to the Governor was soon attended to. We saw here huge snowy mountains on the north-east beyond Teheran.[466]

June 5.—Reached Kum;[801] the country uniformly desolate. The chief Moojtahid in all Persia, being a resident of this city, I sent to know if a visit would be agreeable to him. His reply was, that if I had any business with him I might come; but if otherwise, his age and infirmities must be his excuse. Intending to travel a double stage, started soon after sunset.

June 8.—Arrived, two hours before daybreak, at the walls of Teheran. I spread my bed upon the high road, and slept till the gates were open; then entered the city, and took up my abode at the ambassador's house.

I lost no time in forwarding Jaffir Ali Khan's letter to the premier, who sent to desire that I would come to him. I found him lying ill in the verandah of the king's tent of audience. Near him were sitting two persons, who, I was afterwards informed, were Mirza Khantar and Mirza Abdoolwahab; the latter being a secretary of state and a great admirer of the Soofi sage. They took very little notice, not rising when I sat down, as is their custom to all who sit with them; nor offering me kalean. The two secretaries, on learning my object in coming, began a conversation with me on religion and metaphysics, which lasted two hours. As they were both well-educated, gentlemanly men, the discussion was temperate, and, I hope, useful.

June 12.—I attended the Vizier's levée, where there was a most intemperate and clamorous controversy kept up for an hour or two; eight or ten on one side, and I on the other. Amongst them were two moollas, the most ignorant of any I have yet met with in either Persia or India. It would be impossible to enumerate all the absurd things they said. Their vulgarity in interrupting me in the middle of a speech; their utter ignorance of the nature of an argument; their impudent assertions about the law[467] and the Gospel, neither of which they had ever seen in their lives, moved my indignation a little. I wished, and I said it would have been well, if Mirza Abdoolwahab had been there; I should then have had a man of sense to argue with. The Vizier, who set us going at first, joined in it latterly, and said, 'You had better say God is God, and Muhammad is the prophet of God.' I said, 'God is God,' but added, instead of 'Muhammad is the prophet of God,' 'and Jesus is the Son of God.' They had no sooner heard this, which I had avoided bringing forward till then, than they all exclaimed, in contempt and anger, 'He is neither born nor begets,' and rose up, as if they would have torn me in pieces. One of them said, 'What will you say when your tongue is burnt out for this blasphemy?'

One of them felt for me a little, and tried to soften the severity of this speech. My book, which I had brought expecting to present it to the king, lay before Mirza Shufi. As they all rose up after him to go, some to the king and some away, I was afraid they would trample on the book; so I went in among them to take it up, and wrapped it in a towel before them, while they looked at it and me with supreme contempt. Thus I walked away alone in my tent, to pass the rest of the day in heat and dirt. What have I done, thought I, to merit all this scorn? Nothing, I trust, but bearing testimony to Jesus. I thought over these things in prayer, and my troubled heart found that peace which Christ hath promised to His disciples.

To complete the trials of the day, a message came from the Vizier in the evening, to say that it was the custom of the king not to see any Englishman, unless presented by the ambassador, or accredited by a letter from him, and that I must, therefore, wait till the king reached Sultania, where the ambassador would be.

June 13.—Disappointed of my object in coming to the camp, I lost no time in leaving it, and proceeded in[468] company with Mr. Canning, who had just joined me from Teheran, towards Kasbin, intending there to wait the result of an application to the ambassador. Started at eleven, and travelled till eleven next morning, having gone ten parasangs or forty miles, to Quishlang. The country all along was well watered and cultivated. The mules being too much tired to proceed, we passed the day at the village; indeed, we all wanted rest. As I sat down in the dust, on the shady side of a walled village by which we passed, and surveyed the plains over which our road lay, I sighed at the thought of my dear friends in India and England, of the vast regions I must traverse before I can get to either, and of the various and unexpected hindrances which present themselves to my going forward. I comfort myself with the hope that my God has something for me to do, by thus delaying my exit.

June 22.—We met with the usual insulting treatment at the caravanserai, where the king's servants had got possession of a good room, built for the reception of the better order of guests; they seemed to delight in the opportunity of humbling an European. Sultania is still but a village, yet the Zengan prince has quartered himself and all his attendants, with their horses, on this poor little village. All along the road, where the king is expected, the people are patiently waiting, as for some dreadful disaster; plague, pestilence, or famine is nothing to the misery of being subject to the violence and extortion of this rabble soldiery.

June 25. (Zengan.)—After a restless night, rose so ill with the fever that I could not go on. My companion, Mr. Canning, was nearly in the same state. We touched nothing all day.

June 26.—After such another night I had determined to go on, but Mr. Canning declared himself unable to stir, so here we dragged through another miserable day. What added to our distress was that we were in danger, if[469] detained here another day or two, of being absolutely in want of the necessaries of life before reaching Tabreez. We made repeated applications to the moneyed people, but none would advance a piastre. Where are the people who flew forth to meet General Malcolm with their purses and their lives? Another generation is risen up, 'who know not Joseph.' Providentially a poor muleteer, arriving from Tabreez, became security for us, and thus we obtained five tomans. This was a heaven-send; and we lay down quietly, free from apprehensions of being obliged to go a fatiguing journey of eight or ten hours, without a house or village in the way, in our present weak and reduced state. We had now eaten nothing for two days. My mind was much disordered from head-ache and giddiness, from which I was seldom free; but my heart, I trust, was with Christ and His saints. To live much longer in this world of sickness and pain seemed no way desirable; the most favourite prospects of my heart seemed very poor and childish; and cheerfully would I have exchanged them all for the unfading inheritance.

June 27.—My Armenian servant was attacked in the same way. The rest did not get me the things that I wanted, so that I passed the third day in the same exhausted state; my head, too, was tortured with shocking pains, such as, together with the horror I felt at being exposed to the sun, showed me plainly to what to ascribe my sickness. Towards evening, two more of our servants were attacked in the same way, and lay groaning from pains in the head.

June 28.—All were much recovered, but in the afternoon I again relapsed. During a high fever Mr. Canning read to me in bed the Epistle to the Ephesians, and I never felt the consolations of that Divine revelation of mysteries more sensibly and solemnly. Rain in the night prevented our setting off.

June 29.—My ague and fever returned, with such a[470] head-ache that I was almost frantic. Again and again I said to myself, 'Let patience have her perfect work,' and kept pleading the promises, 'When thou passest through the waters I will be with thee,' etc.; and the Lord did not withhold His presence. I endeavoured to repel all the disordered thoughts that the fever occasioned, and to keep in mind that all was friendly; a friendly Lord presiding;

and nothing exercising me but what would show itself at last friendly. A violent perspiration at last relieved the acute pain in my head, and my heart rejoiced; but as soon as that was over, the exhaustion it occasioned, added to the fatigue from the pain, left me in as low a state of depression as ever I was in. I seemed about to sink into a long fainting fit, and I almost wished it; but at this moment, a little after midnight, I was summoned to mount my horse, and set out, rather dead than alive. We moved on six parasangs. We had a thunder-storm with hail.

July 1.—A long and tiresome march to Sarehund; in seven parasangs there was no village. They had nothing to sell but buttermilk and bread; but a servant of Abbas Mirza, happening to be at the same caravanserai, sent us some flesh of a mountain cow which he had shot the day before. All day I had scarcely the right recollection of myself from the violence of the ague. We have now reached the end of the level ground which we have had all the way from Teheran, and are approaching the boundaries of Parthia and Media; a most natural boundary it is, as the two ridges of mountains we have had on the left and right come round and form a barrier.

July 2.—At two in the morning we set out. I hardly know when I have been so disordered. I had little or no recollection of things, and what I did remember at times of happy scenes in India or England, served only to embitter my present situation. Soon after removing into the air I was seized with a violent ague, and in this state I[471] went on till sunrise. At three parasangs and a half we found a fine caravanserai, apparently very little used, as the grass was growing in the court. There was nothing all round but the barren rocks, which generally roughen the country before the mountain rears its height. Such an edifice in such a situation was cheering. Soon after we came to a river, over which was a high bridge; I sat down in the shade under it, with two camel drivers. The kafila, as it happened, forded the river, and passed on without my perceiving it. Mr. Canning seeing no signs of me, returned, and after looking about for some time, espied my horse grazing; he concluded immediately that the horse had flung me from the bridge into the river, and was almost ready to give me up for lost. My speedy appearance from under the bridge relieved his terror and anxiety. Half the people still continue ill; for myself, I am, through God's infinite mercy, recovering.

July 4.—I so far prevailed as to get the kafila into motion at midnight. Lost our way in the night, but arriving at a village we were set right again. At eight came to Kilk caravanserai, but not stopping there, went on to a village, where we arrived at half-past nine. The baggage not coming up till long after, we got no breakfast till one o'clock. In consequence of all these things, want of sleep, want of refreshment, and exposure to the sun, I was presently in a high fever, which raged so furiously all the day that I was nearly delirious, and it was some time before I could get the right recollection of myself. I almost despaired, and do now, of getting alive through this unfortunate journey. Last night I felt remarkably well, calm and composed, and sat reflecting on my heavenly rest, with more sweetness of soul, abstraction from the world, and solemn views of God, than I have had for a long time. Oh, for such sacred hours! This short and painful life would scarcely be felt could I live thus at heaven's gate. It being impossible to continue my[472] journey in my present state, and one of the servants also being so ill that he could not move with safety, we determined to halt one day at the village, and sent on a messenger to Sir Gore, at Tabreez, informing him of our approach.

July 5.—As soon as it was day we found our way to the village where the Doctor was waiting for us. Not being able to stay for us, he went on to Tabreez, and we as far as Wasmuch, where he promised to procure for us a fine upper room furnished; but when we arrived, they denied that there was any such place. At last, after an hour's threatening, we got admittance to it. An hour before break of day I left it, in hopes of reaching Tabreez before sunrise. Some of the people seemed to feel compassion for me, and asked me if I was not very ill. At last I reached the gate, and feebly asked for a man to show me the way to the ambassador's.

July 9.—Made an extraordinary effort, and as a Tartar was going off instantly to Constantinople, wrote letters to Mr. Grant for permission to come to England, and to Mr. Simeon and Lydia, informing them of it; but I have scarcely the remotest expectation of seeing it, except by looking at the almighty power of God.

Dined at night at the ambassador's, who said he was determined to give every possible *éclat* to my book, by presenting it himself to the king. My fever never ceased to rage till the 21st, during all which time every effort was made to subdue it, till I had lost all my strength and almost all my reason. They now administer bark, and it may please God to bless the tonics; but I seem too far gone, and can only say,[473] 'having a desire to depart and be with Christ, which is far better.'

TO LYDIA GRENFELL.

Tabreez: July 12, 1812.

My dearest Lydia,—I have only time to say that I have received your letter of February 14. Shall I pain your heart by adding, that I am in such a state of sickness and pain, that I can hardly write to you? Let me rather observe, to obviate the gloomy apprehension my letters to Mr. Grant and Mr. Simeon may excite, that I am likely soon to be delivered from my fever. Whether I shall gain strength enough to go on, rests on our Heavenly Father, in whose hands are all my times. Oh, His precious grace! His eternal unchanging love in Christ to my soul never appeared more clear, more sweet, more strong. I ought to inform you that in consequence of the state to which I am reduced by travelling so far overland, without having half accomplished my journey, and the consequent impossibility of returning to India the same way, I have applied for leave to come on furlough to England. Perhaps you will be gratified by this intelligence; but oh, my dear Lydia, I must faithfully tell you that the probability of my reaching England alive is but small; and this I say, that your expectations of seeing me again may be moderate, as mine are of seeing you. Why have you not written more about yourself? However, I am thankful for knowing that you are alive and well. I scarcely know how to desire you to direct. Perhaps Alexandria in Egypt will be the best place; another may be sent to Constantinople, for though I shall not go there, I hope Mr. Morier will be kept informed of my movements. Kindest love to all the saints you usually mention. Yours ever most faithfully and affectionately,

H. MARTYN.

[474]

TO REV. C. SIMEON

Tabreez: July 12, 1812.

My dearest Friend and Brother,—The Tartar courier for Constantinople, who has been delayed some days on our account, being to be despatched instantly, my little strength also being nearly exhausted by writing to Mr. Grant a letter to be laid before the court: I have only to notice some of the particulars of your letter of February of this year. It is not now before me, neither have I strength to search for it among my papers; but from the frequent attentive perusals I gave it during my intervals of ease, I do not imagine that any of it has escaped my memory. At present I am in a high fever, and cannot properly recollect myself. I shall ever love and be grateful to Mr. Thornton for his kind attention to my family.

The increase of godly young men is precious news. If I sink into the grave in India, my place will be supplied an hundredfold. You will learn from Mr. Grant that I have applied for leave to come to England on furlough; a measure you will disapprove; but you would not, were you to see the pitiable condition to which I am reduced, and knew what it is to traverse the continent of Asia in the destitute state in which I am. If you wish not to see me, I can say that I think it most probable that you will not; the way before me being not better than that passed over, which has nearly killed me.

I would not pain your heart, my dear brother, but we who are in Jesus have the privilege of viewing life and death as nearly the same, since both are one; and I thank a gracious Lord that sickness never came at a time when I was more free from apparent reasons for living. Nothing seemingly remains for me to do but to follow the rest of my family to the tomb. Let not the book written against Muhammadanism be published till approved in India. A[475] European who has not lived amongst them cannot imagine how differently they see, imagine, reason, object, from what we do. This I had full opportunity of observing during my eleven months' residence at Shiraz. During that time I was engaged in a written controversy with one of the most learned and temperate doctors there. He began. I replied what was unanswerable, then I subjoined a second more direct attack on the glaring absurdities of Muhammadanism, with a statement of the nature and evidences of

Christianity. The Soofis then as well as himself desired a demonstration, from the very beginning, of the truth of any revelation. As this third treatise contained an examination of the doctrine of the Soofis, and pointed out that their object was attainable by the Gospel, and by that only, it was read with interest and convinced many. There is not a single Europeanism in the whole that I know of, as my friend and interpreter would not write anything that he could not perfectly comprehend. But I am exhausted; pray for me, beloved brother, and believe that I am, as long as life and recollection lasts, yours affectionately,

H. MARTYN.

Tabreez: August 8.

My dearest Brother and Friend,—Ever since I wrote, about a month, I believe, I have been lying upon the bed of sickness; for twenty days or more the fever raged with great violence, and for a long time every species of medicine was tried in vain. After I had given up every hope of recovery, it pleased God to abate the fever, but incessant head-aches succeeded, which allowed me no rest day or night. I was reduced still lower, and am now a mere skeleton; but as they are now less frequent, I suppose it to be the will of God that I should be raised up to life again. I am now sitting in my chair, and wrote the will with a strong hand; but as you see I cannot write so now.[476] Kindest love to Mr. John Thornton, for whose temporal and spiritual prosperity I daily pray.—Your ever affectionate friend and brother,

H. MARTYN.

Lydia Grenfell's letter, to which Martyn's of July 12, written in such circumstances, is a reply, was really dated February 1, 1812, and was the last received from her by him. Her *Diary* notes that she 'wrote to India, August 30, September 30, 1812'; and on December 12 of that year, thus remarks on his letter of July 12:

Heard from Tabreez from Mr. Martyn with an account of his dangerous state of health and intention of returning to England if his life was spared. This intelligence affected me variously. The probability of his death, the certainty of his extreme sufferings, and distance from every friend, pressed heavily on my spirits; I was enabled to pray, and felt relieved. Of his return no very sanguine expectations can be entertained. Darkness and distress of mind have followed this information. I cannot collect my thoughts to write, or apply as I ought to anything. Oh, let me consider this as a call to prayer and watchfulness and self-examination. Lord, assist me!

December 16.—A season of great temptation, darkness, and distress. At no period of my life have I stood more in need of Divine help, and oh! may I earnestly seek it. Lord, I would pray, give me a right understanding, and enable me seriously to consider and weigh in the balance of the sanctuary all I do—yea, let my thoughts be watched. Sleep has fled from mine eyes, and a fearful looking for of trial and affliction, however this affair ends, possesses my mind. Oh! let me cast my burden on the Lord—it is too heavy for me. Lord, let me begin afresh to call upon Thy name, and, taking hold of Thee, I shall be borne up above[477] my trials, carried through the difficulties I see before me, and be delivered.

December 17.—I desire, O Thou blessed God, to seek Thy face, to call on Thy name. Thou hast been my refuge; I have been happy in the sense of Thy love. With all my sins, my weaknesses and miseries, I come to Thee, and most seriously would I seek Thy guidance in the perplexing and difficult circumstances I am in. O Lord, suffer me not to run counter to Thy will nor to dishonour Thee.

December 25.—Bless the Lord, O my soul; bless His holy name for ever and ever. I sought the Lord in my distress, and He gave ear unto me. Gracious and merciful art Thou, O Lord, for Thou didst bend Thine ear to the most worthless of all creatures. This is for the glory of Thy name alone, to show how great Thy mercy is, how sure Thy truth. After a night of clouds and darkness, behold the clear sky.

December 26.—This joyful, holy season calls upon me for fresh praises, and a renewed dedication of myself to God. I rejoice in believing Christ was born; I rejoice in the end proposed of His appearance in the flesh, the recovery of mankind to holiness and to God. I welcome this salvation as that I most desire. My happiness, I know, consists in holiness and in the favour of God. Thought much to-day of my dear friend. I cannot think of him as having gained the heavenly crown, but as struggling with dangers and difficulties. Secure in them all of Thy favour, and defended by Thy power, he is safe, and pass but a few years or days, and he will enter into the rest of God. Let me, too, follow after him as he follows Christ.

1813, January 4.—After a night and day spent in great conflict and agony of mind, I, this evening, enjoy a respite from distressing apprehensions. I was reduced to the lowest, as to animal spirits and spiritual life, when it occurred to me I would go to the meeting, where I found a sweet—oh, may it be a lasting! relief from my cares.[478]Having better things proposed for my consideration, my burden has chiefly been from a sense of inward weakness and a conviction of having lost the presence of God. The state of my beloved friend less occupies my mind than I sometimes think is reconcilable with a true affection for him; but the truth is, the concerns of my soul are the more pressing. Oh! may this trial truly answer this purpose of driving me to God, my refuge and rest.

January 6.—Still harassed and without strength to resist. I seem divested of the Spirit, yet, oh, let me not give way to this! I will try, as a helpless sinner, to seek Divine aid. Thou canst command peace within and increase my faith. I am amazed at the state of my mind—instead of having my thoughts exercised about my dear friend, I am filled with distressing fears for my soul, and left so to myself that all I can do is to pray for the Lord to return and lift upon me the light of His countenance. O Thou blessed Redeemer! hear my sighs and put my tears into Thy bottle. My wanderings are noted down in Thy book. Oh, have pity on my wretched state and revive Thy work, increase my faith. Thou art the resurrection and the life—let me rest on this Scripture.

February 1.—My beloved friend remembered every hour, but to-day with less distressing fears and perplexity of mind. I do from my inmost soul, O Lord, desire Thy will to be done, and that Thou mayest be glorified in this concern. Oh, direct us!

February 7.—I have been convinced to-day how by admitting into my heart, and suffering my first, my last, and every thought to be engrossed by an earthly object, I have grieved the Holy Spirit, and hindered God from dwelling in me. Oh! let me have done with idols and worship God.

More than six weeks after his letter of July 12, the fever-stricken missionary recovered strength to write to Lydia once again:[479]

TO LYDIA GRENFELL

Tabreez: August 28, 1812.

I wrote to you last, my dear Lydia, in great disorder. My fever had approached nearly to delirium, and my debility was so great that it seemed impossible I could withstand the power of disease many days. Yet it has pleased God to restore me to life and health again; not that I have recovered my former strength yet, but consider myself sufficiently restored to prosecute my journey. My daily prayer is, that my late chastisement may have its intended effect, and make me all the rest of my days more humble, and less self-confident. Self-confidence has often let me down fearful lengths, and would, without God's gracious interference, prove my endless perdition. I seem to be made to feel this evil of my heart more than any other at this time. In prayer, or when I write or converse on the subject, Christ appears to me my life and strength, but at other times I am as thoughtless and bold as if I had all life and strength in myself, Such neglect on our part works a diminution of our joys; but the covenant, the covenant! stands fast with Him, for His people evermore.

I mentioned my conversing sometimes on Divine subjects, for though it is long enough since I have seen a child of God, I am sometimes led on by the Persians to tell them all I know of the very recesses of the sanctuary, and these are the things that interest them. But to give an account of all my discussions with these mystic philosophers must be reserved to the time of our meeting. Do I dream, that I venture to think and write of such an event as that? Is it possible that we shall ever meet again below? Though it is possible, I dare not indulge such a pleasing hope yet. I am still at a tremendous distance; and the countries I have to pass through are many of them dangerous to the traveller, from the hordes of banditti, whom a feeble govern[480]ment cannot chastise. In consequence of the bad state of the road between this and Aleppo, Sir Gore advises me to go first to Constantinople, and from thence to pass into Syria. In favour of this route, he urges that, by writing to two or three

Turkish Governors on the frontiers, he can secure me a safe passage, at least half-way, and the latter half is probably not much infested. In three days, therefore, I intend setting my horse's head towards Constantinople, distant above thirteen hundred miles. Nothing, I think, will occasion any further detention here, if I can procure servants who know both Persian and Turkish; but should I be taken ill on the road, my case would be pitiable indeed. The ambassador and his suite are still here: his and Lady Ouseley's attentions to me, during my illness, have been unremitted. The Prince Abbas Mirza, the wisest of the king's sons, and heir to the throne, was here some time after my arrival; I much wished to present a copy of the Persian New Testament to him, but I could not rise from my bed. The book will, however, be given to him by the ambassador. Public curiosity about the Gospel, now for the first time, in the memory of the modern Persians, introduced into the country, is a good deal excited here, at Shiraz, and other places; so that, upon the whole, I am thankful for having been led hither and detained, though my residence in this country has been attended with many unpleasant circumstances. The way of the kings of the East is preparing. This much may be said with safety, but little more. The Persians also will probably take the lead in the march to Zion, as they are ripe for a revolution in religion as well as politics.

Sabat, about whom you inquire so regularly, I have heard nothing of this long time. My friends in India have long since given me up as lost or gone out of reach, and if they wrote they would probably not mention him, as he is far from being a favourite with any of them. ——, who is himself of an impatient temper, cannot tolerate him;[481] indeed, I am pronounced to be the only man in Bengal who could have lived with him so long. He is, to be sure, the most tormenting creature I ever yet chanced to deal with—peevish, proud, suspicious, greedy; he used to give daily more and more distressing proofs of his never having received the saving grace of God. But of this you will say nothing; while his interesting story is yet fresh in the memory of people, his failings had better not be mentioned. The poor Arab wrote me a querulous epistle from Calcutta, complaining that no one took notice of him now that I was gone; and then he proceeds to abuse his best friends. I have not yet written to reprove him for his unchristian sentiments, and when I do I know it will be to no purpose after all the private lectures I have given him. My course from Constantinople is so uncertain that I hardly know where to desire you to direct to me; I believe Malta is the only place, for there I must stop in my way home. Soon we shall have occasion for pen and ink no more; but I trust I shall shortly see thee face to face. Love to all the saints.

Believe me to be yours ever, most faithfully and affectionately,

H. MARTYN.

These were Henry Martyn's last words to Lydia Grenfell. Hasting home to be with her, in a few weeks his yearning spirit was with the Lord—

Love divine, all love excelling.

Tabreez was at this time the centre of diplomatic activity. While the Shah and his camp were not far off, the Turkish Ambassador was in the city, and Sir Gore Ouseley was busily mediating between the Turkish and Persian Governments after their hostilities on the Baghdad frontier. Turkey, moreover, had just before concluded a[482] treaty with Russia, with consequences most offensive to the Shah. Only the personal influence and active interference of the British Ambassador prevented the renewal of hostilities. Mr. Morier, the Secretary of Embassy, gives us this contemporary picture of Martyn's arrival:[181] 'We had not long been at Tabreez before our party was joined by the Rev. William Canning and the Rev. Henry Martyn. The former was attached to our Embassy as chaplain; the latter, whom we had left at Shiraz employed in the translation of the New Testament into the Persian language, having completed that object, was on his way to Constantinople. Both these gentlemen had suffered greatly in health during their journey from Shiraz. Mr. Martyn had scarcely time to recover his strength before he departed again.'

Had Henry Martyn been induced by his hospitable friends to rest here for a time, had the physician constrained him to wait for a better season and more strength, he might have himself presented his sacred work to the Shah—might have repeated in the north what he had been permitted to do in one brief year in the south of Persia, and might have again seen the beloved Lydia and his Cambridge friends. For Tabreez, 'the fever-dispeller,' is said to

189

have been so named by Zobeidah, the wife of the Kaliph Haroon'r Rashheed, who, at the close of the eighth century, beautified the ancient Tauris, capital of Tiridates III., King of Armenia in 297, because of its healthy climate. In spite of repeated earthquakes the city has been always rebuilt, low and mean, covering an area like that of Vienna, but the principal emporium from which[483] Persia used to receive its European goods till the coasting steamers of India opened up the Persian Gulf and, of late, the Euphrates, Tigris, and Karoon rivers. Only the ark, or citadel of Ali Shah, a noble building of burnt brick, and the fine ruin of the Kabood Masjeed, or mosque of beautifully arabesqued blue tiles, redeemed the city in Martyn's time from meanness. The Ambassador, his host, was then lodged in the house of its wealthiest citizen, Hajji Khan Muhammed, whom the Prince had turned out to make room for Sir Gore Ouseley. Now the British Consulate of Tabreez is a spacious residence, with a fine garden, and the city has become flourishing again. Henry Martyn left Tabreez on his fatal journey at the very time when the climate began to be at its best. All around, too, and especially in the hills of Sahand to the south, with the air of Scotland and of Wales, or on the natural pastures of Chaman, where the finest brood mares are kept, sloping down to the waters of Lake Ooroomia, he would have found in the hot season the loveliest land in Asia.[182]

Before we hasten on with the modern apostle of the Persians to the bitter but bright end, we must trace the history of the influence of his translation of the New Testament. The 20th August, 1812, he joyfully entered in his *Journal* as a day much to be remembered for the remarkable recovery of strength. He learned from Mirza Aga Meer that his 'work,' that is, his reply to Mirza Ibrahim, had been read to the Shah by Mirza Abdoolwahab, and that the king had observed to Mirza Boozong,[484]his son's vizier, that the Feringhis' (Franks') Government and army, and now one of their moollas, was come into the East. The Shah then directed Mirza Boozong to prepare an answer. In consequence of this information Sir Gore Ouseley, who doubtless desired to spare the little strength of his guest, directed that a certain moolla, who greatly wished to be introduced to the man of God, should not be brought to him. Nevertheless, 'one day a moolla came and disputed a while for Muhammedan, but finished with professing Soofi sentiments.'

The great Shah, Fateh Ali Khan himself, and his son, were thus prepared for the Divine gift of Henry Martyn in due form through the British Ambassador. How it reached His Persian Majesty from Sir Gore Ouseley, and how the Shah-in-Shah received it, these letters tell, so honourable to the writers, even after all allowance is made for the diplomatic courtliness of the correspondence.[183] The Soofi controversialists and friends of the translator, who by that time had entered on his rest, must have, moreover, predisposed the eclectic mind of the always liberal Shah to treat with reverence the *Injil*, or Gospel.

From His Excellency Sir Gore Ouseley, Bart., Ambassador Extraordinary from His Britannic Majesty to the Court of Persia. Addressed to the Right Hon. Lord Teignmouth, President of the British and Foreign Bible Society.

St. Petersburg: September 20, 1814.

My dear Lord,—Finding that I am likely to be detained here some six or seven weeks, and apprehensive that my letters from Persia may not have reached your Lordship, I conceive it my duty to acquaint you, for the information of[485] the society of Christians formed for the purpose of propagating the Sacred Writings, that, agreeably to the wishes of our poor friend, the late Rev. Henry Martyn, I presented in the name of the Society (as he particularly desired) a copy of his translation of the New Testament into the Persian language to His Persian Majesty, Fateh Ali Shah Kajar, having first made conditions that His Majesty was to peruse the whole, and favour me with his opinion of the style, etc.

Previous to delivering the book to the Shah, I employed transcribers to make some copies of it, which I distributed to Hajji Mahomed Hussein Khan, Prince of Maru, Mirza Abdulwahab, and other men of learning and rank immediately about the person of the king, who, being chiefly converts to the Soofi philosophy, would, I felt certain, give it a fair judgment, and, if called upon by the Shah for their opinion, report of it according to its intrinsic merits.

The enclosed translation of a letter from His Persian Majesty to me will show your Lordship that he thinks the complete work a great acquisition, and that he approves of the simple style adopted by my lamented friend Martyn and his able coadjutor, Mirza Sayyed Ali, so appropriate to the just and ready conception of the sublime morality of the Sacred Writings. Should the Society express a wish to possess the original letter from the Shah, or a copy of it in Persian, I shall be most happy to present either through your Lordship.

I beg leave to add that, if a correct copy of Mr. Martyn's translation has not yet been presented to the Society, I shall have great pleasure in offering one that has been copied from and collated with the original left with me by Mr. Martyn, on which he had bestowed the greatest pains to render it perfect.

I also promise to devote my leisure to the correction of the press, in the event of your thinking proper to have it printed in England, should my Sovereign not have|486|immediate occasion for my services out of England.—I am, etc.

GORE OUSELEY.

Translation of His Persian Majesty's Letter, referred to in the preceding.
In the Name of the Almighty God, whose glory is most excellent.

It is our august command that the dignified and excellent our trusty, faithful, and loyal well-wisher, Sir Gore Ouseley, Baronet, His Britannic Majesty's Ambassador Extraordinary (after being honoured and exalted with the expressions of our highest regard and consideration), should know that the copy of the Gospel, which was translated into Persian by the learned exertions of the late Rev. Henry Martyn, and which has been presented to us by your Excellency on the part of the high, dignified, learned, and enlightened Society of Christians, united for the purpose of spreading abroad the Holy Books of the religion of Jesus (upon whom, and upon all prophets, be peace and blessings!), has reached us, and has proved highly acceptable to our august mind.

In truth, through the learned and unremitted exertions of the Rev. Henry Martyn, it has been translated in a style most befitting sacred books, that is, in an easy and simple diction. Formerly, the four Evangelists, Matthew, Mark, Luke, and John, were known in Persia; but now the whole of the New Testament is completed in a most excellent manner: and this circumstance has been an additional source of pleasure to our enlightened and august mind. Even the four Evangelists which were known in this country had never been before explained in so clear and luminous a manner. We, therefore, have been particularly delighted with this copious and complete translation. If it please the most merciful God, we shall|487|command the Select Servants, who are admitted to our presence, to read[84] to us the above-mentioned book from the beginning to the end, that we may, in the most minute manner, hear and comprehend its contents.

Your Excellency will be pleased to rejoice the hearts of the above-mentioned dignified, learned, and enlightened Society with assurances of our highest regard and approbation; and to inform those excellent individuals who are so virtuously engaged in disseminating and making known the true meaning and intent of the Holy Gospel, and other points in sacred books, that they are deservedly honoured with our royal favour. Your Excellency must consider yourself as bound to fulfil this royal request.

Given in Rebialavil, 1229.
(Sealed) FATEH ALI SHAH KAJAR.

Even here we see Martyn and Carey once more linked together. The same volume from which we have taken these letters contains, a few pages before them, these words written by Dr. Carey from Serampore: 'Religion is the only thing in the world worth living for. And no work is so important as serving God in the Gospel of His Son; if, like the Apostle, we do this with one spirit, great will be our enjoyment and abundant our reward.'

Sir Gore Ouseley carried the original MS. to St. Petersburg, where, happening to mention the fact to the President of the Russian Bible Society, Prince Galitzin at once begged that his Society, always an honourable exception to the intolerance of the Tsar's Greek Church, might be|488| allowed to publish it. A set of Persian types was specially procured. Sir Gore Ouseley, assisted by the Persian Jaffir Khan, corrected the proofs, and the Rev. R. Pinkerton, one of the Scottish Mission to Karass, carefully superintended the printing. Several Persians, resident in that city, bespoke copies for their friends. The British and Foreign Bible Society granted 300*l*. towards the expenses of an edition of 5,000 copies.

The first edition appeared there in September, 1815, on which Prince Galitzin wrote to Mr. Pinkerton, as representing the Bible Society in London:

Praise be given to the incomprehensible counsels of God, who, for the salvation of man, gave His Word, and causeth it to increase among all nations: who useth as His instruments the inhabitants of countries of different languages and tribes, not unfrequently the most distant from each other and altogether unacquainted with those for whom they labour! This is a true sign of the holy will of God respecting this work, who worketh all and in all. This is the case with the finished edition of the Persian New Testament, which was translated into that language in a far distant part of Asia, and prepared to be printed in another, but brought into Russia (where nothing of the kind was ever thought of) and printed off much sooner than was at first intended. Here men were found endowed with good-will and the requisite qualifications for the completion of this work, which at first seemed to be so difficult.

Meanwhile, Martyn himself having directed that a copy of the manuscript translation should be sent to Calcutta from Shiraz, when he left that city, four copies were made, lest any accident should befall it on the way to Bengal. It reached the Calcutta Corresponding Committee in 1814, and they invited Mirza Sayyid Ali to join them and pass[489] it through the press. This second edition accordingly appeared at Calcutta in 1816. Professor Lee, of Cambridge, published a third edition of it in London in 1827, and a fourth in 1837. The most beautiful and valuable of all is the fifth, now before the writer, which Thomas Constable printed in Edinburgh in 1846 (corresponding to 1262 of the *Hijrah*) in three royal octavo volumes. This was also the most important because it accompanied a Persian translation of the Old Testament. Mirza Sayyid Ali had early informed the Calcutta Committee that he had his master's original translation of the Psalter, and this also appeared at Calcutta in 1816. This formed the nucleus of the Persian Old Testament prepared by Dr. W. Glen, of the Scottish Missionary Society's Mission, at Karass, Astrakhan, and printed along with Henry Martyn's New Testament in the memorable and beautiful Edinburgh edition. That edition of the whole Bible was presented by Dr. Glen to the present Shah of Persia, Nassr-ed-Deen, on his accession to the throne in 1848. With Martyn's New Testament His Majesty seemed to be well acquainted. Of the volume containing the Old Testament we read that 'on handing the book to the servant in waiting he just kissed and then put it to his forehead, with the same indication of reverence which he would have shown had it been their own sacred book, the Koran.' Archdeacon Robinson, of Poona, published another Persian translation of the Old Testament. The Church Missionary Society's distinguished missionary at Julfa, Dr. Robert Bruce, has been for years engaged on a revision, or rather new translation of the Old Testament into Persian, the two versions of which are far inferior, in the opinion of one who is at the head of all living experts, to Henry Marty[490]n's translation of the New. Dr. Bruce's work has now been completed.

I know no parallel to these achievements of Henry Martyn's, writes Canon W.J. Edmonds, closing a survey of his powers and services as a translator of the Scriptures. There are in him the things that mark the born translator. He masters grammar, observes idioms, accumulates vocabulary, reads and listens, corrects and even reconstructs. Above all, he prays. He lives 'in the Spirit,' and rises from his knees full of the mind of the Spirit. Pedantry is not in him, nor vulgarity. He longs and struggles to catch the dialect in which men may speak worthily of the things of God. And so his work lives. In his own Hindustani New Testament, and in the recovered parts of the Old Testament in which he watched over the labours of Fitrut, his work is still a living influence; men find 'reasons for reverting' to it. His earlier Persian, and what is demonstrably distinct from it, his Persic translation, or rather Sabat's, done under his superintendence, these indeed have gone. They did not survive his visit to Persia. Nor did the Arabic, which was the chief acknowledged motive of his journey. But what a gifted man is here, and what a splendid sum total of work, that can afford these deductions from the results of a five or six years' struggle with illness, and still leave behind translations of the New Testament in Hindustani and in Persian; the Hindustani version living a double life, its own and that which William Bowley gave it in the humbler vocabulary of the Hindi villages! We live in hurrying times; our days are swifter than a shuttle. New names, new saints, new heroes ever rise and dazzle the eyes of common men. So it should be, for God lives, and through Him men live and manifest His unexhausted power. But Martyn is a perennial. He springs up fresh to every generation. It is time, though, to take care that he does not become simply the shadow of an[491] angel passing by. His pinnacle is that lofty one which is only assigned to eminent goodness, but it rests upon, and is only the finial of, a broad-based tower of sound and solid intellectual endowment.

Henry Martyn's Persian Testament called forth, in 1816, two Bulls from Pope Pius VIII., addressed to the Archbishops of Gnesne and Moghilev, within the Russian dominions, and letters from the Propaganda College at Rome to the Vicars Apostolic and Missionaries in Persia, Armenia, and other parts of the East. Wherever the Persian language was known the people were warned 'against a version recently made into the Persian idiom.' The Archbishops were told 'that Bibles printed by heretics are numbered among the prohibited books by the rules of the Index (Nos. II. and III.), for it is evident, from experience, that from the Holy Scriptures which are published in the vulgar tongue, more injury than good has arisen through the temerity of men.' Bible Societies in Russia and Great Britain are denounced as a 'most crafty device, by which the very foundations of religion are undermined.' So the Latin Church has ever put from it 'The Great Missionary' which the Reformation was the first to restore to Christendom and the world, and Henry Martyn gave to the Mohammedans in their own tongue.

FOOTNOTES:

[79]*Journeys in Persia and Kurdistan, &c.*, by Mrs. Bishop (Isabella C. Bird), two vols., John Murray, 1891.

[80]The fanatical shrine of Fatima. See Mrs. Bishop's first volume and Mr. Curzon's second.

[81]*A Second Journey through Persia, &c., between the years 1810 and 1816*, p. 223.

[82]'Were I,' writes Mr. Baillie Fraser, 'to select a spot the best calculated for the recovery of health, and for its preservation, I know not that I could hit upon any more suited to the purpose than Tabreez, at any season. A brighter sky and purer air can scarcely be found. To me it seems as if there was truly health in the breeze that blows around me.'

[83]See the *Eleventh Report of the British and Foreign Bible Society*, 1815, Appendix, No. 51.

[84]I beg leave to remark that the word 'Tilawat,' which the translator has rendered 'read,' is an honourable signification of that act, almost exclusively applied to the perusing or reciting the Koran. The making use, therefore, of this term or expression shows the degree of respect and estimation in which the Shah holds the New Testament.—*Note by Sir Gore Ouseley.*

[492]

CHAPTER XIII

IN PERSIA AND TURKEY—TABREEZ TO TOKAT AND THE TOMB

On the evening of September 2, 1812, Henry Martyn left Tabreez for Constantinople, on what he describes as 'my long journey of thirteen hundred miles.' The route marked out for him by Sir Gore Ouseley, who gave him letters to the Turkish governors of Erivan, Kars, and Erzroom, and to the British Minister at Constantinople, as well as to the Armenian Patriarch and Bishop Nestus at Etchmiatzin, was the old Roman road into Central Asia. Professor W.M. Ramsay describes it as clearly marked by Nature,[85] and still one of the most important trade routes. It was the safest and speediest, as well as the least forbidding. 'Sir Gore, wishing me not to travel in the same unprotected way I had done, procured from the Prince a *mehmandar* for me, together with an order for the use of *chappar* horses all the way to Erivan.' Thence he was passed on to Kars similarly attended, and thence to Erzroom. He took with him 'near three hundred *tomans* in money,' or about 130*l.* On the eve of his departure he wrote:[493] 'The delightful thought of being brought to the borders of Europe, without sustaining any injury, contributed more than anything else, I believe, to restore my health and spirits.'

But travelling in Persia and Asiatic Turkey, even at the best and for the strongest, is necessarily a work of hardship. The *chappar*, or post-stations, occur at a distance of from twenty to twenty-five miles, measured by the *farsakh*, the old parasang in Greek phrase, of four miles each. What Mrs. Bishop has recently described has always been true: 'The custom is to ride through all the hours of daylight, whenever horses are to be got, doing from sixty to ninety miles a day.' Henry Martyn rode his own horses, and his party of two Armenian servants (a groom and Turkish interpreter), with the *mehmandar*, had the post-horses. Out of the cities he had to trust, for rest and accommodation, to the post-stations, which at the best were enclosures of mud walls on three sides, deep in manure, with stabling on two sides, and two dark rooms at the entrance for the servants. Occasionally an erection (*balakhana*) above the gateway is available for the master, but how seldom Martyn was lodged in any way better than the animals, will be seen from his *Journal*. He had travelled in this way, in the heats of two summers, from Bushire to Shiraz, and from Shiraz to Tabreez, the whole extent of the Persian plateau from south to north. He had nearly died at Tabreez.

Yet now, with his Persian New Testament ready for the press and his longing for Lydia, he again set forth, sustained by 'the delightful thought.' With intensest interest we follow him in every step of his march north-west through the Persian province of Azerbaijan, Armenia, and Eastern Asia Minor, the unconquerable spirit sustaining the feeble body for forty-five days, as Chrysostom's was fed in his[494] southern journey to the same place of departure almost within sight of the Euxine Sea.

1812, September 2.—At sunset we left the western gate of Tabreez behind us. The horses proved to be sorry animals. It was midnight before we arrived at Sangla, a village in the middle of the plain of Tabreez. There they procured me a place in the Zabit's house. I slept till after sunrise of the 3rd, and did not choose to proceed at such an hour; so I passed most of the day in my room. At three in the afternoon proceeded towards Sofian. My health being again restored, through infinite and unbounded mercy, I was able to look round the creation with calm delight. The plain of Tabreez, towards the west and south-west, stretches away to an immense distance, and is bounded in these directions by mountains so remote as to appear, from their soft blue, to blend with the skies. The baggage having been sent on before, I ambled on with my *mehmandar*, looking all around me, and especially towards the distant hills, with gratitude and joy. Oh! it is necessary to have been confined to a bed of sickness to know the delight of moving freely through the works of God, with the senses left at liberty to enjoy their proper object. My attendant not being very conversant with Persian, we rode silently along; for my part, I could not have enjoyed any companion so much as I did my own feelings. At sunset we reached Sofian, a village with gardens, at the north-west end of the plain, which is usually the first stage from Tabreez. The Zabit was in his corn-field, under a little tent, inspecting his labourers, who were cutting the straw fine, so as to be fit to be eaten by cattle; this was done by drawing over it a cylinder, armed with blades of a triangular form, placed in different planes, so that their vertices should coincide in the cylinder.

The Zabit paid me no attention, but sent a man to[495] show me a place to sleep in, who took me to one with only three walls. I demanded another with four, and was accordingly conducted to a weaver's, where, notwithstanding the mosquitoes and other vermin, I passed the night comfortably enough. On my offering money, the *mehmandar* interfered, and said that if it were known that I had given money he should be ruined, and added: 'They, indeed, dare not take it;' but this I did not find to be the case.

September 4.—At sunrise mounted my horse, and proceeded north-west, through a pass in the mountains, towards Murun. By the way I sat down by the brook, and there ate my bread and raisins, and drank of the crystal stream; but either the coldness of this unusual breakfast, or the riding after it, did not at all agree with me. The heat oppressed me much, and the road seemed intolerably tedious. At last we got out from among the mountains, and saw the village of Murun, in a fine valley on the right. It was about eleven o'clock when we reached it. As the *mehmandar* could not immediately find a place to put me in, we had a complete view of this village. They stared at my European dress, but no disrespect was shown. I was deposited at last with a Khan, who was seated in a place with three walls. Not at all disposed to pass the day in company, as well as exposed, I asked for another room, on which I was shown to the stable, where there was a little place partitioned off, but so as to admit a view of the horses. The smell of the stable, though not in general disagreeable to me, was so strong that I was quite unwell, and strangely dispirited and melancholy. Immediately after dinner I fell fast asleep and slept four hours, after which I rose and ordered them to prepare for the next journey. The horses being changed here, it was some time before they were brought, but, by exerting myself, we moved off by midnight. It was a most mild and delightful night, and the pure air, after the smell of[496] the stable, was quite reviving. For once, also, I travelled all the way without being sleepy; and beguiled the hours of the way by thinking of the 14th Psalm, especially the connection of the last three verses with the preceding.

September 5.—In five hours we were just on the hills which face the pass out of the valley of Murun (Marand), and in four hours and a half more emerged from between the two ridges of mountains into the valley of Gurjur. Gurjur is eight parasangs from Murun, and our course to it was nearly due north. This long march was far from being a fatiguing one. The air, the road, and my spirits were good. Here I was well accommodated, but had to mourn over my impatient temper towards my servants; there is nothing that disturbs my peace so much. How much more noble and godlike to bear with calmness, and observe with pity, rather than with anger, the failings and offences of others! Oh, that I may, through grace, be enabled to recollect myself in the time of temptation! Oh, that the Spirit of God may check my folly, and at such times bring the lowly Saviour to my view!

September 6.—Soon after twelve we started with fresh horses, and came to the Aras, or Araxes, distant two parasangs, and about as broad as the Isis, and a current as strong as that of the Ganges. The ferry-boat being on the north side, I lay down to sleep till it came; but observing my servants do the same, I was obliged to get up and exert myself. It dawned, however, before we got over. The boat was a huge fabric in the form of a rhombus. The ferryman had only a stick to push with; an oar, I dare say, he had never seen or heard of, and many of my train had probably never floated before;—so alien is a Persian from everything that belongs to shipping. We landed safely on the other side in about two minutes. We were four hours in reaching Nakshan, and for half an hour more I was led from street to street, till at last I was lodged in a wash-house belonging to a great man, a corner of which[497] was cleaned out for me. It was near noon and my baggage was not arrived, so that I was obliged to go without my breakfast, which was hard after a ride of four hours in the sun. The baggage was delayed so long that I began to fear; at last, however, it arrived. All the afternoon I slept, and at sunset arose, and continued wakeful till midnight, when I aroused my people, and with fresh horses set out again. We travelled till sunrise. I scarcely perceived that we had been moving, a Hebrew word in the 16th Psalm having led me gradually into speculations on the eighth conjugation of the Arabic verb. I am glad my philological curiosity is revived, as my mind will be less liable to idleness.

September 7.—Arrived at Khok, a poor village, distant five and a half parasangs from Nakshan, nearly west. I should have mentioned that, on descending into the plain of Nakshan, my attention was arrested by the appearance of a hoary mountain opposite to us at the other end, rising so high above the rest that they sank into insignificance. It was truly sublime, and the interest it excited was not lessened when, on inquiring its name, I was told it was Agri, or Ararat. Thus I saw two remarkable objects in one day, the Araxes and Ararat. At four in the afternoon we set out for Shurour. The evening was pleasant; the ground over which we passed was full of rich cultivation and verdure, watered by many a stream, and containing forty villages, most of them with the usual appendage of gardens. To add to the scene, the great Ararat was on our left. On the peak of that hill the whole Church was once contained; it was now spread far and wide, even to the ends of the earth, but the ancient vicinity of it knows it no more. I fancied many a spot where Noah perhaps offered his sacrifices; and the promise of God, that seed-time and harvest should not cease, appeared to me to be more exactly fulfilled in the agreeable plain in which it was spoken than elsewhere, as I had not seen such fertility[498] in any part of the Shah's dominions. Here the blessed saint landed in a new world; so may I, safe in Christ, out-ride the storm of life, and land at last on one of the everlasting hills!

Night coming on we lost our way, and got intercepted by some deep ravines, into one of which the horse that carried my trunks sunk so deep that the water got into one of them, wetted the linen and spoiled some books. Finding it in vain to attempt gaining our *munzil*, we went to another village, where, after a long delay, two aged men with silver beards opened their house to us. Though it was near midnight I had a fire lighted to dry my books, took some coffee and sunk into deep sleep; from which awaking at the earliest dawn of

September 8, I roused the people, and had a delightful ride of one parasang to Shurour, distant four parasangs from Khok. Here I was accommodated by the great man with a stable, or winter room, for they built it in such a strange vicinity in order to have it warm in winter. At present, while the weather is still hot, the smell is at times overpowering. At eleven at night we moved off, with fresh horses, for Duwala; but though we had guides in abundance, we were not able to extricate ourselves from the ravines with which this village is surrounded. Procuring another man from a village we happened to wander into, we at last made our way, through grass and mire, to the pass, which led us to a country as dry as the one we had left was wet. Ararat was now quite near; at the foot of it is Duwala, six parasangs from Nakshan, where we arrived at seven in the morning of

September 9.—As I had been thinking all night of a Hebrew letter, I perceived little of the tediousness of the way. I tried also some difficulties in the 16th Psalm without being able to master them. All day on the 15th and 16th Psalms, and gained some light into the difficulties. The villagers not bringing the horses in time, we were not|499| able to go on at night, but I was not much concerned, as I thereby gained some rest.

September 10.—All day at the village writing down notes on the 15th and 16th Psalms. Moved at midnight, and arrived early in the morning at Erivan.

September 11.—I alighted at Hosein Khan, the governor's palace, as it may be called, for he seems to live in a style equal to that of a prince. Indeed, commanding a fortress on the frontier, within six hours of the Russians, he is entrusted with a considerable force, and is nearly independent of the Shah. After sleeping two hours I was summoned to his presence. He at first took no notice of me, but continued reading his Koran, it being the Mohurrum. After a compliment or two he resumed his devotions. The next ceremony was to exchange a rich shawl dress for a still richer pelisse, on pretence of its being cold. The next display was to call for his physician, who, after respectfully feeling his pulse, stood on one side: this was to show that he had a domestic physician. His servants were most richly clad. My letter from the ambassador, which till now had lain neglected on the ground, was opened and read by a moonshi. He heard with great interest what Sir Gore had written about the translation of the Gospels. After this he was very kind and attentive, and sent for Lieutenant M., of the Engineers, who was stationed, with two sergeants, at the fort. He ordered for me a *mehmandar*, a guard, and four horses with which a Turk had just come from Kars.

September 12.—The horses not being ready, I rode alone and found my way to Etchmiatzin (or Three Churches|861|), two and a half parasangs distant. Directing my course to the largest church, I found it enclosed by some other buildings and a wall. Within the entrance I found a large court, with monks cowled and gowned|500|moving about. On seeing my Armenian letters they brought me to the Patriarch's lodge, where I found two bishops, one of whom was Nestus, at breakfast on pilaos, kuwabs, wine, arrak, etc., and Serst (Serope) with them. As he spoke English, French, and Italian, I had no difficulty in communicating with my hosts.

Serope, considering the danger to which the cathedral-seat is exposed from its situation between Russia, Persia, and Turkey, is for building a college at Tiflis. The errors and superstitions of his people were the subject of Serope's conversation the whole morning, and seemed to be the occasion of real grief to him. He intended, he said, after a few more months' trial of what he could do here, to retire to India, and there write and print some works in Armenian, tending to enlighten the people with regard to religion, in order to introduce a reform. I said all I could to encourage him in such a blessed work: promising him every aid from the English, and proving to him, from the example of Luther and the other European reformers, that, however arduous the work might seem, God would surely be with him to help him. I mentioned the awful neglect of the Armenian clergy in never preaching; as thereby the glad tidings of a Saviour were never proclaimed. He made no reply to this, but that 'it was to be lamented, as the people were never called away from vice.'

September 13.—I asked Serope about the 16th Psalm in the Armenian version; he translated it into correct Latin. In the afternoon I waited on the Patriarch; it was a visit of great ceremony. He was reclining on a sort of throne, placed in the middle of the room. All stood except the two senior bishops; a chair was set for me on the other side, close to the Patriarch; at my right hand stood Serope, to interpret. The Patriarch had a dignified rather

196

than a venerable appearance. His conversation consisted in protestations of sincere attachment, in expressions of his hopes of deliverance from the Mohammedan[501] yoke, and inquiries about my translations of the Scriptures; and he begged me to consider myself as at home in the monastery. Indeed, their attention and kindness are unbounded: Nestus and Serope anticipate my every wish. I told the Patriarch that I was so happy in being here that, did duty permit, I could almost be willing to become a monk with them. He smiled, and fearing, perhaps, that I was in earnest, said that they had quite enough. Their number is a hundred, I think. The church was immensely rich till about ten years ago, when, by quarrels between two contending patriarchs, one of whom is still in the monastery in disgrace, most of their money was expended in referring their disputes to the Mohammedans as arbitrators. There is no difficulty, however, in replenishing their coffers: their merchants in India are entirely at their command.

September 15.—Spent the day in preparing, with Serope, for the mode of travelling in Turkey. All my heavy and expensive preparations at Tabreez prove to be incumbrances which must be left behind: my trunks were exchanged for bags; and my portable table and chair, several books, large supplies of sugar, etc., were condemned to be left behind. My humble equipments were considered as too mean for an English gentleman; so Serope gave me an English bridle and saddle. The roads in Turkey being much more infested with robbers than those of Persia, a sword was brought for me.

September 16.—Upon the whole I hardly know what hopes to entertain from the projects of Serope. He is bold, authoritative, and very able; still only thirty-one years of age; but then he is not spiritual: perhaps this was the state of Luther himself at first. It is an interesting time in the world; all things proclaim the approach of the kingdom of God, and Armenia is not forgotten. There is a monastery of Armenian Catholics at Venice, which they employ merely in printing the Psalter, book of prayers, etc.[502] Serope intends addressing his first work to them, as they are the most able divines of the Armenians, to argue them back from the Roman Catholic communion, in which case he thinks they would co-operate with him cordially; being as much concerned as himself at the gross ignorance of their countrymen. The Archbishop of Astrakhan has a press, also an agent at Madras and one at Constantinople, printing the Scriptures and books of prayers: there is none at Etchmiatzin. At Constantinople are three or four fellow-collegians of Serope, educated as well as he by the Propaganda, who used to entertain the same sentiments as he, and would, he thinks, declare them if he would begin.

September 17.—At six in the morning, accompanied by Serope, one bishop, the secretary, and several servants of the monastery, I left Etchmiatzin. My party now consisted of two men from the governor of Erivan, a *mehmandar*, and a guard; my servant Sergius, for whom the monks interceded, as he had some business at Constantinople; one trusty servant from the monastery, Melcom, who carried my money; and two baggage-horses with their owners. The monks soon returned, and we pursued our way over the plain of Ararat. At twelve o'clock reached Quila Gazki, about six parasangs from Etchmiatzin. The *mehmandar* rode on, and got a good place for me.

September 18.—Rose with the dawn, in hopes of going this stage before breakfast, but the horses were not ready. I set off at eight, fearing no sun, though I found it at times very oppressive when there was no wind. At the end of three hours we left the plain of Ararat, the last of the plains of modern Persia in this quarter. Meeting here with the Araxes again, I undressed and plunged into the stream.[87] While hastening forward with the trusty Melcom[503] to rejoin my party, we were overtaken by a spearman with a lance of formidable length. I did not think it likely that one man would venture to attack two, both armed; but the spot was a noted one for robbers, and very well calculated, by its solitariness, for deeds of privacy; however, he was friendly enough. He had, however, nearly done me a mischief. On the bank of the river we sprang a covey of partridges; instantly he laid his lance under him across the horse's back, and fired a horse-pistol at them. His horse, starting at the report, came upon mine, with the point of the spear directly towards me, so that I thought a wound for myself or horse was inevitable; but the spear passed under my horse. We were to have gone to Haji-Buhirem, but finding the head-man of it at a village a few furlongs nearer, we stopped there. We found him in a shed outside the walls, reading his Koran, with his sword, gun, and pistol by his side. He was a good-natured farmer-looking man, and spoke in Persian. He chanted the Arabic with great readiness, and asked me whether I knew what that book was: 'Nothing less than the great Koran!'

September 19.—Left the village at seven in the morning, and as the stage was reputed to be very dangerous, owing to the vicinity of the famous Kara Beg, my *mehmandar* took three armed men from the village in addition to the one we brought from Erivan. We continued going along through the pass two or three parasangs, and crossed the Araxes three times. We then ascended the mountains on the north by a road, if not so steep, yet as long and difficult as any of the *kotuls* of Bushire. On the top we found a table-land, along which we moved many a tedious mile, expecting every minute that we should have a view of a fine champaign country below; but dale followed dale, apparently in endless succession, and though at such a height there was very little air to relieve the heat, and nothing to be seen but barren rocks. One part, however, must be excepted, where the prospect opened to the north,|504| and we had a view of the Russian territory, so that we saw at once, Persia, Russia, and Turkey. At length we came to an Armenian village, situated in a hollow of these mountains, on a declivity. The village presented a singular appearance, being filled with conical piles of peat, for they have no fire-wood. Around there was a great deal of cultivation, chiefly corn. Most of the low land from Tabreez to this place is planted with cotton, *Palma Christi*, and rice. This is the first village in Turkey; not a Persian cap was to be seen, the respectable people wore a red Turkish cap. The great man of the village paid me a visit; he was a young Mussulman, and took care of all my Mussulman attendants; but he left me and my Armenians, where he found us, at the house of an Armenian, without offering his services. I was rather uncomfortably lodged, my room being a thoroughfare for horses, cows, buffaloes, and sheep. Almost all the village came to look at me. The name of this village is Fiwik, it is distant six parasangs from the last; but we were eight hours accomplishing it, and a kafila would have been twelve. We arrived at three o'clock; both horses and men much fatigued.

September 20.—From daybreak to sunrise I walked, then breakfasted and set out. Our course lay north, over a mountain, and here danger was apprehended. It was, indeed, dismally solitary all around. The appearance of an old castle on the top of a crag was the first occasion on which our guard got their pieces ready, and one rode forward to reconnoitre: but all there was as silent as the grave. At last, after travelling five hours, we saw some men: our guard again took their places in front. Our fears were soon removed by seeing carts and oxen. Not so the opposite party: for my baggage was so small as not to be easily perceived. They halted therefore at the bottom, towards which we were both descending, and those of them who had guns advanced in front and hailed us. We answered peaceably; but they, still distrusting us as we|505| advanced nearer, cocked their pieces. Soon, however, we came to a parley. They were Armenians, bringing wood from Kars to their village in the mountain: they were hardy, fine young men, and some old men who were with them were particularly venerable. The dangerous spots being passed through, my party began to sport with their horses: galloping across the path, brandishing their spears or sticks, they darted them just at that moment of wheeling round their horses, as if that motion gave them an advantage. It struck me that this, probably, was the mode of fighting of the ancient Parthians which made them so terrible in flight. Presently after these gambols the appearance of some poor countrymen with their carts put into their heads another kind of sport; for knowing, from the ill-fame of the spot, that we should be easily taken for robbers, four of them galloped forward, and by the time we reached them one of the carters was opening a bag to give them something. I was, of course, very much displeased, and made signs to him not to do it. I then told them all, as we quickly pursued our course, that such kind of sport was not allowed in England; they said it was the Persian custom. We arrived at length at Ghanikew, having ridden six hours and a half without intermission. The *mehmandar* was for changing his route continually, either from real or pretended fear. One of the Kara Beg's men saw me at the village last night, and as he would probably get intelligence of my pretended route, it was desirable to elude him. But after all we went the shortest way, through the midst of danger, if there was any, and a gracious Providence kept all mischief at a distance. Ghanikew is only two parasangs from Kars, but I stopped there, as I saw it was more agreeable to the people; besides which I wished to have a ride before breakfast. I was lodged in a stable-room; but very much at my ease, as none of the people of the village could come at me without passing through the house.[506]

September 21.—Rode into Kars. Its appearance is quite European, not only at a distance but within. The houses all of stone; streets with carts passing; some of the houses open to the street; the fort on an uncommonly high rock; such a burying-ground I never saw, there must be thousands of gravestones. The *mehmandar* carried me directly to the governor, who, having just finished his breakfast, was of course asleep, and could not be disturbed; but his head-man carried me to an Armenian's house, with orders to live at free quarter there. The room at the Armenian's was an excellent one, upstairs, facing the street, fort, and river, with a bow containing five windows under which were cushions. As soon as the Pacha was visible, the chief Armenian of Kars, to whom I had a letter from Bishop Nestus, his relation, waited upon him on my business. On looking over my letters of recommendation from Sir Gore Ouseley, I found there was none for Abdallah, the Pacha of Kars; however, the letter to the Governor of Erivan secured all I wanted. He sent to say I was welcome; that if I liked to stay a few days he should be happy, but that if I was determined to go on to-morrow, the necessary horses and ten men for a guard were all ready. As no wish was expressed of seeing me, I was of course silent upon that subject.

September 22.—Promises were made that everything should be ready at sunrise, but it was half-past nine before we started, and no guard present but the Tartar. He presently began to show his nature by flogging the baggage-horse with his long whip, as one who was not disposed to allow loitering; but one of the poor beasts presently fell with his load at full length over a piece of timber lying in the road. While this was setting to rights, the people gathered about me, and seemed more engaged with my Russian boots than with any other part of my dress. We moved south-west, and after five hours and a half reached Joula. The Tartar rode forward and got the coffee-room[507] at the post-house ready. The coffee-room has one side railed and covered with cushions, and on the opposite side cushions on the ground; the rest of the room was left with bare stones and timbers. As the wind blew very cold yesterday, and I had caught cold, the Tartar ordered a great fire to be made. In this room I should have been very much to my satisfaction, had not the Tartar taken part of the same bench, and many other people made use of it as a public room. They were continually consulting my watch to know how near the hour of eating approached. It was evident that the Tartar was the great man here; he took the best place for himself; a dinner of four or five dishes was laid before him. When I asked for eggs they brought me rotten ones; for butter they brought me ghee. The idle people of the village came all night and smoked till morning. It was very cold, there being a hoar frost.

September 23.—Our way to-day lay through a forest of firs, and the variety of prospect it afforded, of hill and dale, wood and lawn, was beautiful and romantic. No mark of human workmanship was anywhere visible for miles, except where some trees had fallen by the stroke of the woodman. We saw at last a few huts in the thickest clumps, which was all we saw of the Koords, for fear of whom I was attended by ten armed horsemen. We frightened a company of villagers again to-day. They were bringing wood and grass from the forest, and on seeing us drew up. One of our party advanced and fired; such a rash piece of sport I thought must have been followed by serious mischief, but all passed off very well. With the forest I was delighted; the clear streams in the valleys, the lofty trees crowning the summit of the hills, the smooth paths winding away and losing themselves in the dark woods, and, above all, the solitude that reigned throughout, composed a scene which tended to harmonise and solemnise the mind. What displays of taste and magnificence are found occasionally on this ruined earth![508] Nothing was wanting to-day but the absence of the Turks, to avoid the sight and sound of whom I rode on. After a ride of nine hours and a half, we reached Mijingui, in the territory of Erzroom, and having resolved not to be annoyed in the same way as last night, I left the Tartar in the undisturbed possession of the post-house, and took up my quarters at an Armenian's, where, in the stable-room, I expected to be left alone; but a Georgian young man, on his way from Etchmiatzin, going on pilgrimage to Moosk, where John the Baptist is supposed to be buried, presumed on his assiduous attentions to me, and contrived to get a place for himself in the same room.

September 24.—A long and sultry march over many a hill and vale. In the way, two hours from the last stage, is a hot spring; the water fills a pool, having four porches. The porches instantly reminded me of Bethesda's pool: they were semicircular arches about six feet deep, intended seemingly for shelter from the sun. In them all the party undressed and bathed. The Tartar, to enjoy himself more perfectly, had his *kalean* to smoke while up to his chin in water. We saw nothing else on the road to-day but a large and opulent family of Armenians—men, women, and children—in carts and carriages returning from a pilgrimage to Moosk. After eleven hours and a half, including the hour spent at the warm spring, we were overtaken by the dusk; so the Tartar brought us to Oghoomra, where I was placed in an Armenian's stable-room.

September 25.—Went round to Husar-Quile, where we changed horses. I was surprised to find so strong a fort and so large a town. From thence we were five hours and a half reaching the entrance of Erzroom. All was busy and moving in the streets and shops—crowds passing along. Those who caught a sight of us were at a loss to define me. My Persian attendants and the lower part of the dress made me appear Persian; but the rest of my dress was new, for those only who had travelled knew it to be[509] European. They were rather disposed, I thought, to be uncivil, but the two persons who preceded us kept all in order. I felt myself in a Turkish town; the red cap, and stateliness, and rich dress, and variety of turbans was realised as I had seen it in pictures. There are here four thousand Armenian families and but one church; there are scarcely any Catholics, and they have no church.

September 29.—Left Erzroom with a Tartar and his son at two in the afternoon. We moved to a village, where I was attacked with fever and ague; the Tartar's son was also taken ill and obliged to return.

September 30.—Travelled first to Ashgula, where we changed horses, and from thence to Purnugaban, where we halted for the night. I took nothing all day but tea, and was rather better, but head-ache and loss of appetite depressed my spirits; yet my soul rests in Him who is 'an anchor to the soul, sure and steadfast,' which, though not seen, keeps me fast.

October 1.—Marched over a mountainous tract; we were out from seven in the morning till eight at night. After sitting a little by the fire, I was near fainting from sickness. My depression of spirits led me to the throne of grace as a sinful abject worm. When I thought of myself and my transgressions, I could find no text so cheering as 'My ways are not as your ways.' From the men who accompanied Sir Gore Ouseley to Constantinople I learned that the plague was raging at that place, and thousands dying every day. One of the Persians had died of it. They added that the inhabitants of Tokat were flying from their town from the same cause. Thus I am passing inevitably into imminent danger. O Lord, Thy will be done! Living or dying, remember me!

October 2.—Some hours before day I sent to tell the Tartar I was ready, but Hassan Aga was for once riveted to his bed. However, at eight, having got strong horses, he set off at a great rate; and over the level ground he[510] made us gallop as fast as the horses would go to Chifflik, where we arrived at sunset. I was lodged, at my request, in the stables of the post-house, not liking the scrutinising impudence of the fellows who frequent the coffee-room. As soon as it began to grow a little cold the ague came on, and then the fever; after which I had a sleep, which let me know too plainly the disorder of my frame. In the night Hassan sent to summon me away, but I was quite unable to move. Finding me still in bed at the dawn, he began to storm furiously at my detaining him so long, but I quietly let him spend his ire, ate my breakfast composedly, and set out at eight. He seemed determined to make up for the delay, for we flew over hill and dale to Sherean, where he changed horses. From thence we travelled all the rest of the day and all night; it rained most of the time. Soon after sunset the ague came on again, which, in my wet state, was very trying; I hardly knew how to keep my life in me. About that time there was a village at hand, but Hassan had no mercy. At one in the morning we found two men under a wain, with a good fire; they could not keep the rain out, but their fire was acceptable. I dried my lower extremities, allayed the fever by drinking a good deal of water, and went on. We had little rain, but the night was pitchy dark so that I could not see the road under my horse's feet. However, God being mercifully pleased to alleviate my bodily suffering, I went on contentedly to the *munzil*, where we arrived at break of day. After sleeping three or four hours, I was visited by an

Armenian merchant for whom I had a letter. Hassan was in great fear of being arrested here; the Governor of the city had vowed to make an example of him for riding to death a horse belonging to a man of this place. He begged that I would shelter him in case of danger; his being claimed by an Englishman, he said, would be a sufficient security. I found, however, that I had no occasion to interfere. He hurried me away from this place without delay, and[511] galloped furiously towards a village, which, he said, was four hours distant, which was all I could undertake in my present weak state; but village after village did he pass till, night coming on, and no signs of another, I suspected that he was carrying me on to the *munzil*, so I got off my horse and sat upon the ground, and told him 'I neither could nor would go any farther.' He stormed, but I was immovable, till, a light appearing at a distance, I mounted my horse and made towards it, leaving him to follow or not, as he pleased. He brought in the party, but would not exert himself to get a place for me. They brought me to an open verandah, but Sergius told them I wanted a place in which to be alone. This seemed very offensive to them. 'And why must he be alone?' they asked, ascribing this desire of mine to pride, I suppose. Tempted at last by money, they brought me to a stable-room, and Hassan and a number of others planted themselves there with me. My fever here increased to a violent degree; the heat in my eyes and forehead was so great that the fire almost made me frantic. I entreated that it might be put out, or that I might be carried out of doors. Neither was attended to; my servant, who, from my sitting in that strange way on the ground, believed me delirious, was deaf to all I said. At last I pushed my head among the luggage, and lodged it on the damp ground, and slept.

From Sherean, or Sheheran, out of which, after a night of burning fever in the stable of the Chifflik post-station, Hassan furiously compelled the dying man to ride, is a mountain track of a hundred and seventy miles to Tokat. 'How wearisome and painful must have been his journey over the mountains and valleys!' wrote the American missionaries, Eli Smith and H.O. Dwight, eighteen years after, when, in the vigour of health and at a better season, they made the same journey, called by his example and[512] memory, to found the Mission to Eastern Anatolia. Think of him, wasting away from consumption, racked with ague, burning with fever, as, pressed by the merciless Turk, he 'flew over hill and dale' all the third day of October, from eight in the morning, then changed horses at Sheheran, then 'travelled all the rest of the day and all night' of the 3rd-4th, while the rain fell amid darkness that could be felt; then, after three or four hours' sleep, on break of day again hurried on, lest his guide should be arrested for a former offence of 'riding to death a horse belonging to a man of this place,' all the fourth day, till almost expiring he sat on the ground and found refuge in a stable, refusing to go farther. 'At last I pushed my head among the luggage, and lodged it on the damp ground, and slept.' Since Chrysostom's ride in the same region, the Church of Christ has seen no torture of a saint like that.

October 5.—Preserving mercy made me see the light of another morning. The sleep had refreshed me, but I was feeble and shaken; yet the merciless Hassan hurried me off. The *munzil*, however, not being distant, I reached it without much difficulty. I expected to have found it another strong fort at the end of the pass, but it is a poor little village within the jaws of the mountain. I was pretty well lodged, and felt tolerably well till a little after sunset, when the ague came on with a violence I had never before experienced; I felt as if in a palsy, my teeth chattering and my whole frame violently shaken. Aga Hosein and another Persian, on their way here from Constantinople, going to Abbas Mirza whom I had just before been visiting, came hastily to render me assistance if they could. These Persians appear quite brotherly after the Turks. While they pitied me, Hassan sat in[513] perfect indifference, ruminating on the further delay this was likely to occasion. The cold fit, after continuing two or three hours, was followed by a fever, which lasted the whole night and prevented sleep.

October 6.—No horses being to be had, I had an unexpected repose. I sat in the orchard and thought with sweet comfort and peace of my God, in solitude my Company, my Friend, and Comforter. Oh! when shall time give place to eternity! When shall appear that new heaven and new earth wherein dwelleth righteousness! There, there shall in no wise enter in anything that defileth: none of that wickedness which has made men worse than wild beasts, none of those corruptions which add still more to the miseries of mortality, shall be seen or heard of any more.

Sitting in the orchard, thinking with sweet comfort and peace of his God, and longing for that new heaven and new earth wherein dwelleth righteousness—such is the last sight we have of Henry Martyn, on October 6, 1812. Two brotherly Persians, on their way from Constantinople, had sought to minister to him the day before. The Turkish Hassan, himself afraid of justice, 'sat in perfect indifference, ruminating on the further delay' caused by his illness. What happened when the dying apostle could write no more—in the ten days till God took him on October 16—who shall now tell? Did the Turk hurry him, as he was expiring, into Tokat, from 'that poor little village within the jaws of the mountain,' in which he was 'pretty well lodged,' or did his indomitable spirit give the poor body strength to ride into the town; and did the plague, then raging, complete what hereditary disease and fever had done? He had at least his Armenian servants, the 'trusty' Melcom and Sergius, with him to minister to his wants.[514] He had written to Lydia of his journey to her by Constantinople, Syria, and Malta, saying: 'Do I dream, that I venture to think and write of such an event as that!... Soon we shall have occasion for pen and ink no more, but I trust I shall shortly see thee face to face.' He dreamed indeed; for He who is the only Love which is no dream, but the one transforming, abiding, absorbing reality, called him, while yet a youth of thirty-one, home to Himself.

FOOTNOTES:

[85]*The Historical Geography of Asia Minor*, vol. iv. of the Royal Geographical Society's *Supplementary Papers*, John Murray, 1890.

[86]In his valuable book *Transcaucasia and Ararat* (1877), Mr. James Bryce, M.P., gives the meaning as 'The Only-Begotten descended.'

[87]A few years after, when Sir R. Ker Porter was on the same route, he wrote: 'This was the spot where our apostolic countryman, Henry Martyn, faint with fever and fatigue, alighted to bathe on his way to Tokat.' There, too, Sir Robert was of opinion, Xenophon and the Ten Thousand Greeks crossed the Araxes 2,300 years ago.

[515]

CHAPTER XIV

THE TWO RESTING-PLACES—TOKAT AND BREAGE

The Armenians were a comparatively strong community in Tokat, where they formed a third of the population, for whom there were seven churches and thirty priests. Henry Martyn was known as a friend of this, the oldest church in Asia. He had sought out their priests and families all over Persia and the Araxes valley, and ministered to many of this oppressed people. The two servants with whom he had journeyed as far as Tokat were Armenians, and he especially trusted Sergius, whom he had engaged at Etchmiatzin, as one about to visit Constantinople, and not unfamiliar with the route. The body of the wearied traveller to the city of the Great King was laid to rest in the extensive cemetery of the church of Karasoon Manoog. Later research revealed the fact that the body was buried in simple and reverent Oriental fashion—not in a coffin, but in such a white winding-sheet as that which for forty hours enwrapped the Crucified. The story afterwards went that the chaplain-missionary of the East India Company was carried to the tomb with all the honours of an Armenian archbishop. That is most probable, for the Armenian clergy of Calcutta, Bushire, and Shiraz always gave him priestly honours during life. The other tradition—that his burial was hardly decent—has arisen from[516] the circumstances that attended the search for his grave and the removal of his dust to the American Mission Cemetery forty years afterwards.

Sir R.K. Porter

TOKAT IN 1812

Far away, in the most distant corner of Asiatic Turkey, or Turkish Arabia, at Baghdad, there was one[88] Anglo-Indian scholar and Christian, who hastened to discharge the pious duty of carving on a limestone slab above the precious remains a Latin inscription. That was the East India Company's civil servant, James Claudius Rich. Born near Dijon in 1787—six years after Martyn—and taken in his infancy to Bristol, he there manifested such extraordinary linguistic powers, even in boyhood, that Joshua Marshman, before he went out to Serampore, helped him with books and introduced him to Dr. Ryland. Robert Hall formed such an opinion of his powers, which the earliest Orientalist, Sir Charles Wilkins, tested, that he received an appointment to the Bombay Civil Service, and was introduced to Sir James Mackintosh. He went to India overland through Turkish Asia, disguised as a[519] Georgian Turk, so that the Mecca pilgrims at Damascus did not discover him. He married Sir James's eldest daughter,[89] and had set out as the Company's Resident at Baghdad and Busrah, not long before Martyn arrived at Bombay. The two men never met, for Martyn's attempt to enter Arabia from Persia through Baghdad was stopped. But the young Orientalist watched Martyn's career with admiration, and seems to have followed his footsteps. In 1821 he himself was cut off by cholera, while ministering to the plague-stricken in Shiraz, leaving a name imperishably associated with that of Sir James Mackintosh, and dear to all Oriental scholars and travellers, but henceforth to be remembered above all as that of the man who was the first to perpetuate the memory of Henry Martyn.[90]

The sacred spot was immediately at the foot of slaty rocks down which the winter snows and summer rains washed enough of stony soil every year to cover up the horizontal slab. The first to visit it with reverent steps after the pious commission of Claudius James Rich had been executed, was Sir Robert Ker Porter. Although only a few years had elapsed, he seems to have failed to see the inscription which fitly commemorated the 'Sacerdos ac Missionarius Anglorum,' so that he thus beautifully wrote: 'His remains sleep in a grave as humble as his own meekness; but while that high pyramidal hill, marked with its mouldering ruins of heathen ages, points to the sky, every European traveller must see in it their honoured countryman's monument.'

In 1830, when the American Board's missionaries, Eli[520] Smith and H.G.O. Dwight, visited Tokat, they had little difficulty in finding the spot, from which they wrote: 'An appropriate Latin inscription is all that distinguishes his tomb from the tombs of the Armenians who sleep by his side.'[91] They urged their Board to make Tokat its centre of operations for the people of Second Armenia, as Cæsarea for those of the First and Third Armenia, and Tarsus for those of Cilicia. As they, reversing his northward journey, reached Tabreez sick, they were cared for, first by Dr., afterwards Sir John McNeill, and then by Dr. Cormick, the same physician who healed Martyn of a similar disease when he was at this city. 'He seemed to have retained the highest opinion of him as a Christian, a companion, and a scholar.'

In 1841 Mr. George Fowler published his *Three Years in Persia*, in which a chapter is filled with reminiscences of Henry Martyn.

Of this distinguished missionary and champion of the Cross, who fearlessly unfolded his banner and proclaimed Christ amongst the bigoted Mahometans, I have heard much in these countries, having made acquaintance with some persons who knew him, and saw (if I may so say) the last of him. At the General's table at Erzroom (Paskevitch), I had the honour to meet graffs and princes, consisting of Russians, Georgians, Circassians, Germans, Spaniards, and Persians, all glittering in their stars and orders, such a *mélange* as is scarcely to be found again under one banner; looking more like a monarch's levy than anything else. My neighbour was an Armenian bishop, who, with his long flowing hair and beard, and austere habits, the cross being suspended to his girdle, presented a great[521] contrast to the military chiefs. There were many other priests at the table, of whom he was the principal. He addressed me in my native tongue very tolerably, asking if I had known anything of the missionary, Martyn. The name was magic to my ear, and immediately our colloquy became to me of great interest.

The bishop was the Serrafino of whom Martyn speaks in his *Journal*, I happening at the time to have it with me. He was very superior to the general caste of the Armenian clergy, having been educated at Rome, and had attained many European languages. He made Martyn's acquaintance at Etchmiatzin, the Armenian monastery at Erivan, where he had gone to pay a visit to the Patriarch or chief of that people, and remained three days to recruit his exhausted strength. He described him to me as being of a very delicate frame, thin, and not quite of the middle stature, a beardless youth, with a countenance beaming with so much benignity as to bespeak an errand of Divine love. Of the affairs of the world he seemed to be so ignorant, that Serrafino was obliged to manage for him respecting his travelling arrangements, money matters, etc. Of the latter he had a good deal with him when he left the monastery, and seemed to be careless, and even profuse, in his expenditure. He was strongly recommended to postpone his journey, but from his extreme impatience to return to England these remonstrances were unavailing. A Tartar was employed to conduct him to Tokat. Serrafino accompanied him for an hour or two on the way—with considerable apprehensions, as he told me, of his ever arriving in his native country.[92] He was greatly surprised, he said, not only to find in him all the ornaments of a refined education, but that he was so eminent a Christian;[522] 'since (said he) all the English I have hitherto met with, not only make no profession of religion, but live seemingly in contempt of it.'

I endeavoured to convince him that his impression of the English character was in this respect erroneous; that although a Martyn on the Asiatic soil might be deemed a phœnix, yet many such existed in that country which gave him birth; and I instanced to him the Christian philanthropy of my countrymen, which induced them to search the earth's boundaries to extend their faith. I told him of our immense voluntary taxation to aid the missionaries in that object, and of the numerous Christian associations,—for which the world was scarcely large enough to expend themselves upon.

He listened with great attention, and then threw in the compliment, 'You English are very difficult to become acquainted with, but when once we know you we can depend on you.' He complained of some part of Martyn's *Journal* referring to himself, respecting his then idea of retiring to India, to write and print some works in the Armenian language, tending to enlighten that people with regard to religion. He said that what followed of the errors and superstitions of the Armenian Church should not have been inserted in the book, nor did he think it would be found in Martyn's *Journal*. His complaint rested much on the compilers of the work in this respect; he said, 'these opinions were not exactly so expressed, and certainly they were not intended to come before the public, whereby they might ultimately be turned against me.'

At Erzroom, on my way to Persia, I had met with an Italian doctor, then in the Pasha's employ, from whom I heard many interesting particulars respecting Martyn. He was at Tokat at the time of our countryman's arrival and death, which occurred on October 16, 1812; but whether occasioned by the plague, or from excessive fatigue by the brutal treatment of the Tartar, he could not determine. His remains were decently interred in the Armenian[523] burying-ground, and for a time the circumstance was forgotten. Some years afterwards, a gentleman, at the request of the British ambassador in Constantinople, had a commemorative stone erected to his memory, and application was made to the Armenian bishop to seek the grave for that purpose. He seemed to have forgotten altogether such an occurrence, but referring to some memoranda which he had made of so remarkable a case as that of interring a Feringhi stranger, he was enabled to trace the humble tablet with which he had distinguished it. It is now ornamented with a white slab, stating merely the name, age, and time of death of the deceased.

I had many reminiscences of Martyn, at Marand particularly. I quitted this place at midnight, just at the time and under the circumstances which he describes. 'It was a most mild and delightful night, and the pure air, after the smell of the stable, was reviving.' I was equally solitary with himself. I had attached great interest to my resting-place, believing it to have been the same on which Martyn had reposed, from his own description, as it was the usual reception for travellers, the *munzil*, or post-house. Here I found myself almost alone, as with Aliverdy, my guide, not three words of understanding existed between us. Martyn says, 'They stared at my European dress, but no disrespect was shown.' Exactly so with me: the villagers stood around questioning my attendant, who was showing me off, I know not why.

Martyn's description of the stable was precisely what I found it; thus—'I was shown into the stable, where there was a little place partitioned off, but so as to admit a view of the horses.' He was 'dispirited and melancholy.' I was not a little touched with this in my solitariness, and sensibly felt with the poet:

Thou dost not know how sad it is to stray
Amid a foreign land, thyself unknown,
And, when o'erwearied with the toilsome day,
To rest at eve and feel thyself alone.
[524]

At Khoi, on my return, I witnessed the Persian ceremony related by Martyn in his *Journal* of the death of Imam Hussein—the anniversary of which is so religiously observed in that country. At Tabreez I heard much of him who was

Faithful found
Among the faithless—faithful only he,
Unshaken, unseduced, unterrifed,
His loyalty he kept—his zeal—his love.

I scarcely remember so bright an ornament to the Christian profession, on heathen land, as this hero of the Cross, who was 'patient in tribulation, rejoicing in hope;' and I heard him thus spoken of by those who could estimate the *man*, and perhaps not appreciate the *missionary*—'If ever there was a saint on earth, it was Martyn; and if there be now an angel in heaven, it is Martyn.' Amidst the contumely of the bigoted Mussulmans, he had much to bear, as to the natural man, amongst whom he was called an 'Isauvi' (the term given to Christians).

I know of no people where, to all human calculation, so little prospect opens of planting the Cross. The moollas are by no means averse to religious discussion, and still remember the 'enlightened infidel,' as Martyn was called; but so bigoted are these benighted Moslems, and show so much zeal, as I noticed at their Ramazan, that they scorn us, and, I may say, they shame us. It is interesting, when looking at those dark regions, to inquire—when shall the Cross triumph over the Crescent? when shall the riches and power of the Gospel spread over their soil, root up the weeds of error, and produce the fruits of righteousness?

Since the days of Martyn but little effort has been made by the Missionary Society to turn the tide of Christian philanthropy towards this country; but I would say, spite of the discouragements, Send your missionaries to this stronghold of Mahomet; here plant your standard[525] of redeeming love to the wretched devotee of the impostor; to the sometime worshipper of the sun hang out the banner of the Sun of Righteousness; kindle in his bosom the flame of Divine truth, that the Holy Spirit, of which his former god was the emblem, may enlighten and guide him into the fold of Christ.

It is gratifying to find from a paper in the *Asiatic Register*, the writer of which spent a few weeks at Shiraz, that the love and work of this distinguished missionary, although he saw no fruits from them, have in one instance proved that his labour has not been in vain in the Lord. He relates that in that city he met with an interesting character, Mahomed Rahim, who had been educated for a moolla; a man of considerable learning, and much attached to the English. He found him reading a volume of *Cowper's Poems*, and was astonished at the precision with which he expressed himself in English; this led to the subject of religion, when he acknowledged himself to be a Christian, and related the following circumstance.

In the year of the Hegira 1223 there came to this city an Englishman, who taught the religion of Christ with a boldness hitherto unparalleled in Persia, in the midst of much scorn and ill-treatment from the moollas as well as the rabble. He was a beardless youth, and evidently enfeebled by disease; he dwelt among us for more than a year. I was then a decided enemy to infidels, as the Christians are termed by the followers of Mahomet, and I visited this teacher of the despised sect, for the purpose of treating him with scorn, and exposing his doctrines to contempt. Although I persevered in this conduct for some time, I found that every interview not only increased my respect for the individual, but diminished my confidence in the faith in which I was educated. His extreme forbearance towards the violence of his opponents, the calm and yet convincing manner in which he exposed the fallacies and sophistries by which he was assailed (for he spoke Persian[526]excellently), gradually inclined me to listen to his arguments, to inquire dispassionately into the subject of them, and finally to read a tract which he had written in reply to *A Defence of Islam*, by our chief moollas. The result of my examination was a conviction that the young disputant was right. Shame, or rather fear, withheld me from this opinion; I even avoided the society of the Christian teacher, though he remained in the city so long. Just before he quitted Shiraz I could not refrain from paying him a farewell visit. Our conversation, the memory of which will never fade from the tablet of my mind, sealed my conversion. He gave me a book; it has been my constant companion; the study of it has formed my most delightful occupation; its contents have often consoled me. Upon this he put into my hand a copy of the New Testament in Persian; on one of the blank leaves was written, 'There is joy in heaven over one sinner that repenteth. HENRY MARTYN.'

The memory of Henry Martyn was borne by Mussulmans to Northern Africa, and south to India again. The late Rev. Mr. Oakley, of St. Paul's, Onslow Square, London, when travelling south of Algiers, met Mohammedans who asked him if he were of the same tribe as Henry Martyn, the man of God whose controversy at Shiraz and books they knew. A Persian of gentle manners, who had a surprising knowledge of the *Mesneri*, that inexhaustible fountain of Soofi philosophy, received a copy of Martyn's Persian New Testament. After fourteen years' study of it, in silence, he applied to the nearest Christian, an Armenian bishop, for baptism unto Christ. Fearing the consequences, the bishop sent on the catechumen to the Armenian priests at Calcutta, who, equally afraid that the news would reach the Persian authorities, handed him over to the Rev. |527|E.C. Stuart, then the Church Missionary Society's secretary there, and a Persian scholar, now Bishop of Waiapu. Mr. Stuart took him as his guest, found that he delighted in instruction in the New Testament, and baptized him. Ultimately the convert went back to Persia as one who 'had gained a sincere faith in Christ from the simple reading of H. Martyn's Persian Testament.'

In 1842 the learned Bombay chaplain, George Percy Badger, visited Tokat on a mission from the Archbishop of Canterbury and the Bishop of London to the Nestorian tribes of Koordistan. He was guided to Henry Martyn's first tomb by the Armenian priest who had performed the rites of Christian burial. While Mrs. Badger sought out and planted wild flowers around the stone, her husband, recalling the fervent zeal and ardent piety of the departed, 'lifted up a secret prayer that God in His mercy would raise up many of a like spirit to labour among the benighted Mohammedans of the East.'[93]

Adopting the report of their missionaries in 1830, the American Board at Boston sent out Dr. Henry J. van Lennep, who first visited Tokat fourteen years after them, and thirty-two years after Henry Martyn's death. The first object of his attention was the grave, which then he had great difficulty in discovering and identifying. It was this experience, and not any earlier facts, that must have led to the publication of these lines:

No stone marks the spot where these ashes are resting,
No tear has e'er hallowed thy cold, lonely grave,
But the wild warring winds whistle round thy bleak dwelling,
And the fierce wintry torrent sweeps o'er it with its wave.

|528|

In his *Travels in Little Known Parts of Asia Minor*,[94] Dr. van Lennep writes:

The Armenian burying-ground, where he was laid, is situated just outside of the town, and hard by the wretched gipsy quarter which forms its eastern extremity. It is a most barren and desolate spot, overhung by lofty cliffs of clay slate. Its only verdure, besides the rank weeds that spring up between the thickly set graves, consists of two scraggy wild pear-trees nearly dead for lack of moisture. The sexton of the church near by could give no information, and I was left to search for it alone. Beginning at the graves lying at the outer edge of the ground nearest the road, I advanced towards the hill, examining each in its turn, until just at the foot of the overhanging cliffs I came upon a slab of coarse limestone, some forty inches by twenty, bearing the following inscription:

Rev . Vir .
Gug[95] . Martino .
Sacer . Ac . Miss . Anglo .
Quem . In . Patr . Redi .
Dominus
Hic . Berisae . Ad . Sb . Voc .
Pium . D . Fidel . Q . Ser .
A.D. MDCCCXII.
Hunc . Lap . Consac .
C. I. R.
A.D. MDCCCXIII.

It was just ten years after this first visit that I was again in Tokat, not on a transient visit, but with the purpose of making that city my permanent abode. A little party of us soon repaired to the hallowed spot. Guided by my recollections and a drawing made at my previous visit, we were soon at the place; but in the last[529] few years it had undergone a remarkable change. Instead of the slab of stone with its inscription, which we expected to see, we only found a smooth surface of pebbly and sandy soil overgrown with weeds, without vestige of stone or mound to indicate the presence of a grave; but the identical surroundings were there, too well remembered to be mistaken. Could it be that, as happens in these lawless regions, the stone had been removed by some ruthless hand and incorporated in the wall of a neighbouring building? We could not accept that unpleasant conclusion, and, calling the sexton, we directed him to dig where we pointed. It was at a depth of two feet from the surface that the stone came into view: the soil and rubbish accumulated upon the grave were then removed, and we hoped the place would hereafter need little attention. But, to our surprise, we found it again, the ensuing spring, covered to the same depth as before. The soil was washed upon it by the rains from the whole mountain side, and we found that were a wall built for its protection, the gipsy boys, who made this their playground, would soon have it down.

Some time after this, a correspondence took place with friends in London, which resulted in a grant being made by the late Hon. East India Company's Board of Directors, for the purpose of erecting a more suitable monument to the memory of Henry Martyn, to be placed with his remains in the Mission Burying-ground. The monument was cut out of native marble, and made by native workmen at Tokat. The remains were removed under the inspection of the missionary physician, and though it was difficult positively to identify them, there can be no doubt that what was found once formed a portion of the earthly tenement of the devoted and lamented missionary. There were no remains of a coffin; Orientals never use them, and he was doubtless laid in immediate contact with the soil, literally 'dust to dust.' The monument under which we laid these remains was the first grave in our little cemetery, and well[530] might it be said that it became sacred ground. The obelisk has four faces, on each of which the name, encircled with a wreath, is cut, severally in English, Armenian, Persian, and Turkish. The four sides of the base contain the following inscription in the same languages:

REV. HENRY MARTYN, M.A.

CHAPLAIN OF THE HON. EAST INDIA COMPANY,
BORN AT TRURO, ENGLAND, FEBRUARY 18, 1781,
DIED AT TOKAT, OCTOBER 16, 1812.

HE LABOURED FOR MANY YEARS IN THE EAST, STRIVING TO
BENEFIT MANKIND BOTH IN THIS WORLD AND THAT TO COME.
HE TRANSLATED THE HOLY SCRIPTURES INTO HINDOSTANEE
AND PERSIAN,
AND PREACHED THE GOD AND SAVIOUR OF WHOM THEY TESTIFY.
HE WILL LONG BE REMEMBERED IN THE EAST, WHERE HE WAS
KNOWN AS A MAN OF GOD.

The grave now lies in a spot every way adapted to foster the holy memories which it recalls. It stands upon a broad and high terrace, overlooking the whole city for whose salvation we cannot doubt that he offered some of the last petitions 'of the righteous man, which avail much.' It is a solitude, immediately surrounded by the thick foliage of fruit trees, among which tall walnuts are conspicuous. We ourselves planted by its side the only weeping willows which exist in the whole region. The place is visited by many, who read the concise inscription and further inquire into the good man's history. It has always been a favourite place of resort of our students and native Christians, and they have many a time sat under its shade and expounded to wondering strangers the very doctrines to propagate which that model of a missionary had sacrificed his life.

TOMB OF HENRY MARTYN

Tokat is now for ever memorable as the centre which links the names of Basiliscus, the martyr, Basil the Great, John Chrysostom, and Henry Martyn. The cloud-crested fortress points almost straight up from the Jeshil-Irmak |533|river, the ancient Iris, which, rising in the Anti-Taurus range of Pontus, finds its way to the Black Sea with a breadth and volume of water second only to the Halys. Still, as of old, the town crowds about the foot of the two spiral crags and straggles out with towered church, mosque and minaret, into the valley. The ruins of the embattled walls crowning every pinnacle of the insulated rocks of which they seem to form a part, tell of the days when Greek and Roman passed along the 'royal road' from Amisos or Samsoon on the Euxine to Sebaste, Caesareia, and Central Asia; and when the Saracens beat off the Emperor Michael (860) from what was then called Daximon.[196] The time is coming when there shall once more be here a highway of civilisation after the barren centuries of the Moslem.

Tokat represents Komana Pontica, six miles off, the oracle and emporium of the royal road, described by Strabo as a little Corinth for vice and traffic. Another step, and the Apostle Paul himself might have visited it from Galatia. In 312, in the persecution under Maximin, Basiliscus, the bishop of Komana, was martyred, being shod with red-hot iron shoes, beheaded, and thrown into the Iris. The *Acta* picture the saint as led on foot by soldiers along the road without food for four days, till he reached Komana; 'and the road was much the same as the modern way, Tokat to Amaseia,' along which Henry Martyn was violently hurried by his Tartar. In the martyrium, built a few miles out of Komana, in memory of Basiliscus, Chrysostom found rest in death, and a grave.

Basilius, the bishop of Caesareia, belonged to the|534| neighbouring province of Cappadocia, but his missionary influence, and that of his bishop brother, Gregory Nyssen, and his sister, Macrina, spread all over Pontus, while Gregory Nazianzen was his fellow-student at Athens, and his admiring friend, as Julian also, the future Emperor, was for a time. Like Martyn, Basil owed to his sister his conversion, his call to the ministry, and his self-sacrifice all through life. It was on the banks of the Iris above Tokat that, secluded for five years, the great Father laid the foundation of the monastic communities of the Greek Church, and learned to be the future defender of orthodoxy against the Arians, and of the unity of the Oriental Church.

But it is the exile and death of John Chrysostom, just fourteen centuries before, that form the most touching parallel to the sufferings of Henry Martyn. Never has there been a greater missionary bishop than the 'golden-mouthed' preacher of Antioch and Constantinople. The victim first of a cabal of bishops, and then of the Empress Eudoxia, whose vices and sacrilege he rebuked, he was driven from Constantinople to the scorching plains of Cappadocia in the midsummer heat. His guard drove on the venerable man day and night, giving him no rest. When a halt was made, it was always in some filthy village where good water was not. Fever and ague were provoked, but still he was forced on to Basil's city of Caesareia, to find Basil's successor his bitter enemy. Taking a physician with him he reached his destination at Kokussos, where the Empress had hoped that the barbarians would make an end of him. As it seemed likely to prove his Tabreez, he was once more driven forth on foot, under two guards selected for their brutality. It took him three months to reach Komana—one long, slow martyrdom to|535| the fever-stricken old man. 'It was evident that Chrysostom's strength was entirely worn out,' writes Canon Venables, in words which exactly describe the experience of the young Henry Martyn. 'But his pitiless guard hurried him through the town "as if its streets were no more than a bridge," without a moment's halt.' Five miles farther on they halted at the chapel of the martyr Basiliscus, of whom Chrysostom dreamed that he saw him and heard him say: 'Be of good cheer, on the morrow we shall be together.' Canon Venables continues, unconsciously, the parallel with the experience of the nineteenth-century saint of the Evangel:

In the morning Chrysostom earnestly begged for a brief respite, but in vain. He was hurried off, but scarcely had he gone three or four miles when a violent attack of fever compelled them to retrace their steps.

On reaching the martyrium, Chrysostom, led within, stripped on his soiled garments, clothed himself in white baptismal vestments, joined in the communion of the body and blood of the Lord Jesus Christ, offered his last prayer 'for present needs,' uttered his accustomed doxology: 'Glory be to God for all things,' and, having said 'Amen,' breathed his last on September 14, 407, in his sixtieth year. His body was laid beside that of Basiliscus. A generation after, the children of the Empress and Emperor who had thus slaughtered the saint brought back his body and gave it imperial sepulture in Constantinople, while they publicly asked Heaven to forgive the wrong of the past.

From Basiliscus, Basil, and Chrysostom to Henry Martyn, the fourteen centuries tell of the corruption of the[536] Church of Christ in the East, and the rise upon its ruins of Mohammedanism, which covered the northern half of Africa, and Spain, and reached as far as Tours and Vienna in Europe. It is to the glory of Henry Martyn that he was the first missionary of the Reformed Church of the West to the Mohammedans, giving those of India and Central Asia the Gospel and the Psalms in two of their own vernaculars, and dying for them before he could complete his work at the Arabic Bible.

We shall see whom his example inspired to follow him. His death became a summons, first to his own evangelical circle in England and India, and then to the whole Church of Christ, to follow in the path that he marked out alike by his toiling and his writing.

Sergius, the Armenian, must at once have pursued the journey from Tokat to Constantinople, which is distant from Tabreez 1,542 miles, and not 1,300 as roundly estimated by Henry Martyn. He presented the letters of his master to Mr. Isaac Morier, in the Sultan's capital, father of Sir Gore Ouseley's secretary and successor. On February 12, 1813, Charles Simeon wrote thus to Mr. Thomason in Calcutta:

The day before yesterday a letter arrived from Mr. Isaac Morier, of Constantinople, announcing that on October 16 (or thereabouts) our beloved brother entered into the realms of glory, and rested for ever in the bosom of his God.... But what an event it is! How calamitous to his friends, to India, and to the world! Methinks I hear God say: 'Be still and know that I am God.' ... I had been forming plans in my mind with a view to the restoration of his health in England, and should now have been able to carry into execution whatever might have[537] been judged expedient; but I am denied the joy of ministering to him!

Again on April 2:

We are making collections for Mr. Martyn's brother's family, who in him have lost their main support. We have got about 400*l.*, and Mr. Thornton has sent you a paper for the purpose of getting them some aid in India.

The news reached Lydia Grenfell on February 14, 1813. She was then for a fortnight at Marazion, where every spot recalled the past. She thus communed with herself and God in her*Diary*:

Marazion: February 20, 1813.

I am fearful to retrace the last week on two accounts, lest the infirmity of nature prevail, and I give way to sorrow,—and lest, in recollecting the wondrous kindness and love of God my Saviour, I increase my pride and not my gratitude. Oh, shall I then remain silent? Shall Thy mercies be forgotten? Teach me, O Lord, to write and speak for Thy glory, and to my own deeper humiliation. Heard on the 14th of the removal of my most tender, faithful, and beloved friend to the joys of heaven. Oh, I could not wish his absence from them prolonged. What I only wished was, and now I am reconciled to that too,—I wished to have been honoured of God so far as to have been near him, or that some friend had been.[97] Lord, if this was wrong, forgive me. I will endeavour, yea, I am enabled to say of this too, 'Thy will be done.' Great has been the peace and tranquillity of my soul, such nearness to God, such a hold of Christ, such hope in the promises, such assurance of bliss and immortality, as I cannot express, and may have to forget. Oh, that I may never[538] lose,—rather would I lose everything I most prize, every earthly friend, every earthly enjoyment, than this. Oh, the fear of doing so, or of the abatement of spiritual perceptions and affections, is the thing I most dread, and makes me long to die. It is not for the sake of rejoining that blessed spirit of my friend, though I have, and do, feel that too,— but to be again shut out from Thy possession is what I fear.

February 28.—A silent Sabbath, at least to me,—to my ears, I should say, for I trust God speaks to my heart. 'Comfort ye, comfort ye, My people,' enables me to take comfort. I feel a submission to the will of God which is more blessed than when I had my own in the ministry of the Word,—yet this is a time which calls for prayer. Lord, pour out the spirit of prayer on me and many, and grant us grace to ask, fervently yet resignedly, the restoration of Thy preached gospel. Suddenly are we deprived of it,—may it be as quickly restored. Very weak in health, so powerless this morning,—I could not but think my earthly bed was preparing for me too, and that my soul would soon return to God, but I am better, and willing to stay my appointed time. True, to perform my work in a little time might be what I should rejoice in, but I am willing to live, so I may have the presence of God with me, and be engaged in His service. I have a pleasure in supposing it possible the blessed spirit of my friend may be, on some occasions, sent to protect, to console, and counsel me,—but this is a weakness, and perhaps should not be indulged. I felt this afternoon as if he was present, as I sat alone in the garden,—the thought only disposed me to solemnity and pensiveness of mind. I am afraid of my dependence on the creature, whether embodied or not, and I will rather trust to the sure support of God's Word.

March 2.—Some sorrowful thoughts will enter my mind respecting my late dear friend, and call forth some sighs and tears from my heart,—yet is that heart resigned[539] to the will of God, and confident of His having done all things well for His beloved servant. Oh, how shall I, with wonder and praise, listen in eternity to the relation of his last days! The excess of affection now, and the unwillingness I feel that he should have suffered, make it amongst my mercies that a veil is drawn over that period of his life. It is mercy all, and God is good to me in everything. I see His hand, I love and I adore. I submit and resign myself to His blessed disposal and to all His dispensations. I have been thinking how necessary for me it was that we are thus separated; for during his life I felt such a desire to please and to be worthy of the regard he entertained for me, that it was my bane, and caused me to forget God as the first object I was to think of and please. I accept the punishment sent for this offence, may it prove an effectual cure of this evil in my heart!

March 8.—During the last few days I have experienced much of the Divine support and consolation of the Gospel. It has been a time of conflict, not inward, blessed be the name of the Lord. I have enjoyed a constant, uninterrupted peace, a peace past an understanding, unless experienced. I never was more sensible of, or rejoiced more in the presence of God, and my heart rises to my Maker with delight and joy, as easily as I breathe. God, 'as soon as sought, is found,' through Jesus Christ,—but I have been put into the hands of a bitter enemy, and that enemy.... She has left me, and I pray that every uneasy feeling excited in my breast by her unkind and injurious treatment may depart with her. Oh, how I rejoice that no storms can molest the dead who die in the Lord,—they rest from their labours of every kind. Since the account reached me of the departure of my dear friend to be with Christ, which is far better than to be here,—every evil I suffer, or fear, is blessed in its purpose, from knowing he can never feel the same; and all I enjoy or behold that is delightful, is the more enjoyed from thinking[540] 'he has all this, and more, in perfection, and without interruption.' May I accomplish my work of suffering, or ending, or labouring, and then enter into rest.

March 13.—Nature has its turn in my feelings. To-day I have been given to feel more of sorrow for the removal of my beloved friend, and, without desiring it to be otherwise, to mourn my own loss. The recollection of his unmerited kindness softens my heart, and I can hardly forbear indulging a tenderness which may weaken but cannot strengthen my mind. O Lord, I beseech Thee preserve me from whatever may injure my soul and unfit me for Thy service. I have the hope of heaven too, and that is enough. In heaven we shall meet and unite for ever in the work of praise. Life, with its trials and cares, will be but short. May I only desire to live to Thee, my God, and finish the work Thou hast given me to do. Lord, make me faithful, self-denying, and submissive to Thy will.

April 3.—My thoughts revert to the possible circumstances of my late dear friend's sufferings and death, and I am sunk low by doing so. It was the last step he had to travel below, and one necessary to be taken, in order to reach the heights of glory. There let me view him triumphing with his Saviour, and through His meritorious sufferings and death made more than conqueror over all his enemies. I must think more of his glorious Lord, and less of the servant, either as suffering and labouring or glorified and resting. Lord, be graciously present, and in the contemplation of Thy perfections, and the review of Thy mercies, let me forget everything beside.

April 21.—A letter from Tabreez, dated August 28, reached me. O Thou who readest my heart, direct and sanctify every feeling. May the anguish of my soul be moderated, and let me endeavour to exercise faith in Thy Divine goodness, mercy, and power, and to believe it was well with him in all respects.[541]

April 24.—I am tormented with fears that even in eternity I shall never be capable of enjoying the same happiness my departed friend does, and it seems as if no other would satisfy me. O Lord Jesus, weary and heavy laden I come to Thee; let me behold the light of Thy countenance, and praise Thee, and lose in the contemplation of Thy glories, and in the sense of Thy love to my soul,—let me lose the remembrance of every other excellence. When the sun shines the light of the stars is eclipsed; thus may it be with me!—Unless the genius which shone in his character make me admire and love God more, let me turn from viewing them. Oh, teach me to love Thy saints, whether living or dead, and for Thy sake and Thyself above them all. I have never felt I was not resigned to the will of God in our separation on earth, but my anxious mind dwells on another, which I cannot bear to think possible.

June 3.—For several days my mind has been occupied with recollections that weaken its hold of spiritual things. I think more of a departed saint than of the King of Saints. It is strange that now I should be more in danger of loving too well a creature passed into the skies than when he lived on earth. But so it is,—continually my thoughts revert to him. I pray God this may not be a snare unto me to divide me from Himself. Let me behold Jesus.

June 13.—Passed a very blessed Sabbath. My soul quickened,—Oh, let it live, and it shall praise Thee! A letter from my dearest Emma containing wholesome, though at first unwelcome, counsel, has been of singular use to me. The snare is seen, if not broken. Yes, I have lost my hold of everything that used, and ought, to support me by allowing, without restraint, the remembrance of my late dear friend to fill my mind. My almost constant thoughts were of him, and pride at the preference he showed me was fed, as well as affection. Now I have a[542] painful, difficult part to act. A sacrifice I must offer of what has become so much my happiness as to interfere with my enjoyment of God. I must fly from the recollection of an earthly object, loved too well, viewed too much. Let me follow his faith, and consider the end of his conversation,—Jesus Christ, the same for ever. I have had the greatest peace to-day in only trying to resolve on this,—how merciful is God!

1814, January 28.—Found great sweetness yesterday and to-day in reading and sweet prayer in the garden; was sensibly refreshed in the exercise, and had a taste that the Lord was gracious. This evening my heart is sad, not from the withdrawing of those consolations, or darkness of soul, as is often the case, but from having the circumstances of my revered friend's death brought to my recollection. I strive not to dwell on them, for oh, what a scope do they give to my busy fancy! I would fly from this subject as too high for me, and take refuge in this: the Lord did not forsake His servant, and precious was his death in His sight. Nature is weak, but faith can strengthen me.

February 12.—A twelvemonth, this day, since I heard of the death of my dear friend. My thoughts revert to this event, but more to the mercies of God to me at that season.

October 16.—My thoughts engaged often to-day by the event of this day in 1812. Twice has the earth performed its annual round since the honoured servant of God received the welcome mandate to cease from his labours, and join those who 'see His face' and 'serve Him,' unencumbered with flesh and blood. He no longer measures time by days and years, and there is no tedious six days between Sabbath and Sabbath, as it is here. 'How blessed are those who die in the Lord.' This expresses my feelings most at the remembrance of this departed saint. May I abide in Christ, and be with Him and His saints for ever. O blessed hope of everlasting life,—I will cherish it, exult in it, and may I pursue till I attain it.

[543]

It was April 18, 1813, when Corrie and Thomason in India learned what they had always feared since the dearest of all friends to them had passed through Calcutta on his way to Arabia. Corrie was at Agra, and he wrote to his brother-in-law, Mr. C. Shaw, in reply to a letter 'containing the affecting intelligence of Martyn's death, to us afflictive, to him happy beyond expression. I could find nothing but lamentations to express—lamentations for us, not for him. He was meet for "the inheritance of the saints in light." My master is taken from me; oh, for a double portion of his spirit! The work of printing and distributing the Scriptures will henceforth go on more slowly.' Again, to Simeon: 'Could he look from heaven and see the Abdool Massee'h, with the translated New Testament in his hand, preaching to the listening throng, ... it would add fresh delight to his holy soul.' Thomason, at once his disciple and his friend, wrote: 'He was in our hearts; we honoured him; we loved him; we thanked God for him; we prayed for his longer continuance amongst us; we rejoiced in the good he was doing. We are sadly bereaved. Where such fervent piety, and extensive knowledge, and vigorous understanding, and classical taste, and unwearied application were all united, what might not have been expected?' When, soon after, Thomason, as chaplain, accompanied the Governor-General, Lord Moira, through North India, and arrived at Cawnpore, he had eyes and thoughts only for his friend.[544] 'In these sandy plains I have been tracing again and again the days of Martyn. Close by me is the house that dear minister occupied, leading to which is the gloomy line of aloes spoken of by Mrs. Sherwood.... Oh, for Martyn's humility and love!... His standard of every duty was the highest, and his feelings of joy, sorrow, love, most intense; whilst his conversation was always in heaven, the savour of his holy disposition was as ointment poured forth.... Woe unto us if we do not pray more, live more above the world and deny ourselves more, and love Christ more!'

John Sargent, Rector of Lavington, the earliest of Henry Martyn's intimate friends, at once undertook to write a memoir of his life, for which Simeon charged himself with collecting 'all possible materials from India and Persia.' Bishop Corrie accordingly addressed Sargent thus:

Agra: November 1, 1813.

It will be of use for you to know that when he left Cawnpore in 1810 to seek change of air I was with him, and persuaded him to leave in my hands a number of memorandums he was about to destroy. They were sealed up, but on his death, being opened, they proved to be journals of the exercises of his mind from January 1803 to 1807 inclusive. They seem to me no less worthy of publication than the journal of Mr. Brainerd, if more books of that kind should be judged necessary. Since the beginning of 1807 Mr. Martyn favoured me with almost a weekly letter, in which his various employments and engagements for the furtherance of the Gospel in this country are detailed, with occasional very interesting remarks. This correspondence ceased on my being ordered by our Commander-in-chief to assist Mr. Martyn in the duties of the station of Cawnpore, when I took up my abode with him from June till his departure, October 1. Other letters passed between us after that time, and it is my intention to send you copies of all the above correspondence, together with his private memorandums. The latter, with copies of Martyn's letters from February to July 1807, were sent off this day to Mr. Thomason in Calcutta, to be forwarded to England by the first oppor[545]tunity, and the copies of the remaining letters shall follow as soon as may be. Of course I have omitted to copy what seems purely personal: yet much remains which you will perhaps judge unnecessary for publication, and will exercise your own judgment on that head. All the extracts seem to me, however, to cast light on the progress of missionary work in this land, and may perhaps be thought interesting to those who take a concern in Indian affairs. These extracts give so full a view of Mr. Martyn's character that nothing remains for me to add. Only I may say a more perfect character I never met with, nor expect to see again on earth. During the four years we were fellow-labourers in this country, I had no less than six opportunities of enjoying his company; the last time for four months together, and under the same roof all the time; and each opportunity only increased my love and veneration for him.

I conclude the above intelligence will plead my excuse for writing to you without previous introduction, and I was anxious it should reach you through the nearest channel. Your brother in Calcutta has told me several times of your welfare, and during beloved Martyn's life I used to hear of you sometimes. Your person, whilst a student at King's College, was well known to me, and your character admired, though I had not steadiness of principle sufficient at that time to imitate you, and consequently had no pretensions to an acquaintance with you, though I often greatly desired it. To that 'Father in Israel,' Mr.

Simeon, I owe all my comfort on earth and all my hopes respecting eternity: for through his instrumentality the seeds of grace, I trust, were, during my residence at Cambridge, especially during the latter part of my residence, implanted in my heart, and have influenced, though alas! unsteadily, my after days.

Lydia Grenfell was of course consulted as the work made progress, but none of her letters to Martyn have seen the light.[546]

1815, December 26.—Wrote this day to Mr. Simeon. I have reason to search into my heart and watch the risings of pride there, both respecting the notice of this blessed saint, and the avowal to be expected of my being the object of so much regard from another still more eminent in the Church of Christ. I have ever stood amazed at this, and now that in the providence of God it seems certain that my being so favoured is likely to be made known, vanity besets me. Oh, how poor a creature am I! Lord, I pray, let me be enabled to trace some evidence of Thine eternal love to me, and let this greater wonder call off my thoughts from every other distinction. But how do I learn that in the whole of this notice my thoughts have not indeed been Thine, O Lord, nor my ways Thy ways? How much above all I could have conceived of have been the designs of God! I sought concealment, and lo! all is made known to many, and much will be even known to the world. It is strange for me to credit this, and strange that, with my natural reserve and the peculiar reasons that exist for my wishing to have this buried in silence, I am nevertheless composed about it. But, Lord, I would resign myself, and all things that concern me, to Thy sovereign will and pleasure. Preserve me blameless to Thine eternal kingdom, and grant me an everlasting union with thy servant above.

1816, January 28.—I feel an increased thankfulness that God has called me to live free from the many cares which fall on all in the married state, and for the peculiarly favourable circumstances He has placed me in here. The privilege of watching over my mother in the decline of life, the charge of a sweet child, the occupation of the schools, and a portion of this world's goods for the use of the poor,—all, all call for more thankfulness and diligence. Lord, help me to abound in both, and with and above all I have peace and hope in God through Jesus Christ, in a measure—though unbelief often robs my soul of both. Oh, let me[547] seek the grace of steadfast faith, and I have all I want or desire.

April 21.—Thought with delight of my loved friends, Mrs. Hoare and H.M., both before the Throne, led by the Lamb to living fountains of waters, and all tears wiped away from their eyes. Oh, I long to be there; yet I could willingly forego the joys of heaven if I might, by suffering or labours here, glorify my Lord and Saviour.

June 30.—Often have I thought, when desirous of pursuing a more consistent deportment, and of introducing spiritual subjects: 'How can I appear so different before those I have been so trifling and merely worldly in all my intercourse with?' The death of my esteemed and beloved brother in Christ, H.M., I thought would have been the period for my maintaining that serious watchfulness so essential to my enjoyment of God; but no, I have been worse since, I think, as a judgment for failing in my keeping my resolution.

In 1817 Lydia Grenfell's *Diary* records the visits of such men as Mr. Fenn, 'who came to preach in the great cause of the Church Missionary Society,' and of Mr. Bickersteth, who at Penzance 'stated what he had met with in Africa.' The author of many immortal hymns, Francis Thomas Lyte, 'opened his ministry' of two years in Marazion at this time, to her joy and spiritual growth. She notes on August 31, 1817, that his hymn 'Penitence' was sung for the first time.

Marazion: March 6, 1819.

Received, a few days since, Mr. Sargent's Memoir, and reading only a few pages has convinced me that, without a greater resemblance in the spirit to our friend, I never can partake of that blessedness now enjoyed by the happy subject of it in the presence of his Saviour. It is chiefly in humility, meekness, and love I see the sad, the[548] total difference. This may be traced to a departure from the fountain of grace, Christ Jesus, to whom, oh, may I return, and I shall be replenished.

October 14.—Indulged a wandering imagination, and am sad in consequence. This season I ought to deem a sacred one. Oh, that, in my remembrance of Thy blessed ... and servant, I could entirely forget what feeds my vanity. Lord, help me to check all earthly sorrow at the recollection of his many sorrows, for were they not the appointed means of fitting him for his present felicity, and of manifesting Thy grace, by which Thou art glorified? I would make this season one of serious preparation for my own departure, and what does that preparation consist in?—faith in Jesus. Oh, strengthen it in me, and by following Thy blessed saint in all virtuous and godly living I may come to those eternal joys prepared for those that love Thee.

1820, June 25.—Oh, what a heaven for a creature, who has no strength, or wisdom, or righteousness, like myself, to be fixed in, beholding the glories of Jehovah manifested in Him who is my Saviour and my Lord. Gladly would I part from this dull clod of earth and come to Thee, and reach the pure pleasures of a spiritual state. There, there dwells the blessed Martyn, who bows before the throne, of a glorious company of saints, washed with him, and clothed in spotless robes. Oh, (that) I may be brought to them.

December 5.—Thought of the holy martyr, so humble, so self-denying, so devoted, and of his early-accomplished prayer for the heavenly country, where he dwells perfect in purity and love. Oh, to be a follower of him as he followed Christ, and to walk in the same paths, influenced by the same holy, humble, heavenly principles, upheld by the same arm of omnipotent grace, till I too reach the rest above.

1821, January 23.—Elevated rather than refreshed and humbled in worship to-day. Imagination has been too|549| active and unrestrained. The remembrance of past events, in which that blessed saint now with God, H.M. (? figured), has been filling my mind. This should not be. This is not communion with him, now a glorified spirit, but merely the indulgence of a vain, sinful imagination. I would turn from all, from the most holy creatures, to the Holy One, and the just; spiritual, and moral, yea, Divine glory and beauty I may behold in Him, who is the chief among ten thousand, and altogether lovely.

October 18.—I have now survived my beloved friend eight years. Eight years have been given me to be prepared for that world of blessedness he has so long entered upon. Alas! I seem less so now than at any period.

1822, October 16.—The remembrance of the event of the day has been rendered useless by my absence from home a great part of it. It should be the occasion for renewed self-dedication, of more earnest prayer, and of humiliation; for the recollection of being the cause of increased sufferings to Thy saint, O Lord, is cause for constant humiliation. I would realise death, and look to eternity, and to that glorious Saviour, for whom the blessed subject of my thoughts lived only to serve and honour. Oh, never more shall I have intercourse with the beloved friend now with Christ, but by faith in Christ. Lord, help me to use the recollection of our earthly regard to promote this end.

October 19.—My birthday (forty-seventh) follows that of the anniversary of the death of Martyn.

December 31.—Read dear Martyn's sermon on the Christian's walk with greater enjoyment and unction than has been vouchsafed unto me for a long season. The holy simplicity of the directions, and persuasive motives to walk in, as well as receive, Christ, had influence in my heart.

1823, January 11.—Placed in my room yesterday the print of dear M. Felt affected greatly in doing so, and|550| my tears, which seldom flow in the presence of anyone, I could not restrain before the person who was fixing it.[98] With the Saviour now, and the Saviour, doubtless, was with him in his greatest agony, even the agony of death—this thought will be the more familiar to me by viewing the representation of Christ's Crucifixion, now placed over the picture of His servant. I trust, by a prudent and not too frequent sight of both, I may derive some advantage from possessing what is so affecting and so admonitory to me, who am declining in religious fervour and spirituality. Thus may I use both, not to exercise feelings, but faith. I cannot behold the resemblance of M. but I am reminded that God wrought powerfully on his soul, meeting him for a state of purity, and love, and spiritual enjoyment, and that he has entered upon it. His faithfulness, and diligence, and self-denial, and devotedness; his love to God, and love for souls; his meekness, and patience, and faith, should stimulate me to earnestness in prayer for a portion of that grace, through which alone he attained them, and was what he was.

January 19.—Read dear Martyn's sermon on 'Tribulation the Way to Heaven,' with, I trust, a blessing attending it.

1825, October 16.—The anniversary of dear H.M. gaining the haven of rest after his labours. Oh, how little do I labour to enter into that rest he enjoyed upon earth.

1826, April 2.—God, the ever gracious and merciful God, Thee would I bless and everlastingly praise for granting me the favour of hearing 'the joyful sound' of[55] His rich love, and abounding grace by Jesus Christ, this day, and by a messenger unexpected, and beloved as a friend and brother. The text was that I once heard preached from by the blessed Martyn, whose spirit I pined to join in offering praises to God after sermon: 'Now then we are ambassadors for Christ.'

June 18.—My friends gone to heaven seem to reproach me, that I aim not to follow them, as they followed Christ. The beloved Martyn, the seraphic Louisa Hoare, and my dear[22] Georgina's spirits are employed in perpetually beholding that God whom I neglect, and remain unconcerned when I do not delight in or serve (Him). Oh, let me be joined to them in the sweet work of adoration and praise to Him who hath loved us, to Jesus, our one Lord and Saviour. Amen.

So ends the *Diary* of Lydia Grenfell, the eight last years of her life afflicted by cancerous disease, and one year by a clouded mind.[100] To the manuscript 'E. H,'—that is, her sister, Emma Hitchins—added these words: 'This prayer was answered September 21, 1829;

And now they range the heavenly plains,
And sing in sweet, heart-melting strains.'

The motto on her memorial stone in the churchyard of Breage, where she lies near another holy woman, Margaret Godolphin, first wife of Queen Anne's prime minister, is 'For a small moment have I forsaken thee, but with great mercies will I gather thee.'

FOOTNOTES:

[88]We must not forget the boyish 'Epitaph on Henry Martyn,' written by Thomas Babington Macaulay in his thirteenth year (*Life*, by his nephew, vol. i. p. 38):

'Here Martyn lies. In manhood's early bloom
The Christian hero finds a Pagan tomb.
Religion sorrowing o'er her favourite son
Points to the glorious trophies that he won,
Eternal trophies! not with carnage red;
Not stained with tears by hapless captives shed,
But trophies of the Cross. For that dear Name,
Through every form of danger, death, and shame,
Onward he journeyed to a happier shore,
Where danger, death, and shame assault no more.'

These lines reflect the impression made on Charles Grant and the other Clapham friends by Henry Martyn's death at a time when they used his career as an argument for Great Britain doing its duty to India during the discussions in Parliament on the East India Company's Charter of 1813.

[89]*Narrative of a Residence in Koordistan, and an Account of a Visit to Sherauz and Persepolis*, by the late Claudius James Rich, Esq., edited (with memoir) by his widow, two vols., London, 1836.

[90]See p. 528 for the earlier, and p. 530 for the later inscription.

[91]*Missionary Researches in Armenia*, London, 1834.

[92]It is a custom in the East to accompany travellers out of the city to bid them God speed, with the 'khoda hafiz shuma,' 'may God take you into His holy keeping.' If an Armenian, he is accompanied by the priest, who prays over him and for him with much fervour.

[93]*The Nestorians and their Rituals in 1842-1844*, 2 vols. London: Joseph Masters, 1852.

[94]New York, 1870, 2 vols. 12mo. Also published by John Murray, London, 1870.

[95]Mr. Rich, British Resident at Baghdad, who had laid this monumental slab, was evidently ignorant of Martyn's Christian name.

[96]Professor W.M. Ramsay's *Historical Geography of Asia Minor*, 1890.

[97]'Paucioribus lacrymis compositus es.'—Tac. quoted on this occasion by Sargent,*Memoir of Martyn*, p. 493.

[98]Her niece writes of her when she received the news of Henry Martyn's death: 'The circumstances of his affecting death, and my aunt's *intense* sorrow, produced an ineffaceable remembrance on my own mind. I can never forget the "upper chamber" in which she took refuge from daily cares and interruptions—its view of lovely Mount's Bay across fruit-trees and whispering white cœlibes—its perfect neatness, though with few ornaments. On the principal wall hung a large print of the Crucifixion of our Lord, usually shaded by a curtain, and at its foot (where he would have chosen to be) a portrait of Henry Martyn.'—*The Church Quarterly Review* for October 1881.

[99]An authoress, and member of the Gurney family, who died in April, 1816.

[100]*Her Title of Honour*, by Holme Lee, in which an attempt is made to tell the story of Lydia Grenfell's life under a fictitious name, is unworthy of the subject and of the writer.

[552]

CHAPTER XV

BAPTIZED FOR THE DEAD

Henry Martyn is, first of all, a spiritual force. Personally he was that to all who came in contact with him from the hour in which he gave himself to Jesus Christ. To Cambridge student and peasant alike; to Charles Simeon, his master, as to Kirke White and Sargent, Corrie and Thomason, his admiring friends; to women like Lydia Grenfell, his senior in years and experience, as to children like his cousin's at Plymouth, and David Brown's at Aldeen; to the rude soldiery of the Cape campaign and the East India Company's raw recruits as to the cultured statesmen and scholars who were broadening the foundations of our Indian empire; to the caste-bound Hindu, but far more to the fanatical Arab and the Mohammedan mystic of Persia—to all he carried the witness of his saintly life and his Divine message with a simple power that always compelled attention, and often drew forth obedience and imitation. His meteor-like spirit burned and flamed as it passed across the first twelve years of the nineteenth century, from the Cam to the Fal, by Brazil and South Africa, by Calcutta and Serampore, by Patna and Cawnpore, by Bombay and Muscat, by Bushire and Shiraz and Tabreez, to the loneliness of the Armenian highlands, and the exile grave of the Turkish Tokat.[553]

From the year in which Sargent published fragments of his *Journal,* and half revealed to the whole Church of Christ the personality known in its deep calling unto deep only to the few, Henry Martyn has been the companion of good men[101] and women of all the Churches, and the stimulus of the greatest workers and scholars of the century. The latest writer, the Hon. George N. Curzon, M.P., in his exhaustive work on Persia (1892), describes him as 'this remarkable man, who impressed everyone, by his simplicity and godliness of character,' though he ascribes the 'effect in the short space of a year' as much to the charm of his personality as to the character of his mission.

Perhaps the most representative of the many whom Martyn is known to have influenced was Daniel Wilson, of Islington and Calcutta. When visiting his vast diocese in 1838 and crossing the Bay of Bengal, Bishop Wilson[102] thus carefully compared the *Journal* with corresponding passages in his own life:

It is consoling to a poor sinner like myself, who has been placed in the full bustle of public business, to see how the soul even of a saint like H. Martyn faints and is discouraged, laments over defects of love, and finds an evil nature still struggling against the law of his mind. I remember there are similar confessions in J. Milner. It is[554] this which explains the seventh of Romans. Henry Martyn has now been in heaven twenty-six years, having died in his thirty-second year. Dearest Corrie was born like myself in 1778, and died in 1837, aged fifty-nine, and after having been thirty-one years in India. He has been at home now a year and five months. When, where, how, I may be called hence I know not. The Lord make me a follower of them who through faith and patience have inherited the promises. In H. Martyn's *Journals* the spirit of prayer, the time he devoted to the duty, and his fervour in it, are the first things which strike me. In the next place, his delight in Holy Scripture, his meditations in it, the large portions he committed to memory, the nourishment he thence derived to his soul, are full of instruction. Then his humility is quite undoubted, unfeigned, profound, sincere. There seems, however, to have been a touch of natural melancholy and depression, which was increased by one of his greatest mistakes, the leaving England with his affections tied to Lydia Grenfell, whom he ought either not to have loved or else to have married and taken her with him. Such an ecstatic, warm creature as Henry Martyn could do nothing by halves. Separation was martyrdom to such a tender heart. But, oh, to imitate his excellences, his elevation of piety, his diligence, his spirituality, his superiority to the world, his love for souls, his anxiety to improve all occasions to do them good, his delight in the mystery of Christ, his heavenly temper! These, these are the secrets of the wonderful impression he made in India, joined as they were with first-rate talents, fine scholarship, habit of acquiring languages, quickness and promptitude of perception, and loftiness of imaginative powers.

Henry Martyn's *Journal* holds a place of its own in the literature of mysticism. It stamps him as the mystic writer and worker of the first quarter of the century of[555] modern missions (1792-1814), as his master, Robert Leighton, was of the more barren period that ended in 1688. The too little known *Rules and Instructions for Devout Exercises*, found among Leighton's papers, written with his own hand and for his own use, was Martyn's 'usual' companion, with results which made that work[103] as supplemented by the *Journal*, what the *De Imitatione Christi* and the *Theologia Germanica* were to the more passive dark ages of Christendom. At the close of the eighteenth century the young and impulsive Cornish student found himself in an age not less, to him, godless and anti-evangelical than that which had wrung from the heart of at least one good man the hopeless longing of the *Theologia Germanica*. He had seen his Divine Master crucified afresh in the person of Charles Simeon, whom he possibly, as Sargent certainly, had at first attended only to scoff and brawl. He had been denied a church in which to preach the goodness of God, in his own county, other than that of a kinsman. In the troopship and the Bengal barrack even his official authority could hardly win a hearing from officer or soldier. The young prophet waxed sore in heart, as the fire burned within him, at the unbelief and iniquity of his day, till his naturally sunny spirit scorched the souls he sought to warm with the Divine persuasiveness. He stood really at the opening of the Evangelical revival of Christendom, and like William Carey, who loved the youth, he was working out his own side of that movement, but, equally like Carey, he knew it not. He was to do as much by his death as by his life, but all he knew in his humility was that he must make haste while he lived to give the millions of Mohammedans the Word, and to reveal to[556]them the Person of Jesus Christ. The multitude of his thoughts within him he committed to a *Journal*, written for himself alone, and rescued from burning only by the interference of his friend Corrie.

The mysticism of Martyn has been pronounced morbid. All the more that his searching introspection and severe judgment on himself are a contrast to the genial and merry conversation of the man who loved music and children's play, the converse of friends and the conflict of controversy for the Lord, does every reader who knows his own heart value the vivisection. Martyn writes of sin and human nature as they are, and therefore he is clear and comforting in the answer he gives as to the remedy for the one and the permanent elevation of the other. Even more than Leighton he is the Evangelical saint, for where Leighton's times paralysed him for service, Martyn's called him to energise and die in the conflict with the greatest apostacy of the world. Both had a passion to win souls to the entrancing, transforming love they had found, but unless on the side against the Stewarts, how could that passion bear fruit in action? Both, like the author of the *De Imitatione*, wrote steeped in the spirit of sadness; but the joy of the dawn of the modern era of benevolence, as it was even then called, working unconsciously on the sunny Cornubian spirit, kept Martyn free alike from the selfish absorption which marked the monk of the Middle Ages, and the peace-loving compromise which neutralised Leighton. The one adored in his cell, the other wrestled in his study at Newbattle or Dunblane, and we love their writings. But Henry Martyn worked for his generation and all future ages as well as wrote, so that they who delight in his mystic communings are constrained to follow him in his self-sacrificing service.[557] Beginning at March 1807, let us add some passages from the *Journal* to those which have been already extracted for autobiographical purposes.

I am thus taught to see what would become of me if God should let go His strong hand. Is there any depth into which Satan would not plunge me? Already I know enough of the nature of Satan's cause to vow before God eternal enmity to it. Yes! in the name of Christ I say, 'Get thee behind me, Satan!'

Employed a great deal about one Hebrew text to little purpose. Much tried with temptation to vanity, but the Lord giveth me the victory through His mercy from day to day, or else I know not how I should keep out of hell.

May the Lord, in mercy to my soul, save me from setting up an idol of any sort in His room, as I do by preferring a work professedly for Him to communion with Him. How obstinate the reluctance of the natural heart to God. But, O my soul, be not deceived, the chief work on earth is to obtain sanctification, and to walk with God.

O great and gracious God, what should I do without Thee? but now Thou art manifesting Thyself as the God of all consolation to my soul. Never was I so near Thee; I stand on the brink, and I long to take my flight! Oh, there is not a thing in the world for which I would wish to live, except because it may please God to appoint me some work. And how shall my soul ever be thankful enough to Thee, O Thou most incomprehensibly glorious Saviour Jesus!

I walk according to my carnal wisdom, striving to excite seriousness by natural considerations, such as the thoughts of death and judgment, instead of bringing my soul to Christ to be sanctified by his spirit.

Preached on Luke xii. 20—'This night thy soul,' etc. The congregation was large, and more attentive than they have ever yet been. Some of the young officers and|558|soldiers seemed to be in deep concern. I was willing to believe that the power of God was present, if a wretch so poor and miserable can be the instrument of good to souls. Four years have I been in the ministry, and I am not sure that I have been the means of converting four souls from the error of their ways. Why is this? The fault must be in myself. Prayer and secret duties seem to be where I fail; had I more power in intercession, more self-denial in persevering in prayer, it would be no doubt better for my hearers.

My heart sometimes shrinks from spiritual work, and especially at an increase of ministerial business; but now I hope, through grace, just at this time, that I can say I desire no carnal pleasure, no ease to the flesh, but that the whole of life should be filled up with holy employments and holy thoughts.

My heart at various times filled with a sense of Divine love, frequently in prayer was blessed in the bringing of my soul near to God. After dinner in my walk found sweet devotion; and the ruling thoughts were, that true happiness does not consist in the gratifying of self in ease or individual pleasure, but in conformity to God, in obeying and pleasing Him, in having no will of my own, in not being pleased with personal advantages, though I might be without guilt, nor in being displeased that the flesh is mortified. Oh, how short-lived will this triumph be! It is stretching out the arm at full length, which soon grows tired with its own weight.

I travel up hill, but I must learn, as I trust I am learning, to do the will of God without any expectation of any present pleasure attending it, but because it is the will of God. Oh, that my days of vanity were at an end, and that all my thoughts and conversation might have that deep tinge of seriousness which becomes a soldier of the cross.

To the women preached on the parable of the ten|559| pieces of silver, and at night to the soldiers on Rev. i. 18. Afterwards in secret prayer drew near to the Lord. Alas! how my soul contracts a strangeness with Him; but this was a restoring season. I felt an indignation against all impure and sinful thoughts, and a solemn serenity of frame. Interceded for dear friends in England; this brought my late dear sister with pain to my recollection, but I felt relieved by resolving every event, with all its circumstances, into the will of God.

Read an account of Turkey. The bad effects of the book were so great that I found instant need of prayer, and I do not know when I have had such divine and animating feelings. Oh, it is Thy Spirit that makes me pant for the skies. It is He that shall make me trample the world and my lusts beneath my feet, and urge my onward course towards the crown of life.

Spent the day in reading and prayer, and found comfort particularly in intercession for friends, but my heart was pained with many a fear about my own soul. I felt the duty of praying for the conversion of these poor heathens, and yet no encouragement to it. How much was there of imagination before, or rather, how much of unbelief now; seeing no means ready now, no Word of God to put into their hands, no preachers, it sometimes seems to me idle to pray. Alas! wicked heart of unbelief, cannot God create means, or work without them? But I am weary of myself and my own sinfulness, and appear exceedingly odious even to myself, how much more to a holy God. Lord, pity and save; vile and contemptible is Thy sinful creature, even as a beast before Thee; help me to awake.

Some letters I received from Calcutta agitated my silly mind, because my magnificent self seemed likely to become more conspicuous. O wretched creature, where is thy place but the dust? it is good for men to trample upon thee. Various were my reveries on the events apparently approaching, and self was the prominent character in every[560] transaction. I am yet a long way from real humility; oh, when shall I be dead to the world, and desire to be nothing and nobody, as I now do to be somebody?

Throughout the 18th enjoyed a solemn sense of Divine things. The promise was fulfilled, 'Sin shall not have dominion over you.' No enemy seemed permitted to approach. I sometimes saw naught in the creation but the works of God, and wondered that mean earthly concerns had ever drawn away my mind from contemplating their glorious Author. Oh, that I could be always so, seeing none but Thee, taught the secrets of Thy covenant, advancing in knowledge of Thee, growing in likeness to Thee. How much should I learn of God's glory, were I an attentive observer of His Word and Providence. How much should I be taught of His purposes concerning His Church, did I keep my heart more pure for Him. And what gifts might I not expect to receive for her benefit, were I duly earnest to improve His grace for my own! Oh, how is a life wasted that is not spent with God and employed for God. What am I doing the greater part of my time; where is my heart?

Sabat lives almost without prayer, and this is sufficient to account for all evils that appear in saint or sinner.

I feel disposed to partake of the melancholy with which such persons (Lady Mary Wortley Montagu) close their lives. Oh, what hath grace done for us! The thought sometimes bursts upon me in a way which I cannot describe. It is not future bliss, but present peace, which we have actually obtained, and which we cannot be mistaken in; the very thing which the world seeks for in vain; and yet how have we found it? By the grace of God we are what we are.

Truly love is better than knowledge. Much as I long to know what I seek after, I would rather have the smallest portion of humility and love than the knowledge of an archangel.[561]

At night I spoke to them on 'Enoch walked with God.' My soul breathed after the same holy, happy state. Oh that the influence were more abiding; but I am the man that seeth his natural face in a glass.

This last short sickness has, I trust, been blessed much to me. I sought not immediately for consolations, but for grace patiently to endure and to glory in tribulation; in this way I found peace. Oh, this surely is bliss, to have our will absorbed in the Divine Will. In this state are the spirits of just men made perfect in heaven. The spread of the Gospel in these parts is now become an interesting subject to you—such is the universal change.

Perpetually assaulted with temptations, my hope and trust is that I shall yet be sanctified in the name of the Lord Jesus, and by the Spirit of my God. 'Purge me with hyssop, and I shall be clean; wash me, and I shall be whiter than snow.' When I really strive after purity of heart—for my endeavours are too often little more than pretence—I find no consideration so effectual as that of the exalted dignity and infinitely precious privileges of the saints. Thus a few verses of 1 Eph. are more influential, purifying, and transforming than the most laboured reasoning. Indeed, there is no reasoning with such temptations, and no safety but in flight.

I would that all should adore, but especially that I myself should lie prostrate. As for self, contemptible self, I feel myself saying, Let it be forgotten for ever; henceforth let Christ live, let Christ reign, let Him be glorified for ever.

Henry Martyn, by service, escaped the weakness and the danger of the mystic who seeks absorption into God, in the mental sense, as the remedy for sin, instead of a free and purified individuality in Christ. He felt that the will sins; he saw the cure to lie not in the destruction of the will, but in its rectification and personal co-working with God.[562] Absorption is spiritual suicide, not service. Martyn realised and taught that a free individuality is the best offering we can make to God after Christ has given it to us to offer to Him. With Martyn moral service helped spiritual contemplation to rise heavenward, and to raise men with it. The saint was also the sacred scholar and translator; the mystic was the prophet preacher, the Persian controversialist, the unresting missionary. His Christian life was guided by the motto, 'To believe, to suffer, and to hope.' His praying realised his own ideal of 'a visit to the invisible world.' His working was ever quickened like St. Paul's by the summons, alike of the Old dispensation and the New, which he cut with a diamond on the window of his college rooms Ἔγειραι, ὁ καθεύδων, καὶ ἀνάστα, 'Awake thou that sleepest and arise.' When the fierce flame of his love and his service had burned out his frail body, his picture, painted at Calcutta the year before he died, spoke thus to Charles Simeon, and ever since it has whispered to every new generation of Cambridge men, 'Be serious, be in earnest; don't trifle—don't trifle.'

The men whom Henry Martyn's pioneering and early death have led to live and to die that Christ may be revealed to the Mohammedans, are not so many as the thousands who have been spiritually stimulated by his *Journal.* Such work is still 'the forlorn hope' of the Church which he was the first to lead. But in Persia and Arabia he has had such followers as Anthony Groves, John Wilson, George Maxwell Gordon, Ion Keith-Falconer, and Bishop French. Where he pointed the way the great missionary societies of the United States of America and of England and the Free Church of Scotland have sent their noblest men and women.[563]

The death of Henry Martyn, followed not many years after by that of her husband, who had been the first to mark his grave with a memorial stone, led Mrs. James Claudius Rich, eldest daughter of Sir James Mackintosh, to appeal in 1831 for 'contributions in aid of the school at Baghdad, and those hoped to be established in Persia and other parts of the territory of Baghdad.' In the same year, 1829, that Alexander Duff sailed for Calcutta, there had gone forth by the Scots Mission at Astrakhan to Baghdad, that Catholic founder of the sect since known as 'The Brethren,' Anthony N. Groves, dentist, of Exeter. Taking the commands of Christ literally, in the spirit of Henry Martyn, he sold all he had, and became the first of Martyn's successors in Persia. The record of his two attempts forms a romantic chapter in the history of Christian missions.[1104] All theories apart, he lived and he worked for the Mohammedans of Persia in the spirit of Henry Martyn. When the plague first, and persecution the second time, extinguished this Mission to Baghdad, Dr. John Wilson,[1105] from his central and commanding position in Bombay, flashed into Arabia and Persia such rays of Gospel light as were possible at that time. He sent Bible colporteurs by Aden and up the Persian Gulf; he summoned the old Church of Scotland to despatch a mission to the Jews of Arabia, Busrah, and Bombay. A missionary was ready in the person of William Burns who afterwards went to China, the support of a missionary at Aden was guaranteed by a friend, and Wilson had found a volunteer 'for the purpose of exploring Arabia,' when the disruption of the Church of Scotland[564] arrested the movement, only, however, vastly to increase the missionary development in India and Africa, as well as church extension in Scotland. What John Wilson tried in vain to do during his life was effected by his death. It was his career that summoned the Hon. Ion Keith-Falconer and his wife to open their Mission in Yemen, at Sheikh Othman and Aden. Like Martyn at Tokat, in the far north, and just at Martyn's age, by his dust in the Aden cemetery Ion Keith-Falconer has taken possession of Arabia for Christ. 'The *Memoirs of David Brainerd*and *Henry Martyn* gave me particular pleasure,' wrote young John Wilson in 1824. 'Mind to get hold of the *Life of John Wilson,* the great Scotch missionary of India,' wrote the young Ion Keith-Falconer in 1878.[1106] So the apostolic succession goes on.

Gordon of Kandahar, 'the pilgrim missionary of the Punjab,' was not the least remarkable of Henry Martyn's deliberate followers, alike in a life of toil and in a death of heroism for the Master. Born in 1839, he was of Trinity College, Cambridge, and had as his fellow-curate Thomas Valpy French, when the future bishop came back from his first missionary campaign in India. Dedicating himself, his culture, and his considerable property to the Lord, he placed his unpaid services at the disposal of the Church Missionary Society, as Martyn once did. Refusing a bishopric after his first furlough, and seeking to prepare himself for the work of French's Divinity School of St. John at Lahore, he returned to India by Persia, to learn the language and to help Dr. Bruce for a little in 1871.[565] The famine was sore in that land, and he lived for its people as 'relieving officer, doctor, purveyor, poorhouse guardian, outfitter and undertaker. There is a cry like the cry of Egypt in the night of the Exodus—not a house in which there was not one dead.' So he wrote.[107] From Julfa he carried relief to Shiraz, where he found himself in the midst of the associations made sacred by Henry Martyn's residence there. 'I have taken up my quarters in a Persian's house, and have a large garden all to myself. I am in the very same house which Henry Martyn was in. I heard to-day that my host is the grandson of his host Jaffir Ali Khan, and that the house has come down from father to son.'

Eight years after Gordon was in Kandahar, sole (honorary) chaplain to the twenty regiments who were fighting the Ameer of Afghanistan. There he found the assistant to the political officer attached to the force to be the same Persian gentleman who had been his host at Shiraz, and with whom when a child Martyn must have played. Gordon learned from him that the roads and sanitary improvements made as relief works, as well as the orphanage started on the interest of the famine relief fund sent from London, were still blessing the people. When, after the black day of Maiwand, the British troops were besieged in Kandahar, till relieved by the march and the triumph of Lord Roberts, Gordon as chaplain attended a sortie to dislodge the enemy. Hearing that wounded men were lying in a shrine outside the Kabul gate, he led out some bearers with a litter, and found that the dying men were in another shrine still more distant. In spite of all[566]remonstrance he dashed through the murderous fire of the enemy, was struck down, and was himself carried back on the litter he had provided for others. He did not live to wear the Victoria Cross, but was on the same day, August 16, laid in a soldier's grave.

It would seem difficult to name a follower more worthy of Henry Martyn than that, but Bishop French was such a disciple. More than any man, as saint and scholar, as missionary and chaplain, as the friend of the Mohammedan and the second apostle of Central Asia, he was baptized for the dead. Born on the first day of 1825, son of an Evangelical clergyman in Burton-on-Trent, a Rugby boy, and Fellow and Tutor of University College, Oxford, Thomas Valpy French was early inspired by Martyn's life and writings. These and his mother's holiness sent him forth to Agra in 1850, along with Edward Stuart of Edinburgh, now Bishop of Waiapu, New Zealand, to found the Church Missionary College there. In the next forty years, till he resigned the bishopric of Lahore that he might give the rest of his life to work out the aspirations of Martyn in Persia and Arabia, he consecrated himself and his all to Christ. It will be a wonderful story if it is well told. He then went home for rest, first of all, but took the way north through Persia and Turkey on Martyn's track, so that in April 1888 he wrote from Armenia: 'Were I ignorant both of Arabic and French, I should subside into the perfect rest, perhaps, which I require.' So abundant were his labours to groups of Mohammedans and among the Syrian Christians, that he had nearly found a grave in the Tokat region.

After counselling the Archbishop of Canterbury as to the project of so reforming the Oriental Churches as to[567] convert them themselves into the true apostles of the Mohammedan race, Bishop French returned to Asia and settled near Muscat, whence he wrote thus on March 10, 1891, his last letter to the Church Missionary Society:

Those three years of Arab study will not, I trust, be thrown away and proved futile. In memory of H. Martyn's pleadings for Arabia, Arabs, and the Arabic, I seem almost trying at least to follow more directly in his footsteps and under his guidance, than even in Persia or India, however incalculable the distance at which the guided one follows the leader!...

I have scarcely expressed in the least degree the view I have of the *extremely serious* character of the work here to be entered upon; and the possible—nay probable— severity of the conflict to be expected and faithfully hazarded by the Church of Christ between two such strong and ancient forces, pledged to such hereditary and deep-grounded hostility. Yet *The Lamb shall overcome them; for He is Lord of Lords, and King of Kings; and they also shall overcome that are with Him, called and chosen and faithful.*

Two months after, on May 14, 1891, at the age of sixty-six, after exposure and toils like Martyn's, he was laid to rest in the cemetery of Muscat by the sailors of H.M.S. Sphinx, to whom he had preached.

Henry Martyn at Tokat, John Wilson at Bombay, George Maxwell Gordon at Kandahar, Ion Keith-Falconer at Aden, and Thomas Valpy French at Muscat, have by their bodies taken possession of Mohammedan Asia for Christ till the resurrection. Of each we say to ourselves and to our generation:

Is it for nothing he is dead?
Send forth your children in his stead!
[568]O Eastern lover from the West!
Thou hast out-soared these prisoning bars;
Thy memory, on thy Master's breast,
Uplifts us like the beckoning stars.
We follow now as thou hast led,
Baptize us, Saviour, for the dead.[108]

Each, like not a few American missionaries, men and women, like Dr. Bruce and his colleagues of the Church Missionary Society, like Mr. W.W. Gardner and Dr. J.C. Young of the Scottish Keith-Falconer Mission, is a representative of the two great principles, as expressed by Dr. Bruce: (1) That the lands under the rule of Islam belong to Christ, and that it is the bounden duty of the Church to claim them for our Lord. (2) That duty can be performed only by men who are willing to die in carrying it out.

Henry Martyn's words, almost his last, on his thirty-first birthday were these: 'The Word of God has found its way into this land of Satan (Persia), and the devil will never be able to resist it if the Lord hath sent it.' We have seen what sort of men the Lord raised up to follow him. This is what the Societies have done. In 1829 the American Board of Commissioners for Foreign Missions began, and in 1871 the Presbyterian Board shared, the mission to Persia and Asiatic Turkey. The former has missionaries at Aintab, Marash, Antioch, Aleppo, and Oorfa, to the south of the Taurus range, being its mission to Central Turkey; at Constantinople, Adrianople, Smyrna, Broosa, Nicomedia, Trebizond, Marsovan, Sivas, *including Tokat*, and Cæsarea, being its mission to Western Turkey; at Erzroom, Harpoot, and Arabkir, uniting with the Assyrian stations of Mardin and Diarbekir, its mission to Eastern[569] Turkey. Taking up the evangelisation at Oroomiah, the American Presbyterians unite with that Tabreez, Mosul, and Salmas as their Western, and Teheran and Hamadan as their Eastern Persia Mission. In 1876 a letter of Henry Venn's and the urgency of its principal missionary, Dr. Bruce, led the Church Missionary Society to charge itself with the evangelisation, by a revised version of the Persian Bible and medical missions, of the whole southern half of the ancient kingdom of Persia, the whole of Nimrod's Babylonia, and the eastern coast of Arabia, from Julfa (Ispahan) and Baghdad as centres. Very recently the independent Arabian Mission of America has made Busrah its headquarters for Turkish Arabia. The Latin Church since 1838 has worked for the Papacy alone. The Archbishop of Canterbury's mission since 1886 has sought to influence the Nestorian or Syrian Church, which in the seventh century sent forth missionaries to India from Seleucia, Nisibis, and Edessa, and now desires protection from Romish usurpation. All these represent a vast and geographically linked organisation claiming, at long intervals, the whole of Turkey, Persia, and Arabia for Christ since Henry Martyn pointed the way. Dr. Robert Bruce, writing to us from Julfa, thus sums up the results and the prospect:

I believe there is a great work going on at present in Persia, and Henry Martyn and his translations prepared the way for it, to say nothing of his life sacrifice and prayers for this dark land. The Babi movement is a very remarkable one, and is spreading far and wide, and doing much to break the power of the priesthood. Many of the Babis are finding their system unsatisfactory, and beginning to see that it is only a half-way house (in which there is no[570] rest or salvation) to Christianity. Ispahan has been kept this year in a constant state of turmoil by the ineffectual efforts of two moollas to persecute both Babis and

Jews.[109] They have caused very great suffering to some of both these faiths, but they have been really defeated, and all these persecutions have tended towards religious liberty. Our mission-house is the refuge of all such persecuted ones, and the light is beginning to dawn upon them.

While the whole Church, and every meditative soul seeking deliverance from self in Jesus Christ, claims Henry Martyn, he is specially the hero of the Church of England. An Evangelical, he is canonised, so far as ecclesiastical art can legitimately do that, in the baptistry of the new cathedral of his native city. A Catholic, his memory is enshrined in the heart of his own University of Cambridge. There, in the New Chapel of St. John's College, in the nineteenth bay of its interior roof, his figure is painted first of the *illustriores* of the eighteenth Christian century, before those of Wilberforce, Wordsworth, and Thomas Whytehead, missionary to New Zealand. In the market place, beside Charles Simeon's church, there was dedicated on October 18, 1887, 'The Henry Martyn Memorial Hall.' There, under the shadow of his name, gather daily the students who[571] join in the University Prayer Meeting, and from time to time the members of the Church Missionary and Gospel Propagation Societies. 'This was the hero-life of my boyhood,' said Dr. Vaughan, the Master of the Temple and Dean of Llandaff, when he preached the opening sermon before the University. In Trinity Church, where Martyn had been curate, the new Master of Trinity preached so that men said: 'What a power of saintliness must have been in Henry Martyn to have affected with such appreciative love one whose own life and character are so honoured as Dr. Butler's!' In the Memorial Hall itself, its founder, Mr. Barton, now Vicar of Trinity Church; Dr., now Bishop, Westcott, for the faculty of Divinity; Dr. Bailey, for St. John's College and the Society for the Propagation of the Gospel; Mr. Barlow, Vicar of Islington, for the Church Missionary Society; and the Christian scholar, Professor Cowell, for all Orientalists and Anglo-Indians, spake worthily.

We would continue his work. The hopes, the faith, the truths which once animated him are still ours. Still, as on the day when he preached his first sermon from this pulpit, is it true that if each soul, if each society, if each heathen nation knew the gift of God, and Who the promised Saviour is, they would for very thirst's sake ask of Him, and He would indeed give them His living water. And still it is the task of each true witness of Christ, and most of all of each ordained minister of His Word and Sacraments, first to arouse that thirst where it has not yet been felt, and then to allay it at once and perpetuate it from the one pure and undefiled spring. And still each true minister will feel, as Martyn felt, as St. Paul himself felt, 'Who is sufficient for these things?' The riper he is in his ministry, the more delicate his touch of human souls,[572] alike in their strivings and in their inertness; the closer his walk with God and his wonder at the vastness and the silent secrecy of God's ways, the more he will say in his heart what Martyn said but a few days after his feet had ceased to tread our Cambridge streets. 'Alas! do I think that a schoolboy or a raw academic should be likely to lead the hearts of men! What a knowledge of men and acquaintance with Scriptures, what communion with God and study of my own heart, ought to prepare me for the awful work of a messenger from God on the business of the soul!'

To these lessons of Martyn's life Dr. Butler added that which the eighty years since have suggested—the confidence of the soldier who has heard his Captain's voice, and knows that it was never deceived or deceiving: *Be of good cheer; I have overcome the world.*

In that confidence let the Church Catholic preach Christ to the hundred and eighty millions of the Mohammedan peoples, more than half of whom are already the subjects of Christian rulers. Thus shall every true Christian best honour Henry Martyn.

FOOTNOTES:

[101]In 1816 Charles Simeon thus wrote from King's College to Thomason, of the *Journal*: 'Truly it has humbled us all in the dust. Since the Apostolic age I think that nothing has ever exceeded the wisdom and piety of our departed brother; and I conceive that no book, except the Bible, will be found to excel this.... David Brainerd is great, but the degree of his melancholy and the extreme impropriety of his exertions, so much beyond his strength, put him on a different footing from our beloved Martyn.'

[102]*Bishop Wilson's Journal Letters*, addressed to his family during the first nine years of his Indian Episcopate, edited by his son Daniel Wilson, M.A., Vicar of Islington, London, 1864.

[103]See *Journal*, passim, especially in February, 1806.

[104]*Journal of Mr. Anthony N. Groves, Missionary to and at Baghdad*, London, 1831.

[105]*The Life of John Wilson, D.D., F.R.S.*, London, 1878.

[106]*Memorials of the Hon. Keith-Falconer, M.A., late Lord Almoner's Professor of Arabic in the University of Cambridge, and Missionary to the Muhammadans of South Arabia*, by Rev. Robert Sinker, D.D., p. 146 of 1st edition, 1888.

[107]*George Maxwell Gordon, M.A., F.R.G.S., a History of his Life and Work, 1839-1880*, by the Rev. Arthur Lewis, M.A., London, 1889.

[108]Archdeacon Moule in the *Church Missionary Intelligencer*.

[109]Even of the Soofis the ablest authority writes: 'The remarkable development, in our own century, which has been given to the story of the death of Hosein should encourage us to hope that the Divine pathos of the New Testament will one day soften these hearts still more, and teach them the secret of which their poets have sung in such ardent strains. A Sufi has already learnt that Islam cannot satisfy the longing soul. He is, by profession, tolerant or even sympathetic in the presence of the Cross. And he believes, like all Moslim, that Isa, the Messiah of Israel, has the breath of life, and can raise the dead from the tomb.... To the reflecting mind, however, the lyric effusions of Hafiz prove that Eastern philosophy is either childlike or retrograde, and its principles at the mercy of those seas of passion upon which it has so long been drifting.'*Quarterly Review*, January 1892.

Made in United States
Troutdale, OR
09/12/2023

12841125R00126